"The difference between Mark Noltir
ence. So many of Mark's reviews of a s
last trip we saw..." or "on the mornings' game drive we counted..." Africa's Top Wildlife Countries doesn't offer rehashed general info gathered from another guide book, but specific information from someone who has been there. This book allows the reader to compare one African park to another by telling the reader where they are most likely to see specific wildlife species. For example, there may be 20 game parks where there are still wild dogs but Mark tells you where you really have a chance to see one."

Tom Leeson
Professional Wildlife Photographer

"As a safari tour leader to Africa for the past 12 years, the only book I need is Mark Nolting's Africa's Top Wildlife Countries. It is my "Bible" for planning my photo safaris, and I recommend it to anyone considering a wildlife safari to sub-Sahara Africa."

Richard L. Henning
Safari Tour Leader

"When it comes to Africa trips, Mark Nolting is the man. He's the first guy I call, and his book is the first one I reach for".

David Noland
Contributor to Outside Magazine and author of TRAVELS ALONG THE EDGE: 40 Ultimate Adventures for the Modern Nomad

"Africa's Top Wildlife Countries is the book to consult for anyone planning an experience of a lifetime in Africa. More than a "must read", Mark Nolting's book has impressive breadth covering game parks in 16 countries in Africa, which enables the reader to make informed choices".

M. T. Hatendi
Zimbabwe Tourist Office-New York

"Faced with the ever-changing scene in Africa, and the increasing variety of options for wildlife trips and safaris, the savviest traveler will reach first for Mark Nolting's Africa's Top Wildlife Countries. With detailed descriptions of game reserves and parks in sixteen African countries, plus an extremely useful introduction defining almost twenty types of safaris and safari activities, this book is one of the most practical travel planners on the market."

Ann H. Waigand, Editor
The Educated Traveler

"Africa's Top Wildlife Countries is required reading for anyone with a safari in mind. First of all, it gives a comprehensive picture of wildlife reserves throughout Africa for intelligent, before-you-go planning. It's also a great portable field reference. Finally it is a memory book, even years after your safari - an enduring testament to the wonder that is Africa".

Marie Speed, Editor
Boca Raton Magazine

"A unique and splendid piece of work - it tells about wildlife, birdlife and the cultural heritage of Africa's top wildlife countries."

Edson P. Tembo
Director of North and South America
Zambia National Tourist Board - New York

AFRICA'S TOP WILDLIFE COUNTRIES

—FIFTH EDITION—

BY

MARK W. NOLTING

GLOBAL TRAVEL PUBLISHERS, INC.

AFRICA'S TOP WILDLIFE COUNTRIES

(Fifth Edition, completely revised and updated)

Copyright:	October, 1997 © by Mark W. Nolting
ISBN:	0-939895-07-2
Edited by:	Alison V. H. Nolting
Proofread by:	Sandy Pearlman
Cover and Interior Design by:	Pearl and Associates
Maps, Icons, Illustrations	
Copyright:	1997 © by Mark W. Nolting
Published by:	Global Travel Publishers, Inc.

Enquiries should be addressed to: Global Travel Publishers, Inc.. P.O. Box 70067, Ft. Lauderdale, FL 33307-0067, U.S.A., Telephone (954)491-8877 or (800)882-9453, Facsimile (954)491-9060.

International Standard Book Number

0-939895-07-2

Library of Congress Catalog Card Number

97-77317

Printed in the United States of America

4 5 6 7 8 9 0

Third Printing

Dedication

This edition is dedicated to all the individuals responsible for the continued success of tourism to the National Parks and Wildlife Reserves of Africa. Without the commitment and efforts of the guides, researchers, camp and lodge staff, tour operators, National Park and Reserve personnel and rangers, wildlife societies, etc., the safari experience in Africa would not be as it is today. Through their work many species have been saved from extinction and much of Africa's landscape has been left "untouched." It is the contributions of these people along with the much needed revenue generated by safari enthusiasts that continue to preserve the wildlife and their natural habitats.

Other Books by Mark W. Nolting

African Safari Journal
—Fourth Edition—

 (See page 613 for details.)

Dear Reader:

As President of The Africa Adventure Company, I have had the pleasure over the last twelve years of sending thousands of people from all walks of life on game-viewing safaris to Africa.

Why do so many people wish to go to Africa? Many seek the wonderful wilderness of a still primitive African continent where wildlife in its natural and exciting environment still abounds. Others seek contact with wild spaces and traditional African cultures which can have a meaningful effect on the human spirit — stirring and stimulating the senses, relaxing and revitalizing the mind.

Visiting Africa means getting back to basics and feeling the thrill of experiencing something entirely different from the world in which we live.

The main allure of Africa is that you can find adventure there. When you go on safari, you never know what you're going to see or what is going to happen. Every safari is exciting.

With the right assistance and guidance from an expert in African travel, it doesn't matter if you go on a tented or lodge safari, hot-air balloon ride, walking safari, canoe safari or go white-water rafting — there's no finer adventure!

There is no better time to venture to Africa than the present, as more and more species of wildlife are becoming endangered.

Growing population pressures in Africa are causing many governments to prove to their people that the wildlife reserves provide more jobs, foreign currency and other benefits than if the land was given to their people for farming, grazing or other uses.

Going on a photographic safari is a donation in itself toward conserving African wilderness regions and wildlife, as tourism gives many people who live near the reserves jobs and an economic incentive to preserve wildlife. This could be the most enjoyable and rewarding donation you will ever make!

Sincerely,

Mark W. Nolting, President
The Africa Adventure Company

P.S. To plan your safari with us and for more information on The Africa Adventure Company , please see following pages.

A REQUEST:

THE AFRICA ADVENTURE COMPANY

Dear Adventurer:

Mark Nolting, president of THE AFRICA ADVENTURE COMPANY, has spent over 25 years exploring and researching the African continent. This valuable experience is reflected in this award-winning book, *Africa's Top Wildlife Countries*, in which Mark chronicles every aspect of the safari experience, and in the *African Safari Journal,* a wildlife/botany guide, trip organizer, safari directory, phrasebook, safari diary, map directory and wildlife checklist all in one!

His tour company, THE AFRICA ADVENTURE COMPANY, offers this same attention to detail when helping to plan your safari. Unlike other companies whose brochures might highlight only a few standardized tours, Mark promises — and delivers — a much more personalized approach.

Mark and his friendly staff will combine their intimate firsthand knowledge of each African country with your ideas to choose a safari, whether a group tour or tailor-made itinerary, to precisely fit your desires and personal expectations.

"The key," says Mark, "is to understand the personal experience an individual wants to have in Africa and to match that experience with the optimum itinerary specifically designed to the client's needs, wants and desires. This can best be accomplished only if the person advising the client has extensive on-site experience in **all** the top safari countries. No amount of office training can substitute for actually having been there."

"Once we have a good feeling for what our clients want," continues Mark, "we then recommend the African countries which can best provide that experience, along with the best parks and reserves. Only then do we pick a few tour options or create special itineraries for our clients to consider with specific hotels, lodges, camps, or mobile tented accommodations, and safari activities that we feel would be of greatest interest to them. Doing anything less would be compromising the best interests of our clients."

With over 100 programs and dozens of extensions from which to choose, the options are almost unlimited!

Prices of programs begin around $3500 per person (land and air) for a 12-day safari.

Dispense with the uncertainties of traveling to Africa. Save yourself and your energies for the adventure of your Africa trip...let Mark and the friendly staff of THE AFRICA ADVENTURE COMPANY go to work for you, just as they have done for many happy, satisfied "safariers."

It's easy to start planning your safari. Call toll-free (from the United States and Canada), 1-800-882-9453 (1-800-882-WILD) or (954) 491-8877, fax us at (954) 491-9060. E-mail us at noltingaac@aol.com, or visit our website at www.africa-adventure.com and e-mail us a completed questionaire. You'll soon be off to Africa!

ACKNOWLEDGMENTS

The completion and accuracy of this guide would not have been possible without the assistance of many people. Many thanks to all who have contributed to this project, including the following: the Embassy of Botswana, the Embassy of Burundi, the Kenyan Tourist Office, the Lesotho Tourist Board, Roselyne Hauchler of the Mauritius Tourism Promotion Authority, the Embassy of Namibia and the Ministry of Trade & Industry, the Embassy of Rwanda, Ambassador Marc Marengo of the Seychelles, the Embassy of Swaziland, the Embassy of Uganda, Edson Tembo and the Zambia National Tourist Board, Mary Hatendi and the Zimbabwe Tourist Development Corporation.

Special thanks to Colin Bell, Russel Friedman, Alex Berrios de Rautenbach, Rene Evans, Dennis Rundle, Tessa Redman, Trevor Earl, Garth Thompson, Yvonne Christian, Jo Pope, John Coppinger, Ian Davidson, Tim Farrell, Phil Ward, Colin Stuart, Shakir and Abbas Molendina, Mike and Mary Atkin, Anita Balletto and Steve Turner for their assistance; to my staff at The Africa Adventure Company including Bill Rivard, Paula Goodnow, Sherri Desilets, Hazel and Wally Mountz and Irene Groden, to all the guides in the field who have shared their in depth knowledge of wildlife in Africa; and especially to my wife, Alison, for her invaluable assistance on the entire project.

PHOTO CREDITS

COLOR

Front cover — Alison Nolting
— Wilderness Safaris
Spine — Lee Wosk
Back cover — Dave Christianson
— Mike Myers
Page 225 — Sherry Unversaw
Page 226 — Duncan Butchart
Page 227 — Duncan Butchart
Page 228 — Duncan Butchart
Page 229 — Duncan Butchart
Page 230 — Upper: Mike Appelbaum
— Lower: Margo & Lisa Day
Page 231 — Upper: Mike Appelbaum
— Lower: Mike Appelbaum
Page 232 — Upper: P. Adamson
— Lower: Tom Milleson
Page 233 — Virginia Misoff
Page 234 — Upper: Wilderness Safaris
— Lower: Margo & Lisa Day
Page 235 — Upper: Kenneth Coe
— Lower: Mike Appelbaum
Page 236 — Alison Nolting
Page 237 — Upper: Mark Nolting
— Lower: Sharon Chen
Page 238 — Upper left: Mark Nolting
— Upper right: Virginia Misoff
— Lower left: Alison Nolting
— Lower right: Mike Appelbaum
Page 239 — Upper: Tom Barrat
— Lower: Amy Schoeman
Page 240 — Upper: Dave Van Smeerdijk
— Lower: Mark Nolting
Page 241 — Upper: Mark Nolting
— Lower: Ker & Downey
Page 242 — Upper: D & S Harris
— Lower left: Alison Nolting
— Lower right: Ann Morrissey
Page 243 — Marilyn Ritz
Page 244 — Upper: Beryl Davey
— Lower: Virginia Misoff
Page 245 — Upper: Charles O'Neil
— Lower: Wilderness Safaris
Page 246 — Upper: Mark Nolting
— Lower: Alison Nolting
Page 247 — Upper: Lydia Edison
— Lower: Ker & Downey
Page 248 — Mark Nolting
Page 249 — Upper: Mark Nolting
— Lower: Wilderness Safaris
Page 250 — Upper: Mark Nolting
— Lower: Alison Nolting
Page 251 — Upper: Saul Singer
— Lower: J & B Pratt
Page 252 — Upper: Mark Nolting
— Lower: Mike Appelbaum
Page 253 — Upper left: Mark Nolting
— Upper right: Mildred Smith
— Lower: Mark Nolting
Page 254 — Upper left: Mike Appelbaum
— Upper right: Mark Nolting
— Lower left: Alison Nolting
— Lower right: Ralph Hope
Page 255 — Upper: Cindy Corcoran
— Lower: Garth Thompson
Page 256 — Mark Nolting

BLACK AND WHITE

Page 33 — Lee Wosk
Page 34 — Mark Nolting
Page 46 — Mark Nolting
Page 48 — Mark Nolting
Page 52 — John Sowers
Page 55 — Virginia Misoff
Page 56 — Upper: Mike Appelbaum
— Lower: Mike Appelbaum
Page 57 — Bob Ehlers
Page 59 — Tom Barrat
Page 60 — Garth Thompson
page 64 — Upper: Marilyn Ritz
— Lower: Robin Pope Safaris
Page 66 — Mike Myers
Page 71 — J & B Pratt
Page 93 — Mark Nolting
Page 96 — Burt Fink
Page 103 — Mike Appelbaum
Page 109 — Upper: Mike Appelbaum
— Lower: Mike Appelbaum
Page 112 — Mark Nolting
Page 114 — Mark Nolting
Page 116 — Mark Nolting
Page 125 — Mark Nolting
Page 134 — Mark Nolting
Page 136 — Sand Rivers
Page 137 — Mwagusi
Page 149 — Lee Wosk
Page 153 — Lee Wosk
Page 154 — Mike Appelbaum
Page 156 — Lonrho Hotels
Page 161 — P & S Brady
Page 166 — Mike Appelbaum
Page 168 — Savannah Lodges
Page 172 — Savannah Lodges
Page 177 — Kenya Tourist Board
Page 181 — Alison Nolting
Page 187 — Bill Knudsen
Page 190 — Virginia Misoff
Page 195 — M & E Mattison

Continued on next page

PHOTO CREDITS
BLACK AND WHITE (Continued)

Page 199 — M & E Mattison
Page 210 — M & E Mattison
Page 213 — Jim Russell
Page 217 — Jim Russell
Page 224 — Mark Nolting
Page 257 — Charles O'Neil
Page 261 — Charles O'Neil
Page 272 — Mark Nolting
Page 277 — M & E Mattison
Page 281 — M & E Mattison
Page 284 — Mike Appelbaum
Page 289 — Alison Nolting
Page 293 — Alison Nolting
Page 297 — Mark Nolting
Page 298 — Victoria Falls Safari Lodge
Page 305 — Brian Worsley
Page 308 — Alison Nolting
Page 309 — Ivan Carter
Page 311 — Brian Worsley
Page 314 — Donna Cook/Mark Slay
Page 319 — Wild Geese Lodge
Page 322 — Zimbabwe Tourist Board
Page 327 — Mark Nolting
Page 328 — Upper: Londa Mela
— Lower: Londa Mela
Page 331 — P & S Brady
Page 335 — P & S Brady
Page 342 — Mark Nolting
Page 343 — Ker & Downey
Page 344 — Okavango Horse Safaris
Page 345 — Wilderness Safaris
Page 348 — Hayden Oake
Page 351 — Wilderness Safaris
Page 358 — Ramona Sergent
Page 361 — Tom Milleson
Page 365 — Tom Milleson
Page 371 — Marek Patzer
Page 372 — Mike Appelbaum
Page 374 — Bryan Jackson
Page 375 — Robin Pope Safaris
Page 377 — Bryan Jackson
Page 385 — Tongabezi Safaris
Page 388 — Tongabezi Safaris
Page 389 — Mark Nolting
Page 393 — Mark Nolting
Page 397 — Livingstonia Beach Hotel
Page 400 — Wilderness Safaris
Page 401 — Wilderness Safaris
Page 403 — Wilderness Safaris
Page 405 — P & S Brady
Page 412 — J & B Pratt
Page 414 — Mike Myers
Page 415 — P & S Brady
Page 416 — P & S Brady
Page 418 — J & B Pratt
Page 427 — Amy Schoeman
Page 429 — J & B Pratt
Page 431 — Pat Chase
Page 435 — Pat Chase
Page 444 — Alison Nolting
Page 446 — Rattray Reserves
Page 448 — Tanda Tula Camp
Page 449 — The Coach House
Page 451 — Sun International
Page 454 — SATOUR
Page 456 — Mark Nolting
Page 457 — Sun International
Page 460 — Roggeland
Page 462 — SATOUR
Page 472 — SATOUR
Page 474 — Wilderness Safaris
Page 477 — Mark Nolting
Page 481 — Mark Nolting
Page 483 — Mark Nolting
Page 487 — Mark Nolting
Page 491 — Mark Nolting
Page 498 — Mary Lippold
Page 503 — Mauritius Government Tourist Office
Page 507 — Mauritius Government Tourist Office
Page 513 — Sun International
Page 514 — Sun International
Page 515 — Mark Nolting
Page 519 — Mark Nolting
Page 526 — Alison Nolting
Page 529 — Tom Milleson
Page 531 — Tom Milleson
Page 557 — Tom Milleson
Page 567 — Tom Milleson
Page 581 — P. Adamson

CONTENTS

MAPS

CONTENTS

CHARTS AND ILLUSTRATIONS

Charts

Animal Profiles

CALL OF THE WILD

CALL OF THE WILD

Feature films like *The Serengeti* (Imax), *Out of Africa, African Queen* and *Gorillas in the Mist* along with countless documentaries have kindled in the hearts of many people the flame of desire for travel to Africa.

A visit to Africa allows you to experience nature at its finest — almost devoid of human interference, living according to a natural rhythm of life that has remained basically unchanged since the beginning of time.

At our deepest roots, the African continent communicates with our souls. Travelers return home, not only with exciting stories and adventures to share with friends and family, but with a feeling of accomplishment, increased self-confidence and broader horizons from having ventured where few have gone. Here's the kind of adventure about which many dream but few experience.

Having visited Africa once, you too will want to return again to the peace, tranquillity and adventure it has to offer. I invite you to explore with me the reasons for this never-ceasing pull as we journey to some of the most fascinating places on earth.

The time to visit Africa is now. In spite of international efforts, poaching is still rampant. In addition, the continent is rapidly becoming westernized, making it more and more difficult to see the indigenous

AFRICA
Tunisia
Morocco
Algeria
Libya
Egypt
Eritrea
Mauritania
Mali
Niger
Chad
Sudan
Djibouti
Senegal
The Gambia
Guinea-Bissau
Guinea
Sierra Leone
Liberia
Ivory Coast
Ghana
Bukina Faso
Togo
Benin
Nigeria
Cameroon
Central African Republic
Ethiopia
Somali Republic
Seychelles
Uganda
Kenya
Rwanda
Burundi
Equatorial Guinea
Gabon
Congo
Democratic Republic of the Congo
Tanzania
Cabinda
Malawi
Angola
Zambia
Mozambique
Madagascar
Mauritius
Namibia
Zimbabwe
Botswana
South Africa
Swaziland
Lesotho
N
0 1125 2250 km
0 700 1400 miles
1 inch = 1400 miles / 2250 km

peoples living as they have for thousands of years. Go now, while Africa can still deliver all that is promised — and more!

Africa has such a tremendous variety of attractions that most everyone can find something fascinating to do. In addition to fabulous wildlife, Africa boasts having one of the world's largest waterfalls by volume (Victoria Falls), the world's longest river (the Nile), the world's largest intact caldera or crater (Ngorongoro) and the world's highest mountain not part of a mountain range (Mt. Kilimanjaro).

Africa is huge. It is the second largest continent on earth, covering over 20 percent of the world's land surface. More than three times the size of the United States, it is also larger than Europe, the United States and China combined. No wonder it has so much to offer!

HOW TO USE THIS BOOK

Africa's Top Wildlife Countries highlights and compares wildlife reserves and other major attractions in the continent's best countries for game viewing.

Most people travel to Africa to see lion, elephant, rhino and other wildlife unique to this fascinating continent in their natural surroundings. *Africa's Top Wildlife Countries* makes planning your adventure of a lifetime easy.

This guide is designed to help you decide the best place or places to go in Africa to do what you want to do, when you want to do it, in a manner of travel that personally suits you best.

Using the easy-to-read **When's The Best Time To Go For Game Viewing** chart (see color insert on page 225), you can conveniently choose the specific reserves and country(ies) that are best to visit during your vacation period. From the **What Wildlife Is Best Seen Where** chart (see page 76), you can easily locate the reserves which have an abundance of the animals you wish to see most. From the **Safari Activities** chart (see page 54), you can choose the reserves that offer the safari options that interest you most. From the **Rainfall and Temperature** charts (see pages 78-79), you can decide how best to dress for safari and have an idea of what weather to expect.

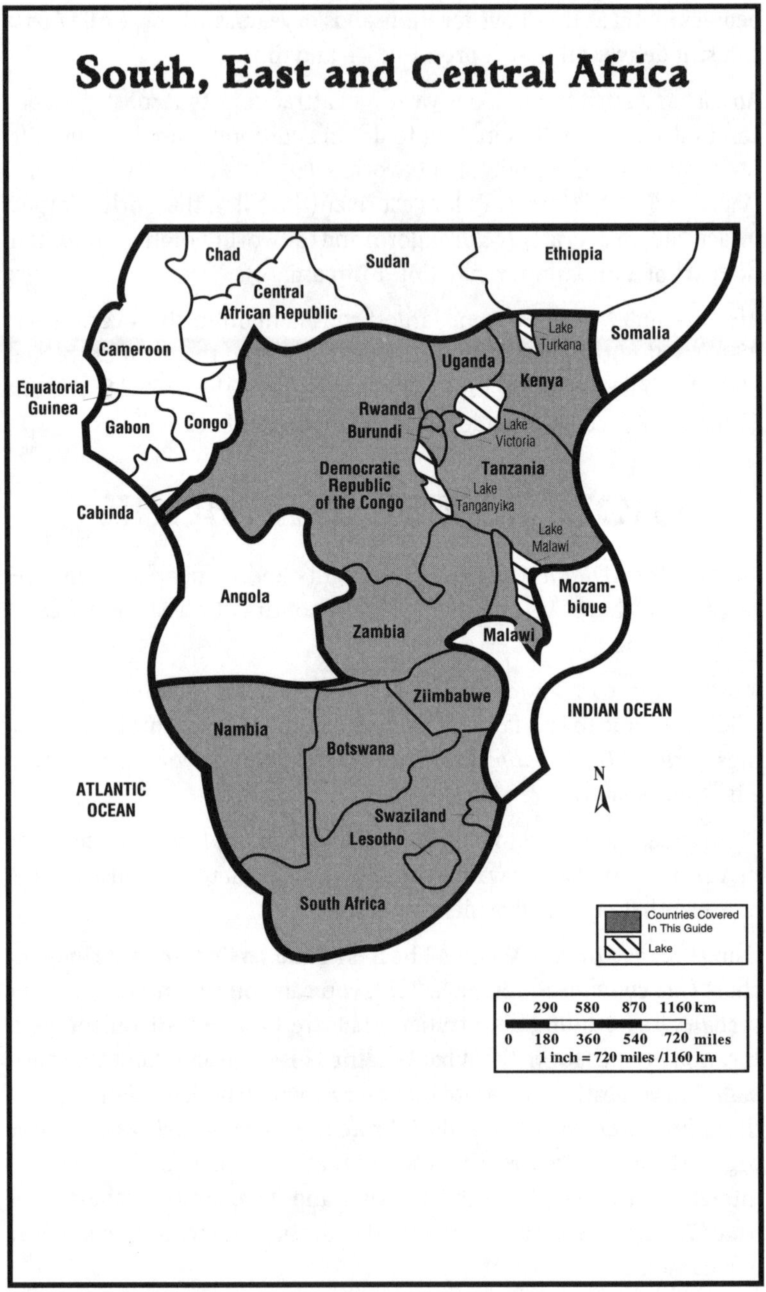
South, East and Central Africa
Chad
Sudan
Ethiopia
Central African Republic
Cameroon
Somalia
Lake Turkana
Uganda
Kenya
Equatorial Guinea
Gabon
Congo
Rwanda
Burundi
Lake Victoria
Democratic Republic of the Congo
Tanzania
Lake Tanganyika
Cabinda
Lake Malawi
Angola
Mozambique
Zambia
Malawi
Ziimbabwe
INDIAN OCEAN
Nambia
Botswana
ATLANTIC OCEAN
N
Swaziland
Lesotho
South Africa
Countries Covered In This Guide
Lake
0 290 580 870 1160 km
0 180 360 540 720 miles
1 inch = 720 miles /1160 km

The **Glossary** contains words commonly used on safari and defines words used throughout the book. English is the major language in most of the countries covered in this guide, so language is in fact not a problem. The **Safari Pages** (a safari directory) provide a veritable gold mine of difficult-to-find information and sources on Africa. The **Suggested Reading List** includes over 100 publications on sub-Sahara Africa.

The safari countries are divided between East Africa and Southern Africa and, in general, appear in their order of importance as safari destinations. The most important safari countries are Tanzania, Kenya and Uganda in East Africa and Zimbabwe, Botswana, Zambia, Malawi, Namibia and South Africa in Southern Africa.

First, complete reading this introduction ("Call of the Wild"). Next, read the chapter or chapters on the countries that you feel offer the kind of *experience* you are looking for in Africa. Then call us at The Africa Adventure Company (toll-free 1-800-882-9453 in the United States and Canada) to discuss your thoughts. We will match the experience you are looking for with one of more than 100 safari programs we have to offer, putting you one step closer to experiencing the safari of your dreams.

WHAT IS A SAFARI LIKE?

"Alephaant, allephanntt," the Masai softly said as he escorted us to dinner that evening. Neither of us could understand him until he shined his flashlight on a tree-sized elephant browsing not 50 feet (15 m) from where we stood. It was then I realized why we were requested to wait for the spear-wielding Masai assigned to our tent to escort us to dinner. The pathway to the dining tent was covered with giant pizza-sized footprints that were not there 45 minutes earlier. Carrying a spear in these parts is not a bad idea!

The dining tent was filled with people from the four corners of the earth, reveling in camaraderie and sumptuous cuisine by candlelight. An excellent selection of wines and desserts complemented the meal.

After dinner we sat around a roaring fire, listening to bush lore from our entertaining host. Later we watched hippo grazing only a few feet from our tent. The night was alive with the sounds and scents of the Africa we had dreamed of — the untamed wilderness where man is but a temporary guest and not a controller of nature. Only then did we retire to our comfortable deluxe tent with ensuite facilities to sleep that gentle sleep which comes with a sigh of contentment.

What is a typical day on safari? Most safaris are centered around guests participating in two activities per day, such as game drives in minivans or four-wheel-drive vehicles. A game drive simply consists of having your guide drive you around a park or reserve in search of wildlife.

Most activities last two to four hours and are done when the wildlife is most active: early in the morning (often before breakfast), just after breakfast, in the late afternoon and at night (where allowed). Midday activities might include lazing around the swimming pool, reading, bird watching or viewing game as it passes by your tent or lodge, or taking a nap. After an exhilarating day on safari, many guests return to revel in the day's adventures over exquisite European cuisine in comfortable lodges and camps.

The kind and quality of experience one has on safari vary greatly from country to country, and even from park to park within the same country. For instance, going on safari in East Africa (Kenya and Tanzania) is completely different from going on safari in Southern Africa (Zimbabwe, Zambia and Botswana).

Simply watching wildlife from a vehicle anywhere in Africa is an experience in itself. However, more and more people are preferring to personally experience more from the safari than just seeing animals.

How can this be done? By choosing a safari that includes parks which are not crowded and offer more of a feeling of being in the bush. Choose reserves that allow you to participate in activities that make you a more integral part of the safari, like walking and canoeing. Choose smaller camps and lodges that are unfenced, allowing wildlife to walk freely about the grounds.

Depending on the park or reserve, safari activities might include day game drives, night game drives, walks, boat safaris, canoeing, kayaking, white-water rafting, ballooning, hiking, mountain climbing, fishing, horseback riding, African elephant back riding — the options are almost endless. See "Safari Activities" and the **Safari Activities Chart** which follow.

Another excellent way to get the most out of your safari is to have a private safari arranged for you. Why? A private safari immediately becomes *your safari*. You do not have to bow to the wishes of the majority of the group or the strictly set itinerary of group departures. With your guide, you are basically free to do (within reason) what you wish!

DISPELLING MYTHS ABOUT TRAVEL ON THE DARK CONTINENT

Many prospective travelers to Africa seem to think that if they go on an African safari, they may have to stay in mud or grass huts or little pup tents and eat strange foods. Nothing could be further from the truth!

Almost all of the top parks and reserves covered in this guide have deluxe or first-class (Class A or B by our grading system) lodges or camps (with ensuite bathroom facilities) that serve excellent food, specifically designed to cater to the discerning traveler's needs. Going on safari can be a very comfortable, fun-filled adventure!

Many prospective travelers to Africa have voiced their fear of being overwhelmed by mosquitoes and other insects or the fear of encountering snakes on safari.

However, most travelers return pleasantly surprised, having found that insects and small snakes are a much greater problem in their own neighborhoods than on safari. In over 20 years of travel to Africa, I have only seen about five snakes — and I had to look for them!

The fact is, most safaris do not take place in the jungle, but on open savannah during the dry season, when the insect populations are at a minimum. In addition, the best time to go on safari for most of the countries is during their winter, which is when many snakes hibernate. Also, many parks are located over 3000 feet (915 m) in altitude, resulting in cool to cold nights, further reducing the presence of any pests.

In any case, except for walking safaris, most all of your time in the bush will be spent in the safety of a vehicle or boat.

ECOTOURS

Over the last few years, the terms "ecotour" and "ecotourism" have hit the travel industry like cholesterol hit the food industry not long ago. Many new companies have sprung up, claiming that their new ecotours are eco-friendly and implying that they have pioneered this type of travel. However, many tour companies have been conducting eco-sensitive tours for years, without the eco-hype.

Ecotours have a very low impact on the environment. Travelers take photos and leave little more than footprints. True ecotourism should ensure that the local peoples living adjacent to parks and reserves benefit directly from tourism in such a way that they have a positive incentive to preserve wildlife and the environment; CAMPFIRE projects in Zimbabwe and camps like Ndumo and Rocktail Bay (South Africa) are excellent examples of this.

CHOOSING ACCOMMODATIONS

There are a great variety of styles and levels of comfort in accommodations available in the major cities and while on safari, ranging from simple bungalows to suites with private swimming pools. Options include hotels, lodges, small camps with chalets or bungalows, fixed tented camps and mobile tented safaris.

The type of accommodation included in a tour of Africa will have a major influence on the type of experience and adventures you will have on safari.

An important factor to consider when choosing accommodations or a tour is the size of the lodge or camp. In general, guests receive more personal attention at smaller camps and lodges than at larger ones. Large properties tend to stick to a set schedule, while smaller properties are often more willing to amend their schedules according to the preferences of their guests. However, larger properties tend to be less expensive, which makes tours using the larger properties more affordable.

Many larger properties (especially in Kenya) are surrounded by electrical fences, allowing guests to move about as they please without fear of bumping into elephant or other wildlife. Travelers (including myself) who enjoy having wildlife roaming about camp should seek properties that are not fenced; these properties are best for travelers who want to experience living in the bush.

Most properties in Kenya and Tanzania have 75–200 beds, whereas most camps in Botswana, Zambia and Zimbabwe have 20 or fewer.

HOTELS AND HOTEL CLASSIFICATIONS

Many African cities such as Nairobi (Kenya), Harare (Zimbabwe) and Cape Town (South Africa) have four- and five-star (first-class and deluxe) hotels comparable to anywhere in the world, with air-conditioning and ensuite facilities, swimming pools and one or more excellent restaurants and bars.

Hotels are categorized as *Deluxe, First Class* and *Tourist Class*. *Ensuite facilities* means bathrooms (toilet plus shower and/or bathtub) are connected to the sleeping rooms/tents. *Private facilities* means that bathrooms are exclusive to guests but are not connected to the sleeping rooms/tents. *Separate facilities* means that bathrooms are shared by guests from more than one room/tent and are separate from the sleeping quarters.

DELUXE: An excellent hotel, rooms with ensuite bathroom (toilet plus shower and/or bathtub), air-conditioning, one or more restaurants serving very good food, swimming pool, bars, lounges, room service — all the amenities of a four- or five-star international hotel.

FIRST CLASS: A very comfortable hotel, rooms with ensuite facilities, air-conditioning, at least one restaurant and bar, and most have a swimming pool.

TOURIST CLASS: A comfortable hotel with simple rooms with ensuite facilities, most with air-conditioning, a restaurant and bar, and most with a swimming pool.

Typical deluxe permanent tented camp accommodation.

LODGES AND CAMPS

Lodges ranging from comfortable to deluxe (many have swimming pools) are located in or near most parks and reserves. Many lodges and camps are located in wildlife areas 3000 feet (915 m) or more above sea level, so air-conditioning often is not necessary.

There is often confusion over the term *camp*. A camp often refers to lodging in chalets, bungalows or tents in a remote location. Camps range from very basic to garishly plush. Deluxe camps often have better service and food, and most certainly a truer safari atmosphere, than large lodges and hotels.

Permanent tented camps or **fixed tented camps** are camps that are not moved. Besides generally having better food and service than lodges, guests of tented camps have more of a "safari experience." They are less isolated from the environment than those who stay in a lodge. **Mobile tented camps** are discussed below under "Types of Safaris."

LODGE AND CAMP CLASSIFICATIONS

Lodges and tented camps are classified as Class A to F. Accommodations have been primarily graded on facilities, food and service. However, the quality of the guides and management have also been taken into account.

Keep in mind that a lower-class accommodation may be preferable over a higher-class one if the lower-class option offers better guides and management, a better location and/or preferable activities.

CLASS A: Deluxe lodge or tented camp, many with swimming pools, excellent food and service, large nicely appointed rooms or tents with ensuite facilities, comfortable beds and tasteful decor; lodges may have air-conditioning.

CLASS A/B: An excellent lodge or tented camp with very good food and service, many with swimming pools; rooms in lodges have ensuite or private facilities.

CLASS B: A comfortable lodge or camp with good food and service, many with swimming pools. Rooms in lodges have ensuite baths; most tents, chalets or bungalows have ensuite or private bathrooms.

CLASS B/C: Most often a "Class B" property that is very rustic or somewhat inconsistent in the quality of accommodation, food and service.

CLASS C: A simple lodge with private bathrooms; a tented camp, chalet or bungalow with ensuite, private or shared facilities and fair food and service; or a "Class B" structure with fair to poor food or service.

CLASS D: A basic lodge or tented camp (lodges, chalets, bungalows and tents seldom have ensuite or private bathrooms) or a "Class C" structure with poor food or service.

CLASS F: Very basic lodge or tented camp with separate bathrooms; often self-service (no restaurant).

FOOD ON SAFARI

Excellent European cuisine along with interesting local dishes are served in the top hotels, lodges, camps and restaurants. Primarily French cuisine is served in Rwanda, the Congo and Burundi, whereas

The dining room of a typical thatched lodge.

British cuisine predominates in the other countries covered in this guide. Restaurants serving cuisines from all over the world may be found in the larger cities in Africa.

Most international travelers are impressed with the quality of the food and drink served on their safari. The fresh air will give you a healthy appetite. Typical meals include:

> Breakfast — Usually fruit and cereal, eggs, bacon and sausage, toast and preserves, tea and coffee
>
> Lunch — Assorted cold meats and salads with cheeses and bread
>
> Dinner — Normally three courses, with an appetizer or soup, main entree and vegetables, and a dessert

Some safari camps and lodges will provide a light breakfast in the early morning (tea, coffee, rusks, cereals) and then serve brunch at about 11:00 a.m. following a game drive or other activity. Tea, coffee and biscuits (cookies) are served at about 3:00 p.m. Following the afternoon game activity, guests return to the lodge for a delicious dinner.

TYPES OF SAFARIS

LODGE SAFARIS

Lodge safaris are simply safaris that use lodges or permanent tented camps as accommodations. Some safaris mix lodges with tented camps or camps with chalets or bungalows, providing a greater range of experience for their guests.

MOBILE TENTED CAMP SAFARIS

Private and group mobile tented camp safaris are, in my opinion, one of the best ways to experience the bush and a great way of getting off the beaten track.

Seeing hippo grazing by your tent at night or elephant walking through your camp by day is an experience not to be missed! When under the guidance of a professional guide, this is not as dangerous as it might sound. Animals will almost never try to enter a closed tent unless tempted by the smell of food. If you keep the tent flaps closed at night, you are generally just as safe as if you were staying in a bungalow or chalet. So why not go where the excitement is!

Tanzania, Zimbabwe and Botswana are excellent countries for mobile tented safaris; Kenya and Zambia are also good destinations for this type of safari.

Mobile tented safaris range from deluxe to first-class, midrange and budget (participation) safaris.

Deluxe Mobile Tented Camp Safaris

Deluxe mobile tented camp safaris are the epitome of mobile safaris. Each tent has a private bush (bucket) shower and toilet tent. Food and service are excellent. Camp attendants take care of everything, including bringing hot water for your shower. Camp is usually set in remote areas of parks and reserves, providing a true *Out of Africa* experience. For a party of four, the cost ranges from $400 to $650 per person per day.

Sleeping tents used on a typical remote first class tented camp safari.

First Class Mobile Tented Camp Safaris

These are similar to deluxe safaris except that the tents are a little smaller, yet very comfortable; less expensive tableware may be used, there are not quite as many staff and there is usually a separate bush shower (hot water) and toilet tent for each sleeping tent. For a party of four, the cost is around $250–$375 per person per day, depending on the country and season.

Midrange Mobile Tented Camp Safaris

Comfortable (and less expensive) midrange mobile tented safaris are available in a number of countries. Like deluxe and first-class mobile tented safaris, camp staff take care of all the chores. The difference is that the tents are a bit smaller but are still large enough in which to stand. The food and service are very good, and guests from one to three sleeping tents may share one toilet tent and one shower tent (with hot water). For a party of four, the cost is usually under $250 per person per day.

Participation Mobile Tented Camp Safaris

On participation mobile tented safaris, participants are required to help with some or all of the camp chores. Park campsites with basic (if any) facilities are often used.

The advantage is price. Participation camping safaris are almost always less expensive than lodge safaris. However, these are recommended only for hardy travelers with previous camping experience. Most participants are under 45 years of age. Hot showers are usually available most nights, but not all. The cost is usually under $200 per person per day.

OVERLAND SAFARIS

Overland safaris cover several countries and last from two to nine months. Participants usually take care of all the chores and sleep in small pup tents. As many of these safaris originate in Europe, where they load up with supplies, only a small amount of the money spent for the safari reaches the local people. This places this type of safari very low on the ecotourism scale.

DRIVING SAFARIS

Driving safaris are simply safaris in which guests are driven by their driver/guide from reserve to reserve. You generally have the same guide throughout the safari, who should have very good knowledge of all the parks and reserves to be visited.

Driving safaris are usually less expensive than flying safaris (see below). However, safariers should take into account the amount of time it takes to get from reserve to reserve, the quality of the roads, and whether or not there will be something en route that will be of interest to them, and compare that to the cost of doing some or all flying on their safari.

FLYING SAFARIS

Flying safaris are safaris in which guests are flown to or near the wildlife reserves to be visited. They are then usually picked up at the airport or airstrip upon arrival and driven to their camp or lodge.

Guides and vehicles are based at the camps and lodges at which guests will be staying. A real advantage here is that the resident guides should have intimate knowledge of the area as they are usually based in the same camp for the season.

This type of safari is very popular in Zimbabwe, Zambia and Botswana and is taken by many travelers to Kenya and Tanzania. Time that would normally be spent on the road driving between the parks and reserves may instead be spent game viewing — the primary reason why most people travel to Africa in the first place!

FLY/DRIVE SAFARIS

As the name implies, these safaris are a combination of some driving and some flying. The general idea is to fly over areas that are not interesting to drive or that you have already covered on the ground, and drive through the areas that have the most to offer.

GROUP SAFARIS

Group safaris are in many cases a more cost-effective way of experiencing the bush than private safaris (see below). The key for group safaris in Africa is to be sure the group size is small. Group size preferably should be limited, in my opinion, to 12 or fewer passengers (8 is preferable) and never over 16.

With large groups, passengers in the lead vehicle see game, while those in the vehicles that follow eat dust. Lots of time is wasted getting under way, and time schedules are very inflexible. Large group tours may be fine for Europe or Asia, but have no place in the bush!

PRIVATE SAFARIS

For those who wish to avoid groups, a private safari is highly recommended for several reasons.

An itinerary can be specially designed according to the kind of experience *YOU* want, visiting the parks and reserves *YOU* wish to see most, and traveling on dates that suit *YOU* best. You may spend your time doing what you wish to do rather than having to compromise with the group.

For instance, if you find a leopard up a tree with a kill, you can stay five minutes or five hours at that location — it's up to you!

What few people realize is that, in many cases, a private safari need not cost more than one with a large group. In fact, I have sent many couples and small groups on private safaris for not much more (and sometimes less) than the cost of group safaris from other tour operators offering the same or similar itinerary.

If you find this difficult to believe, call or write us with what you have in mind, and we'll be happy to send you an itinerary (see introduction pages).

HONEYMOON SAFARIS

There is no more romantic setting for a honeymoon than an African safari. Most honeymooners begin with a few days to relax and recover from the wedding in a five-star hotel or lodge — then it's off on safari!

Honeymoon safaris, like all safaris, can include as plush or rustic accommodations as you wish. Most camps and small lodges have a "honeymoon tent" or "honeymoon suite" located to ensure maximum privacy. Please keep in mind that most tented camps and small lodges have two single beds per room/tent, so be sure to have your tour operator let them know you are indeed honeymooners.

The epitome of a honeymoon safari, in my opinion, is a private mobile tented and lodge safari, with a private guide. Tenting at a remote private campsite is truly the *Out of Africa* experience!

FAMILY SAFARIS

More and more parents and grandparents are taking their children and grandchildren on safari. Seeing nature in all its abundance as a child is an experience that cannot be underestimated.

In most cases, the best option for families is a private safari with your own vehicle(s) and guides. You may travel at your own pace and choose camps and lodges that offer amenities like swimming pools that will provide the kids with some play time as well as help them burn off some of that endless energy they seem to possess. In addition, visits to local schools and villages provide insights into how children of their own age live in the countries you are visiting — and will hopefully make them more thankful for what they have!

Mark Nolting on safari with his son Miles (14 months).

Many of the smaller camps and lodges in Africa have minimum age restrictions (ranging from 7 to 16 years of age) and/or have minimum age restrictions (i.e., 16 years old) for activities offered, such as walks in the bush with professional guides and canoeing. However, if, for instance, your family takes over the camp or entire canoe safari departure or does a private mobile safari, you can in most instances get around the minimum age requirements. As some safari camps and lodges cater to a maximum of 6 to 20 guests, taking over a camp may be easier than you think. Just try to book your safari well in advance to ensure availability.

SELF-DRIVE SAFARIS

In Africa, self-drive safaris are a viable option for general sightseeing in countries such as South Africa which have excellent road systems. However, self-drive safaris into wildlife parks and reserves are, in general, not a good idea for several reasons.

One major disadvantage of a self-drive safari is that one misses the information and experience a driver/guide can provide. A good guide is also an excellent game spotter and knows when and where to look for the animals you wish to see most. He can communicate with other guides to find out where the wildlife has most recently been seen. This also leaves you free to concentrate on photography and game viewing instead of on the road and eliminates the anxiety of perhaps getting lost.

Self-drive safaris, especially ones requiring four-wheel-drive vehicles, are most often more expensive than joining a group safari. Petrol is generally several times the cost of what it is in North America. Vehicle rental costs are high.

Finally, self-drive safaris by people without extensive experience in the bush can be dangerous. Lack of knowledge of wildlife and the bush can result in life-threatening situations. For instance, if a lion sees you out of your vehicle changing a tire, it may very well attack.

Carnet de Passage is required by most countries to take your own vehicle across borders without paying import duty or leaving a deposit with Customs; a *carnet* must be purchased before arrival.

An International Driver's License is required by some of the countries covered in this book. Contact the tourist offices, consulates, or embassies of the countries in which you wish to drive for any additional requirements.

SAFARI ACTIVITIES

Africa can be experienced in a myriad of exciting ways. What follows are a number of types of safari activities. For additional information, refer to the country or countries mentioned.

PHOTO SAFARIS

The term *photo safari* generally means any kind of safari *except* hunting safaris.

In its strictest sense, a photo safari is a safari escorted by a professional wildlife photographer, especially for the serious photographer. These safaris are mainly about learning wildlife photography and getting the best photos possible. These are recommended only for the serious shutterbug.

SAFARI ACTIVITIES

VEHICLES – NIGHT GAME DRIVES – WALKING SAFARIS
BOAT SAFARIS – CANOE SAFARIS

COUNTRY	PARK OR RESERVE	VEHICLE TYPE ALLOWED			NIGHT DRIVES	WALKING SAFARIS	BOAT SAFARIS	CANOE SAFARIS
		OPEN	HATCHES	CLOSED				
EAST & CENTRAL AFRICA								
TANZANIA	Arusha		X			X		
	Lake Manyara		X					
	Tarangire		X			*5		
	Ngorongoro		X			*5		
	Serengeti		X			*5		
	Selous	X				X	X	
	Ruaha	X						
	Mahale & Gombe					X		
KENYA	Masai Mara		X		*1	*1		
	Mount Kenya					X		
	Samburu		X			*1		
	Other parks		X					
	Private game reserves	X			X	X		
UGANDA	Murchison Falls		X				X	
	Queen Eliz. N.P.		X				X	
	Bwindi Impent. Forest		X			X		
	Kibale		X			X		
	Ruwenzori Mountains					X		
RWANDA	Volcano					X		
CONGO	Kahuzi-Biega, Bukima & Djomba Gorilla Sanctuary					X		
	Rwindi (Virunga)		X					
SOUTHERN AFRICA								
ZIMBABWE	Chizarira	X				X		
	Hwange	*3			*1,*3	X		
	Mana Pools	*3				X	*1	X
	Matusadona	*3			*1,*3	X	X	X
BOTSWANA	Chobe	X					X	
	Moremi	X			*1	*1,*2	X	*4
	Okavango Delta	X				X	X	*4
	Savute	X			*1	*1		
ZAMBIA	South and North Luangwa	*3			*3	X		
	Lower Zambezi N.P.	*3			*3	X	X	X
NAMIBIA	Etosha	*3	*3		*1	*1		
SOUTH AFRICA	Kalahari - Gemsbok			X				
	Kruger			X	*1 *3	*1 *3		
	Private Reserves	X			X	X		

*1: Activity is conducted on outskirts of park or reserve.
*2: Activity is conducted at a few camps within the reserve.
*3: Licensed tour operators only.
*4: Mokoro.
*5: Activity is conducted in certain areas of the park or reserve.

Game viewing by open vehicle.

The best option by far for the serious photographer is to have a private vehicle and guide (see "Private Safaris" above). Group safaris generally move too quickly from place to place, allowing insufficient time to get the best shots.

GAME DRIVES

The type of vehicle used on game drives varies from country to country.

Open vehicles usually have two or three rows of elevated seats behind the driver's seat. There are no side or rear windows or permanent roof, providing unobstructed views in all directions and a feeling of being part of the environment instead of on the outside looking in. This is my favorite type of vehicle for viewing wildlife. Open vehicles are used in Botswana, Zambia, Zimbabwe, southern Tanzania, some reserves in Namibia and private reserves in Kenya and South Africa.

In **vehicles with roof hatches or pop-top roofs**, riders may stand up through the hatch for game viewing and photography. If the vehicle is full, riders usually must take turns using the hatches, making tours which guarantee window seats for every passenger (i.e., maximum of seven passengers in a nine-seat minivan) imperative. These vehicles are primarily used in Kenya, Tanzania and Uganda.

Game viewing from a land cruiser with roof hatches in the Masai Mara, Kenya.

Game viewing from a mini-van with a pop-top roof.

Walking up to elephant with a professionally licensed guide.

Wildlife viewing, and especially photography, is more difficult where **closed vehicles** are required. In South Africa (except private reserves), closed vehicles are generally required.

NIGHT GAME DRIVES

Night game drives open up a new world of adventure. Nocturnal animals, seldom if ever seen by day, are viewed with the aid of the vehicle's powerful search light. Bushbabies, night apes, leopard, civet, genet and many other species can be seen.

Night drives are conducted in Zambia, Malawi, private concession areas in Botswana, and private reserves in Kenya, Namibia and South Africa.

WALKING SAFARIS

Walking safaris put one in closest touch with nature. Suddenly your senses come alive — every sight, sound and smell becomes intensely meaningful. Could that flash of bronze in the dense brush ahead be a lion? I wonder how long ago these rhino tracks were made? Can that herd of elephant ahead see or smell us approaching?

Accompanied by an armed wildlife expert or professional guide, walking safaris last anywhere from a few hours to several days. The bush can be examined up close and at a slower pace, allowing more attention to its fascinating detail than a safari by vehicle.

Participants can often approach game quite closely, depending on the direction of the wind and the cover available. This is experiencing the excitement and adventure of the bush at its best. Zambia and Zimbabwe are the top countries for walking safaris. Walking is also available in some parts of Botswana, Tanzania, Kenya and South Africa.

GORILLA SAFARIS

Gorilla trekking is one of the most exciting adventures one can have on the "dark continent" and is certainly one of the most exciting experiences of my life.

Mountain gorillas are currently best seen in Bwindi Impenetrable Forest (Uganda). At the time of this writing, gorilla trekking in Rwanda and the Congo is not recommended, due to lack of security in these countries. Permits for gorilla trekking are limited; gorilla safaris should be booked well in advance.

BALLOON SAFARIS

At 5:30 in the morning, we were awakened by steaming hot coffee and tea brought to our bedsides by our private tentkeeper. We were off at 6:00 for a short game drive to where the hot-air balloons were being filled. Moments later we lifted above the plains of the Masai Mara for the ride of a lifetime.

Silently viewing game from the perfect vantage point, we brushed the tops of giant acacias for close-up views of birds' nests and baboons. Most animals took little notice, but somehow the hippos knew we were there. Maybe it was our shadow or the occasional firing of the burners necessary to keep us aloft.

Our return to earth was an event in itself. One hour and 15 minutes after lift-off, our pilot made a perfect crash landing. By the way, all landings are crash landings, so just follow your pilot's instructions and join in the fun.

Ballooning safaris are available in Kenya, Tanzania and Namibia.

Minutes later, a champagne breakfast appeared on the open savannah within clear view of herds of wildebeest, buffalo, and zebra. Our return to camp was another exciting game drive, only a little bumpier than the trip out.

Hot-air balloon safaris are available in Kenya in the Masai Mara Game Reserve, at Taita Hills near Tsavo West National Park, in Serengeti National Park (Tanzania), near Namib-Naukluft National Park (Namibia) and in Pilanesberg Nature Reserve (South Africa).

BOAT/CANOE/KAYAK/MOKORO SAFARIS

Wildlife viewing by boat, canoe, kayak or mokoro from rivers or lakes often allows one to approach wildlife closer than by vehicle. Game viewing by **boat** is available in Chobe National Park, the Linyanti Swamps and the Okavango Delta (Botswana), along the shores of Lake Kariba including Matusadona National Park, and on the Zambezi River upstream from Victoria Falls and downstream from the Kariba Dam, including Mana Pools National Park (Zimbabwe), on the Lower Zambezi National Park (Zambia) and in Liwonde National Park (Malawi).

A highlight of a safari – canoeing along the Lower Zambezi River.

Canoe safaris from three to nine days are operated along the Zambezi River below Kariba Dam on both the Zimbabwe and Zambia sides of the river. Wildlife is best in the area along Mana Pools National Park and Lower Zambezi National Park. This is definitely one of my favorite adventures. Motorboats are not allowed along Mana Pools National Park; however, they are allowed along the Lower Zambezi National Park.

Short excursions are also available upstream from Victoria Falls (Zimbabwe/Zambia), along Matusadona National Park (Zimbabwe) and Kafue National Park (Zambia).

One- to three-day **kayak safaris** are operated along Zambezi River in Zambezi National Park upstream from Victoria Falls, Zimbabwe.

Mokoro safaris from a few hours to several days in length are available in the Okavango Delta (Botswana).

WHITE-WATER RAFTING

For white-water enthusiasts and newcomers alike, the Zambezi River (Zambia/Zimbabwe) below Victoria Falls is one of the most challenging rivers in the world. Some rapids are *Class Five* — the highest class runable. Rafting safaris from one to eight days are available. No previous experience is required. Just hang on and have the time of your life! If this is an adventure that interests you, definitely go as soon as possible; a dam is planned downstream of Victoria Falls, and once built, the gorge will be flooded, and that will be the end of the rafting! See the chapter on Zimbabwe for more details.

ELEPHANT-BACK SAFARIS

For years only available in Asia, elephant-back safaris on African elephants are a fabulous way to explore the bush. Clients may ride these well-trained elephants, which are much larger than Indian elephants, in the Okavango Delta (Botswana) and at Victoria Falls, near Matobo National Park and at Imire Game Ranch (Zimbabwe).

HORSEBACK SAFARIS

Game viewing by horseback is yet another intriguing way to experience the bush. Horseback safaris from 3 to 10 days in length are conducted in the Okavango Delta (Botswana), from a half day to 10 days in length on the Nyika Plateau (Malawi) and up to 16 days in length in Kenya.

Half-day or full-day horseback safaris are available in Matobo National Park, Mutirikwe Recreational Park , Nyanga and Victoria Falls (Zimbabwe), Maputaland Coastal Forest Reserve and Cape Town (South Africa), and several private reserves in Kenya.

BIRD WATCHING

If you are not a bird watcher now, there's a good chance you will be converted before the end of your safari. Bird watching in Africa is almost beyond belief. Some countries have recorded over 1000 different species and some parks over 500.

The best time of year for bird watching, as shown on the "When's the Best Time to go for Birdwatching Chart (page 77) is November–March in most areas covered in this guide. However, bird watching is very good year-round.

Keen birders planning to visit southern Africa (Botswana, Lesotho, Namibia, South Africa, Swaziland and Zimbabwe) will find *Newman's Birds of Southern Africa* by Kenneth Newman (Southern Book Publishers) invaluable. *Collins Field Guide to the Birds of East Africa* by

J. G. Williams and N. Arlott (Harper Collins) is very good for eastern Africa. *Birds of Kenya & Tanzania* by Zimmerman, Turner and Pearson, (A & C Black, Russel Friedman Books, Africa, 1996) is the best book currently available.

MOUNTAIN CLIMBING

Africa has mountains to challenge the tenderfoot and the expert as well. Mt. Kilimanjaro (Tanzania), 19,340 feet (5895 m) in altitude, is the highest mountain in Africa, followed by Mt. Kenya at 17,058 feet (5199 m). The Ruwenzoris, or *Mountains of the Moon* (Uganda/Congo), are the highest mountain chain in Africa, rising to 16,762 feet (5109 m). All of these mountains lie within a few degrees of the equator yet are snowcapped year-round. Hiking through fascinating and unique Afro-alpine vegetation found on all of these mountains gives one the feeling of being on another planet.

SCUBA DIVING AND SNORKELING

Kenya, Tanzania, South Africa, Mauritius and the Seychelles offer excellent coral reef diving in the warm waters of the Indian Ocean. Lake Malawi offers a fascinating freshwater dive experience.

The Malindi-Watamu Marine National Reserve is probably the best choice in Kenya and Pemba Island the best choice in Tanzania.

The Natal coast of South Africa has excellent coral reefs, while the Southern Cape offers the ultimate underwater thrill of diving with great white sharks!

Mauritius and the Seychelles offer numerous coral reefs and a variety of dive options.

FISHING

Some of the finest **deep-sea fishing** in the world is found in the Indian Ocean off the coast of Kenya, off Pemba and Mafia Islands (Tanzania), and off the island countries of Seychelles and Mauritius.

Freshwater fishing for Nile perch (200+ pounds/ 90+ kg) and tigerfish (one of the best fighting fish in the world) is excellent in Lake Tanganyika (especially near Zambia), Lakes Turkana and Victoria (Kenya), and Lake

Kariba (Zimbabwe). Trout fishing is very good in parks such as Nyanga (Zimbabwe) and on remote lakes on the slopes of Mt. Kenya. Most freshwater fishing requires a license, which can usually be obtained from your hotel, lodge or camp for a small fee.

OTHER SAFARIS

Additional options for the special-interest traveler include anthropology, archeology, art, backpacking and camel safaris.

COST OF A SAFARI

African currencies have been historically weak against the U.S. and Canadian dollars, making Africa an especially attractive destination when the value of the dollar is down against the currencies of Europe, the Far East and other destinations overseas.

The cost per day is most dependent on how comfortably you wish to travel (the level of accommodation), the remoteness of the safari, type of transportation used, whether you're on a private safari or on a tour and the countries involved. Deluxe accommodations and transportation are normally more expensive in countries off the beaten track than in the more popular tourism spots.

For example, deluxe (Class A) safari camps in Botswana and Zimbabwe are often more expensive than Class A lodges in Kenya. Camps in Botswana and Zimbabwe cater to smaller groups and are generally situated in more remote locations, and charter aircraft are often used to reach them.

Transportation is more costly in Tanzania, for instance, than in South Africa because in Tanzania petrol is more expensive and poor roads mean greater wear-and-tear on vehicles.

As in Europe and other parts of the world, general-interest tours cost less than tours with more unique itineraries. Getting off the beaten track may dip a bit more into the wallet, but many travelers find it well worth it.

For current costs on package tours and tailor-made itineraries, contact The Africa Adventure Company (see introduction pages).

How much closer can you get?

Night photography — a leopard is always a lucky find.

LANGUAGE

English is widely spoken in all these countries except Burundi, Rwanda and the Congo, where French is the international language.

Travel Journal Africa (see **Catalog**) has illustrations of 125 mammals, birds, reptiles and trees, along with words and phrases in French, Kiswahili (Kenya, Tanzania), Shona (Zimbabwe), Tswana (Botswana) and Zulu (Southern Africa). Your guide will love it if you start naming the animals spotted in his native language!

PHOTOGRAPHY

For wildlife photography, a 200mm zoom lens is the smallest that should be used; a 300–400mm zoom is preferable. A 500mm or larger lens is necessary for bird photography. A wide-angle lens (28–35mm) is great for scenic shots.

I prefer an autofocus 35mm camera which can also be adjusted manually. On my most recent safari, I took two camera bodies, a 28–85mm and 100–300mm zoom lenses, and a 500mm lens and was satisfied with the results.

ASA 64 and 100 are best during the day when there is plenty of light. ASA 200–ASA 400 is often needed in early mornings and late afternoons, especially when using telephoto or zoom lenses. With very low light, use a flash or ASA 1000 or higher film.

Bring extra camera and flash batteries and plenty of film, as film and batteries are very expensive and difficult to obtain in Africa. At least 30 rolls of film should be brought (per couple) for a two-week safari.

Bring a beanbag on which to steady your camera. If weight is a problem, then bring the beanbag without the beans and fill it with sand, rice, etc. when you arrive at your destination.

Also consider bringing a small tripod to help steady your camera when shooting from the roof of your vehicle. Monopods (one-legged support) are also useful, especially on walking safaris.

Vehicle vibrations can cause blurry photos, so ask your guide to turn off the engine for those special shots. Protect lenses with UV filters. A polarizer helps

Young cubs are such fun to watch – usually up to some kind of mischief!

cut glare and is especially effective when you have lots of sky and water in the photo. Store cameras and lenses in plastic bags to protect them from dust and humidity, and clean them regularly with lens paper or lens brushes.

If you bring a camcorder or video recorder, be sure to bring at least three extra batteries and a charging unit and converter (Africa uses 220–240 volts). Batteries can usually be recharged at your lodge or permanent camp while the generator is running or from your vehicle while you are being driven around.

Do *not* take photographs of airports, bridges, railway stations, government buildings, telecommunication installations and offices, military and police installations and personnel. You may have your camera confiscated and waste a lot of time having to explain why you were taking the photos in the first place.

SAFARI TIPS

Read the **Safari Glossary** to become familiar with the terminology used in the bush. Once on safari, you will notice that when you ask people what animals they saw on their game drive, they might reply, "Elephant, lion, leopard and oryx," when in fact they saw several members of each species. This use of the singular form when more than one of that species was seen is common. However, one exception to this rule is saying *crocs* for *crocodile*. This form of "Safariese" will be used throughout this guide to help separate you from the amateur.

Obtain detailed maps of the countries you intend to visit. This will not only increase your awareness of the geography before and during your safari, but will better enable you to relate the story of your safari to family and friends upon your return. For a catalog of difficult-to-find maps of Africa, please call the Africa Adventure Company (see introduction pages).

It is often better to sit quietly at a few water holes than to rush around in an attempt to visit as many locations as possible. Don't just look for large game; there is an abundance of reptiles, amphibians, smaller mammals, birds and insects that are often fascinating to observe. Do not disturb the animals. Remember, we are guests in their world.

Instead of just checking species of animals off your checklist and then moving on, concentrate on observing the behavior of the animals around you. Asking your guide about the animal behavior you are observing will open up a whole new level of exploration for you. Most people who take the time to really look, find animal behavior fascinating!

Put your valuables in a safety deposit box at your lodge or hotel.

Do not call out to a person, signaling with an index finger. This is insulting to most Africans. Instead, use four fingers with your palm facing downward.

Wear colors that blend in with your surroundings (brown, tan, light green or khaki). Do not wear perfume or cologne while game viewing. Wildlife can detect unnatural smells for miles and unnatural colors for hundreds of yards (meters), making close approaches difficult.

The very few tourists who get hurt on safari are almost always those travelers who ignore the laws of nature and most probably the advice and warnings of their guides. Common sense is the rule.

Do not wade or swim in rivers, lakes or streams unless you know for certain they are free of crocodiles, hippos, and bilharzia (a disease). Fast-moving areas of rivers are often safe, but can still be a bit risky. Bilharzia, fortunately, is not the dreaded disease that it once was; if detected early it can be easily cured.

Do not walk along the banks of rivers near dawn, dusk or at night. Those that do so may inadvertently cut off a hippo's path to its water hole, and the hippo may charge. Hippos are responsible for more human deaths in Africa than any other game animal, most often from this type of occurrence.

Malaria is present in almost all the parks and reserves covered in this guide. Malarial prophylaxis (pills) should be taken and must be prescribed by a physician. As malaria-carrying mosquitos come out at dawn, dusk and at night, during this period you should use mosquito repellent and wear long pants and long-sleeve shirt, shoes (not sandals) and socks. For further information see the section on "Health" in the "Safari Pages" section of this book.

Wear closed-toed shoes or boots at night and also during the day if venturing out into the bush. Bring a flashlight and always have it with you at night.

Don't venture out of your lodge or camp without your guide, especially at night, dawn or dusk. Remember that wildlife is not confined to the parks and reserves in many countries.

Resist the temptation to jog in national parks, reserves or other areas where wildlife exists. To lion and other carnivores, we are just "meat on the hoof" like any other animal — only much slower and less capable of defending ourselves.

WHAT TO WEAR – WHAT TO TAKE

Countries close to the equator (Burundi, Kenya, Rwanda, Tanzania, Uganda, and the Congo) have small differences in seasonal temperatures, with June-August being the coolest time of the year; the main factor affecting temperature is altitude.

Countries in southern Africa (Lesotho, Namibia, South Africa, Swaziland, Zambia, Zimbabwe and Malawi) have more pronounced seasons, often cold (sometimes freezing) in winter (June-August) and hot in summer (October-February).

Casual clothing is usually worn by day. Dresses for ladies and coats and ties for men are only required in a few top restaurants in Kenya, South Africa and Zimbabwe. In some restaurants, gentlemen's coats are available on request.

Bring at least one camera and lots of film, binoculars, sun block, electric converter and adapter, a copy of *Travel Journal Africa*, alarm clock, insect repellent, brown, khaki or light green cotton clothing including at least two pairs of long pants and two long-sleeve shirts, wide-brimmed hat, rain gear, good walking shoes, flashlight and extra batteries, two pairs of sunglasses, two pairs of prescription glasses (one for contact-lens wearers) and a copy of the prescription with a letter from your doctor verifying your need, medical summary from your doctor if medical problems exist, Band-aids (plasters), motion-sickness tablets, medicine for traveler's diarrhoea, antimalarial prophylaxis, decongestant tablets, laxative, headache tablets, throat lozenges, antacid, and antibiotic ointment.

Bring along a comfortable pair of walking shoes. If you are going on walking safaris, be sure to have a pair of earth colored shoes (not white tennis shoes!) for your walks.

Each person going on safari should definitely have his own pair of binoculars. I am amazed at the number of Africa travelers who have paid thousands of dollars each for a game viewing safari, yet take with them a poor-quality pair of binoculars which limits the enjoyment of the primary function of the trip.

If your budget will allow, I suggest spending from $150 to $375 for a medium to high quality pair of binoculars that could be used on subsequent Africa safaris and safaris to other continents, and possibly provide you with a lifetime of use. I recommend binoculars with 8 to 10 power, such as Steiner 8X30 Safaris or 10x28 Rockys.

Leave your dress watch at home and buy an inexpensive (under U.S. $50) waterproof watch with a light and alarm. Do not wear or bring any camouflage or dark green clothing; in many countries these colors are reserved for the military.

For a more comprehensive packing list and trip organizer for your safari, obtain a copy of *Travel Journal Africa*. To obtain a catalog of valuable books, maps, binoculars and safari clothing, see the end of the book.

WILDLIFE

HABITATS

Animals are most often found in and nearby the habitats in which they feed or hunt. These habitats fall roughly into four categories — savannah, desert, wetlands and forest.

Savannah is a very broad term referring to dry land which can be open grasslands, grasslands dotted with trees, or wooded areas. Grazers (grass-eaters) and carnivores (meat-eaters) adept at hunting in savannah are most easily found here. Some browsers (leaf-eaters) also make the savannah their home.

Deserts have little or no standing water and very sparse vegetation. Many desert animals do not drink at all but derive water only from the

The fastest running land mammal is the cheetah.

plants they eat and the condensation formed on them. Some savannah grazers and carnivores can be found in the desert.

African **forests** are thickly vegetated, often with grasses and shrubs growing to about ten feet (3 m) in height, shorter trees 20-50 feet (6-15 m) high, and a higher canopy reaching to 150 feet (45 m) or more.

It is usually more difficult to spot animals in forests than in the other habitats. Many forest animals such as the elephant are more easily seen in open savannah areas. Forest herbivores (plant-eaters) are browsers, preferring to feed on the leaves of plants and fruits usually found in forests. Carnivores have adapted to a style of hunting where they can closely approach their prey under cover.

Wetlands consist of lakes, rivers and swamps which often are part of a larger savannah or forest habitat. Many rivers wind through savannah regions, providing a habitat within a habitat. Wetlands are good places not only to see wetland species, but also other habitat species that come there to drink.

The **Eco Map** (see page 226 of the color insert pages) shows the location of different eco-zones. Following the map are detailed descriptions and representative photos of nine different zones. When reading the description of a park or reserve, use these photos to help visualize what the park or reserve may look like.

The animals listed in the **Animals by Habitat** chart that follows are classified according to the habitat where most of their time is spent – their most dominant habitat. The animals are listed in order of size by weight.

The major parks and reserves listed in the **Major Wildlife Areas By Habitat** chart are classified according to their most dominant habitats.

Many of these wildlife areas are composed of more than one habitat, so consult the text of this book for in-depth descriptions. Keep in mind that savannah and forest animals may visit wetland habitats to drink and that many forest animals are more easily seen on the open savannah.

A well-rounded safari includes visits to several types of habitats and parks, giving the visitor an overall picture of wildlife and ecosystems.

Use the **What Wildlife Is Best Seen Where** chart as a guide in finding the major parks and reserves that are most likely to have the animals you are most interested in seeing on safari.

WHEN'S THE BEST TIME TO GO?

The **When's The Best Time To Go For Game Viewing** chart (see p. 225 of the color insert) shows at a glance when best to go to see the greatest numbers or concentration of large mammals in the countries, parks and reserves of your choice. Alternatively, the chart shows the best places to go in the month(s) in which your vacation is planned. In other words, how to be in the right place at the right time.

For example, your vacation is in February and your primary interest is game viewing on a photographic safari. Find the countries on the chart in which game viewing is "excellent," "good," or "fair" in February. Turn to the respective country chapters for additional information and choose the ones that intrigue you the most. In this example, for instance, Tanzania would be an excellent choice. Use this chart as a general guideline as conditions vary from year to year.

Timing can make a world of difference. For example, Hwange National Park in Zimbabwe is well-known for its population of over 25,000 elephant. I once spent Christmas there (during the rainy season), and we didn't see one elephant. But during the dry season, they're everywhere.

ANIMALS BY HABITAT

The animals listed below are classified according to the habitat where most of their time is spent. The animals are listed in order of size by weight.

SAVANNAH/ SAVANNAH WOODLAND

GRAZERS	BROWSERS	CARNIVORES
White rhino	Elephant	Lion
Eland	Giraffe	Hyena
Zebra	Kudu	Leopard
Waterbuck	Nyala	Cheetah
Roan antelope	Bushbuck	African wild dog
Gemsbok (oryx)	Gerenuk	Jackal
Topi	Duiker	Serval
Hartebeest	Dikdik	Bat-eared fox
Wildebeest		Mongoose
Tsessebe		Genet
Warthog		
Reedbuck		
Grant's gazelle		
Impala		
Springbok		
Thomson's gazelle		
Klipspringer		
Steenbok		

FOREST

PRIMATES	BROWSERS	CARNIVORES
Gorilla	Elephant	Leopard
Chimpanzee	Nyala	Serval
Colobus monkey	Bongo	Genet
Syke's monkey	Bushbuck	
	Duiker	

WETLANDS

BROWSERS	CARNIVORES
Hippopotamus	Crocodile
Buffalo	Otter
Sitatunga	

DESERTS

See savannah grazers, browsers and carnivores above

MAJOR WILDLIFE AREAS BY HABITAT

P - Primary Habitat S - Secondary Habitat [R] - Riverine [L] - Lake

EAST AND CENTRAL AFRICA

COUNTRY	WILDLIFE AREA	SAVANNAH	FOREST	WETLAND
Tanzania	Arusha (N.P.)		P	S
	Lake Manyara	S		P[L]
	Ngorongoro	P		S[L]
	Serengeti	P		S [R]
	Tarangire	P		S [R]
	Mt. Kilimanjaro		P	
	Selous	P		S [R]
	Ruaha	P		S [R]
	Mikumi	P		
	Gombe Stream		P	S [L]
	Mahale Mountains		P	S [L]
Kenya	Nairobi (N.P.)	P		
	Amboseli	P		S
	Tsavo	P		
	Masai Mara	P		S [R]
	Mt. Elgon		P	
	Aberdere		P	
	Mt. Kenya		P	
	Meru	P	S	
	Lake Naivasha			P [L]
	Lake Nakuru	S		P [L]
	Lake Bogoria			P [L]
	Lake Baringo			P [L]
	Samburu	P		S [R]
	Lewa Downs	P		
Uganda	Murchison Falls	P		S [R]
	Queen Elizabeth N.P.	P		S [L]
	Bwindi		P	
	Kibale		P	
Rwanda	Volcano Nat. Park		P	
Congo	Virunga (Rwindi area)	P		S [L]
	Virunga (other areas)	S	P	
	Kahuzi-Biega		P	

MAJOR WILDLIFE AREAS BY HABITAT

P - Primary Habitat S - Secondary Habitat [R] - Riverine [L] - Lake

SOUTHERN AFRICA

COUNTRY	WILDLIFE AREA	SAVANNAH WOODLAND	FOREST	WETLAND	DESERT
Zimbabwe	Hwange	P			
	Matusadona	S		P [L]	
	Chizarira	P			
	Mana Pools	S		P [R]	
	Matobo	P			
Botswana	Okavango Delta			P	
	Moremi	P		S	
	Linyanti	S		P	
	Savute	P			
	Chobe	P		S [R]	
	Kalahari Desert	S			P
Zambia lower	North & South Luangwa	P		S [R]	
	Zambezi	S		P [R]	
	Kafue	P		S	
Namibia	Etosha	P			S
	East Caprivi	P		S	
	Damavraland				P
	Namib-Naukluft				P
South Africa	Kruger	P		S [R]	
	Private Reserves (Kruger)	P			
	Kalahari-Gemsbok				P
	Hluhluwe Umfolozi	P			

In most cases the best game viewing, as exhibited on the chart, also corresponds to the dry season. Wildlife concentrates around water holes and rivers, and vegetation is less dense than in the wet season, making game easier to find. There are, however, exceptions. For instance, the Serengeti migration (to the north and west) often begins at the height of the rains in Tanzania.

During the rainy season the land is often luxuriously green, the air clear. People interested in scenery or with dust allergies may wish to plan their visits shortly after the rains are predicted to have started or soon after the rains are predicted to have stopped. Game is usually more difficult to find, but there are usually fewer travelers in the parks and reserves.

WHAT WILDLIFE IS BEST SEEN WHERE?

(Ratings pertain to the best time to go to each park or reserve)

COUNTRY	MAJOR PARK OR RESERVE	Lion	Leopord	Cheetah	Elephant	Black rhino	White rhino	Hippo	Buffalo	Eland	Greater kudu	Sable antelope	Gemsbok/Oryx	
EAST AFRICA														
Tanzania	Lake Manyara	B	D	D	A	X	X	A+	B	X	X	X	X	
	Ngorongoro	A	C	C	A	A	X	A	A	B	X	X	B[3]	
	Serengeti	A	A	A	B	X	X	B	A	B	X	X	B	
	Tarangire	A	C	B	A+	X	X	B	B	B	X	X	A	
	Selous	B	C	X	A	F	X	A	B	B	B	X	X	
	Ruaha	A	C	C	A	D	X	A	A	B	B	B	B	
Kenya	Amboseli	B	C	B	A	X	X	B	A	C	X	X	C	
	Masai Mara	A	B	A	B	C	X	B	B	B	X	X	X	
	Samburu	A	B[1]	B	A	X	X	X	A	B	X	X	A	
	Tsavo	B	D	C	A	D	X	B	A	C	X	X	C	
	Lewa Downs	D	B2	C	B	A+	A+	X	B	D	B	X	A	
SOUTHERN AFRICA														
Zimbabwe	Chizarira	C	C	F	B	C[4]	X	X	B	D	B	D	X	
	Hwange	A	B	C	A	D	C	B	A	B	B	A	D	
	Mana Pools	B	B	F	A+	F	X	A+	A	B	B	F	X	
	Matusadona	B	C	D	A	C	X	A	A+	X	B	F	X	
	Matobo	X	C	F	X	B	A	B	X	B	B	A	X	
Botswana	Chobe	A	C	B	A+	X	X	A	A	D	B	C	F	
	Moremi	A	B	B	A	X	F	A	B	F	A	C	X	
	Okavango Delta	C	D	D	B	X	X	A+	B	F	B	D	X	
	Linyanti	A	C	C	A	X	X	A	B	D	A	B	X	
	Savute	A	C	C	A	X	X	F	C	D	A	C	X	
Zambia	S. Luangwa	A	A[2]	F	A	F	X	A	A	C	B	F	X	
	N. Luangwa	A	C	X	B	X	X	A	A	B	B	F	X	
	Lower Zambezi	B	B	F	A	X	X	A	A	B	B	X	X	
Namibia	Etosha	A	B	B	A	B	X	X	X	B	A	X	A	
South Africa	Kruger	B	C	B	A	C	B	A	A	C	A	C	X	
	Private Reserves	A	A[2]	B	A	C	A	A	A	C	A	C	X	

A+ - Best reserves
A - Almost always seen (seen on most game drives)
B - Frequently seen (usually seen on every two - six game drives)
C - Occasionally seen (seen every one-two weeks)
D - Seldom seen (seen every two-four weeks)
F - Present but almost never seen
X - Not seen in this reserve
[1] At lodges that bait for leopard
[2] Seen most often on night game drives
[3] In Ngorongoro Conservation Area near Serengeti National Park
[4] Seen more often on walks than on game drives

When's the Best Time to Go For Bird Watching

AFRICA'S TOP WILDLIFE RESERVES

EXCELLENT | GOOD | FAIR | POOR | CLOSED

COUNTRY	PARK/RESERVE	JAN	FEB	MAR	APR	MAY	JUN	JUL	AUG	SEP	OCT	NOV	DEC
EAST AFRICA													
TANZANIA	LAKE MANYARA	Excellent	Excellent	Excellent	Good	Good	Fair	Poor	Poor	Fair	Good	Excellent	Excellent
	NGORONGORO	Excellent	Excellent	Excellent	Good	Good	Fair	Poor	Poor	Fair	Good	Excellent	Excellent
	SERENGETI (S.E.)	Excellent	Excellent	Excellent	Good	Good	Fair	Poor	Poor	Fair	Good	Excellent	Excellent
	SERENGETI (N. & N..W.)	Excellent	Excellent	Excellent	Good	Good	Fair	Poor	Poor	Fair	Good	Excellent	Excellent
	TARANGIRE	Excellent	Excellent	Excellent	Good	Good	Fair	Poor	Poor	Fair	Good	Excellent	Excellent
	SELOUS & RUAHA	Excellent	Excellent	Excellent	Good	Good	Fair	Poor	Poor	Fair	Good	Excellent	Excellent
KENYA	AMBOSELI	Excellent	Excellent	Excellent	Good	Good	Fair	Poor	Poor	Fair	Good	Excellent	Excellent
	TSAVO	Excellent	Excellent	Excellent	Good	Good	Fair	Poor	Poor	Fair	Good	Excellent	Excellent
	MASAI MARA	Excellent	Excellent	Excellent	Good	Good	Fair	Poor	Poor	Fair	Good	Excellent	Excellent
	ABERDERES & MERU	Excellent	Excellent	Excellent	Good	Good	Fair	Poor	Poor	Fair	Good	Excellent	Excellent
	SAMBURU, BUFFALO SPRINGS & SHABA	Excellent	Excellent	Excellent	Good	Good	Fair	Poor	Poor	Fair	Good	Excellent	Excellent
	LEWA DOWNS	Excellent	Excellent	Excellent	Good	Good	Fair	Poor	Poor	Fair	Good	Excellent	Excellent
SOUTHERN AFRICA													
ZIMBABWE	CHIZARIRA	Excellent	Excellent	Excellent	Good	Fair	Fair	Fair	Good	Good	Excellent	Excellent	Excellent
	HWANGE	Excellent	Excellent	Excellent	Good	Fair	Fair	Fair	Good	Good	Excellent	Excellent	Excellent
	MATUSADONA	Excellent	Excellent	Excellent	Excellent	Good	Good	Good	Good	Good	Excellent	Excellent	Excellent
	MANA POOLS	Closed	Closed	Closed	Closed	Good	Good	Good	Good	Excellent	Excellent	Excellent	Closed
	MATOBO	Excellent	Excellent	Excellent	Good	Fair	Fair	Fair	Good	Good	Excellent	Excellent	Excellent
BOTSWANA	MOREMI & OKAVANGO DELTA	Excellent	Excellent	Excellent	Good	Good	Good	Good	Good	Excellent	Excellent	Excellent	Excellent
	LINYANTI	Excellent	Excellent	Excellent	Good	Good	Good	Good	Good	Excellent	Excellent	Excellent	Excellent
	SAVUTE	Excellent	Excellent	Excellent	Good	Fair	Poor	Poor	Poor	Good	Good	Excellent	Excellent
	CHOBE	Excellent	Excellent	Excellent	Excellent	Good	Good	Good	Good	Excellent	Excellent	Excellent	Excellent
	NXAI PAN	Excellent	Excellent	Excellent	Excellent	Good	Fair	Fair	Fair	Fair	Good	Good	Good
	MAKGADIKGADI	Excellent	Excellent	Excellent	Excellent	Good	Fair	Fair	Fair	Fair	Good	Good	Good
ZAMBIA	SOUTH LUANGWA (NORTHERN PART)	Closed	Closed	Closed	Closed	Fair	Fair	Fair	Good	Good	Excellent	Closed	Closed
	SOUTH LUANGWA (CENTRAL)]	Excellent	Excellent	Good	Good	Fair	Fair	Fair	Good	Good	Excellent	Excellent	Excellent
	LOWER ZAMBEZI	Excellent	Excellent	Excellent	Excellent	Good	Good	Good	Good	Excellent	Excellent	Excellent	Excellent
NAMIBIA	ETOSHA	Excellent	Excellent	Excellent	Excellent	Good	Good	Good	Good	Good	Excellent	Excellent	Excellent
SOUTH AFRICA	KRUGER	Excellent	Excellent	Excellent	Excellent	Good	Good	Good	Good	Good	Excellent	Excellent	Excellent
	PRIVATE RESERVES	Excellent	Excellent	Excellent	Excellent	Good	Good	Good	Good	Good	Excellent	Excellent	Excellent
	NATAL GAME RESERVES	Excellent	Excellent	Excellent	Excellent	Excellent	Good	Good	Good	Excellent	Excellent	Excellent	Excellent

AVERAGE MONTHLY TEMPERATURES

MIN/MAX IN CENTIGRADE

CITY	JAN	FEB	MAR	APR	MAY	JUN	JUL	AUG	SEP	OCT	NOV	DEC
EAST AFRICA												
Dar-es-Salaam	25/32	25/32	24/32	23/31	22/29	20/29	19/28	19/28	19/28	21/29	23/31	24/31
Dodoma	18/29	18/29	18/28	18/28	16/28	15/27	13/27	14/27	15/29	17/31	18/31	18/31
Kigoma	19/27	20/27	20/27	19/27	19/28	188/29	17/28	18/29	19/30	21/29	20/27	19/26
Nairobi	12/25	13/26	14/25	14/24	13/22	12/21	11/21	11/21	11/24	14/25	13/24	13/24
Mombasa	24/32	24/32	25/32	24/31	23/28	23/28	22/27	22/27	22/28	23/29	24/29	24/30
Kampala	18/28	18/28	18/27	18/26	25/17	26/18	26/18	26/17	27/17	27/17	27/17	27/17
Kabale	9/24	11/24	11/24	11/24	11/23	10/23	9/23	10/23	10/24	11/24	11/24	10/24
Kigali	6/20	9/21	8/20	6/20	5/20	3/20	5/20	4/21	3/21	9/20	3/20	4/20
Bujumbura	19/28	19/28	19/28	19/28	19/28	18/29	18/29	18/31	19/32	20/31	19/29	19/29
SOUTHERN AFRICA												
Harare	17/27	17/27	15/27	13/27	10/24	8/22	7/22	8/24	12/27	14/29	16/28	16/27
Bulawayo	17/28	17/28	16/27	14/27	10/24	8/22	8/22	10/24	12/28	15/30	16/31	16/29
Victoria Falls	18/29	17/29	17/29	14/29	9/27	5/24	7/27	12/31	16/32	18/32	18/31	18/30
Hwange	18/29	18/29	17/29	14/29	9/27	5/24	5/25	7/27	12/31	16/32	18/32	18/30
Kariba	22/31	21/31	21/31	19/31	15/29	12/27	11/26	14/29	19/33	23/35	24/34	22/32
Mana Pools	22/32	21/32	21/32	20/31	17/29	14/27	13/27	15/30	19/34	23/36	23/35	22/33
Maun	19/32	19/31	18/31	14/31	9/28	6/25	6/25	9/28	13/33	18/35	19/34	19/34
Lusaka	17/26	17/26	17/26	15/26	13/25	10/24	10/23	12/25	15/30	18/31	18/30	18/28
S. Luangwa	20/32	20/31	19/32	18/32	19/31	12/30	11/29	12/30	15/35	20/40	22/37	22/33
Windhoek	17/30	17/29	15/27	13/25	9/22	7/20	7/20	8/23	12/26	14/29	16/29	17/31
Swakopmund	12/25	12/23	12/23	15/25	15/25	18/28	15/28	15/28	12/25	12/25	12/25	12/25
Johannesburg	15/26	14/25	13/24	11/22	8/19	5/16	5/16	7/19	9/22	12/24	13/25	14/25
Durban	21/28	21/28	20/28	17/26	13/24	10/23	10/23	12/23	15/23	17/24	18/25	20/27
Cape Town	16/26	15/26	14/25	12/23	10/20	8/18	7/17	7/18	8/19	10/21	13/24	15/25

AVERAGE MONTHLY TEMPERATURES

MIN/MAX IN FAHRENHEIT

CITY	JAN	FEB	MAR	APR	MAY	JUN	JUL	AUG	SEP	OCT	NOV	DEC
EAST AFRICA												
Dar-Es-Salaam	77/88	76/87	76/89	74/87	72/85	68/85	66/84	66/84	68/84	68/86	73/87	76/88
Dodoma	66/86	66/85	64/84	64/84	62/83	57/82	57/79	57/81	59/85	63/88	64/89	65/88
Kigoma	67/81	68/82	68/82	67/82	68/83	67/82	63/83	65/85	67/86	69/85	68/81	67/80
Nairobi	55/78	56/80	58/78	58/76	56/73	54/70	51/70	52/71	53/76	55/77	56/74	55/75
Mombasa	75/88	76/88	77/89	76/87	75/84	74/83	71/81	71/81	72/83	74/85	75/86	76/87
Kampala	65/84	65/83	64/82	64/81	63/79	63/78	63/78	62/78	63/81	63/82	62/81	62/81
Kabale	49/76	50/76	50/75	51/74	51/73	50/73	48/75	49/75	50/76	51/75	50/73	50/73
Kigali	43/68	48/68	46/68	43/68	41/68	37/68	41/68	39/70	37/70	48/68	37/68	39/68
Bujumbura	66/83	66/83	66/83	66/83	66/83	65/85	64/85	65/87	67/89	68/87	67/83	67/83
SOUTHERN AFRICA												
Harare	61/79	61/79	59/79	56/79	50/75	45/71	45/71	47/75	54/80	58/84	60/82	61/79
Victoria Falls	65/85	64/85	62/85	57/84	49/81	43/76	42/77	47/82	55/89	62/91	64/90	64/86
Hwange	64/85	64/84	62/85	56/83	47/80	42/76	40/76	45/81	54/88	61/90	64/89	64/85
Kariba	71/88	71/88	69/88	65/87	58/84	53/80	52/79	57/84	67/91	74/95	74/93	72/89
Mana Pools	71/89	71/89	70/89	67/88	62/85	57/81	56/81	59/86	66/92	73/97	74/95	72/91
Bulawayo	61/82	61/81	60/80	57/80	50/75	46/70	46/71	49/75	55/82	59/86	61/85	61/83
Maun	66/90	66/88	64/88	57/88	48/82	43/77	43/77	48/82	55/91	64/95	66/93	66/90
Lusaka	63/78	63/79	62/79	59/79	55/78	50/73	49/73	53/77	59/84	64/88	64/85	63/81
S. Luangwa	68/90	68/88	66/90	64/90	66/88	54/86	52/84	54/86	59/95	68/104	72/99	72/91
Windhoek	63/86	63/84	59/81	55/77	48/72	45/68	45/68	46/73	54/79	57/84	61/84	63/88
Swakopmund	54/77	54/73	54/73	59/77	59/77	64/82	59/82	59/82	54/77	54/77	54/77	54/77
Johannesburg	59/79	57/77	55/75	52/72	46/66	41/61	41/61	45/66	48/72	54/75	55/77	57/77
Durban	70/82	70/82	68/82	63/79	55/75	50/73	50/73	54/73	59/73	63/75	64/77	68/81
Cape Town	61/79	59/79	57/77	54/73	50/68	46/64	45/63	45/64	46/66	50/70	55/75	59/77

AVERAGE MONTHLY RAINFALL

IN INCHES

EAST AFRICA												
CITY	JAN	FEB	MAR	APR	MAY	JUN	JUL	AUG	SEP	OCT	NOV	DEC
Dar-es-Salaam	2.6	2.6	5.1	11.4	7.4	1.3	1.2	1.0	1.2	1.6	2.9	3.6
Dodoma	6.0	4.3	5.4	1.9	0.2	0	0	0	0	0.2	0.9	3.6
Kigoma	4.8	5.0	5.9	5.1	1.7	0.2	0.1	0.2	0.7	1.9	5.6	5.3
Nairobi	1.5	2.5	4.9	8.3	6.2	1.8	0.7	0.9	1.3	2.2	4.3	3.4
Mombasa	1.1	0.8	2.4	7.7	12.7	4.7	3.5	2.6	2.6	3.4	3.8	2.4
Kampala	1.8	2.4	5.1	6.9	5.8	2.9	1.8	3.4	3.6	3.8	4.8	3.9
Kabale	2.4	3.8	5.2	4.9	3.6	1.2	0.8	2.4	3.7	3.9	4.4	3.4
Kigali	3.5	3.5	4.1	6.5	4.9	1.0	.3	.8	2.4	3.9	3.9	3.5
Bujumbura	3.7	4.4	4.8	4.9	2.3	0.4	0.3	0.4	1.5	2.5	3.9	4.4
SOUTHERN AFRICA												
Harare	7.7	7.1	4.5	1.2	0.5	0.2	0	0.1	0.3	1.2	3.8	6.4
Bulawayo	5.6	4.4	3.3	0.8	0.4	0.1	0	0	0.2	0.8	3.3	4.9
Victoria Falls	6.6	5	2.8	1.0	0.1	0	0	0	0.7	1.1	2.5	6.8
Hwange	5.7	5.1	2.3	0.8	0.1	0	0	0	0.1	0.8	2.2	5.0
Kariba	7.5	6.2	4.4	1.2	0.2	0	0	0	0	0.7	2.9	6.9
Mana Pools	8.7	7.1	4.2	1.0	0.2	0	0	0	0	0.5	2.3	9.1
Maun	4.3	3.2	2.8	1.0	0.3	0.1	0	0	0	1.2	2.0	3.8
Lusaka	9.1	7.6	5.7	0.7	0.2	0	0	0	0	0.4	3.6	5.9
S. Luangwa	7.7	11.3	5.6	3.6	0	0	0	0	0	2.0	4.3	4.3
Windhoek	1.7	2.0	2.2	1.1	0.2	0.1	0.1	0.1	0.1	0.4	0.9	1.0
Swakopmund	0.5	0.5	0.5	0.4	0.4	0.4	0.3	0.4	0.4	0.6	0.6	0.4
Johannesburg	4.5	3.8	2.9	2.5	0.9	0.3	0.3	0.2	0.1	2.7	4.6	4.3
Durban	5.1	4.5	5.3	4.2	2.0	1.2	1.4	1.7	2.4	3.9	4.5	4.6
Cape Town	0.6	0.7	0.7	2.0	3.5	3.3	3.5	3.1	2.0	1.4	0.5	0.6

AVERAGE MONTHLY RAINFALL

IN MILLIMETERS

EAST AFRICA												
CITY	JAN	FEB	MAR	APR	MAY	JUN	JUL	AUG	SEP	OCT	NOV	DEC
Dar-es-Salaam	66	66	130	292	188	33	33	26	31	42	74	91
Dodoma	152	110	138	49	5	0	0	0	0	5	24	92
Kigoma	123	128	150	130	44	5	3	5	19	28	143	135
Nairobi	39	65	125	211	158	47	15	24	32	53	110	87
Mombasa	25	19	65	197	320	120	90	65	65	87	98	62
Kampala	47	61	130	175	148	73	45	85	90	96	122	99
Kabale	58	97	130	125	92	28	20	58	98	99	110	87
Kigali	90	90	105	165	125	25	7	20	60	100	100	90
Bujumbura	95	110	121	125	56	11	5	11	37	65	100	115
SOUTHERN AFRICA												
Harare	196	179	118	28	14	3	0	3	5	28	97	163
Bulawayo	143	110	85	19	10	3	0	0	5	20	81	123
Victoria Falls	168	126	70	24	3	1	0	0	2	27	64	174
Hwange	145	129	57	20	3	0	0	0	2	21	56	127
Kariba	192	158	113	30	4	1	1	0	1	18	74	175
Mana Pools	221	181	107	26	4	0	0	0	1	13	59	231
Maun	110	80	70	25	7	3	0	0	0	30	50	95
Lusaka	232	192	144	18	3	0	0	0	0	11	92	150
S. Luangwa	195	287	141	91	0	0	0	0	0	50	108	110
Windhoek	43	53	56	28	5	3	3	3	3	10	23	26
Swakopmund	12	15	12	10	10	10	7	9	11	15	16	11
Johannesburg	112	96	74	61	23	8	8	5	3	69	117	109
Durban	130	114	135	107	54	31	36	43	61	99	114	117
Cape Town	15	18	18	50	90	85	90	80	50	36	13	15

Many camps and lodges offer low-season rates, making travel during those times economically attractive. The low season in Kenya and Tanzania is April-June (except for Easter) and November, while the low season in Botswana is November-June.

Generally speaking, game viewing is best in Kenya and Tanzania mid-December-March and July-September, while the best game viewing in Zimbabwe, Zambia, Malawi and South Africa is June-October. Game viewing in Botswana is best May-November.

In summary, the best time for *you* to go may be a combination of the best time to see the wildlife that interests you most (large mammals vs. birds), the relative costs involved (low or high season), and when you can get vacation time.

Most reserves in Africa are simply heaven for bird watchers. The best times for bird watching, as shown in the **When's the Best Time To Go For Bird Watching Chart** (page 77) are often the opposite of the best times for big game viewing. Bird watching, however, is good year-round in many regions.

The **Temperature and Rainfall Chart** gives average high and low temperatures and average rainfall for each month of the year for a number of locations. Keep in mind that these are *average* temperatures; you should expect variations of at least 7° F (5° C) from the averages listed on the chart. Also keep in mind that at higher altitudes you should expect cooler temperatures. This is why many parks and reserves in Africa can be warm during the day and cool to cold at night. The most common packing mistake safariers make is not bringing enough warm layers of clothing!

AFRICA'S TOP WILDLIFE COUNTRIES

EAST AND CENTRAL AFRICA

TANZANIA

THE LION'S FEAST

On a game drive you will most often see lion either lying in the shade, too sleepy to raise their heads, or grouped around a recent kill, eating their "share."

It may seem that, since the females do most of the hunting (the males simply help drive the prey to the waiting females), the females should be the first to gorge. However, this is not the lion's pecking order. The male will select his preferred contents, usually the lungs, liver and kidneys, followed by the rump, and moving up toward the head. Skin and hair are also eaten, which gives the lion the roughage it needs. When food is plentiful, the females and cubs will feed next.

However, there are usually lots of cat fights, snarls, hisses and arguments during feeding, with the males expressing their views with roars. The males will retire, satisfied (of course); the females survive on the remains, while the cubs frequently go hungry or may be killed in the scramble.

If a small pride is feeding together on a kill, the dominant male will control who eats where and what. Any females or cubs that overstep this order will be disciplined by a snarl or a slap of the paw. Inevitably, the younger cubs will try all sorts of tricks to distract the male, who will usually tolerate these antics. He is not as fierce as he appears.

When they have finished their feast, lions will either wander off for a drink or commence grooming themselves, and all becomes peaceful, once again, in the lion pride.

TANZANIA

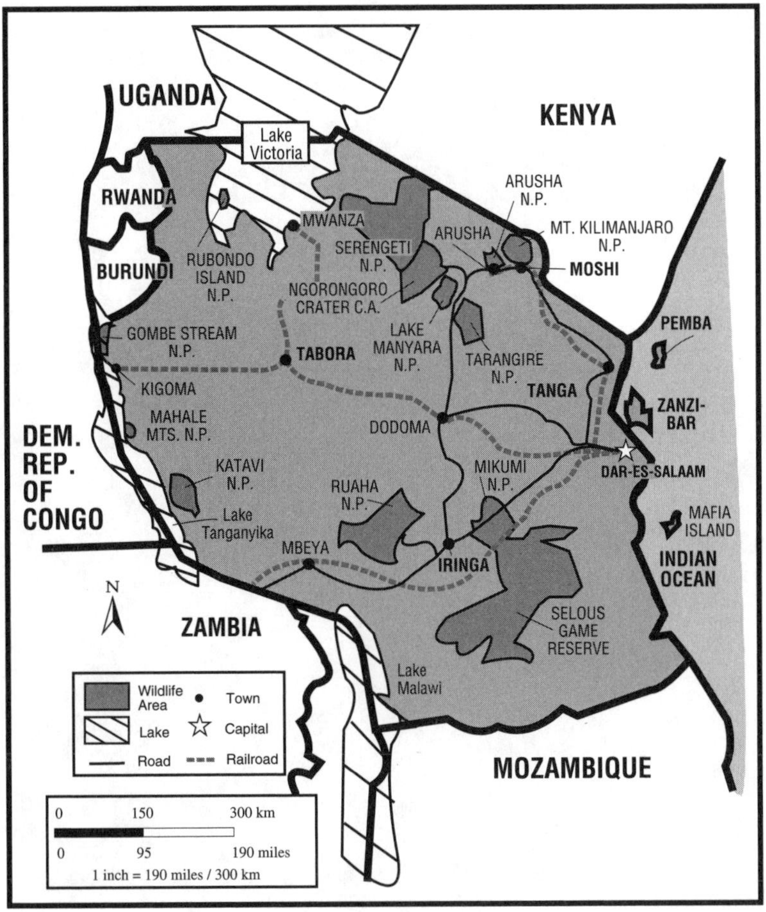

FACTS AT A GLANCE

AREA:	364,864 SQ. MI. / 945,000 SQ. KM.
APPROXIMATE SIZE:	TEXAS PLUS OKLAHOMA OR FRANCE
POPULATION:	27.4 MILLION
CAPITAL:	NOMINAL: DODOMA (POP. EST. 200,000) FUNCTIONAL: DAR ES SALAAM (POP. EST. 1.4 MILLION)
OFFICIAL LANGUAGE:	SWAHILI; ENGLISH WIDELY SPOKEN

TANZANIA

Between Africa's highest mountain (Kilimanjaro) and Africa's largest lake (Victoria) lies one of the best game-viewing areas on the continent. This region also includes the world's largest unflooded intact volcanic caldera or crater (Ngorongoro) and the most famous wildlife park (the Serengeti). To the southeast lies one of the world's largest game reserves — the Selous.

Volcanic highlands dominate the north, giving way southward to a plateau, then semidesert in the center of the country and highlands in the south. The coastal lowlands are hot and humid with lush vegetation. One branch of the Great Rift Valley passes through Lakes Manyara and Natron in northern Tanzania to Lake Malawi (Lake Nyasa) in the south, while the other branch passes through Lakes Rukwa and Tanganyika in the west.

Heavy rains usually occur in April and May and lighter rains in late October and November. Altitude has a great effect on temperature. At Arusha (4600 feet/1390 m) and the top of Ngorongoro Crater (7500 feet/2285 m), nights and early mornings are especially cool. Tanzania's highest temperatures occur in December–March and lowest in July.

Evidence suggests East Africa was the cradle of mankind. The earliest known humanoid footprints, estimated to be 3.5 million years old, were discovered at Laetoli by Dr. Mary Leakey in 1979. Dr. Leakey also found the estimated 1.7-million-year-old skull *Zinjanthropus boisei* at Oldupai (formerly Olduvai) Gorge in 1957.

From around as far back as the tenth century, Arabs, Persians, Egyptians, Indians and Chinese were involved in heavy trading on the coast. The slave trade began in the mid-1600s and was abolished in 1873.

British explorers Richard Burton and John Speke crossed Tanzania in 1857 to Lake Tanganyika. Speke later discovered Lake Victoria, which he felt was the source of the Nile.

The German East Africa Company gained control of the mainland (then called German East Africa) in 1885, and the German government held it from 1891 until World War I, when it was mandated to Britain by the League of Nations. Tanganyika gained its independence from Britain in 1961, and Zanzibar gained its independence in 1963. Zanzibar, once the center of the East African slave trade, was ruled by sultans until its union with Tanganyika in 1964, forming the United Republic of Tanzania.

There are 120 tribes in Tanzania. Bantu languages and dialects are spoken by 95 percent of the population, with Kiswahili the official and national language. Over 75 percent of the people are peasant farmers. Export of coffee, cotton, sisal, tea, cloves and cashews bring 70 percent of the country's foreign exchange.

WILDLIFE AND WILDLIFE AREAS

Reserves cover over 95,000 square miles (250,000 km^2) of area; only a few countries on earth can boast having a greater amount of land devoted to parks and reserves. The 12 national parks, 17 game reserves and 1 conservation area comprise over 15 percent of the country's land area. Tanzania's great variety of wildlife can be at least partially attributed to its great diversity of landscapes, with altitudes ranging from sea level to 19,340 feet (5895 m).

Tanzania is one of the best wildlife countries in Africa for mobile tented camp safaris. Vehicles with roof hatches or pop-tops are used on safari. If accompanied by a national park guide, walking is allowed in Arusha, Gombe Stream, Mahale Mountains and Rubondo Island National Parks, the Selous Game Reserve and in designated areas of Tarangire and the Serengeti. Walking is also allowed in the Ngorongoro Conservation area (but not within the Ngorongoro Crater itself) if accompanied by a conservation ranger.

The best weather for viewing game in northern Tanzania is July-September and December–March. January, February and August are the busiest months. Heavy rains falling in April and May hamper travel and game viewing, and a four-wheel-drive vehicle is highly recommended. Light rains usually fall October–November. In southern Tanzania the best months for game viewing are July–October.

The country contains 35 species of antelope and over 1.5 million wildebeest — over 80 percent of the population of this species in Africa. The calving season for wildebeest is from mid-January to mid-March.

THE NORTH

This region from Mt. Kilimanjaro in the east to Serengeti National Park in the west is the area most visited by tourists and contains the country's most famous parks.

Many visitors reach Arusha on a four to five-hour drive from Nairobi (Kenya) via Namanga or fly into Kilimanjaro International Airport and then are transferred to Arusha. Kilimanjaro International Airport, located 34 miles (54 km) east of Arusha and 22 miles (35 km) west of Moshi, has a bank, bar and restaurant.

The "Northern Circuit" includes Arusha National Park, Lake Manyara National Park, Ngorongoro Conservation Area, Oldupai Gorge, Serengeti National Park and Tarangire National Park.

From Arusha the Northern Circuit runs 45 miles (73 km) west on a good tarmac road, across the gently rolling Masai Plains with scattered acacia trees, to Makuyuni. You may then either continue on the main road toward Dodoma for another 20 miles (32 km) to Tarangire National Park or turn right (northwest) on an all-weather dirt road to Mto wa Mbu (Mosquito Creek).

En route you pass many Masai bomas (villages) and Masai in their colorful traditional dress walking on the roadside, riding bicycles, herding their cattle and driving overloaded donkey carts.

Masai Morani completing the circumcision ritual are sometimes seen clad in black with white paint on their faces. They leave the village as children for a period of training and instruction by elders and return as men.

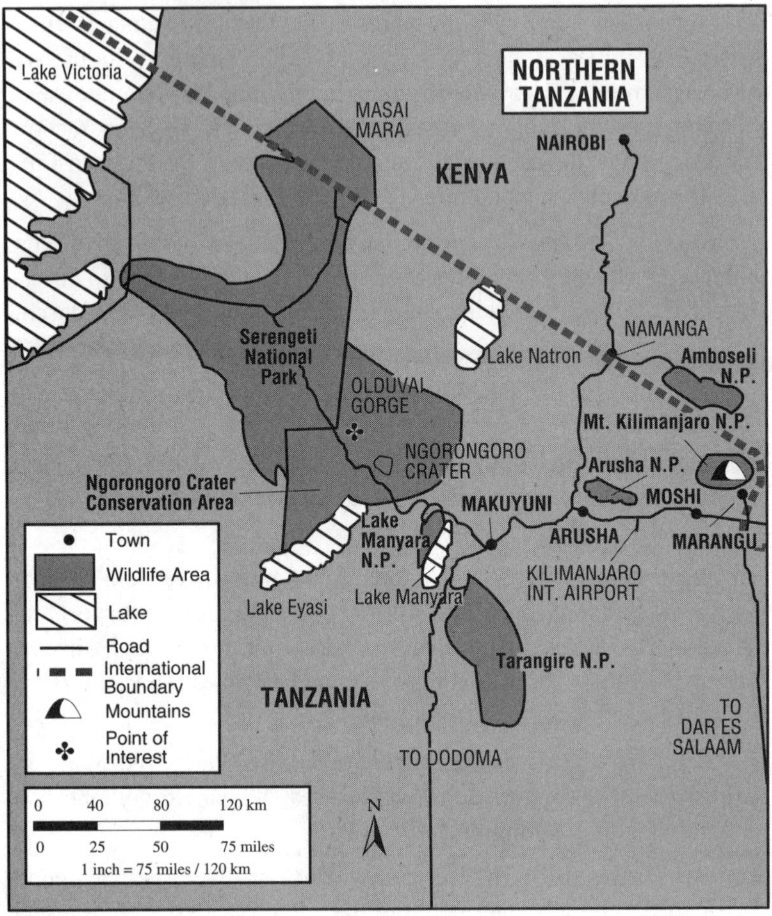

Mto wa Mbu is a village with many roadside stands filled with wood carvings and other local crafts for sale. Be sure to bargain. If you take a few minutes to walk into the village behind the stands, you will get a more realistic (and less touristic) view of village life.

Continuing west, you soon pass the entrance to Lake Manyara National Park. The road becomes quite rough as it climbs up the Rift Valley escarpment past huge baobab trees and numerous baboons looking for handouts. Fabulous views of the valley and Lake Manyara Park below can be seen. You then pass through beautiful cultivated uplands and small villages and on up the slopes of the Crater Highlands to

Masai herding cattle.

Ngorongoro Crater. The road then follows the rim of the crater and finally descends the western side of the crater to Oldupai Gorge and Serengeti National Park.

ARUSHA

This town is the center of tourism for northern Tanzania and is situated in the foothills of rugged Mt. Meru. Named after one of the Arusha tribes, it is located on the Great North Road midway between Cairo and Cape Town. *Makonde* carvings and other souvenirs are available in the numerous craft shops at the center of town. Walking around the Arusha Market, located behind the bus station, is an interesting way to spend a few hours.

ACCOMMODATION: Also see "Accommodation" under "Arusha National Park."

FIRST CLASS: * *Mountain Village* has 40 bungalows (doubles) and three triples with ensuite facilities. The lodge is set in lovely gardens and is located 6 miles (10 km) east of Arusha overlooking Lake Duluti. Horseback riding and fishing are available. * *Ngare Sero Mountain Lodge* is a farm house situated on the slopes of Mt. Meru, with rooms with private facilities. * *Dik Dik Hotel* has nine bungalows with two double rooms in each bungalow, with ensuite facilities, and a swimming pool. * *Mt. Meru Hotel* is a 200-room hotel with ensuite facilities and a swimming pool.

TOURIST CLASS: * *The Impala Hotel* has 45 rooms with ensuite facilities. * *New Arusha Hotel,* located in the center of town, has 72 rooms with ensuite facilities. * *Hotel 77* is Tanzania's largest hotel, with 400 double rooms with ensuite facilities.

ARUSHA NATIONAL PARK

This highly underrated park is predominantly inhabited by forest animals, while in the other northern parks savannah animals are the most prevalent. Arusha National Park is the best place in northern Tanzania to spot black and white colobus monkeys and bushbuck and to photograph larger species with Mt. Kilimanjaro or Mt. Meru in the background. Early mornings are best for this since Mt. Kilimanjaro is less likely to be covered with clouds.

Wildlife is more difficult to spot here than in the other northern parks; do not expect to see large herds of game. However, you are allowed to walk in the western part of this park when accompanied by a park ranger, and there are a number of hikes and picnic sites to enjoy. The best time to visit is July–March.

This 53-square-mile (137-km^2) park is actually the merger of three regions: Meru Crater National Park, Momela Lakes and Ngurdoto Crater National Park. The wide range of habitats, from highland rain forest to acacia woodlands and crater lakes, hosts a variety of wildlife. Armed park guides are required to accompany you for walks in the park or for climbing Mt. Meru; guides are available at Park Headquarters at Momela Gate.

The turnoff to the park entrance is 13 miles (21 km) east of Arusha and 36 miles (58 km) west of Moshi. Continue another 7 miles (11 km) to Ngurdoto Gate.

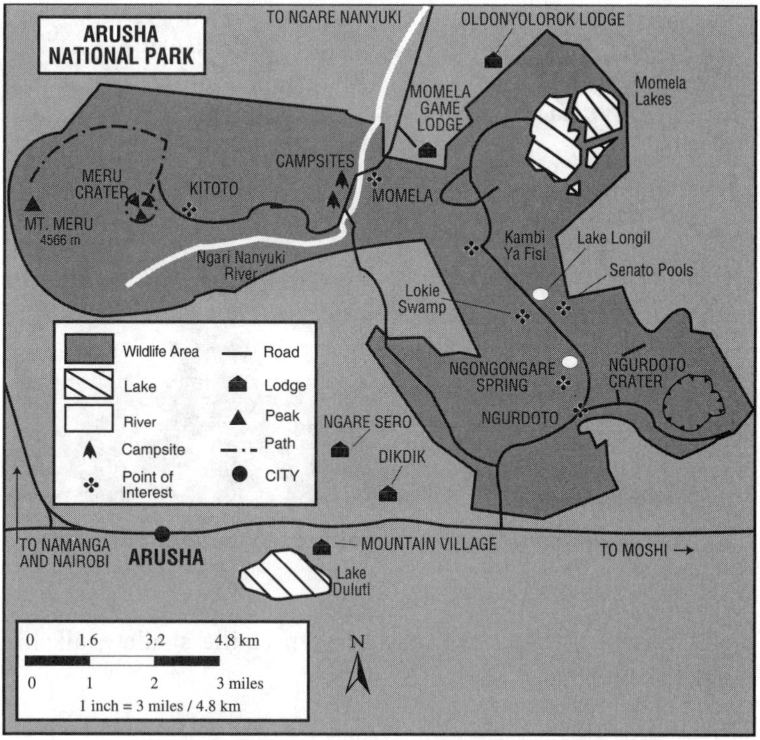

On the open grassland near the entrance to the park, Burchell's zebra are often seen. High in the forest canopy of the Ngurdoto Forest is a good place to find blue monkeys and black and white colobus monkeys. Olive baboons are common and red duiker are sometimes seen.

Walking is not allowed in the 2-mile- (3-km) wide Ngurdoto Crater, which is in essence a reserve within a reserve. However, there may be good views (especially in the early morning) of the crater, Momela Lakes and Mt. Kilimanjaro.

Driving north from Ngurdoto, you pass Ngongongare Spring, the Senato Pools (sometimes dry) and Lokie Swamp and are likely to see common waterbuck and maybe Bohor reedbuck. Buffalo are often seen around Lake Longil.

As you continue past Kambi Ya Fisi (hyena's camp), the landscape becomes more open, and elephant and giraffe may be seen. Hippo

Black and white colobus monkeys–Ngurdoto Forest.

and a variety of waterfowl may be seen at the shallow, alkaline Momela Lakes.

From Kitoto, a four-wheel-drive vehicle is needed to reach Meru Crater. The sheer cliff rises about 4920 feet (1500 m) and is one of the highest in the world.

At the base of Mt. Meru, you may encounter elephant and buffalo. Kirk's dikdik, banded mongoose and klipspringer may also be seen in the park. On a recent visit we saw giraffe lying down—very unusual indeed! Over 400 species of birds have been recorded.

Mt. Meru (14,977 feet/4566 m) is an impressive mountain classified as a dormant volcano; its last eruption was just over 100 years ago. The mountain can be climbed in two days, but it is more enjoyable to take three days, allowing more time for exploration.

On the morning of the first day of a three-day climb, walk for about three hours from Momela Gate (about 5000 feet/1500 m) to Miriakamba Hut. In the afternoon, hike to Meru Crater. On the second day, hike three hours to the Saddle Hut and in the afternoon walk for about one and one-half hours to Little Meru (12,530 feet/3820 m). On day three, reach the summit and return to Momela Gate.

The best months to climb are October and December–February. Bring all your own gear and make your reservations in advance.

ACCOMMODATION IN THE RESERVE — CLASS F: One self-service resthouse (five beds) is located near Momela Gate.

ACCOMMODATION NEAR THE RESERVE — CLASS A/B: * *Oldonyolorok Lodge* is a small lodge with six bungalows (doubles) and ensuite facilities.

CLASS C/D: * *Momela Game Lodge,* located just outside Arusha National Park, has rondavels (40 beds) with ensuite facilities.

CAMPING: One campsite is located near Ngurdoto Gate in the forest and three are at the foot of Tululusia Hill. All have water, long-drop toilets and firewood.

LAKE MANYARA NATIONAL PARK

Once one of the most popular hunting areas of Tanzania, this 125-square-mile (325 km^2) park has the Great Rift Valley escarpment for a dramatic backdrop. Two-thirds of the park is covered by alkaline Lake Manyara, which is situated at an altitude of 3150 feet (960 m).

The turnoff to Lake Manyara is past Mto wa Mbu on the road from Makuyuni to Ngorongoro Crater, about 75 miles (120 km) west of Arusha.

Five different vegetation zones are found in the park. The first zone reached from the park entrance is ground-water forest fed by water seeping from the Great Rift Wall, with wild fig, sausage, tamarind and mahogany trees. Elephant prefer these dense forests as well as marshy glades. The other zones include the marshlands along the edge of the lake, scrub on the Rift Valley Wall, open areas with scattered acacia, and open grasslands.

Manyara, like Ishasha in the Ruwenzori National Park in Uganda, is well known for its tree-climbing lions found lazing on branches of acacia trees. Some people believe that lions climb trees in Manyara to avoid tsetse flies and the dense undergrowth while remaining in the cool shade, while lions of the Ruwenzori National Park in Uganda climb trees to gain a hunting advantage. Finding lion in the trees is very rare, so don't set your heart on it — look at it as an unexpected bonus.

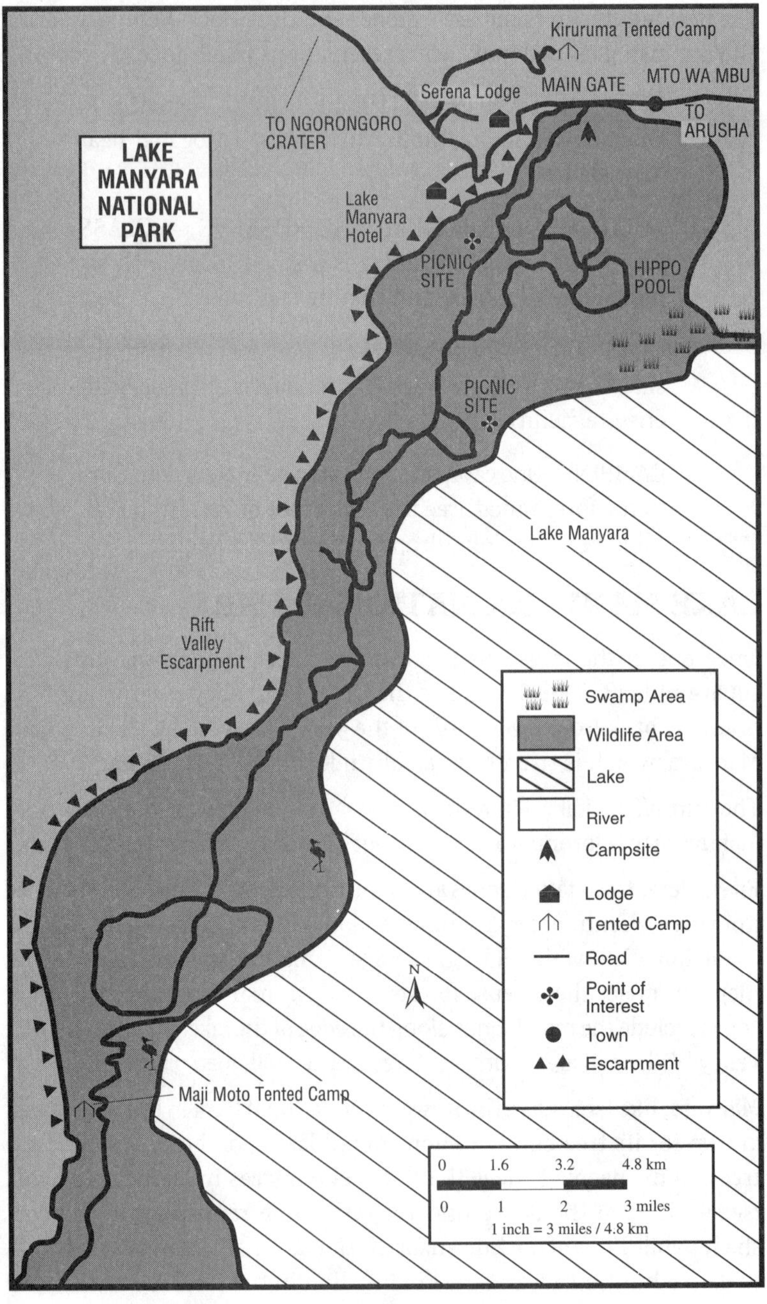
LAKE MANYARA NATIONAL PARK
Kiruruma Tented Camp
MAIN GATE
MTO WA MBU
Serena Lodge
TO ARUSHA
TO NGORONGORO CRATER
Lake Manyara Hotel
PICNIC SITE
HIPPO POOL
PICNIC SITE
Lake Manyara
Rift Valley Escarpment
Maji Moto Tented Camp
Swamp Area
Wildlife Area
Lake
River
Campsite
Lodge
Tented Camp
Road
Point of Interest
Town
Escarpment
N
0 1.6 3.2 4.8 km
0 1 2 3 miles
1 inch = 3 miles / 4.8 km

Manyara features large concentrations of elephant and buffalo. Other wildlife includes common waterbuck, Masai giraffe, zebra, impala, baboons and blue monkeys. Over 380 species of birds, including over 30 birds of prey, have been recorded.

The traditional migration route from Lake Manyara to Tarangire National Park has been all but cut off by new villages. Much of the wildlife is resident year-round, making this a good park to visit any time. The best time to visit is December–February and May–July; August–September is also good.

On a visit to the hippo pool, we saw over 20 gregarious hippos lying all over each other in a large pile on the bank. Something finally spooked them, and a mad rush ensued as they joined other hippos in the pool. In a matter of minutes we spotted over 20 species of birds without moving from that spot.

On our most recent visit we encountered a pride of lion lying only a few yards (meters) from the road. Later, as we were rounding a bend, we almost ran right into two huge bull elephants that were sparring with tusks locked, pushing each other from one side of the road to the other, trumpeting and kicking up mounds of dust in their fight for dominance.

Birds spotted included white-breasted cormorant, red-billed oxpecker, African spoonbill, lesser flamingo, white pelican, grey-headed gull, wood sandpiper, black-winged stilt, white-faced duck, white-crowned plover, blacksmith plover, long-toed plover, avocet, water dikkop, cattle egret, common sandpiper, painted snipe and sacred ibis.

Roads in the northern part of the park are good year-round and four-wheel drive is not needed, although in the rainy season some side tracks may be temporarily closed. Four-wheel-drive vehicles are sometimes necessary in the more remote southern part of Lake Manyara. There is a small museum at the gate with a large number of mounted birds commonly seen in the park.

ACCOMMODATION — CLASS A: * *Lake Manyara Serena Lodge*, magnificently set on the Rift Valley Escarpment overlooking the park and the Rift Valley 1000 feet (300 m) below, has 67 rooms with ensuite facilities and a swimming pool.

ACCOMMODATION — CLASS A/B: * *Maji Moto Camp* is located within the park and has ten tents with ensuite facilities. * *Kirurumu Camp* is set on the escarpment overlooking the Rift Valley outside the reserve and has 20 tents covered by thatched roofs, with ensuite facilities.

ACCOMMODATION — CLASS B/C: * *Lake Manyara Hotel,* set on the escarpment overlooking the park, has 212 rooms with private facilities and a swimming pool.

ACCOMMODATION — CLASS C: * *Migunga Camp* is located near the park and has eight tents with ensuite chemical toilet and communal showers.

CLASSES D & F: * *National Park Self-Service Bandas* (ten doubles) are located near the park entrance. Some bandas have private facilities and everyone shares a communal kitchen.

CAMPING: Two campsites are located near the park entrance, both with toilet and shower facilities. One campsite is situated within the park with no facilities; this site requires a special permit.

ACCOMMODATION BETWEEN LAKE MANYARA AND NGORONGORO CRATER — CLASS A/B: * *Kifaru Safari Lodge,* a converted farmhouse located on a working coffee, flower seed and dairy plantation, has rooms with ensuite facilities (24 beds).

CLASS B: * *Gibb's Farm* has cottages with ensuite facilities (30 beds). Walks to nearby waterfalls can be arranged.

NGORONGORO CRATER CONSERVATION AREA

Ngorongoro Crater is the largest unflooded, intact caldera (collapsed cone of a volcano) in the world. Known as the eighth wonder of the world, its vastness and beauty are truly overwhelming, and it is

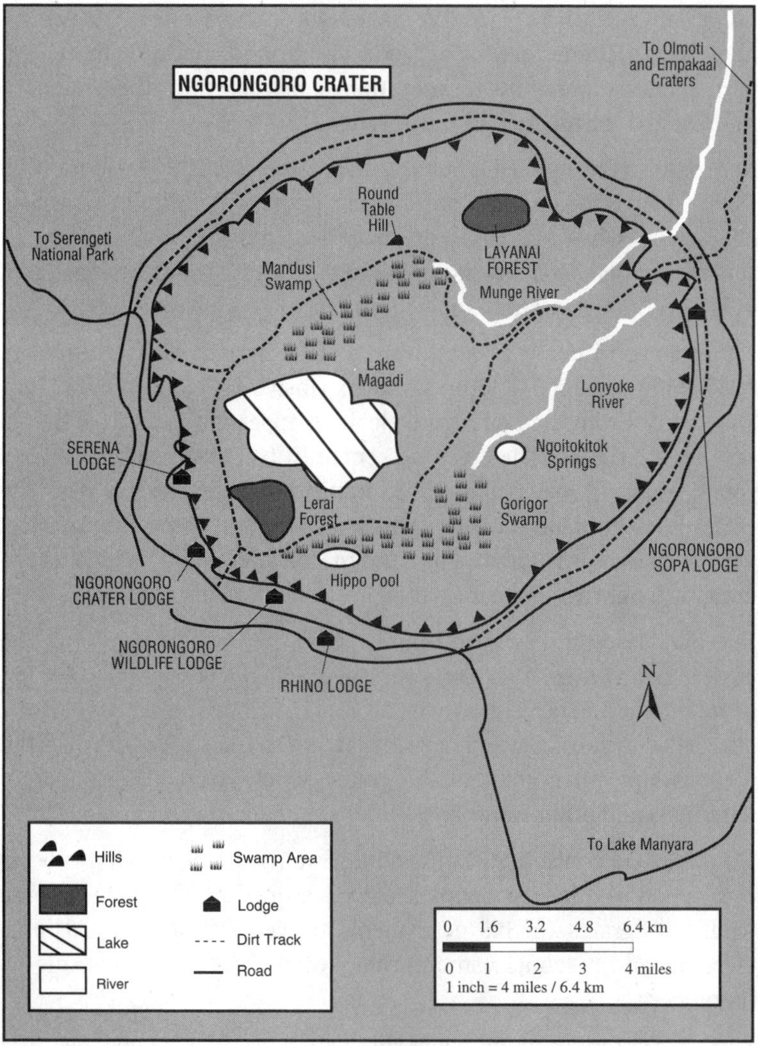

believed by some to have been the proverbial Garden of Eden. Many scientists suggest that before its eruption, this volcano was larger than Mt. Kilimanjaro.

Ngorongoro contains possibly the largest permanent concentration of wildlife in Africa, with an estimated average of 30,000 large mammals. In addition, this is one of the best reserves in Africa to see black rhino.

Large concentrations of wildlife make Ngorongoro Crater their permanent home. Game viewing is good year-round. Because there is a permanent source of fresh water, there's no reason for the wildlife to migrate as they must do in the Serengeti.

Ngorongoro Crater itself is but a small portion of the 3200-square-mile (8288-km^2) Ngorongoro Conservation Area, a World Heritage Site characterized by a highland plateau with volcanic mountains as well as several craters, extensive savannah and forests. Altitudes range from 4430 to 11,800 feet (1350 to 3600 m).

Ngorongoro Crater is about 12 miles (19 km) wide and its rim rises 1200–1600 feet (365–490 m) off its expansive 102-square-mile (265-km^2) floor. From the crater rim, elephant appear as small dark specks on the grasslands. The steep descent into the crater along narrow, rough, winding roads takes 25–35 minutes from the crater rim. The crater floor is predominantly grasslands (making game easy to spot) with two swamps fed by streams and the Lerai Forest. The walls of the crater are lightly forested.

You may descend on a road beginning on the western rim or on the eastern rim. Once on the floor, your driver will more than likely turn left on a dirt road and travel clockwise around the crater floor. Lake Magadi, also called Crater Lake and Lake Makat, is a shallow soda lake near the western rim entry point of the crater which attracts thousands of flamingos and other water birds.

The dirt road continues past Mandusi Swamp. Game viewing is especially good in this area during the dry season (July–October) as some wildlife migrates to this permanent source of fresh water. Hippo, elephant and reedbuck, among many other species, can usually be found here.

You then come to Round Table Hill, which provides a good view and excellent vantage point to get one's bearings. The circular route continues over the Munge River, whose source is in the Olmoti Crater north of Ngorongoro Crater, to Ngoitokitok Springs. From there, you journey past Gorigor Swamp, fed by the Lonyokie River, to the Hippo Pool, which is probably the best place to see hippo.

The Lerai Forest, primarily composed of fever trees (a type of acacia), is a good place to spot elephant and, if you are very lucky, leopard.

Two fine males of the species.

There are two picnic areas here with long-drop toilets and running water. The exit only road climbing the wall of the crater is behind the forest. The road from the eastern rim may be used as both a down and up road into the crater.

On a full-day's game drive during a visit, we saw 7 black rhino (including one mother with her baby); 27 lion; several golden jackal and spotted hyena; numerous elephant, buffalo, zebra and wildebeest; an ostrich guarding the eggs in her nest; flamingo; baboon; monkey; bat-eared fox at their den; kori bustard and a host of other species. Later we spotted a leopard crossing the rim road around the crater. Bull elephant are also found in the wooded areas and on the slopes of the crater. Cheetah are present, but there are no giraffe, topi or impala.

Over 350 species of birds have been recorded. Birds commonly sighted include ostrich, crowned crane, Egyptian geese, and pelican.

At the picnic site, vervet monkeys are very aggressive in getting at your food. Kites (a species of bird) made many swooping attempts at our lunches. You may wish to eat inside your vehicle. Camping has not been allowed on the crater floor since 1992.

One important thing to remember: game is not confined to the crater; wildlife is present throughout the conservation area, including near hotels and lodges. This I learned the hard way on my first visit to Ngorongoro over 20 years ago. One evening, just outside the Ngorongoro Wildlife Lodge, I walked blindly to within 20 feet (6 m) of three large buffalo. One buffalo appeared as if it was going to charge, but fortunately it ran off. "Welcome to Africa!" I thought, relieved beyond words.

Game viewing in the Ngorongoro Conservation Area west of the crater bordering the Serengeti is best between December and May, when the Serengeti migration is usually in the area.

Ngorongoro Crater is about 112 miles (180 km) west of Arusha. An airstrip is located further along the crater rim, but fog often keeps it closed in the mornings. Four-wheel-drive vehicles are required for game drives into the crater, and guests must be accompanied by a licensed guide or ranger.

The Serengeti Plains cover the western part of the conservation area. Since this is classified as a conservation area and not a national park, wildlife, human beings and livestock exist together. Ground cultivation is not allowed. The Masai are allowed to bring in their cattle for the salts and permanent water available on the crater floor, but must leave the crater at night.

An interesting excursion is to take the beautifully scenic drive past **Olmoti Crater** through Masailand to the 10,700-foot- (3260-m) high **Empakaai Crater**, situated 20 miles (32 km) northwest of Ngorongoro Crater on a road that is difficult to negotiate even with a four-wheel-drive vehicle. **Ol Doinyo Lengai** (10,600 feet/3231 m) — an active volcano and holy mountain of the Masai — Lake Natron and possibly even Mt. Kilimanjaro may be seen. Hiking Olmoti Crater and Empakaai Crater is allowed if accompanied by an armed wildlife guard.

About 30 miles (50 km) west of Ngorongoro Crater and a few miles off the road to the Serengeti is **Oldupai Gorge**, site of many archeological discoveries including the estimated 1.7-million-year-old *Zinjanthropus boisei* fossil. The fossil is housed in the National Museum in Dar es Salaam.

A small museum overlooks the gorge itself, and a guide there will tell you the story of the Leakeys' research and findings. For a small tip, the guide will take you down into the gorge and show you where the *Zinjanthropus boisei* fossil was found.

ACCOMMODATION — CLASS A: * *Ngorongoro Serena Lodge,* situated on the western rim of the crater, has 75 rooms with ensuite facilities and a swimming pool. * *Ngorongoro Crater Lodge* is being completely rebuilt at the time of this writing and is expected to have 30 rooms with ensuite facilities.

CLASS A/B:* *Ngorongoro Sopa Lodge,* located on the eastern rim of the crater, has 92 suites with ensuite facilities and a swimming pool. There is a down and up access road into the crater nearby.

CLASS B: * *Ngorongoro Wildlife Lodge,* a 78-room hotel with ensuite facilities, has a wonderful view of the crater.

CLASS C: * *Ngorongoro Rhino Lodge* is a small lodge with no view of the crater. Two rooms share one toilet and shower.

CAMPING: Campsites are located on the crater rim.

SERENGETI NATIONAL PARK

This is Tanzania's largest and most famous park, and it has the largest concentration of migratory game animals in the world. It is also famous for its huge lion population and is one of the best places on the continent to see them. The park has received additional notoriety through Professor Bernard Grzimek's book, *Serengeti Shall Not Die,* and the feature film Serengeti (IMAX).

Serengeti is derived from the Masai language and appropriately means "endless plain." The park's 5700 square miles (14,763 km^2) makes it larger than the state of Connecticut. Altitude varies from 3120 to 6070 feet (950 to 1850 m).

The park, a World Heritage Site, comprises most of the Serengeti ecosystem, which is the primary migration route of the wildebeest. The Serengeti ecosystem also includes Kenya's Masai Mara National Reserve, bordering on the north; the Loliondo Controlled Area, bordering on the northeast; the Ngorongoro Conservation Area, bordering on the southeast; the Maswa Game Reserve, bordering on the southwest; and the Grumeti and Ikorongo Controlled Areas, bordering on the northwest. The "western corridor" of the park comes within 5 miles (8 km) of Lake Victoria.

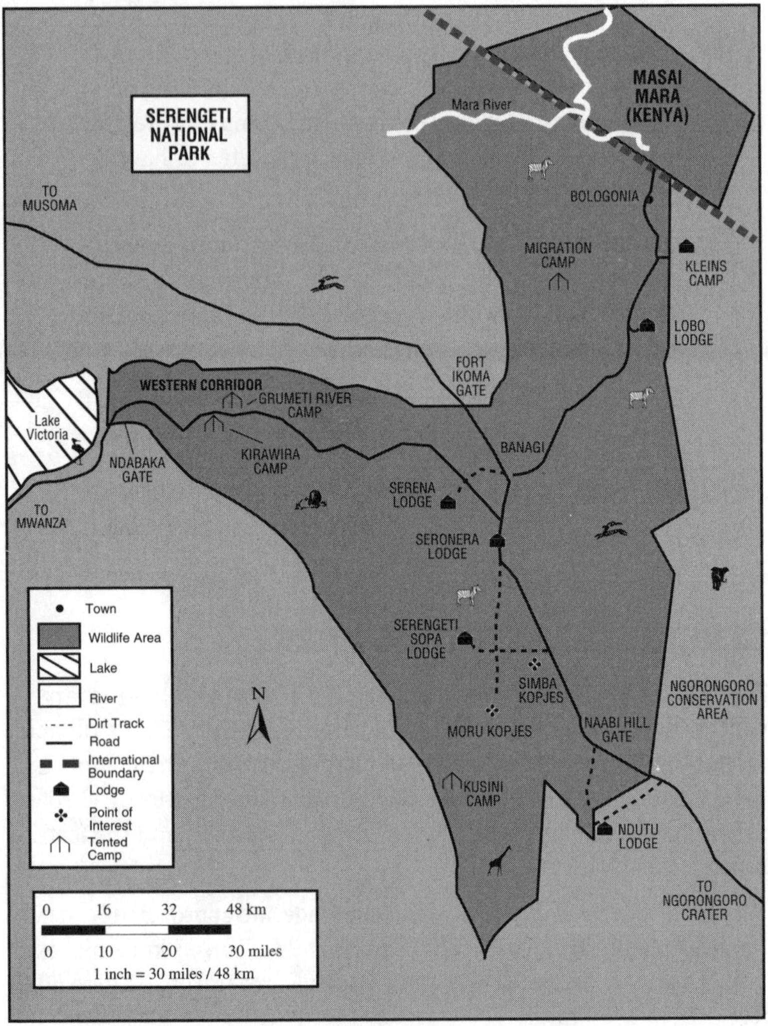

Nearly 500 species of birds and 35 species of large plains animals can be found in the Serengeti. The park may contain as many as 1.3 million wildebeest, 250,000 Thomson's gazelle, 200,000 zebra, 70,000 topi, 30,000 Grant's gazelle, 20,000 buffalo, 9000 eland, 8000 giraffe, 1500 lion and 800 elephant.

Most of the Serengeti is a vast open plain broken by rocky outcrops (kopjes). There is also acacia savannah, savannah woodland, riverine forests, some swamps and small lakes.

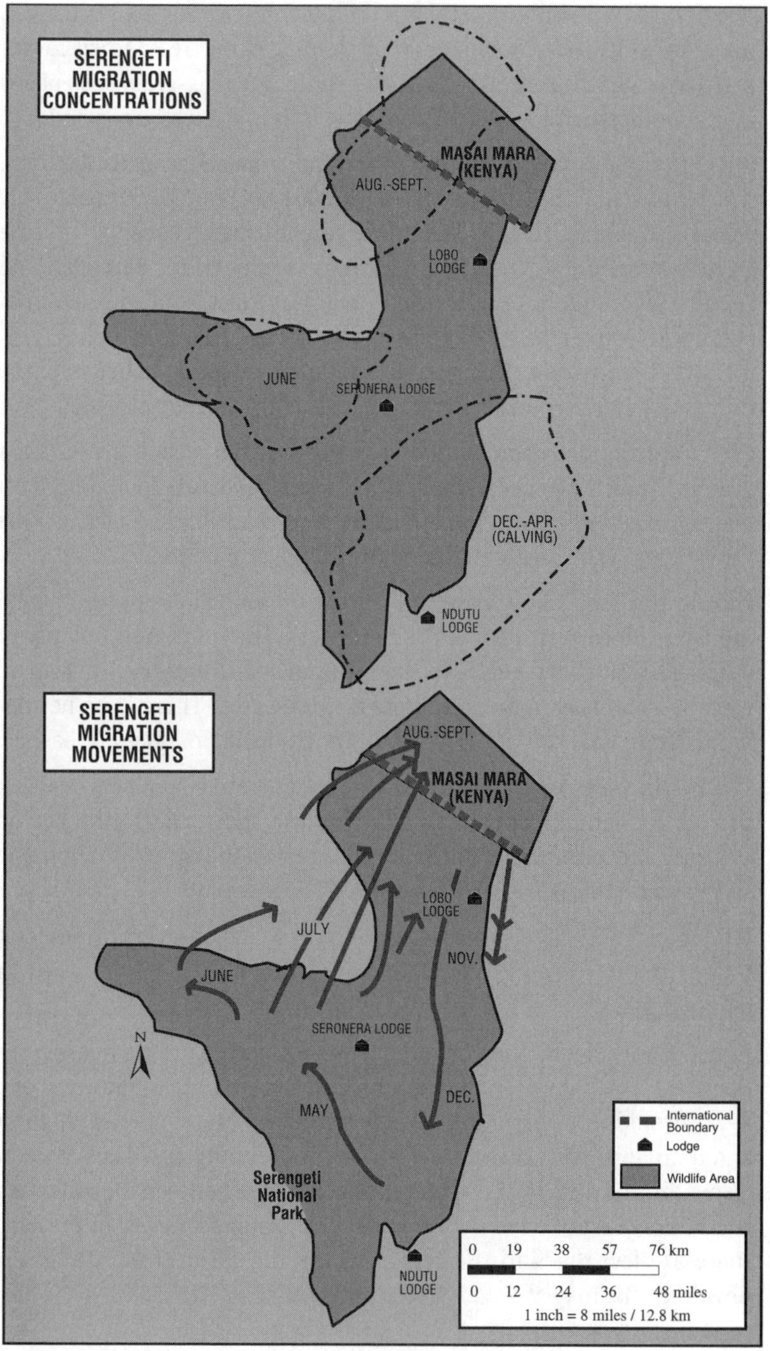
SERENGETI MIGRATION CONCENTRATIONS
MASAI MARA (KENYA)
AUG.-SEPT.
LOBO LODGE
JUNE
SERONERA LODGE
DEC.-APR. (CALVING)
NDUTU LODGE
SERENGETI MIGRATION MOVEMENTS
AUG.-SEPT.
MASAI MARA (KENYA)
LOBO LODGE
JULY
JUNE
NOV.
SERONERA LODGE
N
MAY
DEC.
Serengeti National Park
NDUTU LODGE
International Boundary
Lodge
Wildlife Area
0 19 38 57 76 km
0 12 24 36 48 miles
1 inch = 8 miles / 12.8 km

The north is more hilly, with thick scrub and forests lining the Mara River, where leopards are sometimes spotted sleeping in the trees. Acacia savannah dominates the central region, with short- and long-grass open plains in the southeast and woodland plains and hills in the western corridor.

It is impossible to predict the exact time of the famous **Serengeti migration**, which covers a circuit of about 500 miles (800 km). From December to May wildebeest, zebra, eland and Thomson's gazelle usually concentrate on the treeless short-grass plains in the extreme southeastern Serengeti and western Ngorongoro Conservation Area near Lake Ndutu in search of short grass, which they prefer over the longer dry-stemmed variety. This is the best time to visit the Serengeti. In April and May, the height of the rainy season, a four-wheel-drive vehicle is highly recommended.

Other species common to the area during this period are Grant's gazelle, eland, hartebeest, topi and a host of predators including lion, cheetah, spotted hyena, honey badger and black-backed jackal. Kori bustard and yellow-throated sandgrouse are also common.

During the long rainy season (April–May), nomadic lions and hyena move to the eastern part of the Serengeti. The migration, mainly of wildebeest and zebra, begins in May or June. Once the dry season begins, wildebeest and zebra must migrate from the area. There is no permanent water, and both of these species must drink on a regular basis.

The mating season for wildebeest is concentrated over a three-week period and generally occurs in May or June. After a gestation period of eight and one-half months, the calves are born, usually on the short-grass plains.

Wildebeest move about six to ten abreast in columns several miles long toward the western corridor. Zebra do not move in columns but in family units.

As a general rule, by June or July the migration has progressed west of Seronera. The migration then splits into three separate migrations: one west through the corridor toward permanent water and Lake Victoria and then northeast; the second due north, reaching the Masai Mara of Kenya around mid-July; and the third northward between the other two to a region west of Lobo Lodge, where the group disperses. At present, there are few roads in the region where the third group disperses; however, this may change.

The great Serengeti migration.

Cheetah mother and her cubs.

During July–September, the Serengeti's highest concentration of wildlife is in the extreme north. The first and second groups meet and begin returning to the Serengeti National Park around late September to late October; the migration then reaches the central or southern Serengeti by December.

Short-grass plains dominate the part of the Ngorongoro Conservation Area bordering the Serengeti. As one moves northwest into the park, the plains change to medium-grass plains and then into long-grass plains around Simba Kopjes north of Naabi Hill Gate. Topi, elephant, Thomson's and Grant's gazelle, bat-eared fox and warthog are often seen here.

There are two saline lakes in the south of the park, **Lake Masek** and **Lake Lagaja**, known mainly for their populations of lesser and greater flamingos.

Seronera

The Seronera Valley is located in the center of the park. Game is plentiful, and the area is famous for lion and leopard. Other wildlife includes hyena, jackal, topi, Masai giraffe and Thomson's gazelle. This is the best part of the park to find cheetah, especially in the dry season. In the wet season, many cheetah are found in the short-grass plains. They are, however, found throughout the park.

Research on African wild dogs is being conducted in the region. Exciting balloon safaris over the Serengeti Plains are operated near Seronera Lodge.

Banagi Hill, 11 miles north of Seronera on the road to Lobo, is a good area for Masai giraffe, buffalo and impala. Four miles (6 km) from Banagi on the Orangi River is a hippo pool.

As of this writing, Park Headquarters and the park village are being moved outside of the park to Fort Ikoma to minimize human impact on the ecosystem within the park.

Lobo

From Banagi northward to Lobo and the Bologonja Gate are rolling uplands with open plains, bush, woodlands and magnificent kopjes. This is the best area of the park to see elephant. Forests of large mahogany and fig trees are found along the rivers where Patas monkeys, kingfishers, fish eagles and turacos may be seen. Other wildlife found in the Lobo area includes grey bush duikers and mountain reedbuck. Large numbers of Masai giraffe are permanent residents.

Large herds of wildebeest are often in the region from August until the rains begin, usually in November. During this period, many wildebeest drown while attempting to cross the Mara River.

On a recent visit, we watched a pride of lion with five cubs play for hours. Later we came upon a fire in the park, where hundreds of storks were feeding on the insects fleeing the flames.

Western Corridor

Beginning three miles north of Seronera, the western corridor road passes over the Grumeti River and beyond to a central range of hills. Eighteen miles (29 km) before Ndabaka Gate is an extensive area of black cotton soil which makes rainy season travel difficult. This area is best visited June–October during the dry season. Colobus monkeys may be found in the riverine areas. Other wildlife includes roan antelope, Patterson's eland, topi, impala, dikdik, hippo and crocodile.

The granite kopjes or rocky outcrops that dot the plains are home to rock hyrax, Kirk's dikdik and klipspringer. Banded, dwarf and slender mongoose are occasionally seen nearby. Verreaux's eagle are sometimes sighted near the Moru Kopjes.

Three species of jackal occur in the Serengeti: black-backed, side-striped and golden. Side-striped jackal are rare, golden jackal are usually found in the short grass plains and black-backed jackal are quite common. The six species of vultures occurring in the park are white-backed, white-headed, hooded, lappet-faced, Ruppell's and Egyptian.

At the time of this writing, the border with Kenya between Serengeti National Park and the Masai Mara is officially closed. There is a dry weather road (often impassable in the rainy season) from Mwanza and Musoma (Lake Victoria) to the west through Ndabaka Gate. The main road from the Ngorongoro Conservation Area via Naabi Hill Gate is open year-round.

Vehicles must stay on the roads within a 10-mile (16-km) radius of Seronera and Lobo. Off-road driving is allowed in the rest of the park, making a safari with a four-wheel-drive vehicle all the more attractive. Travel in the park is only allowed from 6:00 a.m. until 7:00 p.m. Visitors

Serengeti Sopa Lodge

may get out of the vehicle in open areas if no animals are present. Do stay close to the vehicle, and keep a careful lookout.

From July to mid-September, when one arm of the migration is usually in the Masai Mara in Kenya, consider concentrating your time in either the Western Corridor or the northern Serengeti. At that time, wildlife may be more concentrated in the Masai Mara (Kenya), but you will most certainly encounter a fraction of the tourists in the Serengeti as you would in the Masai Mara. Having those expansive Serengeti Plains almost to yourself is a priceless experience for travelers looking for more out of a safari than just seeing animals.

ACCOMMODATION — CLASS A: * *Kirawira Camp*, located in the western corridor approximately 55 miles (90 km) west of Seronera and 6 miles (10 km) east of the Kirawira Ranger Post, has a classic Victorian atmosphere, with 25 luxury tents with ensuite facilities. * *Serengeti Serena Lodge*, set on a hill overlooking the Serengeti Plains about 18 miles (29 km) northwest of Seronera Lodge, has 66 rooms with ensuite facilities and a swimming pool.

ACCOMMODATION — CLASS A/B: * *Migration Camp,* located 14 miles (22 km) west of Lobo Lodge, has 16 tents with ensuite facilities and a swimming pool. **Serengeti Sopa Lodge,* located 25 miles (40 km) southwest of Seronera Lodge and 60 miles (96 km) from Naabi Hill Gate, has 75 suites with ensuite facilities and a swimming pool. * *Mashado Kusini Camp* is a fixed tented camp (20 beds) with ensuite facilities. Guests are flown into the park and have game drives with resident guides. * *Grumeti River Camp,* located in the Western Corridor 53 miles (85 km) west of Seronera Lodge and 31 miles (50 km) east of Lake Victoria, has ten tents with ensuite facilities. As of this writing, the camp is being renovated and is expected to be a Class A/B camp when completed.

CLASS B: * *Lobo Wildlife Lodge,* located in the north of the park 43 miles north of Seronera, is uniquely designed around huge boulders and has a swimming pool carved out of solid rock. All 75 double rooms have ensuite facilities. * *Seronera Wildlife Lodge,* situated in the center of the park 90 miles (145 km) from Ngorongoro Crater, has 75 double rooms with ensuite facilities.

ACCOMMODATION ON THE PERIPHERY OF THE PARK — CLASS A: * *Kleins Camp* is situated in a 25,000-acre (10,000-hectare) private reserve bordered on the west by Serengeti National Park and the north by the Masai Mara in Kenya. Each of the eight chalets has ensuite facilities. Day and night game drives and walks are offered.

CLASS B: * *Ndutu Safari Lodge* is a rustic lodge with 32 rooms (doubles) with ensuite facilities, located on the edge of the park in Ngorongoro Conservation Area. Six tents with separate facilities are available December–March.

CAMPING: Campsites are available at Seronera, Ndutu, Naabi Hill Gate, Moru Kopjes, Kirawira and Lobo. Camping in other areas requires permission from the warden and higher fees. It is best to book well in advance.

Wildebeest among baobab trees in Tarangire National Park.

TARANGIRE NATIONAL PARK

Large numbers of baobab trees dotting the landscape give the park a prehistoric look the likes of which I have never seen before. This park has a different feel to it than any other northern park — and an eerie feeling at that, making it one of my favorites.

Tarangire is the best park on the northern circuit to see elephant. On a recent visit, Cynthia Moss, author of *Elephant Memories* and *Portraits in the Wild*, identified over 500 individual elephants within the park in a week!

Fewer tourists visit this park than Manyara, Ngorongoro and Serengeti, allowing a better opportunity to experience it as the early explorers did — alone. This park should not be missed; wildlife viewing is excellent, especially from July to October, when many animals concentrate near the only permanent water source in the area — the Tarangire River and its tributaries.

At the beginning of the short rainy season (October/November), migratory species including wildebeest and zebra, soon followed by elephant, buffalo, Grant's gazelle, Thomson's gazelle and oryx, begin migrating out of the park. However, as most migration routes have been cut off

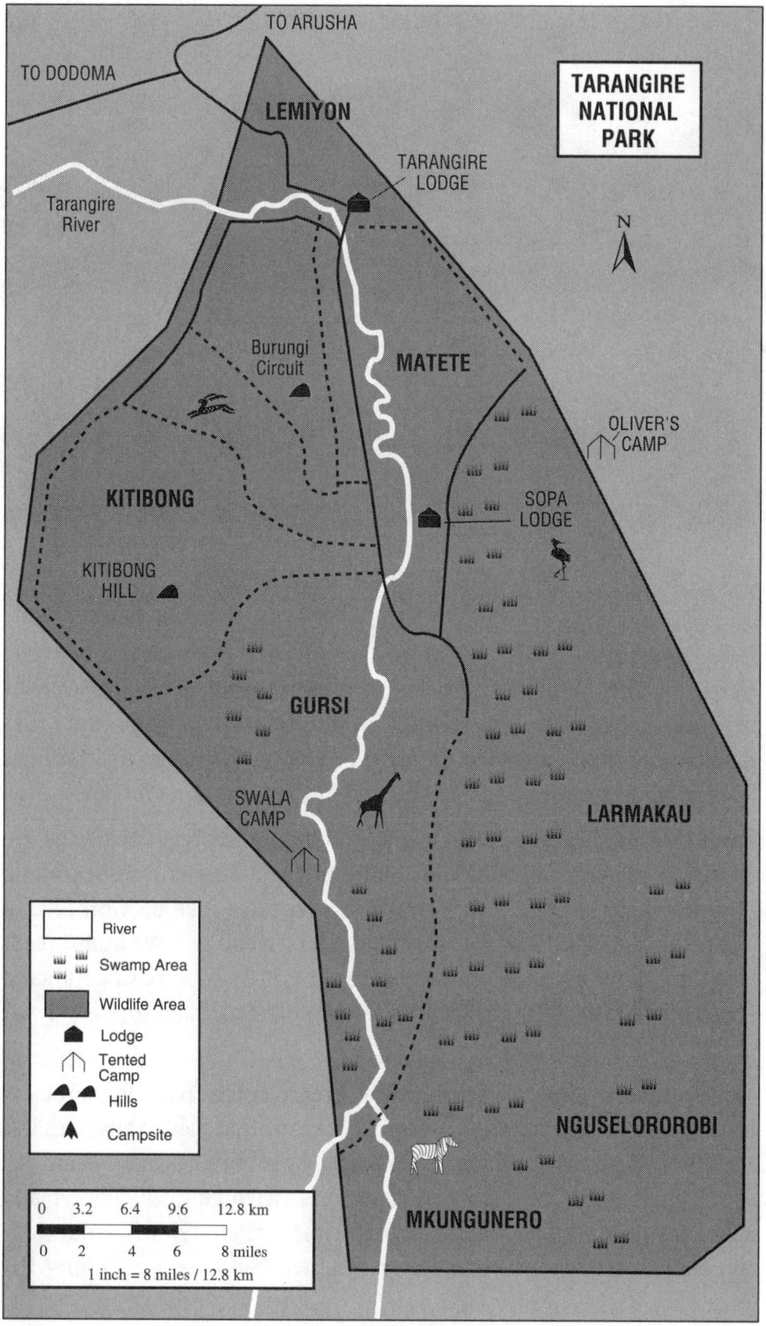
TARANGIRE NATIONAL PARK
TO ARUSHA
TO DODOMA
LEMIYON
TARANGIRE LODGE
Tarangire River
N
Burungi Circuit
MATETE
OLIVER'S CAMP
KITIBONG
SOPA LODGE
KITIBONG HILL
GURSI
SWALA CAMP
LARMAKAU
River
Swamp Area
Wildlife Area
Lodge
Tented Camp
Hills
Campsite
NGUSELOROROBI
0 3.2 6.4 9.6 12.8 km
0 2 4 6 8 miles
1 inch = 8 miles / 12.8 km
MKUNGUNERO

Mobile tented camp in Tarangire.

from the expansion of man's presence, many of these animals are in fact remaining in the park and few are migrating out of the park or far beyond the park's borders. Giraffe, waterbuck, lesser kudu and other resident species remain in the park. The migratory animals that have left the park usually return at the end of the long rains in June.

Tarangire wildlife populations include approximately 30,000 zebra, 25,000 wildebeest, 5000 buffalo, 5000 eland, 3000 elephant, 2500 Masai giraffe and 1000 oryx. Other prominent species include Grant's and Thomson's gazelle, hartebeest, impala, lesser and greater kudu, reedbuck and gerenuk. Lion and leopard are frequently seen. Cheetah and spotted hyena are also present, as are the banded, black-tipped, dwarf and marsh mongoose.

The **Lemiyon region**, the northernmost region of the park, is characterized by a high concentration of baobab trees unmatched in any park I've seen. This unique landscape is also dotted by umbrella acacia trees with some open grasslands and wooded areas. Elephant, wildebeest and zebra are often seen. Visitors with little time for game viewing may want to concentrate on the Matete and the Lemiyon areas, including the Tarangire River.

The **Matete region** covers the northeastern part of the park and is characterized by open grasslands with scattered umbrella acacia and baobab trees and the Tarangire River. Lion, fringe-eared oryx and klipspringer are seen quite often. Bat-eared fox are also present.

On the 50-mile (80-km) **Burungi Circuit**, you pass through acacia parklands and woodlands. You are likely to see a number of species, including elephant, eland and bushbuck.

The eastern side of the **Kitibong area** is a good place to find large herds of buffalo. The eastern side is mainly acacia parklands, and the western side is thicker woodlands.

The **Gursi section** is similar to the Kitibong area with the addition of rainy season wetlands, which are home to large populations of water birds.

Hippo are found in the extensive swamps of the **Larmakau region**, located in the central eastern part of the park. **Nguselororobi**, in the south of the park, is predominantly swamp with some woodlands and plains. The **Mkungunero section** has a few freshwater pools and a variety of bird life.

On one visit, we spotted eland, giraffe, buffalo, a few lion, oryx, elephant, impala, Grant's gazelle, zebra, hartebeest, warthog, baboon and ostrich.

Elephants have destroyed many baobab trees. A baobab tree with a huge hole through the center of its trunk can be seen near Tarangire Safari Lodge.

Game viewing is excellent in this 1003-square-mile (2600-km^2) park during the dry season from July-October, and is in fact good year-round — especially for elephant. Over 300 species of birds have been recorded in the park. Bird watching is best December–May. During the rainy seasons, many roads become impassable.

ACCOMMODATION — CLASS A/B: * *Tarangire Sopa Lodge* has 75 rooms with ensuite facilities and a swimming pool. * *Mashado Swala Camp* is a fixed tented camp with 10 tents (20 beds) with ensuite facilities. Guests are generally flown into the park and have game drives with resident guides.

CLASS B: * *Tarangire Safari Lodge* has 35 tents (doubles) and 6 bungalows (triples) with private facilities and a large swimming pool. Wildlife viewing can be excellent in the late afternoon from the veranda.

ACCOMMODATION ON THE PERIPHERY OF THE PARK —CLASS B: * *Oliver's Camp*, located just outside the eastern border of the reserve, has six tents with private bush showers and bush toilets. Day game drives are offered within the park, while night drives and walks are offered outside the park.

CAMPING: There are campsites with no facilities.

LAKE NATRON REGION

Lake Natron, located between the Ngorongoro Conservation Area and the Kenya border, is a shallow, alkaline lake approximately 38 miles long and 15 miles wide (60 x 25 km). This remote lake is one of East Africa's largest breeding areas for flamingos.

South of Lake Natron is **Oldoinyo Lengai**, the only active carbonatite volcano in the world and holy mountain of the Masai. This steep mountain takes about ten hours to climb and return to its base. The **Gol Mountains**, located between Lake Natron and the Serengeti, is an interesting area for hiking.

MT. KILIMANJARO NATIONAL PARK

Known to many through Ernest Hemingway's book *The Snows of Kilimanjaro*, Mt. Kilimanjaro is the highest mountain in the world that is not part of a mountain range and is definitely one of the world's most impressive mountains. Kilimanjaro means "shining mountain"; it rises from an average altitude of about 3300 feet (1000 m) on the dry plains to 19,340 feet (5895 m), truly a world-class mountain. On clear days, the mountain can be seen from over 200 miles (320 km) away.

The mountain consists of three major volcanic centers: Kibo (19,340 feet/5895 m), Shira (13,650 feet/4162 m) to the west and Mawenzi (16,893 feet/5150 m) to the east. The base of the mountain is 37 miles (60 km) long and 25 miles (40 km) wide. The park is a World Heritage Site and covers 292 square miles (756 km^2) of the mountain above 8856 feet (2700 m). The park also has six corridors that climbers may use through the Forest Reserve.

Hikers pass through zones of forest, alpine and semidesert to its snow-capped peak, situated only three degrees south of the equator. It was once thought to be an extinct volcano, but due to recent rumblings, it is now classified as dormant.

Climbing Mt. Kilimanjaro was definitely a highlight of my travels. For the struggle to reach its highest peak I was handsomely rewarded with a feeling of accomplishment and many exciting memories of the climb.

Kilimanjaro may in fact be the easiest mountain in the world for a climber to ascend to such heights. But it is still a struggle for even fit adventurers. On the other hand, it can be climbed by people from all walks of life who are in good condition and have a strong will. Mind you, reaching the top is by no means necessary; the flora, fauna and magnificent views seen en route are fabulous.

A Christian missionary, Johann Rebmann, reported his discovery of this snow-capped mountain, but the Europeans didn't believe him. Hans Meyer was the first European to climb Kilimanjaro, doing so in 1889.

The most unique animal in this park is the Abbot's duiker, which is found in only a few mountain forests in northern Tanzania. Other wildlife includes elephant, buffalo, eland, leopard, hyrax, and black and white colobus monkeys. However, very little large game is seen.

The best time to climb is January–March, August and October, during the drier seasons when the skies are fairly clear. January and February are warmer, while October is cooler.

July, November and December are also good, while April and May should be avoided because of heavy rains and overcast skies. I, of course, happened to be in Tanzania in April, but I still made the climb and thoroughly enjoyed it.

From April to May, during the long rainy season, the summit is often covered in clouds, with snow falling at higher altitudes and rain at lower altitudes. The short rains (October–November) bring afternoon thunderstorms, but evenings and mornings are often clear.

Many routes to the summit require no mountaineering skills. Mountaineers wishing to ascend by technical routes may wish to get a copy of *Guide to Mt. Kenya and Kilimanjaro*, edited by Iain Allan.

The Park Headquarters is located in Marangu, about a seven-hour drive from Nairobi, two and one-half hours from Arusha. Children under ten years of age are not allowed over 9843 feet (3000 m).

Travelers wishing to see Mt. Kilimanjaro but not climb it may do so (provided the weather is clear) from within the park, from Arusha National Park or Amboseli National Park (Kenya).

Zones

Mt. Kilimanjaro can be divided into five zones by altitude: (1) cultivated lower slopes, (2) forest, (3) heath and moorland/lower alpine, (4) highland desert/alpine and (5) summit. Each zone spans approximately 3300 feet (1000 m) in altitude. As the altitude increases, rainfall and temperature decrease; this has a direct effect on the vegetation each zone supports.

The rich volcanic soils of the **lower slopes** of the mountain around Moshi and Marangu up to the park gate (6000 feet/1830 m) are intensely cultivated, mostly with coffee and bananas.

The **forest zone** (5900–9185 feet/1800–2800 m) receives the highest rainfall of the zones, with about 80 inches (2000 mm) on the southern slopes and about half that amount on the northern and western slopes. The upper half of this zone is often covered with clouds, and humidity is high, with day temperatures ranging from 60 to 70°F (15 to 21°C). Don't be surprised if it rains while walking through this zone; in fact, expect it.

In the lower forest, there are palms, sycamore figs, bearded lichen and mosses hanging from tree limbs, tree ferns growing to 20 feet (6 m) in height, and giant lobelia which grow to over 30 feet (9 m). In the upper forest zone, giant groundsels appear. Unlike many East African volcanic mountains, no bamboo belt surrounds Kilimanjaro.

Black and white colobus and blue monkey, olive baboon and bushbuck may be seen. Elephant, eland, giraffe, buffalo and suni may be seen on the northern and western slopes. Also present but seldom seen are bushpig, civet, genet, bush duiker, Abbot's duiker and red duiker.

Zone three, a lower alpine zone ranging from 9185 to 13,120 feet (2800 to 4000 m), is predominantly **heath** followed by **moorlands**. Rainfall decreases with altitude from about 50 inches to 20 inches (1250 to 500 mm) per year. Giant heather (10–30 feet/3–9 m high), grasslands with scattered bushes and beautiful flowers, including "everlasting" flowers, protea and colorful red-hot pokers, characterize the lower part of this zone.

You then enter the moorlands with tussock grasses and groups of giant senecios and lobelias — weird prehistoric-looking Afro-alpine vegetation that would provide a great setting for a science fiction movie. With a lot of luck, you may spot eland, elephant, buffalo or klipspringer.

The **highland desert/alpine zone** is from around 13,120 to 16,400 feet (4000 to 5000 m) and receives only about 10 inches (250 mm) of rain per year. Vegetation is very thin and includes tussock grasses, "everlasting" flowers, moss balls and lichens. The thin air makes flying too difficult for most birds, and the very few larger mammals that may be seen do not make this region their home. What this zone lacks in wildlife is compensated for by the fabulous views. Temperatures can range from below freezing to very hot, so be prepared.

The **summit** experiences arctic conditions and receives less than 4 inches (100 mm) of rain per year, usually in the form of snow. It is almost completely void of vegetation.

Kibo's northern summit is covered by the Great Northern Glacier. On Kibo there is an outer caldera about one and one-half miles (2.5 km) in diameter. Uhuru peak is the highest point on the outer caldera and also the highest point on the mountain.

Within the outer caldera is an inner cone which contains the Inner or Reusch Crater, which is about one-half mile (1 km) in diameter. Vents (fumaroles) spewing steam and sulfurous gasses are located at the Terrace and the base of the crater. Within the Inner Crater is an ash cone with an ash pit about 1100 feet (335 m) across and about 400 feet (120 m) deep.

ROUTES

Climbing Kibo Peak via the routes described below requires no mountaineering skills. A guide for each climbing party is required. Porters are highly recommended. The Marangu, Machame and Shira Plateau Routes are the most popular. It is more interesting (and more expensive) to take other routes up and return via the Marangu Route, which offer additional variety to the climb.

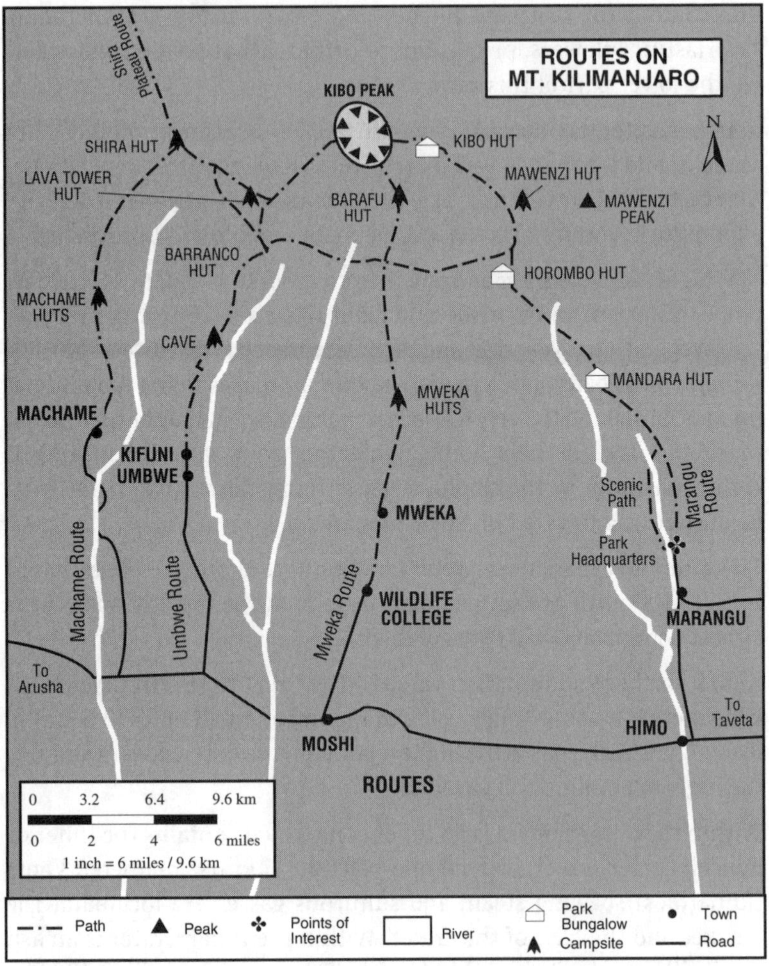

Little firewood is available. Do bring fuel (kerosene) for cooking and heating; this will help minimize deforestation. The national park guides are not qualified to lead glacier- or ice-climbing routes. The services of a professional guide must be arranged in advance.

The park has a rescue team based at the Park Headquarters for immediate response to emergencies on the Marangu Route. If using another route, descend the mountain and contact Park Headquarters (telephone: Marangu 50), which will send a rescue team to assist.

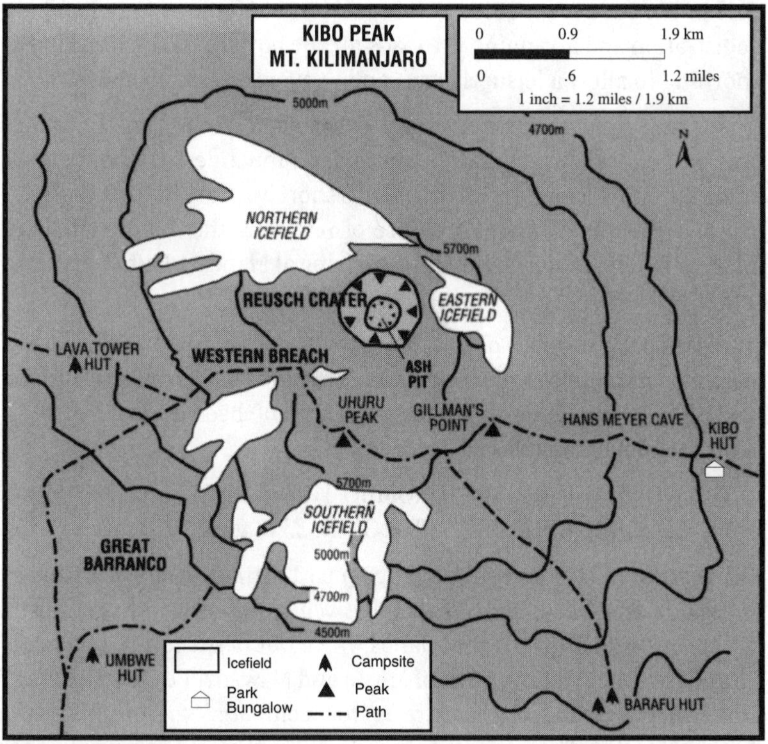

Marangu Route

The Marangu Route is the route most often used; it has the best accommodations and is the easiest (most gradual) route to the summit.

This route may be completed in five days, but it's best to take six days, spending an extra day at Horombo hut to allow more time to acclimatize to the altitude. The huts are dormitory-style with common areas for cooking and eating.

Most climbing tours originate in Nairobi, Arusha or Kilimanjaro Airport and are for seven or eight days. The night before and the night after the climb are usually spent in the village of Marangu or in Arusha.

DAY ONE: MARANGU (6004 feet/1830 m) to MANDARA HUT (8856 feet/ 2700 m) — REGULAR ROUTE: THREE–FOUR HOURS; FOREST ROUTE: FOUR–FIVE HOURS. ALTITUDE GAIN: 2854 feet (870 m).

An hour or so is spent at Park Headquarters at Marangu Gate handling registration and arranging the loads for the porters. Try to leave in the morning to allow a leisurely pace and to avoid afternoon showers.

The fastest route and the one most often taken is along an old vehicle track. The forest trail takes longer but has much less traffic than the main trail; this trail veers off to the left a short way past the gate and runs along a stream. You have a choice of rejoining the main trail about halfway to (about one hour before) arriving at Mandara Hut. Both paths are often muddy.

Mandara has a number of small wooden A-frame huts that sleep eight persons each, four to a room, and a main cabin with a dormitory upstairs and dining room downstairs, for a total of 200 beds. Kerosene lamps, stoves and mattresses are provided.

DAY TWO: MANDARA to HOROMBO HUT (12,205 feet/3720 m) — FIVE–SEVEN HOURS. ALTITUDE GAIN: 3346 feet (1020 m).

On day two, you pass through the upper part of the rain forest to tussock grassland and fascinating Afro-alpine vegetation of giant groundsels and giant lobelias to the moorlands. Once out of the forest, you begin to get great views of the town of Moshi and Mawenzi Peak (16,893 feet/5149 m). If you can spare an extra day for acclimatizing, Horombo is the best hut for this. There are some nice day hikes that will help you further acclimatize. Kibo is too high to allow a good night's sleep. Horombo also has 200 beds and is similar to Mandara.

DAY THREE: HOROMBO HUT to KIBO HUT (15,430 feet/4703 m) — FIVE–SIX HOURS. ALTITUDE GAIN: 3225 feet (983 m).

On the morning of day three, the vegetation begins to thin out to open grasslands. You pass "Last Water" (be sure to fill your water bottles as this is the last source of water). The landscape becomes more barren as you reach "the saddle," a wide desert between Kibo and Mawenzi Peak. Kibo Hut does not come in view until just before you reach it. Kibo Hut has 120 beds and is located on the east side of Kibo Peak.

With the wind-chill factor, it can be very cold, so dress warmly. This is the day many hikers feel the effects of the altitude and may begin to experience some altitude sickness. Most people find it impossible to sleep at this height because of the lack of oxygen and the bitter cold, not to mention the possibility of altitude sickness. Get as much rest as you can.

The author at Uhuru Peak, Mt. Kilimanjaro.

DAY FOUR: KIBO HUT to GILLMAN'S POINT (18,635 feet/5680 m) and UHURU PEAK (19,340 feet/5895 m) AND DOWN TO HOROMBO HUT — TEN–TWELVE HOURS.

Your guide will wake you shortly after midnight for your ascent, which should begin around 1:00 a.m. Be sure not to delay the start; it is vital that you reach the summit by sunrise. The sun quickly melts the frozen scree, making the ascent all the more difficult.

The steep ascent to Gillman's Point on the edge of the caldera is a grueling four- to five-hour slog up scree. Hans Meyer Cave is a good place to rest before climbing seemingly unending switchbacks past Johannes Notch to Gillman's Point.

From Gillman's Point, Uhuru Peak is a fairly gradual climb of 705 feet (215 m) in altitude. It will take another hour to hour and a half. Uhuru Peak is well marked, and there is a book in which you may sign your name.

If you are still feeling strong, ask your guide to take you down into the caldera to the inner crater, which has some steam vents. You return to Gillman's Point by a different route.

On my climb, our guide woke us late, and we didn't start the climb until after 2:00 a.m. We made it all right to Gillman's Point, but the final hike to Uhuru (Freedom) Peak was a killer. Instead of walking across the frozen crust, I fell through knee-deep snow on every step. Had we arrived an hour earlier, this may not have been a problem.

The feeling of accomplishment upon reaching the summit is one of the highlights of my life. I was amazed at the tremendous size of the glaciers so close to the equator. Standing over 16,000 feet (4900 m) above the surrounding plains, the view was breathtaking in every direction. Sunrise over Mawenzi is a beautiful sight. You truly feel you're on the top of the world!

Shortly after sunrise, you begin the long walk down the mountain to Kibo Hut for a short rest, then continue onward to Horombo Hut. Provided you are not completely exhausted, the walk down is long but pretty easy going. From Gillman's Point to Horombo takes about four hours and from Uhuru Peak about five.

The entire descent is made in two days, and one's knees take a hard pounding; you may want to wrap your knees with elastic bandages or use elastic knee supports.

DAY FIVE: HOROMBO HUT TO MARANGU

Another long day of hiking as you descend past Mandara Hut to Park Headquarters, where you receive a diploma certifying your accomplishment. Many climbers spend the night at Kibo or Marangu Hotel and have the pleasure of sharing their experiences with unwary visitors planning to begin their Kilimanjaro adventure the following day.

Machame Route

This is possibly the most beautiful route up the mountain. The park gate is located a few miles above Machame village. Hike four to six hours through rain forest to Machame Huts (9843 feet/3000 m).

The following day hike five to seven hours to the defunct Shira Hut (12,467 feet/3800 m) on the Shira Plateau (see Shira Plateau Route for description of the area). Continue hiking about four hours to Lava Tower Hut. From Lava Tower Hut follow the directions from the Umbwe Route to the summit.

Shira Plateau Route

This is a very scenic and yet seldom-used route, providing great views of Kilimanjaro and the Rift Valley and probably the best wildlife viewing on the mountain. A four-wheel-drive vehicle is needed, and the roads may be impassable in the rainy seasons. The route is hard to find. Be sure to have a guide who knows the way.

Drive north from the Moshi-Arusha road at Boma la Ng'ombe to Londorossi Gate, located on the western side of Kilimanjaro. Continue on to a campsite. The track ends shortly thereafter, at 12,200 feet (3720 m). The defunct Shira Hut (12,467 feet/3800 m) is only a one-and-one-half-hour's walk away. You may want to take two days to acclimatize before continuing on.

From Shira Hut it is about a four-hour hike to the remains of Lava Tower Hut. The vegetation changes on the Shira Plateau are fabulous as you walk through open grasslands and moorlands dotted with giant senecios over 30 feet (9 m) high and past the impressive Shira Cone, Cathedral and Needle Peaks. From Lava Tower Hut follow the directions from the Umbwe Route to the summit.

Mweka Route

This is the steepest and most direct route to Uhuru Peak. It starts at Mweka village near the College of Wildlife Management (4593 feet/1400 m) and runs along an old logging road through banana and coffee plantations for about three miles, then along a seldom-used path for another three and one-half miles to Mweka Hut at 9515 feet (2900 m). This hike takes six to eight hours. There is water nearby.

After a five- to six-hour climb the following day through heathlands and alpine desert, you reach Barafu Hut (14,435 feet/4400 m). The third day is a steep climb between Ratzel and Rebmann Glaciers to Kibo Rim (six to seven hours) and Uhuru Peak (one more hour).

Umbwe Route

The Umbwe Route is very steep and strenuous. The route begins at Umbwe (about 4600 feet/1400 m), a village ten miles from Moshi. Walk two miles to Kifuni village and into the forest. Follow the path for another three and one-half miles and then branch left into a mist-covered forest until you reach the forest cave (Bivouac #1) at 9515 feet (2900 m), six to seven hours from Umbwe. Overhanging ledges extending about five feet from the cliff provide reasonable protection for about six people; however, it is recommended you use your own tents. The wood is usually very damp and water is available, but not close by.

Continue through moorlands and along a narrow ridge with deep valleys on either side. The thick mist and vegetation covered with "Old Man's Beard" moss creates an eerie atmosphere. The second caves at 11,483 feet (3500 m) are still another two- to three-hour hike from Bivouac #1. The vegetation thins out, and you branch right shortly before arriving at Barranco Hut (12,795 feet/3900 m) about two hours later.

From Barranco you can backtrack to the fork and turn right (north) and hike for three hours to where Lava Tower Hut (15,092 feet/4600 m) used to stand. From there the climb is up steep scree and blocks of rock to the floor of the crater and Uhuru Peak via the Great Western Breach. The climb from Lava Tower Hut to the caldera takes about nine hours. An alternative from Barranco Hut is to traverse the mountain eastward and join the Mweka Route.

Summit Circuit

There is a circuit between 12,139 and 15,092 feet (3700 and 4600 m) completely around the base of Kibo Peak. Horombo, Barranco and Moir Huts are on the circuit, while Lava Tower, Shira, Kibo and Mawenzi Huts are on side trails not far from the circuit. A tent is needed since there is no hut on the northern side of Kibo. Be sure to bring a well-insulated pad for your sleeping bag.

Huts

Mandara, Horombo and Kibo Huts are described under the Marangu Route above. The other huts are prefab metal huts, either 10 or 15 feet (3 or 4.5 m) in diameter in varying states of disrepair; some are basically uninhabitable. Many of the wooden floors have been ripped up and used for firewood. It is best to bring your own tents and let the guides and porters use the huts. Drinking water should be filtered, treated and/or boiled, as some sources on the mountain are polluted.

MAWENZI HUT (15,092 feet/4600 m): From "The Saddle" on the Marangu Route just after passing East Lava Hill, hike one and one-quarter miles east-northeast (050 degrees) to the hut at the base of the West Corrie. Mawenzi Hut sleeps five and is about a three-hour hike from Horombo or Kibo Huts. There are no toilets. Mawenzi Peak should only be attempted by well-equipped, experienced mountaineers.

MAWENZI TARN HUT (14,206 feet/4330 m): This hut is situated northeast of Mawenzi Hut; it is an easy hike around the foot of the peak. The hut sleeps six.

MWEKA HUTS (9515 feet/2900 m): There are two large huts that sleep 12 persons each. There is a stream nearby.

BARAFU HUT (15,092 feet/4600 m): The hut sleeps 12 and there is no wood or water.

BARRANCO HUT (12,795 feet/3900 m): The hut sleeps eight and there is a bivouac site about a 600-foot walk above the hut under a rock overhang. Some wood may be available in the vicinity, and a stream is nearby.

MOIR HUT (13,780 feet/4200 m): This hut is located on the northwest side of Kibo north of the Shira: it sleeps ten and there is water nearby.

Climbing Tips

There are a number of ways of increasing your chances of making it to the top. One of the most important things to remember is to *take your time. Polepole* is Swahili for "slowly," which is definitely the way to go. There is no prize for being the first to the hut or first to the top.

Pace yourself so that you are never completely out of breath. Exaggerate your breathing, taking deeper and more frequent breaths than you feel you actually need. This will help you acclimatize and help keep you from exhausting yourself prematurely or developing pulmonary or cerebral edema.

Ski poles make good walking sticks; they can be rented at Park Headquarters and are highly recommended. Bring a small backpack to carry the items you wish to have quick access to along the trail, such as a water bottle, snacks and a camera. Most importantly, listen to what your body is telling you. Don't overdo it! Many people die each year on the mountain because they don't listen or pay attention to the signs and keep pushing themselves.

On steep portions of the hike, use the "lock step" method to conserve energy. Take a step and lock the knee of the uphill leg. This puts your weight on the leg bone, using less muscle strength. Pause for a few seconds, letting your other leg rest without any weight on it, and breath deeply. Then repeat. This technique will save vital energy that you may very well need in your quest for the top.

Some climbers take the prescription drug diamox, a diuretic which usually reduces the symptoms of altitude sickness, but there are side effects from taking the drug, including increased urination. You should discuss the use of diamox with your doctor prior to leaving home.

Drink a lot more water than you feel you need. High-altitude hiking is very dehydrating, and a dehydrated body weakens quickly. Climbers should drink three to four liters (quarts) of liquids daily.

Most hikers find it difficult to sleep at high altitude. Once you reach the hut each afternoon, rest a bit, then hike to a spot a few hundred feet in altitude above the hut and relax for a while. Acclimatizing even for a short time at a higher altitude will help you get a more restful night's sleep. Remember, "Climb high, sleep low!"

Consume at least 4000 calories per day on the climb. This can be a problem. Most climbers lose their appetite at high altitude. Bring along trail mix (mixed nuts and dried fruit), chocolate and other goodies that you enjoy to supplement the meals prepared for you.

Forget about drinking alcoholic beverages on the climb. Altitude greatly enhances the effects of alcohol. Plus, alcohol causes dehydration. A headache caused by altitude sickness can be bad enough without having a hangover on top of it.

Park Headquarters is located in Marangu, 29 miles (47 km) from Moshi, 63 miles (101 km) from Kilimanjaro Airport and 75 miles (120 km) from Arusha.

EQUIPMENT CHECKLIST

The better equipped you are for the climb, the higher your chances of making the summit. When it comes to clothing, the "layered effect" works best. Bring a duffel bag to pack your gear in for the climb. Wrap your clothes in heavy garbage bags to keep them dry. Keep the weight under the porter's maximum load of 33 pounds (15 kg). Here's a checklist of items to consider bringing:

CLOTHING

- ❑ Gortex jacket (with hood) and pants
- ❑ polypropylene long underwear - tops and bottoms, medium and heavy weight
- ❑ wool sweater (one or two)
- ❑ Gortex gaiters (to keep the scree out of your boots at higher altitudes)
- ❑ tennis shoes or ultralight hiking boots (for lower altitudes)
- ❑ medium-weight insulated hiking boots for warmth and to help dig into the scree during the final ascent
- ❑ heavy wool or down mittens with Gortex outer shell and glove liners
- ❑ several pairs of wool socks and polypropylene liner socks
- ❑ several pairs of underwear
- ❑ track or warm-up suit (to relax and sleep in)
- ❑ long trousers or knickers (wool or synthetic)
- ❑ light, loose-fitting cotton trousers
- ❑ shorts (with pockets)
- ❑ wool long-sleeve and cotton long sleeve shirts
- ❑ T-shirts or short-sleeve shirts
- ❑ turtleneck shirt
- ❑ down vest
- ❑ balaclava (wool or synthetic)
- ❑ wide-brimmed hat or cap for protection from the sun
- ❑ bandana
- ❑ wool hat
- ❑ sleeping pad (for all routes except the Marangu Route)

MISCELLANEOUS

- ❑ day pack large enough to carry extra clothing, rain gear, two plastic water bottles (1 liter/quart each), camera and lunch
- ❑ sleeping bag (rated at least 0° F (-18° C)
- ❑ pocket flask for summit climb
- ❑ flashlight with extra bulb and batteries. (some prefer head lamps)
- ❑ light towel
- ❑ sunglasses and mountaineering glasses
- ❑ camera and film
- ❑ strong sunblock
- ❑ protective lip balm, such as Chapstick brand
- ❑ body lotion (otherwise skin may get dry and itchy)
- ❑ water purifiers
- ❑ duffle bag
- ❑ half-dozen heavy garbage bags in which to wrap clothes
- ❑ toilet paper
- ❑ moist towelettes
- ❑ pocket knife with scissors
- ❑ granola bars, trail mix and sweets that travel well
- ❑ powered drink mix

FIRST AID KIT

- ❑ malaria pills
- ❑ moleskin
- ❑ plastic bandage strips, such as Band-Aid brand
- ❑ elastic bandages
- ❑ gauze pads (4" X 4")
- ❑ diuretics (diamox) - by prescription from your doctor
- ❑ broad-spectrum antibiotics (pills) - as above
- ❑ laxative
- ❑ antihistamine tablets
- ❑ antibiotic cream
- ❑ antidiarrheal preparation - Imodium or Lomotil
- ❑ iodine
- ❑ aspirin or acetaminophen for headache/muscle pain
- ❑ throat and cough lozenges
- ❑ decongestant (can be found in combination with antihistamine tablets)

Equipment is available for rent from Park Headquarters and Kibo and Marangu Hotels, but it may not be of top quality. I recommend that you bring your own gear.

ACCOMMODATION — CLASS C: * *Kibo Hotel,* situated less than a mile (1.6 km) from Marangu village, has rooms with private facilities (150 beds). * *Marangu Hotel,* located a mile and a half (2.4 km) from Marangu village, is a rustic lodge with 29 double rooms with ensuite facilities.

THE SOUTH

The "Southern Circuit" of wildlife reserves includes the Selous Game Reserve, Ruaha National Park and Mikumi National Park. The Selous and Ruaha are less visited than the northern Tanzania parks and offer a great opportunity to explore wild and unspoiled bush.

SELOUS GAME RESERVE

This little-known reserve happens to be the second largest game reserve in Africa and a World Heritage Site. Over 21,000 square miles (55,000 km^2) in area, the Selous is more than half the size of the state of Ohio, twice the area of Denmark and three-and-three-fourths times larger than Serengeti National Park. Unexploited and largely unexplored, no human habitation is allowed in this virgin bush except for limited tourist facilities.

The Selous is a stronghold for over 50,000 elephant, 150,000 buffalo (herds often exceed 1000), and large populations of lion, leopard, Lichtenstein's hartebeest, greater kudu, hippo, crocodiles, and numerous other species including giraffe, zebra, wildebeest, waterbuck, African wild dog, impala and a small number of black rhino. Colobus monkey can be found in the forests along the Rufiji River. Over one million large animals live within its borders. Over 350 species of birds and 2000 plant species have been recorded.

Almost 75 percent of this low-lying reserve (360–4100 feet/110–1250 m) is composed of miombo woodlands, with the balance being grasslands, floodplains, marshes and dense forests.

Giraffe on the dry floodplains of the Rufiji River.

Morning walks accompanied by an armed ranger and guide are popular and are conducted by all the camps. Fly camping for a few nights as well as portered safaris up to two weeks in length are also available.

This reserve may give you the feeling of exploring the bush for the first time, as you will encounter few other visitors during your safari.

The Rufiji River, the largest river in East Africa, roughly bisects the park as it flows from the southwest to the northeast. The Rufiji and its tributaries, including Great Ruaha and Luwego, have high concentrations of hippo and crocs. Fish eagles are numerous.

Exploring the Rufiji River, its channels, swamps and lakes by boat is another great way to view game and experience the reserve. One should consider adding the Selous onto a northern Tanzania itinerary, as game viewing by boat is not possible in the Serengeti, Ngorongoro, Lake Manyara or Tarangire. Fishing is also popular.

On our last visit, we encountered numerous lion including two females and four cubs on a Defassa waterbuck kill; a pack of wild dogs; large herds of elephant, eland, buffalo and giraffe; banded mongoose; Defassa waterbuck; and very healthy blue wildebeest that one could almost classify as handsome. Bird life was prolific; our sightings on a boat game drive included African spoonbill, black-winged stilt, fish eagle, gray heron, great white heron, little heron and open-billed stork.

All tourist activities are restricted to the northern 20 percent of the reserve. The best time to visit the reserve is during the dry season, June–November. Game viewing from December to February is good, although it is quite hot during that period. During the rainy season, many of the roads are impassable and wildlife is scattered. The reserve is usually closed from March to May.

Most visitors fly to camps in the Selous from Dar es Salaam by charter aircraft. Access by road is difficult and only possible in the dry season.

ACCOMMODATION: The camps are located about 160–235 miles (260–380 km) from Dar es Salaam, requiring a 6 to 12-hour drive in a four-wheel-drive vehicle. All camps have private airstrips and flying is highly recommended.

CLASS A: * *Mbuyuni Safari Camp*, a luxury tented camp set on the banks of the Rufiji River, has 12 tents with ensuite facilities and a swimming pool. The camp also has a "dungo," a large elevated platform overlooking the Rufiji River for relaxing and watching game and bird life during the midday. Game drives, escorted walks, boat safaris, fishing and fly camping are offered. * *Sand Rivers* has eight luxury chalets with ensuite facilities and a swimming pool. Game drives, walks, boat safaris, fishing, fly camping and long-distance portered walking safaris (up to two weeks) are offered.

CLASS B: * *Rufiji River Camp*, a comfortable tented camp with 15 tents (doubles) with ensuite facilities, offers game drives, fishing, walking and boat safaris.

CAMPING: Sites are available.

Sand Rivers' main lodge area, Selous.

RUAHA NATIONAL PARK

Ruaha, known for its great populations of elephant, buffalo, greater and lesser kudu, hippo, crocs and magnificent scenery, is one of the country's newest and best national parks, and because of its location, it is one of the least visited.

Ruaha's scenery is spectacular, and its 5000-square-mile (12,950-km^2) area makes it almost as large as Serengeti National Park. The landscape is characterized by miombo woodland with rocky hills on a plateau over 3300 feet (1000 m) in altitude. Park elevation ranges from 2460 feet (750 m) in the Ruaha Valley to 6230-foot (1900-m) Ikingu Mountain in the west of the park.

The Great Ruaha River with its impressive gorges, deep pools and rapids runs for 100 miles (160 km) close to the park's eastern boundary and is home to many hippo and crocodiles. The black rocks of the riverbed contrasted against the golden grass on the riverbank dotted with baobob trees is a beautiful sight indeed.

The dry season, June–November, is the best time to visit the park, when game is concentrated along the Ruaha River. Large numbers of greater and lesser kudu, elephant, wildebeest and impala can be seen,

Mwagusi Safari Camp, Ruaha.

along with eland, sable antelope, roan antelope, buffalo, Defassa waterbuck, ostrich and giraffe. Lion, leopard, spotted and striped hyena, black-backed jackal, bat-eared fox and African wild dog are also present in significant numbers. Black rhino are present but seldom seen. Over 400 species of birds have been recorded.

On our most recent visit, we saw 25 greater kudu, 2 eland and herds of buffalo and zebra on the drive from the airstrip to the camp alone. Other game spotted includes leopard, lion, elephant, lesser kudu and wild dog.

During the wet months of December to March, wildlife is scattered but viewing is still good. Game viewing from February to June is difficult due to high grass.

The park is about a two-and-one-half-hour charter flight from Dar es Salaam, or a two-hour drive from Iringa through the villages of Mloa and Idodi and across the Ruaha River via the Ibuguziwa Ferry. Park Headquarters and an airstrip are located at Msembe, 70 miles (112 km) from Iringa and 385 miles (615 km) from Dar es Salaam.

ACCOMMODATION — CLASS B: * *Mwagusi Safari Camp* has eight tents with ensuite facilities. * *Ruaha River Camp*, located in the park 6 miles (10 km) south of Msembe, has 29 stone and thatch bandas and tents in a natural setting, most with ensuite facilities.

CLASS F: * *National Park Rondavels* (self-service) are situated at Msembe.

CAMPING: Campsites are available.

MIKUMI NATIONAL PARK

Mikumi is the closest park to Dar es Salaam (180 miles/288 km), and it takes about four hours to drive on tarmac from Dar es Salaam via Morongoro.

The park covers 1247 square miles (3230 km^2) and borders the Selous Game Reserve to the south along the Tazara Railroad line, which runs down to Zambia and divides the park.

The park is dominated by the Mkata River floodplain, with swamps and grasslands dotted with baobab trees and miombo woodlands at an average altitude of 1800 feet (550 m) above sea level. Elephant, buffalo, lion, hippo, zebra, wildebeest and Masai giraffe are prevalent. Sable antelope, common waterbuck, Lichtenstein's hartebeest, eland, Bohor reedbuck and impala may also be seen. Black and white colobus monkey are frequently seen in the south of the park.

During a two-day stay, we saw elephant, zebra, six lion, giraffe, buffalo, impala, ground hornbill and guinea fowl, among other species. There is a variety of bird life, as Mikumi is in the transition zone between north and south.

The long rains are from March to May and the short rains from November to December. Rainfall within the park ranges from 20 to 40 inches (510 to 1070 mm) yearly.

It is difficult to say when is the best time to visit Mikumi. Unlike most parks, wildlife is concentrated in this park in the wet season, when the vegetation is the thickest, making game viewing more difficult. Fewer animals are present in the dry season, but the ones present are easier to spot. Considering this, the best time to visit is June–February.

This park is open all year, although some roads are closed during the rainy season. There is an airstrip, petrol station and garage at Park Headquarters.

ACCOMMODATION — CLASS B/C: * *Mikumi Wildlife Lodge* has 50 double rooms with ensuite facilities and a swimming pool.

CLASS D: * *Mikumi Wildlife Camp* has self-contained bandas and a restaurant and bar.

CAMPING: Campsites are available.

THE WEST

LAKE TANGANYIKA

Lake Tanganyika forms much of the western border of Tanzania and is indeed an "inland sea." This is the world's longest lake (446 miles/714 km) and the world's second deepest lake (over 4700 feet/1433 m). Only Lake Baikal in Russia is deeper, at over 5700 feet (1738 m). More than 400 species of fish inhabit Lake Tanganyika's clear waters. Easiest access to the lake in Tanzania is by flying to Kigoma.

KIGOMA

Kigoma is the country's major port on huge Lake Tanganyika. From here you can catch a steamer to Burundi or Zambia. Kigoma is the closest town to Gombe Stream National Park and many travelers stay here while in transit to and from the park. Kigoma can be reached by air, by road or by a two-and-one-half-day train ride from Dar es Salaam.

Ujiji, a small town six miles south of Kigoma, is where the line "Dr. Livingstone, I presume" was spoken by Stanley in 1872. Buses run there regularly from the Kigoma Rail Station.

ACCOMMODATION — TOURIST CLASS: * *Aqua Lodge*, located 50 yards (50 m) from the lake, has nine rooms with private facilities.

RUBONDO ISLAND NATIONAL PARK

Located in the southwestern part of Lake Victoria, the main attraction of this 93-square-mile (240-km^2) island is sitatunga, which is indigenous to Rubondo. In addition, walking is allowed and the wildlife may be approached very closely.

Also indigenous to the park are hippo, bushbuck, crocodile, marsh mongoose and python. Chimpanzee, black and white colobus monkey, black rhino, giraffe and roan antelope have been introduced. There are no large predators. Bird watching, especially for waterfowl, is very good here.

In addition to the main island, there are about a dozen small islands that make up the park. Habitats include papyrus swamps, savannah, open woodlands and dense evergreen forests. Visitors, accompanied by a guide who is usually armed, may walk along forested trails in search of wildlife or wait patiently at a number of hides. The best time to visit is November–February. A few boats are available for hire.

Flying by air charter is the only easy way to get to the park. An airstrip is located at Park Headquarters. From Mwanza, it is a seven-hour drive by vehicle and a two-hour boat ride by one route and a ten-hour drive and half-hour boat ride by another route. Visitors are not allowed to bring their vehicles to the island.

ACCOMMODATION — CLASS F: Two self-service bandas are available; bring your own food.

CAMPING: Sites are available, but bring your own supplies.

GOMBE STREAM NATIONAL PARK

Gombe Stream is the setting for Jane Goodall's chimpanzee studies and her films and books, including *In the Shadow of Man*. This remote 20-square-mile (52-km^2) park is situated along the eastern shores of Lake Tanganyika 10 miles (16 km) north of Kigoma in remote northwestern Tanzania.

This tiny park covers a thin strip of land 3 miles (5 km) wide and stretches for 10 miles (16 km) along Lake Tanganyika. A mountain range ascends steeply from the lake at an altitude of 2235 feet (681 m) to form part of the eastern wall of the western branch of the Great Rift Valley, rising to 5000 feet (4524 m).

Thick gallery forests are found along Gombe Stream and many other permanent streams in the valley and lower slopes of the mountains. Higher up the slopes are woodlands, with some grasslands near the upper ridges.

The experience of seeing chimpanzees in the wild is by far the major attraction of this park. Other primates include red colobus monkey, blue monkey and baboon. Other wildlife of note includes buffalo, Defassa waterbuck and leopard.

Chimpanzees can usually be found around the research station and are quite habituated to humans. Two-hour morning and afternoon hikes into the forest searching for chimps can be arranged. The Kakombe Waterfall is worth a visit. There is also a nice walk along the lake shore northward from the guest house.

You may reach the park by water taxi (about three hours) from Ujiji or Kigoma.

ACCOMMODATION — CLASS F: There is a basic self-service guest house with rooms with separate facilities. Book well in advance or bring a tent, as the guest house may be full. Only basic supplies are available in Kigoma.

CAMPING: Allowed on special request.

MAHALE MOUNTAINS NATIONAL PARK

Like Gombe Stream, the main attraction of this remote park, which was only recently gazetted in 1985, is being able to walk among large populations of chimpanzees. The chimps have been studied by Japanese researchers for more than 30 years, and over 100 of them have been habituated to humans.

Located about 95 miles (150 km) south of Kigoma, this 609-square-mile (1577-km^2) park is situated on the eastern shores of Lake Tanganyika. The Mahale Mountains, with deep ravines, permanent streams and waterfalls, run through the center of the park, forming the eastern wall of the Great Rift Valley with altitudes up to 8075 feet (2462 m) above sea level. The western side of the mountains, where the chimp trekking occurs, is primarily composed of semitropical rain forest with brachystygia (semideciduous) woodland on the ridges and montane forest at higher altitudes.

Trekking in the park occurs in the range of the M Group, which consists of about 80 individuals that have been habituated to human presence. Once found, trekkers may watch them naturally go about their normal daily activities from often just a few yards (meters) away.

In addition to over 1000 chimpanzees, the park is also home to eight other species of primates including red colobus monkey and Angolan black and white colobus monkey. Other wildlife includes bushbuck, otters, banded mongoose, Sharpe's grysbok and blue duiker.

Seasons are fairly predictable. The main dry season usually runs from mid-May to mid-October, with mid-December to mid-February also being quite dry. Rainy seasons are usually mid-October to mid-December and mid-February to mid-May. Nights are often cool and rainfall ranges from 60 to 100 inches (1500 to 2500 mm) per year. The best time to visit is during the two dry seasons mentioned above.

There is no easy way to reach this seldom-visited park except by air charter from Nairobi, Arusha or any Tanzanian park. To reach Mahale by boat from Kigoma (not recommended), take the weekly steamer *MV Liemba* for eight to ten hours to the village of Lagosa (Mugambo). You usually arrive in the middle of the night and must be transferred ashore. From here you may be able to charter a boat for a three-hour ride to Kasoge (Kasiha village) in the park. Small boats from Kigoma make this journey in about 16 hours. The park cannot be reached by vehicle.

ACCOMMODATION — CLASS A/B: * *Mahale Mountains Tented Camp* is a 12-bed luxury tented camp located on the shores of Lake Tanganyika, with private bush (bucket) showers and long-drop toilets. Hikes to see chimpanzees, sailing by dhow, dugout canoeing, snorkeling and fishing are offered. The camp is open June to mid-October and mid-December to mid-February.

CLASS F: There is a basic guest house, but you will need to bring your own food, crockery and cutlery, bed linens and stove. No supplies are available in the park.

CAMPING: Camping sites are available.

KATAVI NATIONAL PARK

This undeveloped 1545-square-mile (4000-km^2) park is located between the towns of Mpanda and Sumbawanga on the main road running through western Tanzania from north to south.

Lake Katavi and its extensive floodplains are in the north of this park which is about 2950 feet (900 m) above sea level. To the southeast is Lake Chada, which is connected with Lake Katavi by the Katuma River and its extensive swampland. Miombo woodlands dominate most of the dry areas, except for acacia woodlands near Lake Chada.

Wildlife includes hippo, crocs, elephant, zebra, lion, leopard, eland, puku, roan antelope and sable antelope. Herds of several thousand buffalo are sometimes seen. Over 400 species of birds have been recorded.

The long rains are March–May. The best time to visit is July–October.

ACCOMMODATIONS — CLASS B: * *Katavi Tented Camp* has four tents with bush showers (hot water) and bush (long-drop) toilets. Activities include game drives, walks and optional fly-camping.

CLASS F: There are only a few huts for shelter. Very basic hotel accommodation is available in Mpanda and Sumbawanga.

CAMPING: Sites are available in the park. Campers must be self-sufficient, as there are no facilities.

THE COAST

DAR ES SALAAM

Dar es Salaam, which means "haven of peace" in Arabic, is the functional capital, largest city and commercial center of Tanzania. Many safaris to the southern parks begin here. Among the more interesting sights are the harbor, National Museum, Village Museum and the Kariakoo Market. Ask at your hotel about traditional dancing troops that may be performing during your stay.

Once the German capital, hub of the slave trade and end point of the slave route from the interior, **Bagamoyo** is an old seaport 46 miles (75 km) north of Dar es Salaam. Fourteenth century ruins, stone pens and shackles that held the slaves may be seen.

ACCOMMODATION — FIRST CLASS: * *Sheraton Hotel* has 250 air-conditioned rooms with ensuite facilities, two restaurants, and a bar, swimming pool and health club.

TOURIST CLASS: * *The Hotel Agip* has 57 air-conditioned rooms with ensuite facilities. * The *Kilimanjaro Hotel* is a large air-conditioned hotel with ensuite facilities, a swimming pool and a fabulous view of the harbor. * *Oyster Bay Hotel* is four miles from town on the coast and has rooms with ensuite facilities.

ACCOMMODATION NEAR DAR-ES-SALAAM — FIRST CLASS: * *Ras Kutani Beach Resort,* located on a beautiful, remote beach 17 miles (28 km) south of Dar es Salaam, has 25 rooms with ensuite facilities. Wind surfing, sailing, snorkeling and fishing are offered. Easiest access is by air charter.

ZANZIBAR

Zanzibar and its sister island, Pemba, grow 75 percent of the world's cloves. A beautiful island relatively unspoiled by tourism, Zanzibar is only 22 miles (35 km) from the mainland — a 25-minute scheduled charter flight from Dar es Salaam or 90-minute hydrofoil ride (beware of thieves).

The narrow streets and Arabic architecture of historical Zanzibar City are exceptionally mystical and beautiful on a moonlit night. Main attractions include the Zanzibar Museum, former British Consulate, Arab Fort, Anglican Cathedral built on the site of the old slave market, Sultan's Palace, clove market and Indian bazaar. Livingstone's and Burton's houses are near the picturesque Dhow Harbour, where 20–30 large Arab dhows may often be seen having their cargos loaded or unloaded.

Antique shops stocked with Arab clocks, kettles, brass trays, Zanzibar beds, carved doors and frames have special atmospheres all their own. Visitors can also take a short boat ride to Slave Island to see the slave trading ruins.

The Spice Tour travels north of Stone Town and includes a visit to one or more spice gardens and farms where you may also see red monkeys. Various spices and plants, including cinnamon, cloves, nutmeg, vanilla, ginger and black pepper, along with fruits such as tamarind, guava, rose apple and up to 10 types of mango and 40 different types of banana, may be seen, touched and smelled.

The Fisherman, a very good restaurant, is located near the Tembo Hotel in Stone Town. The Chit Chat is a nice Goan restaurant located near the Roman Catholic Church in Stone Town.

ACCOMMODATION IN ZANZIBAR TOWN — DELUXE: * *Serena Hotel*, located on the waterfront, has 80 rooms with ensuite facilities and a swimming pool.

ACCOMMODATION — TOURIST CLASS: * *Dhow Palace* is located 300 yards (300 m) from the waterfront and has tastefully decorated rooms with ensuite facilities. No alcohol is served in the restaurant. * *Tembo Hotel* has 40 rooms, some with ensuite facilities, and a swimming pool. From its waterfront location, ships are constantly seen, passing en route to and from the harbor. No alcohol is served in the restaurant. * *Emersons* is a very basic hotel situated in the heart of Stone Town on a narrow alleyway, with a restaurant on the roof. Some rooms have ensuite facilities.

ACCOMMODATION ON THE BEACH — FIRST CLASS: * *Mapenzi Beach Resort*, located on a beautiful beach on the east coast 28 miles (45 km) from the airport, has 60 spacious rooms (most with air-conditioning) with ensuite facilities and tennis courts and a swimming pool. Activities include mountain biking, archery, snorkeling, beach volleyball, table tennis, wind surfing, canoeing and deep-sea fishing.* *Karafuu Hotel Village*, located on the east coast of Zanzibar about a 75-minute drive from the airport or Stone Town, has 59 air-conditioned rooms with ensuite facilities and swimming pool, disco and dive center. Activities include tennis, snorkeling, scuba diving, deep-sea fishing, wind surfing, canoeing, volleyball, mountain biking, water skiing, minisailing and boat excursions. * *Mbweni Ruins Hotel,* located on the west coast of the island and a 15-minute drive from Stone Town, has 13 rooms with ensuite facilities and a swimming pool.

TOURIST CLASS: * *Uroa Bay Village,* located on the mid-east coast on a mile-long (1.6 km) beach, has 36 rooms with private facilities. Wind surfing, snorkeling, scuba diving and big-game fishing are offered. * *Matamwe Bungalows,* located on cliffs overlooking the northeast coast, has 12 bandas, some with private facilities.

MNEMBA ISLAND

Mnemba is a private island located 2 miles (3 km) northeast of the Zanzibar mainland. The island is only 1 mile (1.5 km) in circumference and is idyllic for anyone who wants to truly get away from it all. Only guests of the Mnemba Club are allowed.

ACCOMMODATION — FIRST CLASS: * *Mnemba Club* is an exclusive island getaway with ten thatched beach cottages with ensuite facilities. Wind surfing, big-game fishing, skiing, snorkeling and scuba diving are available.

PEMBA ISLAND

Pemba is located 16 miles (25 km) north of Zanzibar Island near the Kenyan border and offers some of the best scuba diving and deep-sea fishing in all of sub-Sahara Africa. The Pemba Channel runs between Pemba and the mainland with depths up to 2625 feet (800 m). Sheer underwater walls drop 150–600 feet (45–183 m) just off the coastline. Divers often see eagle ray, grouper, tuna and a variety of tropical fish.

The only quick access to the island is by private charter flight.

ACCOMMODATION — CLASS C: * *Manta Reef Camp* has 15 cottages built on raised platforms with ensuite facilities and a dive shop. Scuba diving and snorkeling are offered.

MAFIA ISLAND

A 40-minute flight south from Dar es Salaam, this island offers some of the best big-game fishing in the world. Species caught include marlin, sailfish, tuna and shark.

ACCOMMODATION — CLASS B/C: * *Kinasi Camp* is a small lodge (20 beds) with ensuite facilities set on a hillside overlooking Chole Bay. Scuba diving, snorkeling, sport fishing, sailing and wind surfing are offered.

ACCOMMODATION — CLASS C: * *Mafia Island Lodge*, located on Chole Bay, has 40 rooms with ensuite facilities. Scuba diving, snorkeling, deep-sea fishing, water skiing, sailing and motor boating are offered.

KENYA

THE HUNTING CHEETAH

Cheetah hunt by day, and you may be fortunate enough to watch them in action. They are most active early in the morning and in the late afternoon (some may even hunt at midday, when the lion and hyena are most likely sleeping).

As animals of the open grassland, the color markings of the cheetah help with the stalking process. If motionless, the cheetah may be obscured, since the underpart of its body is in shadow, making the lighter, lower part as dark as the upper body. This makes it difficult for the cheetah's prey to notice its spots. The stalking process may take from a few minutes to several hours as cheetah approach to within 100 yards (100 m) of their prey. From this vantage point, they prepare for their attack.

This is when you see the speed of the cheetah. The acceleration from 0 to 45 mph (0 to 70 km/h) in a couple of seconds is made possible by its huge strides, which are six times its body length. At three strides per second, the hind feet strike the ground far in front of the head to reach a top speed of 70 mph (110 km/h). The cheetah uses its tail as a rudder to help it keep its balance at these high speeds.

As sprinters, cheetah have up to 15 seconds to catch their prey. Maximum speed may not be reached, however, since the cheetah must often slow down to swerve in order to follow the zigzag path of its prey. At this speed, cheetah also have to judge the timing of their strike. They do this either by swiping the legs from under the prey with a front paw or by hooking a dew claw into the animal's side.

Your patience may be rewarded by witnessing this spectacle—but if you approach too closely, you may distract the prey, or you may be too far away to witness the kill by the time the cheetah has covered ground in the chase.

KENYA

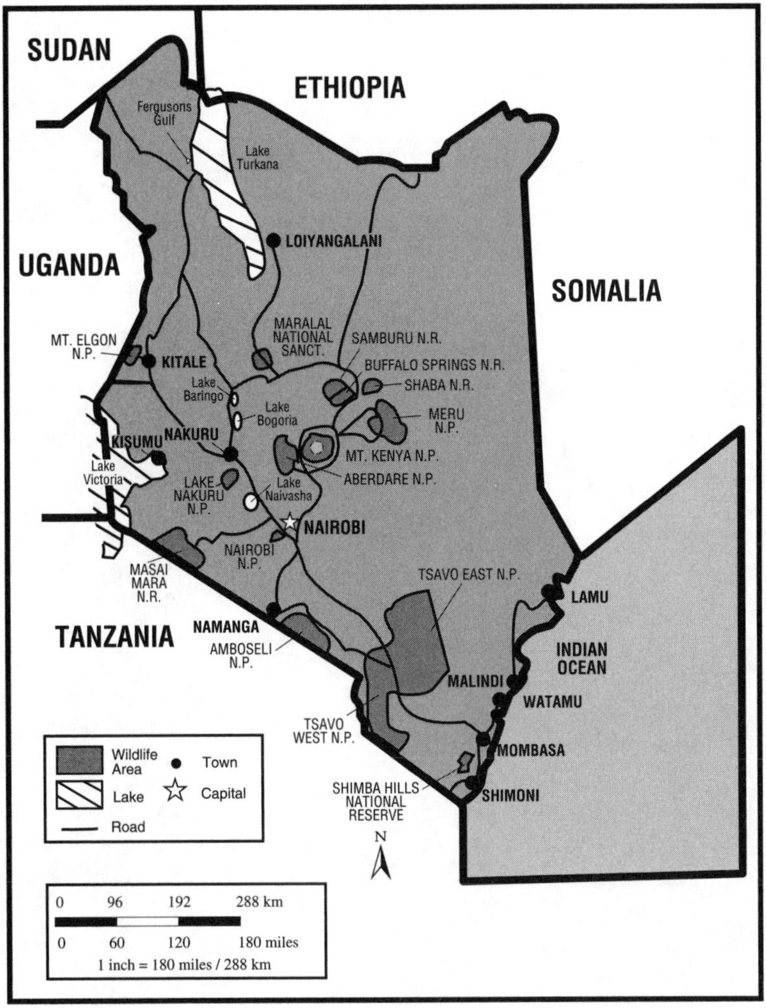

FACTS AT A GLANCE

AREA:	224,960 SQ. MI. / 582,750 SQ. KM.
APPROXIMATE SIZE:	TEXAS OR FRANCE
POPULATION:	28 MILLION
CAPITAL:	NAIROBI (POP. EST. 2 MILLION)
OFFICIAL LANGUAGE:	KISWAHILI AND ENGLISH

KENYA

The word "safari" is Swahili for "travel," and Kenya is where it all began. Great historical figures like Theodore Roosevelt and Ernest Hemingway immortalized this country. Visitors to Kenya can enjoy game viewing, bird watching, hot-air ballooning, mountaineering, scuba diving, freshwater and deep-sea fishing, and numerous other activities.

Kenya is well known for the magnificent Serengeti migration (shared with Tanzania) of more than one million wildebeest and zebra and for the colorful Masai, Samburu and other tribes that contribute so much to making this a top safari destination.

Kenya has one of the most diversely majestic landscapes on the continent. The Great Rift Valley, with the steep walled valley floor dropping as much as 2000–3000 feet (610–915 m) from the surrounding countryside, is more breathtakingly dramatic here than anywhere else in Africa.

The eastern and northern regions of the country are arid. Most of the population and economic production are in the south, which is characterized by a plateau ranging in altitude from 3000 to 10,000 feet (915 to 3050 m) sloping down to Lake Victoria in the west and a coastal strip to the east.

Over half the country is Christian, about 25 percent indigenous beliefs, and 6 percent Muslim concentrated along the coast. The Masai are found mainly to the west and south of Nairobi, the Kikuyu in the highlands around Nairobi, and the Samburu in the north.

Bantu and Nilotic peoples moved into the area before Arab traders arrived on the Kenyan coast by the first century A.D. The Swahili

Samburu Morani.

language was created out of a mixture of Bantu and Arabic and became the universal trading language.

The Portuguese arrived in 1498 and took command of the coast, followed by the Omani in the 1600s and the British in the late nineteenth century. Kenya gained its independence within the Commonwealth from Britain on December 12, 1963. Key foreign exchange earners are tourism, coffee, tea and horticulture (flowers and vegetables for Europe, especially in the European winter).

WILDLIFE AND WILDLIFE AREAS

Kenya is one of the best countries on the continent for seeing large amounts of game. In addition, group lodge safaris in which guests are driven from park to park are generally less expensive here than in Tanzania, Botswana or Zimbabwe. Prices are even more attractive in Kenya's low season (April–June and November), when game viewing is still quite good due to the fact that game is fairly easy to spot on the wide open plains of the Masai Mara and several other reserves.

Kenya's only major drawback is that many of the well-known parks can be crowded, so don't expect to be out there in the more popular parks on your own. However, it is possible to get away from the crowds by visiting private reserves and some of the less popular national parks or traveling during the low season.

The Kenya Wildlife Services organization, formed to monitor the national parks and reserves, has instituted changes which have reduced poaching and limited the building of new lodges and camps in reserves.

The Masai Mara is the best park in Kenya for game viewing and should, if at all possible, be included in your itinerary unless you will be touring the Serengeti National Park in Tanzania at the times of the year when wildlife is more concentrated there.

In general, game viewing is best during the dry seasons, mid-December–March and July–early October. Game is easiest to spot in the Masai Mara, Amboseli and Nairobi National Parks, which have great wide-open plains. Samburu National Reserve and Lewa Downs are the country's best northern reserves and are also excellent for game viewing.

The country is an ornithologist's paradise, with over 1000 species of birds recorded within its borders. Greater and lesser flamingos migrate along the Rift Valley and prefer the alkaline lakes of Magadi, Elmenteita, Nakuru, Bogoria or Turkana. Lakes Naivasha and Baringo are freshwater lakes. Bird watching is good year-round and excellent in the rainy season.

Flying safaris are available to many of the parks and reserves. Camel safaris are operated in the north, where guests walk down dry river beds or ride these "ships of the desert."

Safariers planning to visit Kenya's reserves should consider also visiting Tanzania's northern parks, which include the Serengeti, Ngorongoro Crater, Lake Manyara, Tarangire and Arusha National Parks.

THE SOUTH

NAIROBI

Nairobi, situated at about 6000 feet (1830 m) altitude, means "place of cool waters" in the Masai language.

The Norfolk Hotel, Nairobi.

The **National Museum** of Nairobi features the Leakey family's paleoanthropological discoveries, botanical drawings and the original tribal paintings of Joy Adamson, and taxidermy displays of wild animals that are good to study to help you identify the live game while on safari. Across from the museum is the **Snake Park**, exhibiting over 200 species of the well-loved reptilian family. At the **Municipal Market** in the center of town on Muindi Buingu Street, vendors sell produce and curios (be sure to bargain). The **Railroad Museum** will be of interest to railroad enthusiasts. The **Nairobi Race Course** has horse racing on Sunday afternoons (in season) and is highly recommended as a place for people-watching and meeting a diverse cross section of Nairobians.

One of the more popular dining and disco spots is the Carnivore, famous for its beef and game meat. The Horseman, located in the suburb of Karen, is also excellent. The Tamarind is known for excellent seafood. Kenya has many great Indian restaurants, with the Minar and Haandi at the Sarit Centre very possibly being the finest. The Thorn Tree Cafe is a renowned meeting place for travelers on safari, who leave messages on a bulletin board; it is one of the best spots in town for people-watching. Other excellent restaurants include Alan Bobbies' Bistro and the Red Bull.

For tips on the best eating establishments in Kenya from the country's leading expert, pick up a copy of *Kathy Eldon's Eating Out Guide to Kenya*. Also look for Kathy's *Specialties of the House,* featuring Kenya's tastiest recipes.

Other attractions include the **Bomas of Kenya** which features daily performances of ethnic dances and 16 varying styles of Kenyan homesteads. At the **Giraffe Centre** guests can feed the Rothschild's giraffes from an elevated platform and learn more about them. The **Karen Blixen Museum** is interesting to visit.

ACCOMMODATION — DELUXE: * *Norfolk Hotel,* a landmark in Nairobi, has traditional safari atmosphere, a swimming pool, the fabulous Ibis Grill, and an open-air bar especially popular on Friday nights. All rooms are air-conditioned with ensuite facilities. * *Safari Park Hotel,* located 7 miles (11 km) from the city center in a quiet country setting, has 228 rooms with ensuite facilities, a huge swimming pool, tennis and squash courts, and several excellent restaurants — all in a lush garden setting. * *The Windsor Golf and Country Club,* located 11 miles (17 km) outside Nairobi, is a colonial-style hotel with 130 rooms with ensuite facilities, an 18-hole golf course, tennis courts, and a health club and gymnasium. * *Grand Regency Hotel* is a 300-room high-rise hotel with ensuite facilities and a swimming pool, restaurant, rooftop lounge, conference center and casino. * *Nairobi Safari Club* is an air-conditioned, all-suite hotel (146 rooms) with ensuite facilities and a health club and swimming pool. * *Nairobi Serena Hotel,* located a ten-minute walk from town, has 200 air-conditioned rooms with ensuite facilities and a swimming pool.

FIRST CLASS: * *Ngong House,* located in the Ngong Hills, has four elevated log cabins set in beautiful natural gardens, with ensuite facilities, and excellent food. * *Giraffe Manor,* located in the suburb of Karen, is famous for having Rothschild's giraffes roaming about the property, often sticking their heads through open windows looking for handouts. This unique lodge has three bedrooms with ensuite facilities and two without. * *Hilton International* is centrally located and has 329 air-conditioned rooms with facilities ensuite and a swimming pool. * *Inter-Continental Hotel,* near the center of town, has a swimming pool, 440 air-conditioned rooms with ensuite facilities and a casino. * *New Stanley Hotel,* located in the center of town, has 240 air-conditioned rooms with ensuite facilities.

TOURIST CLASS: * *Boulevard Hotel,* located on the edge of town, is set in lovely gardens and has 70 rooms with ensuite facilities and a swimming pool. * *Landmark Hotel,* located just outside the city center, has 124 rooms with ensuite facilities. * *Mayfair Court Holiday Inn* has 108 rooms with ensuite facilities, two swimming pools, a restaurant and a casino.

LUNATIC EXPRESS

Train buffs might consider taking the overnight train between Nairobi and Mombasa. The quality of the food, service and accommodation is unfortunately not what it used to be, with "first-class" compartments being rated "tourist class" at best. Dinner and breakfast are served on this journey which passes Mt. Kilimanjaro in the night. There are daily departures from both Nairobi and Mombasa.

NAIROBI NATIONAL PARK

Nairobi National Park is only 8 miles (13 km) south of Nairobi and sporadically has an abundance of game (depending on the weather) including lion, cheetah, hippo and a variety of antelope — a bit of everything except elephant. The park has one of the highest concentrations of black rhino in Africa, with a current population of over 60.

There is something very strange about being in the midst of wild game and still within sight of a city skyline. Altitude ranges from 4950 to 5850 feet (1500 to 1785 m) above sea level.

The Animal Orphanage (a small zoo) near the main park entrance cares for hurt, sick or stray animals. The side of the park facing Nairobi is fenced. A four-wheel-drive vehicle is recommended in the rainy season.

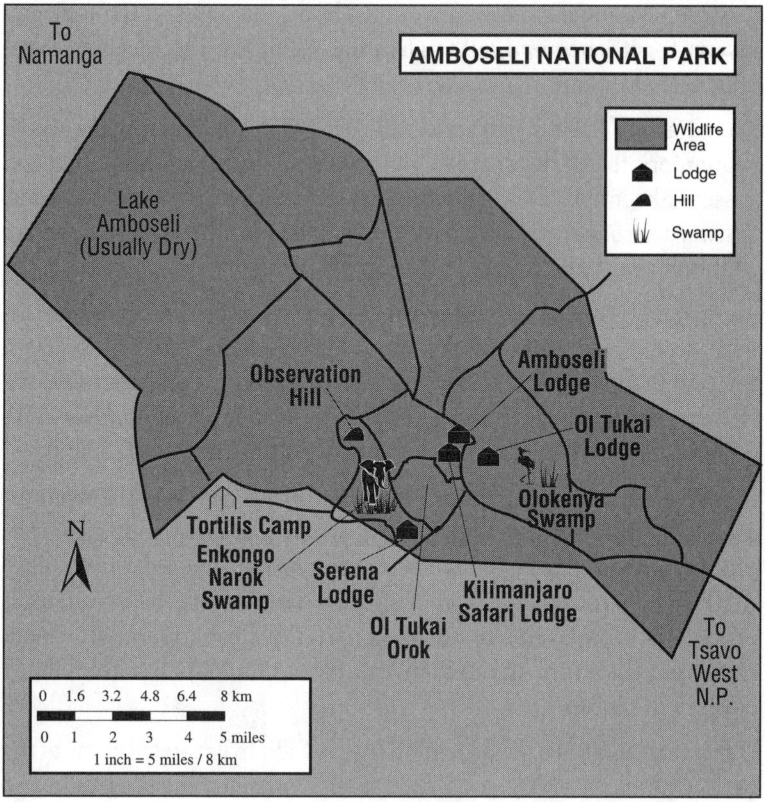

AMBOSELI NATIONAL PARK

The real attraction of this park is the spectacular backdrop of Mt. Kilimanjaro. Also, this may be the best park in Kenya to see elephant. *Elephant Memories*, a fascinating book by Cynthia Moss, is based primarily on her research in Amboseli.

This 150-square-mile (390-km^2) park is probably the most crowded in the country, and a large portion of it has been turned into a dust bowl. However, elephant and giraffe are easily found, and watching (and photographing) them as they pass in front of majestic Mt. Kilimanjaro is a sight to behold. The mountain seems so close, but it is actually located in Tanzania, more than 30 miles (48 km) from the park.

Amboseli National Park is surrounded by a game reserve; the park and reserve together cover 1259 square miles (3260 km^2) and average about 3900 feet (1190 m) in altitude.

From Nairobi travel south across the Athi Plains inhabited by the Masai. One enters the park on a badly corrugated road from Namanga and passes Lake Amboseli (a salt pan), bone dry except in the rainy seasons, eastward across sparsely vegetated chalk flats to Ol Tukai. Mirages are common under the midday sun.

Approaching the center of the park, the barren landscape turns refreshingly green from springs and swamps fed by underground runoff from the overshadowing Mt. Kilimanjaro. These swamps provide water for nearby grasslands and acacia woodlands, attracting an abundance of game and waterfowl, which give life to an otherwise parched land.

Large herds of elephant and buffalo are often seen around the swamps, especially at **Enkongo Narok Swamp**, where it is easy to obtain photos of animals (especially elephant) in the foreground and Mt. Kilimanjaro in the background. Early morning is best, before Kilimanjaro is covered in clouds; the clouds may partially clear in late afternoon. However, there are days when the mountain remains completely covered in clouds.

Observation Hill is a good location from which to get an overview of the park. One has a pretty good chance of spotting cheetah, giraffe and impala. Oryx and gerenuk are less likely to be seen. Over 420 species of birds have been recorded. Game viewing is best from mid-December to March (also best views of Kilimanjaro) and from July to October.

In order to limit destruction to the environment, driving off the roads is forbidden, and heavy fines are being levied against those who break the rules. Please do not ask your driver to leave the road for a closer look at wildlife. The park is about 140 miles (225 km) from Nairobi.

ACCOMMODATION — CLASS A: * *Tortilis Camp* is located just outside the reserve and has 17 luxury tents with ensuite facilities and a swimming pool. Games drives within the park and walks on the concession area are offered. * *Ol Tukai Lodge* has 80 rooms with facilities ensuite and a swimming pool.

Tortilis Camp, Amboseli National Park.

CLASS A/B: * *Amboseli Serena Lodge,* located in the south of the park, is a modern lodge with 96 rooms with ensuite facilities and a swimming pool.

CLASS C: * *Amboseli Lodge* has 112 rooms with facilities ensuite and a swimming pool.

CAMPING: Campsites are located outside the park on Masai land, 4 miles (6 km) past Observation Hill. No facilities exist except long-drop (pit) toilets. Bring your own water.

TSAVO WEST NATIONAL PARK

Halfway between Nairobi and Mombasa lie **West** and **East Tsavo National Parks**, which together with **Chyulu Hills National Park** total 8217 square miles (21,283 km^2). Large herds of over 100 elephant, with a total of over 15,000 in Tsavo West and East combined, over 60 species of mammals and 400 species of birds have been recorded. The park has a number of large prides of lion and a good leopard population. Also present are caracal, giraffe, zebra and a variety of antelope.

Less game is usually seen here than in Amboseli National Park. However, the park's rugged terrain is quite impressive in itself.

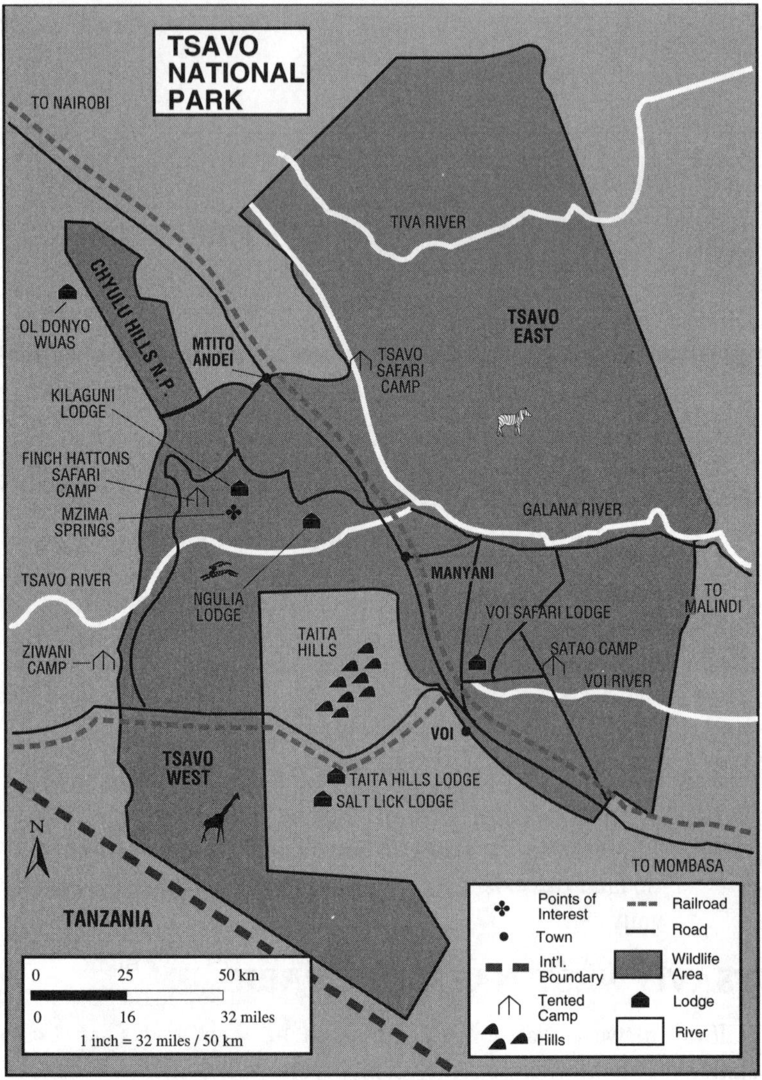

Tsavo West National Park is predominantly extensive semiarid plains broken by occasional granite outcrops. Lava fields are located near Kilaguni Lodge. Altitudes range from 1000 feet (305 m) to nearly 6000 feet (1830 m) in the Ngulia Mountains in the northern region of the park.

From the Mzima Springs underwater viewing platform, located just south of Kilaguni Lodge, visitors may be lucky enough to watch hippo swim about the clear waters with grace and ease. Crocs and numerous species of fish can also be seen. The best viewing is early in the morning. Kilaguni Lodge is about 180 miles (290 km) from Nairobi.

ACCOMMODATION — CLASS A: * *Finch Hattons Safari Camp,* one of the most luxurious camps in Africa, overlooks a hippo pool. It has 35 tents with ensuite facilities and a swimming pool.

CLASS B/C: * *Kilaguni Lodge* has 50 rooms with facilities ensuite and a swimming pool. * *Ngulia Lodge* has 52 rooms with ensuite facilities and a swimming pool.

CLASS D: * *Ngulia Safari Camp* is located near Ngulia Lodge and has self-service bandas. * *Kitani Lodge* is located near Mzima Springs and has self-service bandas.

CAMPING: Campsites are available at Kitani, Kamboyo and Kangechwa and at the following park gates: Mtito Andei, Chyulu (Kilaguni), Kasigau and Tsavo. Chyulu has showers and toilets; the other campsites have basic (if any) facilities.

ACCOMMODATION NEAR TSAVO NATIONAL PARK — CLASS A: * *Ol Donyo Wuas* is a 250,000-acre (100,000-hectare) game ranch situated in the Chyulu Hills. Guests are accommodated in thatched cottages with open fireplaces and ensuite facilities. Day and night game drives in open vehicles, escorted walks and horseback riding are offered.

CLASS A/B: * Taita Hills Lodge and Salt Lick Lodge are situated between the southern extensions of Tsavo East and West Parks, about 240 miles (390 km) from Nairobi. * *Salt Lick Lodge,* built on stilts to enhance viewing of wildlife visiting the salt lick, has 64 rooms with facilities ensuite and a swimming pool. * *Taita Hills Lodge* has 60 rooms with ensuite facilities and a swimming pool and golf course.

CLASS B/C: * *Ziwani Tented Camp* overlooks a hippo pool and has 16 tents with ensuite showers and long-drop toilets. The camp is situated just outside the south-western boundary of the park and offers day and night game drives, walks and excursions to Lake Chala.

TSAVO EAST NATIONAL PARK

Tsavo East is mostly arid bush dotted with rocky outcrops traversed by seasonal rivers lined with riverine forest. Tsavo East is generally hotter, drier and lies at a lower altitude (about 1000 feet/305 m) than its western counterpart. The 3000 square miles (7770 km^2) south of the Galana River is the main region open to the public.

East Tsavo's only permanent water hole is at Aruba Dam, and the drive from Voi makes for a good game run. Just north of the dam is an isolated hill, Mudanda Rock, another good spot for game. The scenic drive along the Galana River often produces sightings of hippo and crocs.

Tsavo East receives fewer visitors than Tsavo West; wildlife is generally more heavily concentrated in Tsavo West. Voi is about 210 miles (340 km) from Nairobi.

ACCOMMODATION — CLASS B/C: * *Satao Camp* is a 32-bed tented camp with ensuite flush toilets and bush (bucket) showers. * *Voi Safari Lodge,* in the hills above the town of Voi, has 52 rooms with facilities ensuite, a swimming pool and photographic hide. * *Tsavo Safari Camp,* located 15 miles (24 km) from Mtito Andei Gate on the Athi River, has 30 tents and 6 bandas with facilities ensuite.

CAMPING: Campsites are available at Voi, Sala and Buchuma Gates. There are few or no facilities.

MASAI MARA NATIONAL RESERVE

This is the finest reserve in Kenya. All the big game is here: elephant, lion, leopard, cheetah and buffalo are prevalent, along with a few black rhino. Other commonly sighted species include zebra, wildebeest, Thomson's gazelle, eland and Masai giraffe. This is the only place in Kenya where topi are common.

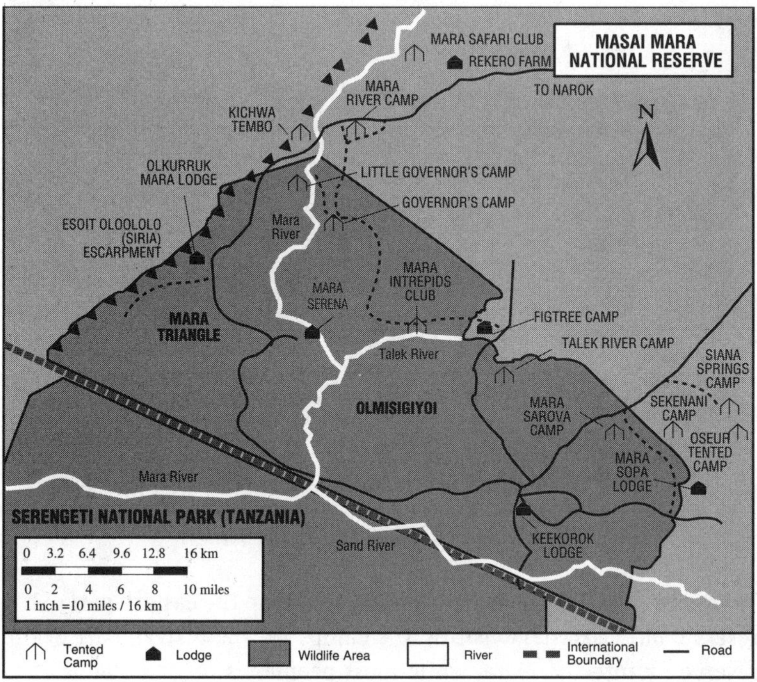

Masai Mara National Reserve, a northern extension of the Serengeti Plains (Tanzania), is located southwest of Nairobi and covers 590 square miles (1530 km^2) of open plains, acacia woodlands and riverine forest along the banks on the Mara and Talek Rivers, which are home for many hippo, crocs and waterfowl.

One of the best places to look for game is in the **Mara Triangle** in the western part of the reserve, bounded by the Siria (Esoit Oloololo) Escarpment rising about 1000 feet (305 m) above the plains on the west, the Tanzanian border to the south and the Mara River to the east. A multitude of savannah animals can be found on these open grasslands and other areas to the northwest of the reserve.

Lion are distributed throughout the park. Cheetah are most often seen on the short-grass plains. Black rhino are most highly concentrated in the Olmisigiyoi Region in the center of the park, in the northwest and in extreme east parts of the park; there are no rhino in the Mara Triangle.

Elephant crossing the Mara River.

The western part of the Mara is less crowed than the eastern part of the reserve. Most safariers visiting the camps in the western part of the reserve fly into the Mara, while most people visiting the lodges and camps in the eastern Mara are driven into the reserve.

The best time to visit is during the Serengeti migration, from approximately mid/late July to mid/late September, when great herds of wildebeest (1.4 million) and zebra (400,000) reside in the Mara and northern Tanzania before returning to Serengeti National Park. At this time, prides of 40 or more lion may be seen. From the Serengeti of Tanzania, a major portion of the migration moves northwest toward Lake Victoria, then north across the Mara River into Kenya in search of grass, usually returning to Tanzania in mid-September/early October. However, as the park teems with resident wildlife, game viewing is in fact very good here year-round.

On our most recent visit, we saw a mother leopard and two cubs with a kill in a tree, several cheetah, numerous prides of lion, thousands of wildebeest and zebra, a large breeding herd of elephant and a variety of other game.

On another visit, we saw wild dog, black rhino, several lion, spotted hyena, a herd of 40 elephant and several smaller herds, buffalo, Masai giraffe, black-backed jackal, wildebeest, zebra, topi and ostrich, among other species.

In the Mara Triangle and the northwestern part of the park, four-wheel-drive vehicles are recommended. There are at least two flights a day from Nairobi servicing the park. Keekorok Lodge is located about 170 miles (275 km) and the Mara Serena about 210 miles (340 km) from Nairobi.

Fishing safaris by private air charter to **Mfangano Island**, **Rusinga Island** and **Takawiri Island** on Lake Victoria are available from all the camps (book in advance).

ACCOMMODATION — All lodges and camps listed below either conduct **hot-air balloon safaris** or will take you to where one is being offered. Many guests fly into the Mara (highly recommended) and are taken game viewing in four-wheel-drive vehicles (preferably) or minivans. Most camps and lodges are a five- to six-hour drive from Nairobi on rough roads.

ACCOMMODATION IN THE RESERVE — CLASS A: * *Little Governor's Camp*, located in the northwest part of the park on the Mara River, has 17 tents with facilities ensuite. Guests reach the camp from Governor's (Main) Camp by crossing the Mara River. Walks are offered outside the reserve.* *Governor's Camp*, located a few miles from Little Governor's Camp on the Mara River, has 38 tents with ensuite facilities and excellent food and service. Walks outside the reserve are offered. * *Mara Intrepids Club* is situated on the Talek River and has 27 tents with four-poster beds, ensuite facilities, and a swimming pool. Groups of two to four tents share a private mess tent with bar and refrigerator. Walks are offered in the adjacent Masai land.

CLASS A/B: * *Mara Serena Lodge*, located in the central western part of the park, has 78 rooms with private facilities and a swimming pool. * *Olkurruk Mara Lodge* has 63 deluxe rondavels with ensuite facilities, overlooking the "Mara Triangle" next to the Esoit Oloololo Escarpment. * *Governor's Paradise Camp* is a semi-permanent camp which is set up in the high seasons, with 20 tents with ensuite flush toilets and bush (bucket) showers. * *Governor's Private Camp*

Mara River Camp, Masai Mara.

caters to private parties of up to 16 guests in tents with ensuite flush toilets and bush (bucket) showers.

CLASS B: * *Talek Camp* has eight tents with ensuite facilities. * *Keekorok Lodge* is an old-style lodge with 72 rooms and 12 tents with ensuite facilities and a swimming pool. * *Mara Sopa Lodge,* located on the eastern border of the park high on a ridge overlooking the Mara near Ololaimutiek Gate, has 72 rooms with facilities ensuite and a swimming pool. * *Sarova Mara Camp* has 75 tents with private facilities and a swimming pool.

ACCOMMODATION ON THE PERIPHERY OF THE RESERVE — CLASS A: * *Kichwa Tembo Camp* has 45 tents and 6 rondavels with ensuite facilities and swimming pool. * *Mara Safari Club* is a deluxe tented camp (40 tents) located north of the park at the base of the Aitong Hills.

CLASS A/B: * *Mara River Camp*, located on the banks of the Mara River, has 27 tents with ensuite facilities and excellent guiding. * *Siana Springs Camp* has 38 tents with facilities ensuite. Walks and day and night game drives are offered. * *Sekenani Camp*, located just outside the park near the Sekenani Gate, has 19 luxury tents with ensuite facilities including full-length bathtubs. Escorted walks outside the reserve are offered.

CLASS B: * *Rekero Farm* caters to a maximum of ten guests in thatched bungalows with ensuite facilities. Game drives, escorted walks and fly camping are offered. * *Oseur Tented Camp*, located 5 miles (8 km) outside the Olemutiak Gate, has 32 tents with ensuite facilities.

CLASS B/C: * *Fig Tree Camp*, located on the Talek River, has 30 basic chalets and 30 tents with facilities ensuite and a swimming pool. Walks and day and night game drives are offered.

CAMPING: Sites are located outside the park along the Talek River.

THE WEST

MT. ELGON NATIONAL PARK

Seldom visited, this 65-square-mile (169-km^2) park is a huge, extinct volcano shared with Uganda, and at 14,178 feet (4321 m) is the second highest mountain in Kenya. Mt. Elgon also has the giant Afro-alpine flora found on Mts. Kenya and Kilimanjaro.

The forests are often so thick that a full-grown elephant could be standing 20 feet (6 m) from the road and not be seen. Buffalo, waterbuck and bushbuck are more likely to be spotted.

Kitum and Makingeny Caves are unique in having a good portion of their size created by elephants. Small herds often enter the caves near dusk to spend several hours in complete darkness mining salts with their tusks. Thousands of bats keep the elephants company. Makingeny is the largest, but Kitum is more frequently visited by elephants. During our visit, elephant droppings were everywhere, foreshadowing the real possibility of their sources being inside.

To explore the caves, be sure to bring two or more strong flashlights. Access to the park is difficult in the rainy season, when four-wheel-drive vehicles are recommended. There are no huts on the mountain; campers must bring their own tents. The park is 255 miles (360 km) from Nairobi.

ACCOMMODATION — CLASS D: * *Mount Elgon Lodge*, situated less than a mile (1.5 km) before the park entrance, has 17 rooms with private facilities.

CAMPING: Several campsites are available in the park.

ACCOMMODATION NEAR THE RESERVE — CLASS B/C: * *Lokiteza Farm* is located on the foothills of Mt. Elgon, 11 miles (19 km) from the town of Kitale. Up to 24 guests are accommodated in the main house and in lodge cottages. The 874-acre (350-hectare) farm primarily produces milk and maize, along with a number of other crops. Over 300 species of birds have been recorded on the farm.

LAKE VICTORIA

Lake Victoria is largest lake in Africa and the second largest freshwater lake in the world (Lake Superior is the largest). The lake is approximately 26,650 square miles (69,000 km^2) in size and is bordered by Kenya, Tanzania and Uganda.

Fishing for giant Nile perch is excellent; the largest one taken from the lake was reported to weigh 520 pounds (236 kg)! Nile perch weighing in excess of 100 pounds (45 kg) are caught on a regular basis.

Over 100 species of birds have been recorded on the islands. Spotted necked otters may also be seen.

Easiest access to the island camps in the lake is by air charter from the Masai Mara.

ACCOMMODATION — CLASS A/B: * *Rusinga Island Club* has five cottages with ensuite facilities. Fishing, boating, bird watching, water skiing, wind surfing and visits to Luo fishing villages are offered. * *Mfangano Island Camp* has six cottages with ensuite facilities.

Fishing, boating, bird watching and visits to Luo fishing villages are offered.

CLASS B/C: * *Takawiri Island Resort* has four cottages, each with two rooms, and ensuite facilities. Fishing, sailing, wind surfing, bird watching and visits to local villages are offered.

KISUMU

Kisumu, located on the shores of Lake Victoria about 215 miles (345 km) from Nairobi, is the third largest city in Kenya, with a population over 125,000.

ACCOMMODATION — TOURIST CLASS: * *Sunset Hotel* has 50 air-conditioned rooms with private facilities and a swimming pool. * *Imperial Hotel* has 87 rooms with ensuite facilities.

THE MOUNT KENYA CIRCUIT

ABERDARE NATIONAL PARK

This 296-square-mile (767-km^2) park of luxuriant forest includes much of the Aberdare (renamed Nyandarua) Range of mountains.

The park can be divided into two sections by altitude. A high plateau of undulating moorlands with tussock grasses and giant heather lies between Ol Doinyo Lasatima (13,120 feet/3999 m) and Kinangop (12,816 feet/3906 m). This region affords excellent views of Mt. Kenya and the Rift Valley. Rhino, lion, hyena, buffalo, elephant, eland, reedbuck, suni, black serval cat, bushpig and, very rarely, the nocturnal bongo can be seen.

On the eastern slopes below lie the forested hills and valleys of the Salient, home to black rhino, leopard, forest elephant, buffalo, waterbuck, bushbuck, giant forest hog, and black and white colobus monkey.

Night temperatures range from cool to freezing, as most of the park lies above 9800 feet (2988 m). A four-wheel-drive vehicle is required for travel within the park. The Ark and Treetops are about 110 miles (175 km) from Nairobi.

Sangare, Aberdare Mountains.

ACCOMMODATION: Guests of two tree hotels, Treetops and the Ark, are entertained by a variety of wildlife visiting their water holes and salt licks.

CLASS B: * The *Ark*, a "tree hotel" overlooking a water hole, has small rooms with ensuite facilities (104 beds total), a glass-enclosed main viewing lounge, outside verandas on each level (floodlit for all-night game viewing) and ground-level photo hide. The area near the Ark is a rhino reserve. Game drives into the Salient are offered. Guests usually have lunch at the Aberdare Country Club before being transferred to the Ark and are transferred back to the Aberdare Country Club by 9:00 the following morning to depart to their next safari destination. Children under seven are not allowed.

CLASS B/C: * *Treetops*, the first of the "tree hotels" (on stilts), is older and more rustic than the Ark. Only suites have ensuite facilities. Guests usually have a buffet lunch at the Outspan Hotel before being transferred to Treetops and are transferred back to the

Outspan by 9:00 the following morning to continue their safari. Children under seven are not allowed.

CAMPING: Only by special permission from the warden. Beware of lions.

ACCOMMODATION NEAR ABERDARE NATIONAL PARK — CLASS B: * *Sangare* is a 6500-acre (2600-hectare) ranch set in the foothills of the Aberdare Mountains. One cottage with two bedrooms and facilities ensuite and four luxury tents with ensuite facilities are set on a small lake. Game drives, walks and horseback riding are offered. An elevated canopy walkway/rope bridge through a beautiful stretch of riverine forest is being constructed for treetop nature walks!

MT. KENYA NATIONAL PARK

Kenya's highest mountain and the second highest on the continent, Mount Kenya lies just below the equator, yet it has several permanent glaciers.

Mt. Kenya's two highest peaks, **Batian** (17,058 feet/5199 m) and **Nelion** (17,023 feet/5188 m), are accessible by about 25 routes and should be attempted only by experienced rock climbers. **Point Lenana** (16,355 feet/4985 m) is a nontechnical climb accessible to hikers in good condition and is best climbed in the dry seasons. January–February is the best time to go, when views are the clearest and temperatures are warmer on top; July–October is also dry but colder. Vegetation changes are similar to those described for the Ruwenzori Mountains (see the Congo) and Mt. Kilimanjaro (see Tanzania).

Rock climbing routes on the south side of the mountain are in best condition from late December to mid-March, while routes on the north side are best climbed from late June to mid-October. Ice routes are best attempted during the same periods but on opposite sides of the mountain. Howell Hut (17,023 feet/5188 m), located on the summit of Nelion, sleeps two.

Although rarely seen, climbers should be on the lookout for buffalo and forest elephant. Other wildlife that may be encountered includes leopard, duiker, bushbuck, giant forest hog, Syke's monkey and colobus monkey.

Because climbers can ascend to high altitudes very quickly, Mt. Kenya claims more than half of the world's deaths from pulmonary edema. My climbing partner had symptoms of pulmonary edema after reaching Austrian Hut (15,715 feet/4790 m), and we had to abandon our attempt of Batian Peak and return to lower altitudes. Therefore, a slow, sensible approach is recommended.

The world's highest altitude scuba diving record was shattered at Two Tarn Lake (14,720 feet/4488 m), one of the more than 30 lakes on the mountain. The previous record of 12,500 feet (3811 m) was set at Lake Titicaca in Bolivia. In addition, climbers are occasionally seen ice skating on the Curling Pond below the Lewis Glacier.

Naro Moru Route

The Naro Moru Route is a steep, quick route up the mountain. The climb to Point Lenana normally takes two or three days up and one or two down. The first night is often spent at Naro Moru Lodge or, better yet, at the Met — Meteorological Station — (10,000 feet/3050 m) to assist altitude acclimatization.

From Nairobi, drive 105 miles (168 km) to Naro Moru, then 10 miles (16 km) on a dirt road to the park gate (7874 feet/2400 m). You may be able to drive to the Met Station unless the road has been washed out by the rains. However, walking is better for acclimatizing to the altitude.

From the park gate, hike for about three and one-half hours (6 miles/10 km) through conifer, hardwood and bamboo forests to the *Met Station*. Beware of buffalo en route. The Met Station has self-service bandas with mattresses, cooking facilities, long-drop toilets and water. In order to help you acclimatize, consider hiking for about an hour up to the tree line (10,500 feet/3200 m) in the afternoon, returning well before dark.

From the Met Station, hike through the muddy **Vertical Bog**, a series of muddy hills with patches of tussock grass. In order to keep your boots dry, you may wish to wear tennis shoes through the bog. Cross the Naro Moru River and continue to **Teleki Valley**, where Mt. Kenya's peaks finally come in clear view (if it is not cloudy). Since leaving the tree line, vegetation has changed to tussock grass and heather moorlands with everlasting flowers, giant groundsel, and giant lobelia sometimes exceeding 30 feet (9 m) in height.

From the Met Station, it takes about six hours to reach *Mackinder's Camp* (1378 feet/4200 m), which has a brick lodge and campsites. *American Camp* (14,173 feet/4320 m), a camping spot one hour from Mackinder's Camp, is used by some campers who bring their own tents. Water is available from a nearby stream.

Austrian Hut (15,715 feet/4790 m) is a three- to four-hour hike from Mackinder's Camp. Another hour is usually required to gain the additional 640 feet (195 m) in altitude needed to reach Point Lenana, only a half-mile away.

Austrian Hut is bitterly cold at night and is most often used by technical rock climbers attempting Nelion or Batian Peaks. Many climbers wishing to conquer Point Lenana begin from their camps in the Teleki Valley (Mackinder's, American) long before sunrise to reach Point Lenana shortly after sunrise and return to Teleki Valley for the night. The view from Point Lenana is the clearest and one of the most magnificent panoramas I've seen from any mountain — and well worth the effort!

Around the Peaks

From Mackinder's Camp, hike two to three hours to *Two Tarn Hut* (14,731 feet/4490 m). Stop for the night or continue for another three or four hours over two passes exceeding 15,000 feet to *Kami Hut* (14,564 feet/4439 m), located on the north side of the peaks. From Kami Hut, it is a five- to six-hour hike up the north ridge of Point Lenana or directly to Austrian Hut. Return via the Naro Moru Route described above.

Chogoria Route

This is the most scenic route on the mountain. From the Chogoria Forest Station on the eastern side of Mt. Kenya, hike or drive 10 miles (16 km) to *Bairunyi Clearing* (8858 feet/2700 m) and camp, or continue for another 4 miles (6 km) (four-wheel-drive required) to *Meru Mt. Kenya Lodge* (9898 feet/3017 m) and stay in its self-catering bandas.

Hike through hagenia forest to *Urumandi Hut* (10,050 feet/3063 m), owned by the Mountain Club of Kenya. Room for camping is available nearby. *Minto's Hut* (14,075 feet/4290 m) is about a six-hour hike from *Meru Mt. Kenya Lodge*. Space for tents is available nearby. *Two Campsites*, situated a mile beyond Minto's Hut, is another good place to camp.

Austrian Hut is a four-hour hike from Minto's Hut. Some climbers descend using the Naro Moru Route.

The access road to the Chogoria Forest Station is very bad, so allow plenty of time for the drive.

Sirimon Route

The Sirimon Route is a long, slow route up the mountain.

Ten miles (16 km) past Nanyuki on the Nanyuki-Timau Road, turn right on a dirt road and drive 6 miles (10 km) to the park gate. Sirimon is the least used and most strenuous of the three major routes on Mt. Kenya.

The northern side of the mountain, being much drier than the western side (Naro Moru Route), has no bamboo or hagenia zone. Acacia grasslands cover much of the northern slopes; zebra and a variety of antelope are likely to be seen.

Although the track continues up to the moorlands to about 13,000 feet (3960 m), it is better to make your first camp around 8000–9000 feet (2440–2745 m) in order to acclimatize. There is another campsite at 10,990 feet (3350 m), 5 miles (8 km) from the park gate. About a mile (1.5 km) further is *Judmeier Camp* (operated by the Mountain Rock Hotel). *Liki North Hut* (13,090 feet/3990 m) is about a four-hour hike from Judmeier. Another four-hour hike brings you to *Shipton's Cave Campsite* (13,450 feet/4100 m). *Shipton's Camp* (operated by Bantu Lodge) is a little further up the mountain. Austrian Hut is a five-hour hike from Shipton's Cave.

Lone climbers are not usually allowed to enter the park. Little equipment is available in Kenya, so bring whatever you need. For climbing tips and equipment checklist, see "Mt. Kilimanjaro" in the chapter on Tanzania.

ACCOMMODATION NEAR THE PARK — CLASS A: * *The Mount Kenya Safari Club*, located on the slopes of Mt. Kenya outside the national park near Nanyuki about 140 (224 km) miles from Nairobi, was partially

Mountain Lodge, Mt. Kenya area.

owned by actor William Holden and became one of the most famous "country clubs" in Africa. The spacious gardens are frequented by many species of exotic birds. Facilities include swimming pool, nine-hole golf course, and very comfortable rooms, suites and luxury cottages with fireplaces (264 beds total). The Animal Orphanage contains a number of rare species such as zebraduiker and bongo. High-altitude flights around the peaks of Mt. Kenya in a Beaver aircraft are available. Game drives are *not* conducted here.

CLASS A/B:* *Lake Rutundu Lodge* is a rustic yet luxurious fishing lodge set on a small tarn (mountain lake) at 10,500 feet (3203 m) altitude. Guests are accommodated in two cedar wood cottages with ensuite facilities and hot tub. The lodge is self-catering, but most tour companies will provide full-service catering. The trout fishing here is some of the finest in the world! Best access is by charter flight to Africa's highest airstrip, at 11,000 feet (3355 m).

CLASS B: * *Mountain Lodge,* about 110 miles (177 km) north of Nairobi, is a "tree hotel" set in a forest outside the park boundary overlooking a water hole and salt lick, similar to Treetops and the Ark (see "Aberdare National Park"). All 42 double rooms have ensuite facilities and face the water hole.

CLASS B/C, D & E: * *Naro Moru River Lodge,* located below the entrance to the park, has chalets (Class B/C) with ensuite facilities and rustic self-service cabins (Class D & E). Climbers often stay here before and after their attempts at Mt. Kenya's peaks. Trout fishing here is good.

CLASS C/D: * *Mountain Rock Hotel.*

CAMPING: Camping is allowed at the Naro Moru Lodge and at sites in the park.

OL PEJETA RANCH

This 110,000-acre (44,000-hectare) private game reserve of savannah and riverine forest has a variety of wildlife, including black rhino, reticulated giraffe, buffalo, zebra, oryx, kongoni and Thomson's gazelle. Walks, day and night game drives, boat rides and camel rides are offered. There is a chimpanzee rehabilitation center that may be visited. A four-wheel-drive vehicle may be necessary to reach the camp from the main road during the rains.

ACCOMMODATION — CLASS A/B: * *Sweetwaters Tented Camp* has 25 large tents with ensuite facilities facing a water hole and a swimming pool. The camp is located 150 miles (240 km) north of Nairobi.

MERU NATIONAL PARK

Meru is best known for where Elsa, the lioness of Joy Adamson's *Born Free,* was rehabituated to the wild. This 300-square-mile (870-km^2) park is located east of Mt. Kenya, 220 miles (355 km) from Nairobi (via Nyeri).

The swamps are host to most of Meru's 5000 buffalo, sometimes seen in herds of more than 200, and a number of elephant. Oryx, eland, reticulated giraffe and Grevy's zebra are plentiful on the plains, where lion are also most likely to be seen. Lesser kudu, gerenuk and cheetah can be found along with hippo and crocs within the Tana River. Leopard are also present, and over 300 species of birds have been recorded.

ACCOMMODATION — CLASS B: * *Patrick's Camp,* located in the western woodlands, has tents with private bush showers and bush toilets located nearby each sleeping tent. The camp is open July–March.

CLASS C: * *Meru Mulika Lodge* was closed at the time of this writing and was undergoing renovations.

CLASS F: Self-service bandas are located at Park Headquarters and at Leopard Rock.

CAMPING: Sites are available at Murera Gate and Park Headquarters.

THE RIFT VALLEY

LAKE NAIVASHA

Lake Naivasha, located 55 miles (89 km) northwest of Nairobi, is a freshwater lake prolific in bird life and a favorite spot for picnics and water sports for Nairobi residents.

Take a boat ride to **Crescent Island** and walk around this game and bird sanctuary, which is host to zebra, giraffe, several antelope species and a few camels.

ACCOMMODATION — CLASS A: * *Longonot Game Ranch* has three double rooms with ensuite facilities. Horseback riding is the main attraction. * *Loldia House,* a cattle ranch located on the northern side of Lake Naivasha, accommodates up to ten guests in rooms in the main house and a cottage with ensuite facilities.

CLASS A/B: * *Crater Lake Camp,* set on a crater lake southeast of Lake Naivasha on the Ndabibi Estate, once the heart of "Happy Valley," accommodates guests in ten tents with ensuite facilities. Day and night game drives and walks are offered.

CLASS B: * *Lake Naivasha Country Club* is a beautifully landscaped hotel with 51 rooms with ensuite facilities and a swimming pool. Sunset cruises are offered and a special Sunday afternoon tea is served.

CLASS C: * *Safariland Club* has 56 rooms with ensuite facilities and a swimming pool. Horseback riding is available.

CAMPING: Campsites are available at the Safariland Lodge and Fisherman's Camp.

HELL'S GATE NATIONAL PARK

Located south of Lake Naivasha, this ruggedly scenic park covers 26 square miles (68 km^2) of high cliffs and scattered grassy areas. The deep gorge is great for hiking and for spotting raptors (birds of prey). Klipspringer, mountain reedbuck, eland, giraffe, and Grant's and Thomson's gazelles may also be seen.

ACCOMMODATION: See "Lake Naivasha" above.

LAKE ELMENTEITA

Lake Elmenteita is a small soda lake located between Lakes Naviasha and Nakuru. Wildlife includes Rothschild's giraffe and Grant's and Thomson's gazelles. Bird life is excellent and includes thousands of lesser and greater flamingos (in season).

ACCOMMODATION — CLASS B: * *Delamere Camp*, located within the Soysambu Game Sanctuary, has 16 tents with ensuite facilities and a rustic four-bed tree house overlooking a water hole. Day game drives, walks and excursions to Lake Nakuru National Park are offered. A variety of nocturnal species may be seen on night drives. The guiding is excellent.

CLASS C/D: * *Lake Elmenteita Lodge* has 33 rondavels with ensuite facilities. Nature walks and ox-wagon rides to the lake shore are offered.

Looking across Lake Elmenteita from Delamere Camp.

LAKE NAKURU NATIONAL PARK

Lake Nakuru National Park encompasses the alkaline lake of the same name and is frequently visited by hundreds of thousands (sometimes more than a million) of greater and lesser flamingos — more than 400 bird species in all. Located 100 miles (160 km) northwest of Nairobi on a fair road, the park covers 73 square miles (188 km^2) — most of which is the lake itself.

Nakuru has been declared a black rhino sanctuary and has a number of these endangered animals under guard. White rhino may also be seen. Other wildlife includes leopard, Rothschild's giraffe (introduced), waterbuck, reedbuck, hippo, baboon, pelican, and cormorant.

ACCOMMODATION — CLASS B/C: * *Sarova Lion Hill Lodge* is located in the park and has air-conditioned cottages (150 beds total) with ensuite facilities and a swimming pool.

CLASS C: * *Lake Nakuru Lodge* has rooms and cottages (120 beds) with ensuite facilities and a swimming pool. Horseback riding just outside the park and nature walks within the park are offered.

CAMPING: Campsites with running water are available in the park.

ACCOMMODATION NEAR LAKE NAKURU — CLASS B: * *Deloraine* is an old colonial home set on a 5000-acre (2000-hectare) farm, with six rooms with ensuite facilities. Horseback riding is offered.

NYAHURURU (THOMPSON'S) FALLS

Thompson's Falls, located at 7745 feet (2360 m) altitude about 115 miles (185 km) from Nairobi, above the Rift Valley between Nanyuki and Nakuru, is a refreshing place to relax.

ACCOMMODATION — CLASS C/D: * *Thompson's Falls Lodge* is a rustic country hotel; rooms have private facilities.

LAKE BOGORIA NATIONAL RESERVE

Lake Bogoria National Reserve, located north of Nakuru, has numerous hot springs and geysers along the lake shore. Thousands of flamingos frequent this alkaline lake, as do greater kudu on the steep slopes of the lake's eastern and southern shores.

ACCOMMODATION — CLASS C/D: * *Lake Bogoria Lodge* has 45 rooms with ensuite facilities.

CAMPING: Campsites are available with no facilities.

LAKE BARINGO

Lake Baringo, a freshwater lake located 20 miles (32 km) north of Lake Bogoria, is a haven for a colorful and mixed variety of bird life (over 400 species recorded) and a sporting center for water skiing, fishing and boating.

The early morning boat ride along the lake shore is one of the finest bird-watching excursions I've experienced. Hippo, crocodile, fishermen and villages along the shore may also be seen.

ACCOMMODATION — CLASS B: * *Island Camp* is located in the center of Lake Baringo on Ol Kokwa Island. All tents have ensuite facilities. Take a walk and you may see a few waterbuck and meet the Njemps tribespeople who also inhabit the island. Boat safaris and water sports (beware of hippo and crocs) are available. * *Lake Baringo Club* has 52 rooms with ensuite facilities and a swimming pool. Boat and fishing trips are offered.

CLASS F: * *Betty Robert's Campsite,* situated on the lake shore, has bandas.

CAMPING: * *Betty Robert's Campsite.*

THE NORTH

LEWA DOWNS

Located between Mt. Kenya and Samburu National Reserve, Lewa Downs is a privately owned ranch with over 1000 head of cattle and a variety of wildlife including a large black and white rhino population (Lewa is a rhino sanctuary), elephant, lion, leopard, cheetah, reticulated giraffe, Grevy's zebra, buffalo, hartebeest, bushbuck, gerenuk, Gunther's dikdik and Somali ostrich. Lewa is one of the few places in Kenya where sitatunga may be seen.

During our visit, we spotted fringe-eared oryx, Grant's gazelle, a large herd of elephant and a few smaller herds, Mt. Kenya hartebeest and Somali ostrich, among other species.

Horseback riding, hiking, and day and night game drives in open four-wheel-drive vehicles are offered.

ACCOMMODATION — CLASS A/B: * *Wilderness Trails* accommodates up to 16 guests in a lodge and six cottages with ensuite facilities. * *Ngarie Niti* is a large two-bedroom stone house and two separate cottages with ensuite facilities. * *Lerai Tented Camp* has 12 tents set on elevated platforms with ensuite facilities. In addition to day and night game drives, walks and horseback riding, camel safaris in tribal lands accompanied by Samburu and Masai warriors lasting from one to several days are offered.

OL MALO RANCH

Ol Malo Ranch, located along the Uaso Nyiro River on the edge of Kenya's North Eastern Province, covers 5000 acres (2000 hectares). Day and night game drives, escorted walks, overnight fly camping and camel treks are offered.

During my last visit we saw lion, giraffe, greater kudu, elephant and a variety of other game while on game drives and on walks.

ACCOMMODATION — CLASS A: * *Ol Malo Lodge,* located on an escarpment with dramatic views of the bush below, has three beautiful chalets, with ensuite bathrooms with large tubs and a swimming pool.

COLCHECCIO RANCH

Colcheccio is a 65,000-acre (26,000-hectare) ranch located on the northern edge of the Laikipia Plateau. Day and night game drives, escorted walks, fly camping and horseback riding are offered.

ACCOMMODATION — CLASS A/B: * *Colcheccio Lodge,* perched on the edge of a cliff overlooking Mt. Kenya in the distance, has seven chalets with private verandas and ensuite facilities and a swimming pool and tennis court.

OL ARI NYIRO RANCH

The ranch is a rhino sanctuary, and Mukutan Retreat is owned by Kuki Gallmann, author of *I Dreamed of Africa.*

The lodge is built on the edge of a gorge on the top of the Rift Valley wall overlooking Lakes Baringo and Bogoria.

The bush is quite thick, which makes game viewing a bit difficult. The real attraction here is to spend time with Kuki herself; however, she does not guarantee that she will be at the lodge. Only one group of guests is accommodated at a time.

ACCOMMODATION — CLASS A: * *Mukutan Retreat* has three stone and thatch cottages with ensuite facilities.

BORANA RANCH

Borana is a 35,000-acre (14,000-hectare) ranch located in the Laikipia area. Elephant, lion, buffalo and a variety of antelope may be seen. Day and night game drives, escorted walks, horseback riding and camel riding are offered.

ACCOMMODATION — CLASS A: * *Borana Lodge* is set on the edge of the escarpment and has six luxury chalets with ensuite facilities and a swimming pool.

SAMBURU NATIONAL RESERVE

This relatively small (64 square mile/165 km^2) but excellent park of scrub desert, thornbush, riverine forest, and swamps along the Ewaso Ngiro River is situated north of Mt. Kenya.

Elephant and lion are plentiful, as are Beisa oryx, Somali ostrich, reticulated giraffe, gerenuk, Grevy's zebra and other species adapted to an arid environment. Leopard are often seen.

Samburu, probably the best park in northern Kenya, is located about 220 miles (355 km) north of Nairobi. Under special arrangement, walking may be offered just outside the reserve.

ACCOMMODATION — CLASS A: * *Samburu Intrepids Camp* has a swimming pool and 25 luxury tents, each with a private terrace and facilities ensuite. * *Larsen's Tented Camp*, situated on the banks of the Ewaso Ngiro River, has 13 double and 4 huge suite tents, all with facilities ensuite (34 beds total).

CLASS B: * *Samburu Serena Lodge*, also situated on the banks of the Ewaso Ngiro River, has 52 rooms with facilities ensuite and a swimming pool. The lodge baits for crocs and leopard. * *Samburu Lodge*, located on the banks of the Ewaso Ngiro River, has rooms, cottages and tents (75 units) with private facilities and a swimming pool. This lodge also baits for crocs and leopard.

CAMPING: Campsites are located along the north bank of the Ewaso Ngiro River between the West Gate and Samburu Lodge. Most sites have long-drop toilets only.

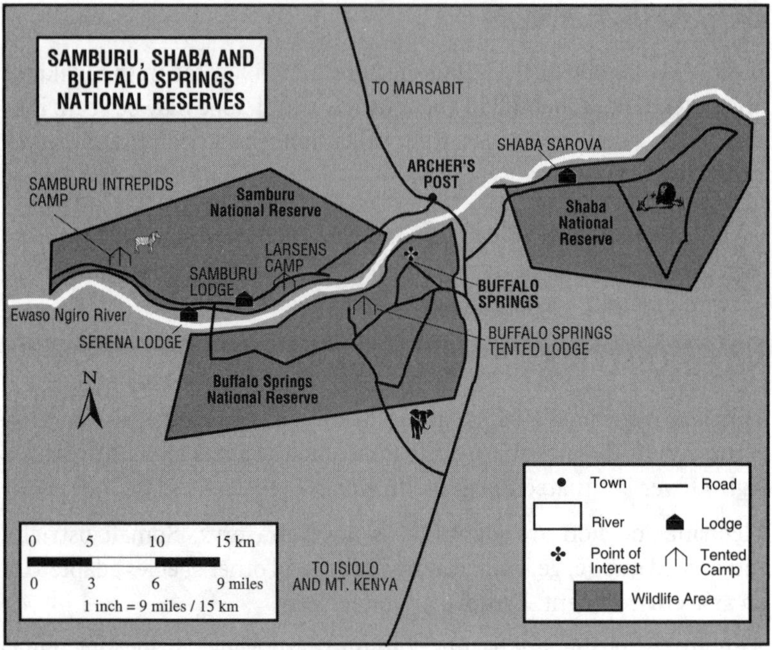

BUFFALO SPRINGS NATIONAL RESERVE

Buffalo Springs is a 50-square-mile (131-km^2) park located south of the Ewaso Ngiro River, which serves as its northern border with Samburu National Reserve. The unusual doum palm, the only palm tree species whose trunk divides into branches, grows to over 60 feet (19 m) in height in this arid park. Wildlife seen here is similar to what is seen in Samburu National Park.

On a two-hour game drive, we encountered oryx, gerenuk, Grant's gazelle, waterbuck, Somali ostrich and two large herds of elephant. Baboon are often found drinking at the springs.

ACCOMMODATION — CLASS C: * *Buffalo Springs Tented Lodge* has basic tents and bandas (76 beds) with ensuite facilities and a swimming pool. The camp baits for crocodile.

CAMPING: Campsites have no facilities.

SHABA NATIONAL RESERVE

The turnoff to the entrance to Shaba National Reserve is located east of Samburu National Reserve, two miles south of Archer's Post. The Ewaso Ngiro River forms the reserve's northwestern border and flows through the western part of the reserve.

This 92-square-mile (239-km^2) park is characterized by rocky hills and scattered thornbush. Volcanic rock is present in many areas. Mt. Shaba, a 5320-foot-(1622-m) high volcanic cone, which the park was named after, lies to the south of the park.

A marsh in the center of the park is a good spot to look for game. During a short visit to this rugged, rocky park, we spotted oryx, gerenuk, common waterbuck, Thomson's and Grant's gazelle, dikdik and ostrich.

The gerenuk or "giraffe antelope"

Wildlife is less abundant and cannot be approached as closely as in the Samburu and Buffalo Springs National Reserves. However, there is much less traffic in this reserve.

ACCOMMODATION — CLASS A/B: * *Shaba Sarova Lodge*, situated on the Ewaso Ngiro River, is a resort-style lodge with 85 rooms with facilities ensuite and a huge swimming pool.

CAMPING: Ask at the gate.

MARALAL NATIONAL SANCTUARY

Maralal National Sanctuary, located northwest of Samburu and 95 miles (153 km) north of Nyahururu (205 miles/330 km from Nairobi) near the town of Maralal, has zebra, buffalo, eland, impala and hyena which come to drink at the water hole adjacent to the Maralal Safari Lodge.

Leopard are baited and can often be seen just before sunset from the blind near the lodge. We fortunately saw two of these fascinating creatures during our visit.

ACCOMMODATION — CLASS C: * *Maralal Safari Lodge* has 12 cottages with fireplaces, ensuite facilities and a swimming pool.

CLASS F & CAMPING: * *Yare Safaris Hostel and Campsite,* located two miles south of Maralal, has bandas, dormitories and campsites.

MATHEWS RANGE

Located northwest of Samburu National Park, this remote wilderness area with lush green vegetation rises above the surrounding semidesert lowlands. Nature walks, fishing and game drives are offered. Four-wheel-drive vehicles are necessary in this region.

ACCOMMODATION — CLASS B * *Kitich Camp* has six tents with ensuite long-drop toilets and bucket showers. Walks in the forests with local Samburu tribesmen are offered.

LAKE TURKANA

Called the Jade Sea because of its deep green color, Lake Turkana is a huge inland sea surrounded by semidesert near the Ethiopian border, three days of hard driving over rough terrain from Nairobi.

Formerly named Lake Rudolf, this huge lake, which is over 175 miles (280 km) long and 10–30 miles (16–48 km) wide, is set in a lunar-like landscape of lava rocks, dried-up river beds and scattered oases.

The brown Omo River flows from the Ethiopian highlands into the northern part of the lake, where the water is fairly fresh but becomes increasingly saline further south due to intense evaporation. The presence of puffer fish implies that the lake was at one time connected to the Mediterranean Sea by the River Nile.

One of the continent's largest populations of crocodile is found here. Because the bitter alkaline waters render their skins useless for commercial trade, crocodile are not hunted and grow to abnormally large sizes. Although the water is very tempting in such a hot, dry climate, swim only at your own risk!

Fishing is a major attraction. Nile perch, the world's largest freshwater fish, can exceed 400 pounds (180 kg). Tigerfish, however, put up a more exciting fight. The El Molo tribe, the smallest tribe in Kenya (about 500 members), can be found near Loiyangalani.

Central Island National Park, a 2-square-mile (5-km^2) island containing three volcanic cones, is the most highly concentrated breeding ground of crocodile in Africa. Excursions to **South Island National Park**, also volcanic and full of crocodile, are available from the Oasis Lodge.

Easiest access to the park is by small aircraft. Four-wheel-drive vehicles are necessary. Loiyangalani is about 415 miles (665 km) and Ferguson's Gulf about 500 miles (805 km) north of Nairobi.

ACCOMMODATION — CLASS C: * *Oasis Lodge*, located on the southeastern shore of the lake at Loiyangalani, has 24 basic cottages with facilities ensuite, two swimming pools, fishing boats and equipment for hire. Excursions to South Island National Park are available.

CLASS D: * *El Molo Lodge* has bandas. There are also self-catering bandas at Koobi Fora.

CAMPING: At El Molo Lodge, Sunset Strip Campsite and El Molo Bay.

Dhows at sunset.

THE COAST

MOMBASA

Mombasa is the second largest city in Kenya, with a population of over 600,000. This island, 307 miles (495 km) from Nairobi on a paved road, is a blend of the Middle East, Asia and Africa.

The **Old Harbor** is haven for dhows carrying goods for trade between Arabia and the Indian subcontinent and Africa, especially from December to April. **Kilindini** ("place of deep water") is the modern harbor and largest port on the east coast of Africa.

Built by the Portuguese in 1593, **Fort Jesus** now serves as a museum. The **Old Town** is Muslim and Indian in flavor, with winding, narrow streets and alleys too narrow for cars, tall nineteenth century buildings with hand-carved doors and overhanging balconies, and small shops. Old Town and Fort Jesus are best seen on foot.

Mombasa is the best place in Kenya for excellent Swahili food. The Tamarind Restaurant, located just north of Mombasa, and the Nomad Restaurant, located in Diani Beach, serve excellent seafood.

The city of Mombasa has no beaches, so most international visitors stay on the beautiful white sand beaches to the south or north of the island. Nyali Beach, Mombasa Beach, Kenyatta Beach and Shanzu Beach lie just to the north of Mombasa, while Diani Beach lies about 20 miles (32 km) to the south.

Most beach hotels on the coast offer a variety of water sports for their guests, including sailing, wind surfing, water skiing, scuba diving and snorkeling on beautiful coral reefs.

ACCOMMODATION IN MOMBASA — TOURIST CLASS: * *Castle Hotel,* located on Mombasa Island, has 60 simple rooms with facilities ensuite.

ACCOMMODATION JUST NORTH OF MOMBASA — DELUXE: * *Nyali Beach Hotel* has 235 air-conditioned rooms with ensuite facilities and minibars and a disco, nightclub and swimming pool. * *Serena Beach Hotel* has 150 air-conditioned rooms with facilities ensuite, a swimming pool and tennis, scuba diving and other water sports. * *Hotel Inter-Continental* has 192 air-conditioned rooms with facilities ensuite, a swimming pool and health club, squash, tennis and a casino.

FIRST CLASS: * *Mombasa Beach Hotel* has 150 air-conditioned rooms with ensuite facilities, a swimming pool, and tennis courts. * *White Sands Hotel* has 346 air-conditioned rooms with private facilities, a swimming pool, tennis and water sports.

ACCOMMODATION JUST SOUTH OF MOMBASA — DELUXE: * *Diani Reef Hotel* has 304 air-conditioned rooms with facilities ensuite and swimming pool, dive school, and tennis courts. * *Pinewood Village* has 20 private villas with ensuite facilities and private chefs. **Indian Ocean Beach Club,* set on a beautiful beach, has 100 air-conditioned rooms with ensuite facilities, a swimming pool, tennis, squash, scuba diving and water sports.

FIRST CLASS: * *Jadini Beach Hotel* has 152 air-conditioned rooms with private facilities and a swimming pool.

TOURIST CLASS: * *Africana Sea Lodge* has 158 air-conditioned rooms with ensuite facilities and a swimming pool.

CAMPING: Campsites available at *Twiga Lodge* (Tiwi Beach) and *Dan's Trench* (Diani Beach).

SOUTH OF MOMBASA

SHIMBA HILLS NATIONAL RESERVE

This 74-square-mile (192-km^2) reserve of rolling hills and forests is located an hour's drive south of Mombasa and ten miles inland. At 1500 feet (460 m) above sea level, this is a good place to cool off from the heat of the coast. From the park one has magnificent views of the Indian Ocean, and Mt. Kilimanjaro can even be seen on exceptionally clear days.

Wildlife includes elephant and buffalo and occasional sightings of genet, civet, serval and leopard. This is the only park in Kenya with sable antelope.

ACCOMMODATION — CLASS B: * *Shimba Hills Lodge* is a three-story "tree hotel" with 80 beds, overlooking a floodlit water hole.

ACCOMMODATION NEAR THE RESERVE — CLASS B: * *Sable Valley*, a privately owned game sanctuary situated along the southern border of Shimba Hills National Park, accommodates up to two adults and two children in a cottage with ensuite facilities. Game drives and walks in the sanctuary, game drives in the park and trips to the beach are offered.

KISITE MPUNGUTI MARINE RESERVE

Kisite Mpunguti Marine Reserve is situated near the small fishing village of **Shimoni** ("place of the caves") where slaves were held before shipment, near the Tanzanian border far from the mainstream of tourism. Delightful boat excursions to **Wasini Island**, an ancient Arab settlement across a channel from Shimoni, and snorkeling excursions are available.

The **Pemba Channel**, just off of Shimoni, is one of the world's finest marlin fishing grounds.

ACCOMMODATION — TOURIST CLASS: * *Pemba Channel Inn and Fishing Club* accommodates up to 14 guests in bungalows with ensuite facilities. Boats are available for hire for deep-sea fishing. The inn is closed from April 1 to July 31st. * *Shimoni Reef Lodge* has ten basic thatched cottages with ensuite facilities, a swimming pool and a PADI scuba diving center.

NORTH OF MOMBASA

MALINDI-WATAMU MARINE NATIONAL RESERVE

Malindi-Watamu Marine National Reserve encompasses the area south of Malindi to south of Watamu, from 100 feet to 3 nautical miles (30 m to 5 km) offshore, and has very good diving and snorkeling.

ACCOMMODATION IN WATAMU — FIRST CLASS: * *Hemingway's* is a 175-bed hotel with ensuite facilities, a swimming pool, and charter boats for deep-sea fishing and diving. * *Turtle Bay Beach Club* has 154 air-conditioned rooms with ensuite facilities.

MALINDI

Malindi, located 75 miles (120 km) north of Mombasa (two hours by car), has numerous beach hotels, nightclubs and shops. The International Bill Fishing Competition is held here every January.

The **Sokoke Arabuko Forest** is Africa's northernmost brachystegia forest and Kenya's last remaining lowland forest. The forest contains a variety of interesting wildlife including Ader's duiker, bushy-tailed mongoose, golden-rumped elephant shrew, the Sokoke scops owl, the Sokoke pipet and Clark's weaver.

The **Gedi Ruins**, last inhabited in the thirteenth century by about 2500 people, is a mystery in that there is no written record in Arabic or Swahili of its existence.

ACCOMMODATION — FIRST CLASS: * *Indian Ocean Lodge* is an exclusive lodge with only six fan-cooled cottages with facilities ensuite and a swimming pool. Activities include snorkeling in the marine park, boating down the shore to secluded beaches for picnics and nature walks into Sokoke Arabuko forest.

TOURIST CLASS: * *Silversands Villas* has 27 air-conditioned rooms and suites with ensuite facilities. * *Driftwood Beach Club* has 27 bandas (some air-conditioned) with ensuite facilities and a swimming pool.

CAMPING: * *Silversands Campsite* is one mile north of town.

LAMU

Swahili culture has changed little in the past few hundred years on the island of Lamu. The only motorized vehicle on the island is owned by a government official, but plenty of donkey carts provide substitutes. Narrow, winding streets and a maze of alleyways add to the timeless atmosphere. Many travelers have compared Lamu to a mini-Katmandu.

The **Lamu Museum** has exhibits of Swahili craftwork. Of the more than 30 mosques on Lamu, only a few are open to visitors. The best beaches are at **Shela**, a 45-minute walk or short boat ride from the town of Lamu to the Peponi Beach Hotel. **Matondoni** is a fishing village where dhows, fishing nets and traps are made. Numerous attractions also lie on nearby islands.

The best way to reach the island is to fly. Driving is not recommended as the road from Malindi is very rough and may be impassable in the rainy season.

ACCOMMODATION — FIRST CLASS: * *Peponi Beach Hotel,* a pleasant beach resort, is located about one mile from the town of Lamu. All 25 rooms are fan-cooled and have facilities ensuite. * *The Island Hotel,* located in the center of Shela Village, has 14 fan-cooled rooms with ensuite facilities.

TOURIST CLASS: * *Lamu Palace Hotel* has air-conditioned rooms (50 beds) with ensuite facilities and is located 200 yards (200 m) from the jetty. * *Petley's Inn* has been a landmark since the nineteenth century. The hotel has a rustic atmosphere and rooms with private facilities.

UGANDA

THE NESTING GORILLA

Gorillas are diurnal and on the move constantly. They find themselves at a different location each night, where they meticulously build their beds (nests) and sleep.

The nests do not appear to offer any decent protection from the rain or cold, and building them seems to be more an activity that has continued from the past, when they were more arboreal, than a necessary part of life.

Females take time and care in the construction of their nests and will frequently build their nests on the ground instead of in trees. The less heavy youngsters may make their nests in trees. Tree nests last longer than those on the ground and can be found from five months to a year after being built.

Males, who are not as careful as females in building their nests, have been observed trying to snuggle into the nest of a female and child to get out of the rain. Hollow tree trunks are good protection from the rain, and they will use them when they can, sometimes lining the nest with moss.

An average nest built by females takes between three to five minutes to construct. They begin by breaking the tips of nonfood vegetation, like *lobelia*, and weave them in a semicircle around their bodies, like the rim of a bathtub, using the leaves as a lining on the bottom. The tasty nettles, thistles, celery and bamboo shoots gorillas like to eat do not make a comfortable mattress for them.

Youngsters make a great pretense at nest building. They begin at about 18 months and practice until they are between three and four years old. They bend and break the pliable stems into their laps, stand up and then quickly try to sit down on them, holding on with their hands. However, their small, light bodies cannot weigh down the springy stems. Signs of frustration are numerous while they learn to master the art of building the rim and using the leafy portion for a mattress. The babies will try to mimic, but their beds are usually a flimsy pile of leaves.

UGANDA

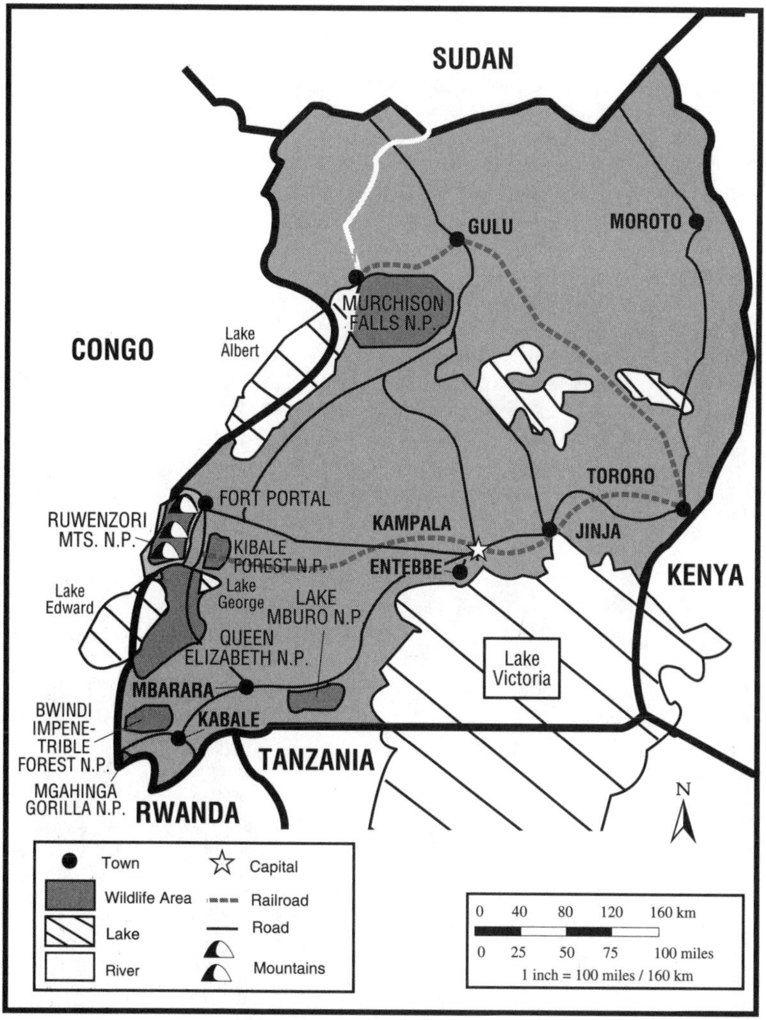

FACTS AT A GLANCE

AREA:	93,050 SQ. MI. / 241,000 SQ. KM.
APPROXIMATE SIZE:	OREGON OR GREAT BRITAIN
POPULATION:	17.5 MILLION
CAPITAL:	KAMPALA (POP. EST. 800,000)
OFFICIAL LANGUAGE:	ENGLISH

UGANDA

Uganda, once the "Pearl of the British Empire in East Africa," is one of the most beautiful countries on the continent. One-sixth of its area is covered by water. Along its western boundary lies Africa's highest mountain range, Ptolemy's fabled "Mountains of the Moon." The Ugandans claim the source of the Nile is at Jinja where it leaves Lake Victoria.

The weather in Uganda is similar to Kenya except that Uganda is wetter. The driest times of the year are December–February and June–July, and the wettest is from mid-March to mid-May, with lighter rains in October–November.

English is spoken as widely here as in Kenya or Tanzania. The main religions are Christianity and Islam.

In the eighteenth century, the Kingdom of Buganda became the most powerful in the region. Together with three other kingdoms and several native communities, it was made a British Protectorate in 1893 and achieved independence in 1962.

Over 90 percent of the population is employed in agriculture. Coffee is the major export.

Uganda has had more than its fair share of turmoil. In spite of this, the people are among the friendliest on the continent. Infrastructure and security in Uganda have greatly improved over the last several years. Adventurous travelers are venturing there and seem to be enjoying their "pioneer" status. A real advantage is that the parks are not anywhere near as crowed as parks in Kenya or Tanzania.

WILDLIFE AND WILDLIFE AREAS

This country was once very rich in wildlife, but much of the larger game was killed during Idi Amin's rule and in the war to oust him in the late 1970s. However, wildlife populations have increased greatly since that time. A real plus is that you meet very few other vehicles on game drives — in essence you have the parks almost to yourself.

Gorillas are the greatest international attraction — especially with Rwanda and the Congo not being safe to travel in, as of this writing. Travelers from all over the world venture to this country to experience these magnificent animals in their native environment. Watching these fascinating creatures on television is exciting enough but nothing in comparison to the thrill of visiting them firsthand.

Uganda has 10 national parks and 15 reserves. The calving seasons for hartebeest and Uganda kob are January–February and for oribi February–March.

NORTHERN AND WESTERN

MURCHISON (KABALEGA) FALLS NATIONAL PARK

This park is named after the famous falls where the Victoria Nile rushes through a narrow, 20-foot- (6-m) wide rock gorge with tremendous force to crash on the rocks 150 feet (45 m) below. Fish dazed by this fall are easy prey to one of the largest concentrations of crocodile on the continent.

Located in northwestern Uganda, this park covers approximately 1500 square miles (3885 km^2) of predominantly grassy plains and savannah woodlands with altitudes ranging from 1650 to 4240 feet (500 to 1292 m). Riverine forest lines some parts of the Victoria Nile, which traverses the park from east to west.

The Rabongo Forest has a population of chimpanzees.

In addition to Murchison Falls, a highlight of the park is the 3-hour, 7-mile (11 km) launch trip from Paraa Lodge to the foot of the falls.

Numerous crocodile and hippo in the river and along its banks, as well as buffalo, elephant, and prolific bird life (over 400 species), can be approached closely.

Another great excursion is a six-hour launch trip from Paraa Lodge to the delta where the Victoria Nile flows into Lake Albert. Shoebills (whale-headed storks) are often seen on this trip.

The park is also home to giraffe, waterbuck, oribi, hartebeest and Uganda kob. Record Nile perch over 200 pounds (90 kg) have been caught in the Nile. Some of the best fishing is just below Karuma Falls and just below Murchison Falls.

The easiest time to spot animals is January–February; the short dry season from June to July is also good. From March to May, the landscape is more attractive but the wildlife is less concentrated.

Park headquarters and the most extensive road system for game viewing are near the Paraa Lodge. The Buligi Circuit takes one to the confluence of the Albert and Victoria Niles. Waterfowl are especially abundant, along with a variety of game. Fuel is often not available.

ACCOMMODATION — CLASS A/B: * *Nile Safari Camp*, set on the south bank of the Nile River on the western edge of the park, has six tents and two chalets with ensuite facilities and a swimming pool. * *Sambiya River Lodge*, located on the Sambiya River 23 miles (20 km) from the falls, has 32 brick bandas with ensuite facilities. * *Paraa Lodge* has 180 rooms with ensuite facilities.

CLASS F: * *Paraa Rest Camp* has simple bandas, long-drop toilets and bucket showers.

CAMPING: Several sites available.

QUEEN ELIZABETH NATIONAL PARK

The park contains about 770 square miles (1995 km^2) of tremendous scenic variety, including volcanic craters and crater lakes, grassy plains, swamps, rivers, lakes and tropical forest. The snowcapped Ruwenzori Mountains lie to the north and are not part of the park itself. The park is being extended to give migratory species more protection while moving to and from Virunga National Park in the Congo.

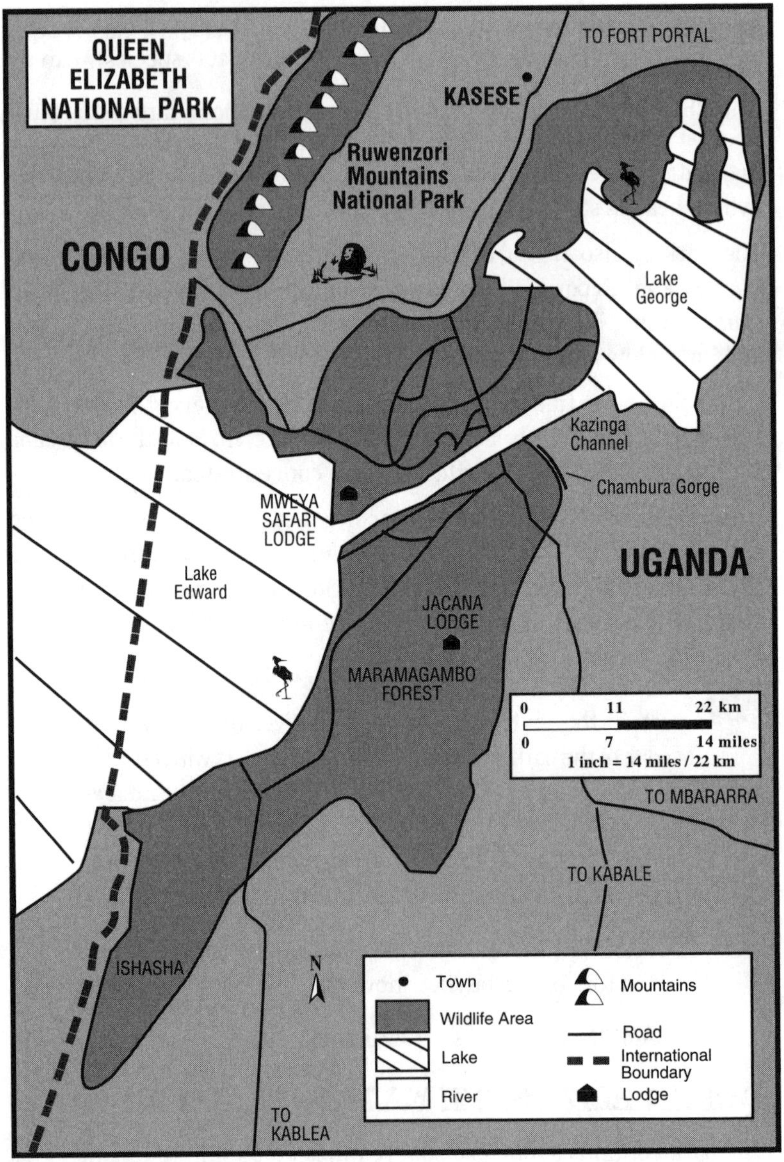

A two-hour launch trip on the **Kazinga Channel**, which joins Lakes Edward (Lake Rwitanzige) and George, affords excellent opportunities for viewing hippo and a great variety of waterfowl at close range. The launch trip departs from just below Mweya Lodge and should not be missed.

The Katwe–Kikorongo area in the north of the park has several saline lakes.

The **Chambura Gorge**, located on the northeast boundary of the park, has a population of chimpanzees. Trekkers descend from the savannah into a tropical rain forest within the gorge.

South of the Kazinga Channel, the **Maramagambo Forest** is home for large numbers of chimpanzees, black and white colobus monkeys, the rare red colobus monkeys, blue monkeys, red-tailed monkeys and baboons. The **Ishasha** region in the south of the park is famous for its tree-climbing lions.

Elephant were heavily poached but are recovering. Many elephants are in fact entering the park from the Congo, where poaching is rampant. Other wildlife includes buffalo, leopard, sitatunga, giant forest hog, Uganda kob, topi and Defassa waterbuck. Over 540 species of birds have been recorded, including the rare prehistoric-looking shoebill (whale-headed stork), which may be sighted along the shores of Lake George and in the Ishasha region.

Interestingly enough, there are no giraffe, zebra, or impala, rhino and only a few crocodile have been sighted in the Kazinga Channel, while none have been seen in Lakes Edward or George. The crocodiles are believed to have been killed long ago by volcanic activity.

From Kampala the park is 260 miles (420 km) via Mbarara and 285 miles (460 km) via Fort Portal. A landing strip is located at Mweya for light aircraft; larger planes can land at Kasese.

ACCOMMODATION — CLASS B: * *Jacana Lodge*, situated in the Maramagambo Forest, has wooden cabins with ensuite facilities.

CLASS B/C: * *Mweya Safari Lodge* is situated on a high bluff overlooking the Kazinga Channel and Lake Edward. All 46 rooms have ensuite facilities.

CLASS F: * *Institute of Ecology Hostel*.

CAMPING: Sites are available near Mweya Lodge and along the Kazinga Channel.

KIBALE FOREST NATIONAL PARK

This 296-square-mile (766-km^2) park consists of marshes, grasslands, crater lakes, lowland tropical rain forest, tropical deciduous forest and montane forest and is the best place in Uganda for chimpanzee trekking.

Kibale is home to ten other species of primates, including black and white colobus monkey, red colobus, white cheeked mangabey and red-tailed monkey. Other wildlife includes blue duiker, Harvey's red duiker, bushbuck, bushpig, over 300 species of birds and over 100 species of butterflies.

The park is located northeast of Queen Elizabeth National Park, 22 miles (35 km) south of Fort Portal.

ACCOMMODATION — CLASS B: * *Mantana Safari Camp* is a permanently based luxury mobile camp with ensuite bush shower (hot water) and long-drop toilet, located 2 miles (3 km) from the park. * *Ndale Lodge,* located on a crater lake a 45-minute drive from the park, has ten cottages with ensuite facilities.

RUWENZORI MOUNTAINS NATIONAL PARK

This is the highest mountain range in Africa and home of the legendary "Mountains of the Moon." They rise 13,000 feet (3963 m) above the western arm of the Rift Valley to 16,762 feet (5109 m) above sea level just north of the equator and are usually covered in mist. See "Ruwenzori Mountains" in the chapter on the Congo for a general description.

Hikers in good condition can enjoy walking strenuous trails that rise to over 13,000 feet (3963 m) in altitude through some of the most amazing vegetation in the world. There is a circuit with huts that takes a minimum of five days to hike — preferably six or seven.

The main trailhead begins near Ibanda. Drive 6 miles north from Kasese on the Fort Portal road, then turn left (west) for 8 miles (13 km). Bring all your own equipment.

The Bujuku Circuit

On day one, follow a dirt road from Ibanda three miles to Nyakalengija (5250 feet/1600 m), then take the path to the Nyabitaba Hut (8700 feet/

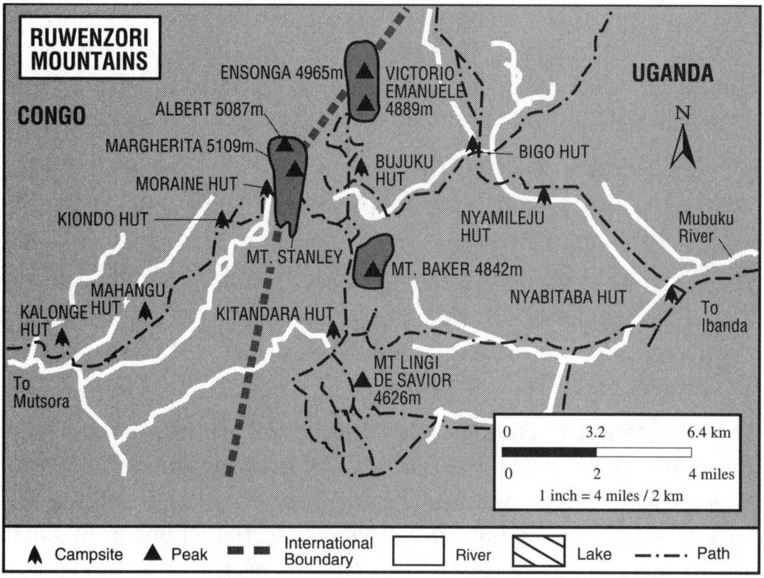

2651 m). Many climbers prefer staying in a nearby rock shelter instead of the aluminum hut which can sleep up to 12 persons. Water and firewood are not available near the hut. Tent spaces are located nearby.

Day two is the most grueling of the circuit. Climbers pass heather and groundsel before reaching Nyamiliju Hut (10,900 feet/3322 m). Again, the rock shelter is often preferred over the hut. Water is available nearby; there is no room for tents. On a clear day you can see Mt. Stanley, Mt. Speak and numerous glaciers.

On day three, hike through giant heather and groundsel forest with colorful mosses and through a muddy bog to Bigo Hut (11,300 feet/3444 m). The hut sleeps up to 12, and it is in good condition. A good rock shelter is nearby. Water and firewood are available. From Bigo Hut, you may hike northeast to Bukurungu Pass, north to Roccati Pass or southwest to Lake Bujuku.

On day four, cross the Kibatsi Bog to Cooking Pot Cave. The left fork of the path leads to Scott Elliot Pass. Take the right fork and hike northwest to Bujuku Hut (13,000 feet/3963 m), near Lake Bujuku, which offers great views of Mt. Baker and Mt. Stanley. Two huts in fair condition can hold up to 14 people. Water is available. A rock shelter for the porters is not far from the hut.

On day five, return to Cooking Pot Cave, take the fork to Scott Elliot Pass and continue past Mt. Baker to Lake Kitandara and Kitandara Hut (13,200 feet/4023 m). Continue on to Kabamba Rock Shelter (12,400 feet/3779 m).

On day six, descend to Kichuchu (a rock shelter) and onward through a bog and across the Mubuku River to Nyabitaba Hut and back to Ibanda.

The best time to climb is December to early February and June to July during the dry season. However, no matter when you climb, you will still get wet. Wood found on the mountain is usually wet, so a camp stove and fuel are highly recommended.

For information on climbing the summits and glaciers, I recommend the books *East Africa International Mountain Guide* by Andrew Wielochowski (1986) and *Guide to the Ruwenzori* by Osmaston and Pasteur (1972), both published by West Col Productions in England. The best maps of the area are "The Central Ruwenzoris" with a scale of 1:250,000 and "Margherita" with a scale of 1:50,000.

ACCOMMODATION — CLASS C/D: See "Kasese" below.

CLASS F: A few huts with dirt floors are available for rent at Ibanda. Many of the huts on the hiking trails are in poor condition but are in the process of being renovated. Bring a ground sheet and insulated pad for your sleeping bag. It is best to bring your own tent.

KASESE

Kasese is the largest town situated near Ruwenzori National Park and the Ruwenzori Mountains and is a good place to purchase supplies. Kasese can be reached by train or by road from Kampala.

ACCOMMODATION — CLASS C/D: * *Margherita Hotel* has rooms with private facilities and is located 2 miles (3 km) out of town.

CENTRAL AND SOUTHERN

KAMPALA

Kampala, the capital of Uganda, is built on seven hills. Points of interest include the Uganda Museum and the Kasubi Tombs of the Kabakas — a shrine to the former Baganda kings and a fine example of Baganda craftsmanship.

The international airport is at Entebbe, about an hour drive from Kampala.

ACCOMMODATION — DELUXE: * *Kampala Sheraton Hotel,* situated in an attractive park setting, has 302 rooms (rooms on the first floor are air-conditioned) with private facilities, a health club, several restaurants and a swimming pool. * *Grand Imperial Hotel* is located in the center of town and has 80 air-conditioned rooms with ensuite facilities, a swimming pool, health club, shops and restaurants.

FIRST CLASS: * *Nile Hotel* contains the International Conference Center and has 85 air-conditioned rooms with ensuite facilities. * *Hotel Equatoria* has rooms (most of them are air-conditioned) with ensuite facilities.

TOURIST CLASS: * *Fairway Hotel* has ensuite facilities and overlooks the Kampala Golf Course.

ACCOMMODATIONS NEAR KAMPALA–DELUXE: * *Lake Victoria Hotel* is located near Entebbe airport overlooking Lake Victoria. The hotel has 99 rooms with facilities ensuite, swimming pool, health club and restaurant.

LAKE MBURO NATIONAL PARK

Formerly a game reserve, Lake Mburo National Park is located in southwestern Uganda between Masaka and Mbarara. This approximately 200-square-mile (520-km^2) park is named after Lake Mburo, the largest of the park's 14 lakes.

The park is characterized by open plains in the north, acacia grassland in the center and lakes and marshes in the south, and is bounded by the Kampala–Mbarara road on the north, Lake Kachera on the east and the Ruizi River on the west.

Wildlife includes hippo, buffalo, leopard, zebra, eland, roan antelope, reedbuck, topi, bushbuck and klipspringer. Impala, which do not exist in any other park in Uganda, are numerous.

ACCOMMODATION — CLASS B: * *Kachira Bush Camp* has five tents with ensuite facilities. Game drives and escorted bush walks are offered.

CLASS F: *Park bandas with shared facilities are available.

CAMPING: Campsites are available in the park.

ACCOMMODATION NEAR THE RESERVE — CLASS D: * *Lake View Hotel* and the * *Katatumba Resort* are located in Mbarara.

KABALE

Kabale is Uganda's highest town, situated in a beautiful area called "The Little Switzerland of Africa" in southwestern Uganda.

ACCOMMODATION — TOURIST CLASS: * *White Horse Inn* has rooms with private facilities. * *Victoria Inn* has basic rooms, some with ensuite facilities.

BWINDI IMPENETRABLE FOREST NATIONAL PARK

The major attraction of the 127-square-mile (330-km^2) Bwindi Impenetrable Forest, which has recently been granted national park status, is the mountain gorilla (*Gorilla gorilla beringei*). Over 300 mountain gorillas are known to inhabit the park.

As of this writing, only two groups are currently being visited by tourists. Group M consists of about 15 gorillas and may be visited by up to six trekkers per day, and permits may be booked up to a year in advance. Group K consists of three gorillas and may be visited by up to four trekkers per day, and permits may only be purchased at park headquarters on the day of departure. Two other groups are being habituated and hopefully will be ready to be visited soon. Once found, visitors spend one hour with the gorillas.

Mountain gorillas form themselves into fairly stable groups of 3–30. They are active by day and sleep in nests at night.

Mountain gorillas eat leaves, buds and tubers (like wild celery). They are continuously on the move, looking for their favorite foods. They eat morning and afternoon, interspacing their dining habits with a midday nap.

Searching for gorillas can be likened to an adventurous game of "hide and seek" in which the guides know where they were yesterday but must find their trail again today and follow it. Finding gorillas can almost be guaranteed for those willing to hike one to four hours or more in search of them.

Each group of visitors is led by a park guide and one tracker. Porters may be hired to carry lunch, drinks, etc. and to assist anyone who may wish to return early.

The search often involves climbing down into gullies, then pulling yourself up steep hills by holding onto vines and bamboo. Even though the pace is slow, you must be in good condition to keep up; the search may take you to altitudes of 3800 to over 6500 feet (1160–1982 m). While this sounds difficult, almost anyone in good physical condition, without a heart problem, can do it.

The guide looks for nests used the night before by the gorillas, and then tracks them from that spot.

Once the gorilla group has been located, the guide communicates with them by making low grunting sounds and imitates them by picking and chewing bits of foliage. Juvenile gorillas are often found playing and tend to approach within a few feet of their human guests. Occasionally our guides had to keep them from jumping into our laps!

Adult females are a little more cautious but may still approach within several feet of you. The dominant male, called a silverback because of the silvery-grey hair on his back, usually keeps more than 20 feet (6 m) from his human visitors.

Silverback gorilla from the M group,
Bwindi National Park.

Gorilla-viewing "etiquette" is important. Do not make eye contact with a silverback. If a silverback begins to act aggressively, look down immediately and take a submissive posture by squatting or sitting, or he may take your staring as aggression and charge. The key is to follow the directions of your well-trained guide. Gorillas are herbivores (vegetarians) and will not attack a human unless provoked. Please do not touch the gorillas as they are very susceptible to catching human colds and diseases.

After spending up to 60 minutes visiting with these magnificent animals, visitors descend to a more open area for a picnic lunch. Use 400 ASA film or higher, as gorillas are often found in the shadow of the forest. You will probably want to "push" 400 ASA to 800 ASA to get enough light. Many trekkers use 1000 and 1600 ASA films. Flash photography is not allowed. Bring several rolls of film on the trek—you very well may need them!

Mornings are almost always cool and misty; even if it doesn't rain, you will undoubtedly get wet from hiking and crawling around wet vegetation. Wear a waterproof jacket or poncho (preferably gortex), leather gloves to protect your hands from stinging nettles, waterproof light- or medium-weight hiking boots to give you traction on muddy slopes and to keep your feet dry and a hat. Bring a waterproof pouch for your camera and plenty of film, a water bottle and snacks. Do not wear bright clothes, perfumes, colognes or jewelry as these distractions may excite the gorillas.

Visiting the gorillas is one of the most expensive yet most rewarding safaris in Africa. The park fees, which are among the highest in Africa, go toward the preservation of these magnificent, endangered creatures.

Other primates include chimpanzee, black and white colobus monkey, red colobus monkey, grey-cheeked mangabey, L'Hoest's monkey and blue monkey. Other wildlife includes elephant, giant forest hog and duiker.

Park Headquarters is based at Buhoma, a three-hour drive (67 miles/108 km) from Kabale. As trekkers must be at the park by 8:30 a.m., it is necessary to overnight at a nearby guest house or camp. Children under 15 years of age are not allowed gorilla trekking, nor are adults who are ill.

ACCOMMODATION — CLASS B: * *Mantana Safari Camp* is a permanently based luxury mobile camp with ensuite bush shower (hot water) and long-drop toilet. * *Buhoma Camp* is a permanently based mobile tented camp with ensuite bush showers and bush toilets.

CLASS C: * *African Pearl Guest House* has simple rooms with shared facilities.

CLASS D: * *National Park bandas* have rooms with separate facilities.

CAMPING: Campsites are available near the park entrance.

MGAHINGA GORILLA NATIONAL PARK

Mgahinga Gorilla National Park is situated on the slopes of Mts. Muhabura and Gahinga in the southwestern corner of Uganda, bordering Rwanda and the Congo.

A joint commission has been set up by Uganda, Rwanda and the Congo to protect the mountain gorilla in the Virunga Mountains where the borders of the three countries meet.

Gorillas are much less likely to be sighted here than in Bwindi Impenetrable Forest National Park. They spend their time in Rwanda and the Congo (especially in the dry season) as well as in Uganda.

Other wildlife in this 12-square-mile (34-km^2) reserve includes blue monkey, black and white colobus monkey, buffalo and bushbuck.

ACCOMMODATION CLASS D: * *Traveller's Rest*, situated about a two-hour drive from the park, has basic rooms with private facilities.

CAMPING: By permission of the landowner. There are no facilities.

RWANDA

THE NILE CROCODILE

Crocodiles are opportunistic feeders and have adapted techniques for acquiring their staple diet, which consists of fish, water birds, terrapins, water monitors and smaller animals.

They will attack and drag smaller animals from the shoreline into deeper water to drown them before feeding. A valve at the back of their throat closes when they have the animal within their jaws, and it prevents them from swallowing water and drowning themselves.

Crocodiles are cold-blooded animals, and they regulate their body temperature by basking in the sun in the early mornings and afternoons, lying in the water during midday to cool off and returning at night to the warmer water. Interestingly enough, they lay their eggs in the sand along the riverbanks, and the difference of a few degrees in temperature within the incubated nest under the sand will determine whether the hatchlings are male or female.

Crocodiles spend their time either underwater or floating low in the water, with only nostrils and eyes showing, searching for prey. While underwater, they can slow their heart rate to one beat per minute, thereby conserving oxygen. While afloat, they are known to ingest stones, which act as ballast to counteract the buoyancy of their lungs.

During a night safari, you may see the red, reflected eyes of the crocodile on the top of the water, waiting...

RWANDA

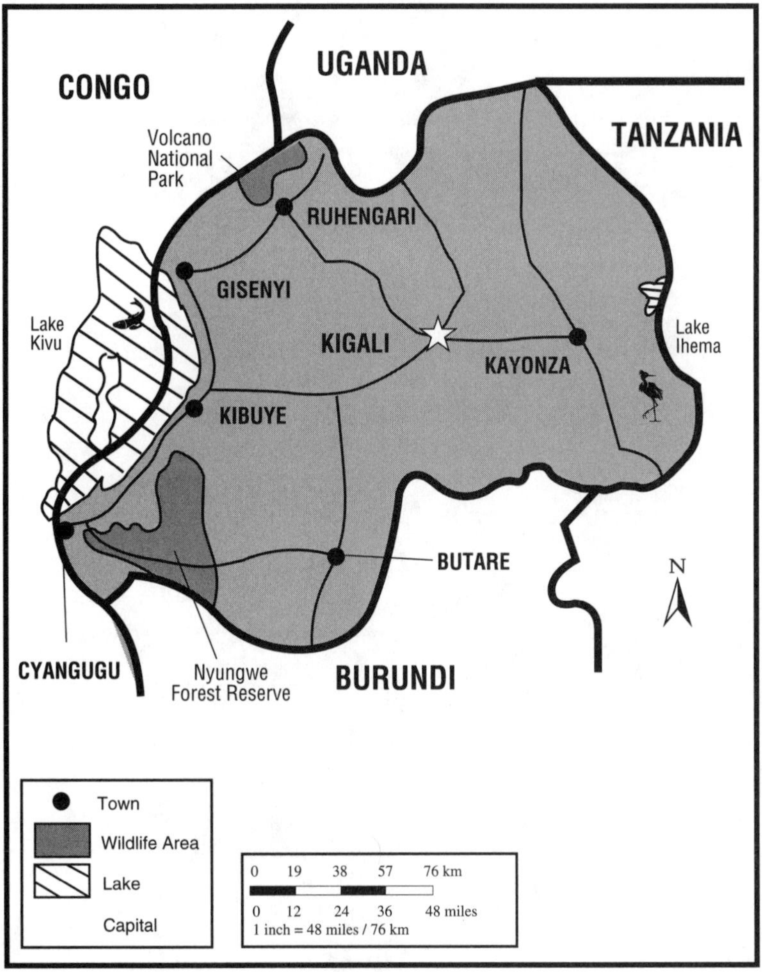

FACTS AT A GLANCE

AREA:	10,160 SQ. MI. / 26,638 SQ. KM.
APPROXIMATE SIZE:	MARYLAND OR BELGIUM
POPULATION:	10 MILLION
CAPITAL:	KIGALI (POP. EST. 3-4 MILLION)
OFFICIAL LANGUAGE:	KINYARWANDA AND FRENCH

RWANDA

Appropriately called "The Country of a Thousand Hills," Rwanda is predominantly grassy uplands and hills, with altitudes above sea level varying from a low of 3960 feet (1207 m) to Mt. Karisimbi, the highest of a range of extinct volcanoes in the northwest, which reach 14,786 feet (4507 m). Lake Kivu forms part of the border with the Congo and is one of the most beautiful lakes in Africa.

Also called "The Country of Perpetual Spring," Rwanda's comfortable climate is temperate and mild with an average daytime temperature of 77°F (25°C). The main rainy season is from mid-February to mid-May, and the shorter one is from mid-October to mid-December.

Ninety-seven percent of the people live in self-contained compounds and work the adjacent land. Sixty percent of the population is Christian (80 percent of which is Catholic), though many people follow traditional African beliefs. About 90 percent of the population is Hutu (Bahutu), 9 percent Tutsi (Batusi) and 1 percent Twa (Batwa) pygmies.

The Tutsi dominated the Hutu farmers with a feudal system analogous to that of medieval England. The system was based on cattle and was surpassed in Africa only by Ethiopia.

Because of its physical isolation and fearsome reputation, Rwanda was not affected by the slave and ivory trade from Zanzibar in the 1800s. The area peacefully became a German protectorate in 1899 and in 1916 was occupied by the Belgians.

Following World War I, Rwanda and Burundi were mandated by the League of Nations to Belgium as the territory of Ruanda-Urundi. Full independence for Rwanda and Burundi was achieved on July 1, 1962.

In 1994 a civil war erupted between the Hutus and the Tutsis, resulting in over a million deaths and even more refugees fleeing primarily to neighboring Zaire (now the Congo) and Tanzania. The Tutsis were victorious and some refugees have returned.

As of this writing, it still not advisable to travel here due to lack of security. The accommodations listed may or may not be open, depending on the security in the region.

High population density is at the root of Rwanda's economic problems. Almost all arable land is under cultivation. Coffee is the country's major export. French and Kinyarwanda are widely spoken, while Kiswahili is spoken in the major towns and regions close to the borders. English is spoken in the deluxe hotels and exclusive shops, but very little English is spoken in the countryside.

WILDLIFE AND WILDLIFE AREAS

Mountain gorilla trekking in Volcano National Park had by far been Rwanda's major international attraction. After the release of the feature film *Gorillas in the Mist* about the late Dian Fossey's pioneering work habituating the gorillas, interest in gorilla trekking reached new heights. Hopefully the area will soon stabilize so that people may once again visit these magnificent creatures in Rwanda. As of this writing, gorillas are being visited by international tourists in Uganda.

THE WEST

VOLCANO NATIONAL PARK (PARC NATIONAL DES VOLCANS)

Volcano National Park is home to the mountain gorilla, discovered by Europeans in the early 1900s. The peaks of the Virunga Mountains, heavily forested extinct volcanoes, serve as a border with the Congo and Uganda and are part of the watershed between the Congo and Nile river systems.

This 46-square-mile (120-km^2) park supports several vegetation zones from lowland forest to luxuriant mountain forest to Afro-alpine. From 8500 to 11,000 feet (2590 to 3350 m) primary forest is dominated by

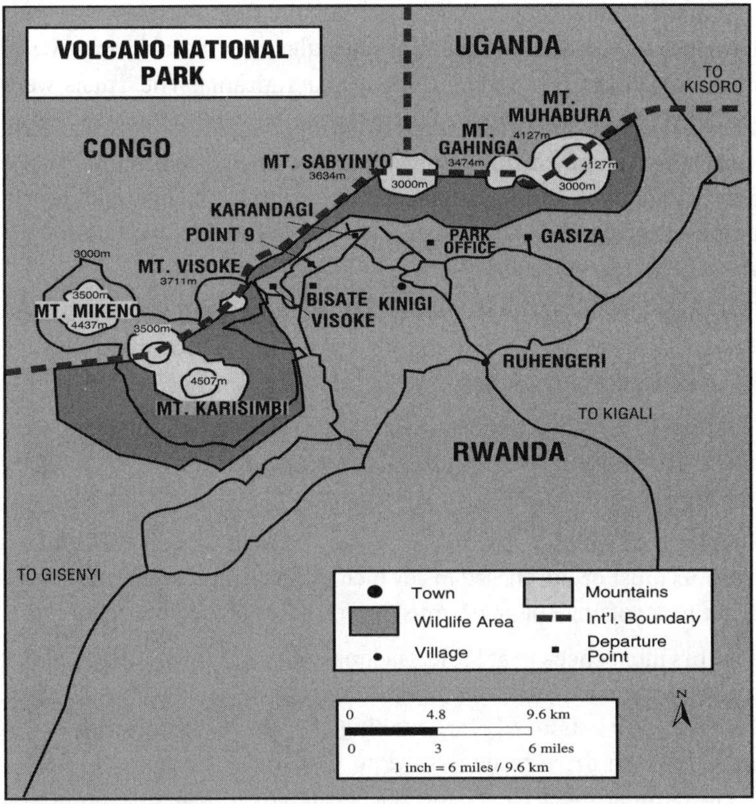

hagenia trees growing 30–60 feet (9–18 m) in height. Hagenia have twisted trunks with low branches covered with lichen, out of which parasitic orchids often grow.

Volcano National Park borders Virunga National Park in the Congo and the Mgahinga Gorilla National Park in Uganda. The park receives a high amount of rainfall, averaging 40 inches (1020 mm) per year. Daytime temperatures average about 50°F (10°C).

The mountain gorilla is larger and has longer hair than the lowland gorilla. It grows to over 6 feet (2 m) in height and weighs more than 440 pounds (200 kg). For a description of gorilla trekking, see the "Bwindi Impenetrable Forest" section of the chapter on Uganda.

Fourteen species of primates are found in these forests, including the red colobus and the crested mangabey. Other wildlife in the park includes forest elephant, giant forest hog, black-fronted duiker (very common), yellow-backed duiker and buffalo. Over 90 species of birds have been recorded, including spectacular mountain touracos and black partridges.

Forest elephants are smaller than those found on the savannah and are most often found in the lower forest zone. Forest elephants do not hesitate to climb the steep slopes of the volcanoes and are known to climb to the bamboo zone where they eat the young bamboo shoots. However, they are seldom seen.

The three gorilla groups currently available to be visited by tourists are Group Sabyinyo, Group Susa and Group 11. Each group may be visited by up to eight tourists each day.

Visitors to Group 11 meet at the Visoke departure point, Group Susa at Gashinga or Cundura, and Group Sabyinyo between Karandaryi and Kinigi.

Children under 15 years of age are not allowed to visit the gorillas. Permits must be purchased in advance in Kigali, and a copy of the first three pages of one's passport must be presented at the time of purchase.

Visitors must check in at Park Headquarters near Kinigi village, about a 45-minute drive from Ruhengeri, between 7:00 and 8:00 a.m. Be sure to have your voucher before making the 30–40-minute (up to 10-mile/16- km) drive to departure points where the searches begin. Visitors must meet their guides at designated departure points no later than 9:00 a.m.

The most popular time to visit the gorillas is during the dry seasons, mid-June–September and December–March.

The park was temporarily closed due to unrest in the country. However, as of this writing, the park is open to international visitors, although visiting here is currently considered very risky.

It is very difficult to get to the park and departure points unless you join a tour (the best option) or rent your own vehicle (expensive). There is no public transportation from Ruhengeri to the Park Headquarters or to the trek departure points.

Mountain Climbing

Hiking in the beautiful Virunga Mountains is in itself an adventure. Trails lead to the craters or peaks of the park's five volcanoes, upward through the unique high vegetation zones of bamboo, hagenia-hypericum forests, giant lobelia and senecio, and finally to alpine meadows. Views from the top, which overlook the lush Rwandan valleys and into the Congo and Uganda, are spectacular.

Some travelers spend a day or two searching for gorillas interspaced with hikes to one or more of the volcanoes.

Karisimbi (14,786 feet/4507 m), which is occasionally snowcapped, is Rwanda's highest mountain. It is the most arduous ascent, requiring two days from the Visoke departure point. The night may be spent in a metal hut at about 12,000 feet (3660 m).

Visoke (12,175 feet/3711 m) has a beautiful crater lake and requires four hours of hiking up a steep trail to reach the summit from the Visoke departure point. The walk around the crater rim is highly recommended. Allow seven hours for the entire trip.

Lake Ngezi (9843 feet/3000 m), a small, shallow crater lake, is the easiest hike in the park, taking only three to four hours round-trip from the Visoke departure point.

Sabyinyo (11,922 feet/3634 m) can be climbed in five to six hours starting at Park Headquarters near Kinigi. A metal hut is located just before you reach the lava beds. The final section is along a narrow rocky ridge with steep drops on both sides.

Gahinga (11,398 feet/3474 m) and **Muhabura** (13,540 feet/4127 m) are both reached from the departure point at Gasiza. The trail rises to a hut in poor condition on the saddle between the two mountains. Gahinga's summit can be reached in four hours, while two days is recommended to reach the summit of Muhabura.

A park guide must accompany each group. Porters are optional. Should you encounter gorillas on your hike, you may not leave the path to follow them. You may only track gorillas if you have previously purchased the proper permits.

Unfortunately, as of this writing, hiking in these mountains is not considered safe and may in fact not be allowed at all by the armed forces.

ACCOMMODATION — FIRST CLASS: See "Gisenyi." Gisenyi is about two hours by road to the gorilla trek points.

TOURIST CLASS: * *Hotel Muhabura* is a very rustic hotel (the best in Ruhengeri) with the most convenient access to Volcano National Park. Ten simple double rooms and two pavilions with bathrooms ensuite, plus a popular local bar, disco and dining room, are available. The hotel is located about 10 miles (16 km) from Park Headquarters, which takes about 45 minutes to drive.

CAMPING: Campsites at Park Headquarters near Kinigi with cold shower and toilet facilities may be available. Beware of thieves.

GISENYI

Gisenyi is a picturesque resort on the northern shores of beautiful Lake Kivu. Lake Kivu has some nice sandy white beaches and is believed to have little or no bilharzia. Crocodiles are absent from the lake due to volcanic action eons ago which wiped them out, making swimming safer.

ACCOMMODATION — TOURIST CLASS: * *Hotel Izuba Méridien* has 68 double rooms and four suites with ensuite facilities and is a 90-minute drive from Volcano National Park. Situated on Lake Kivu, the hotel has a swimming pool, tennis courts and solarium. * *Hotel Palm Beach* has 112 rooms, some with ensuite facilities, and is located on the lakeshore drive.

KIBUYE

Kibuye, located on Lake Kivu midway between Gisenyi and Cyangugu, is a small town with an attractive beach. Be sure not to miss the over 330-foot- (100-m) high **Ndaba Waterfall** (Les Chutes des Ndaba), not far from Kibuye.

ACCOMMODATION — TOURIST CLASS: * *Centre Bethanie Mission* has 24 rooms, half of which have facilities ensuite. * *Kibuye Guest House* is located on Lake Kivu and has 18 double rooms with private facilities, tennis courts and sports activities on the lake.

NYUNGWE FOREST RESERVE (LA FORET DE NYUNGWE)

The Nyungwe Forest is one of the most biologically diverse high-altitude rain forests in Africa. Located in southwestern Rwanda bordering the country of Burundi, this 375-square-mile (970-km^2) reserve is home for 12 species of primates including a rare subspecies of black and white colobus monkey, the rare golden monkey, blue monkey, grey-cheeked mangabey and chimpanzee.

In addition to a variety of butterflies and orchids, over 275 species of birds have been recorded. Some of the over 250 species of trees and shrubs grow to over 165 feet (50 m) in height.

This mountainous reserve has a variety of habitats including wetlands, forested valleys and bamboo zones. Elevation ranges from 5250 to 9680 feet (1600 to 2950 m).

Although Nyungwe Forest Reserve is situated at a lower altitude and is drier (receives less rain) than Volcano National Park, hiking is more difficult in Nyungwe. The vegetation at Nyungwe is much thicker and many slopes are steeper, if not impossible, to ascend. Colobus and the other primates may be difficult to approach closely.

ACCOMMODATIONS: Day trips to Nyungwe Forest Reserve can be made from Butare. See "Accommodations" under "Butare" below.

CAMPING: Campsites have no facilities.

BUTARE

Located in southern Rwanda not far from the border with Burundi, Butare is the intellectual capital of Rwanda. Here you find the **National Museum** (good archeology and ethnology exhibits) and the **National University** and **National Institute of Scientific Research** (ask about folklore dances).

Several craft centers are located in villages within 10 miles of Butare. The **Ballet National du Rwanda** is located in Nyanza, 22 milles (35 km) from Butare.

ACCOMMODATION — TOURIST CLASS: * *Hotel Faucon* has 13 rooms with ensuite facilities. * *Hotel Ibis* has 15 rooms with facilities ensuite.

Impala.

CENTRAL AND EAST

KIGALI

The capital of Rwanda, Kigali, is the commercial center of the country. A number of very good restaurants are located in the deluxe hotels.

ACCOMMODATION — FIRST CLASS: . * *Hotel des Mille Collines* has 112 rooms with ensuite facilities, video and a swimming pool. * *Umubano Méridien*, located a few miles outside the city center, has 100 rooms with ensuite facilities.

TOURIST CLASS: * *Hotel Des Diplomates* has 24 double rooms and 16 apartments, all with ensuite facilities, private terraces, video and tennis. * *Hotel Isimbi* has 27 rooms with ensuite facilities.

When's the Best Time to Go For Game Viewing

AFRICA'S TOP WILDLIFE RESERVES

Key: EXCELLENT | GOOD | FAIR | POOR | CLOSED

COUNTRY	PARK/RESERVE	JAN	FEB	MAR	APR	MAY	JUN	JUL	AUG	SEPT	OCT	NOV	DEC
EAST AFRICA													
TANZANIA	LAKE MANYARA	Excellent	Excellent	Excellent	Fair	Fair	Good	Good	Good	Good	Fair	Fair	Excellent
	NGORONGORO	Excellent	Excellent	Excellent	Good	Good	Good	Excellent	Excellent	Excellent	Good	Good	Excellent
	SERENGETI (S.E.)	Excellent	Excellent	Excellent	Excellent	Good	Good	Poor	Poor	Poor	Poor	Fair	Good
	SERENGETI (N. & N..W.)	Fair	Fair	Fair	Fair	Good	Good	Excellent	Excellent	Excellent	Excellent	Good	Fair
	TARANGIRE	Good	Good	Good	Fair	Fair	Good	Excellent	Excellent	Excellent	Excellent	Good	Good
	SELOUS & RUAHA	Good	Good	Fair	Closed	Closed	Good	Excellent	Excellent	Excellent	Excellent	Good	Good
KENYA	AMBOSELI	Excellent	Excellent	Excellent	Fair	Fair	Good	Excellent	Excellent	Excellent	Excellent	Good	Good
	TSAVO	Good	Good	Good	Poor	Poor	Fair	Excellent	Excellent	Excellent	Fair	Fair	Good
	MASAI MARA	Excellent	Excellent	Excellent	Good	Good	Good	Excellent	Excellent	Excellent	Excellent	Good	Excellent
	ABERDERES & MERU	Excellent	Excellent	Good	Poor	Poor	Good	Excellent	Excellent	Excellent	Good	Fair	Good
	SAMBURU, BUFFALO SPRINGS & SHABA	Excellent	Excellent	Excellent	Good	Fair	Good	Excellent	Excellent	Excellent	Good	Fair	Good
	LEWA DOWNS	Excellent	Excellent	Excellent	Fair	Fair	Good	Excellent	Excellent	Excellent	Good	Fair	Good
SOUTHERN AFRICA													
ZIMBABWE	CHIZARIRA	Poor	Poor	Poor	Fair	Fair	Good	Excellent	Excellent	Excellent	Excellent	Fair	Closed
	HWANGE	Fair	Fair	Fair	Fair	Good	Good	Excellent	Excellent	Excellent	Excellent	Good	Fair
	MATUSADONA	Good	Good	Good	Good	Good	Excellent	Excellent	Excellent	Excellent	Excellent	Excellent	Good
	MANA POOLS	Closed	Closed	Closed	Fair	Fair	Good	Excellent	Excellent	Excellent	Excellent	Good	Closed
	MATOBO	Good	Good	Good	Good	Good	Excellent	Excellent	Excellent	Excellent	Excellent	Excellent	Good
BOTSWANA	MOREMI & OKAVANGO DELTA	Good	Good	Good	Good	Excellent	Excellent	Excellent	Excellent	Excellent	Excellent	Excellent	Good
	LINYANTI	Good	Good	Good	Good	Excellent	Excellent	Excellent	Excellent	Excellent	Excellent	Excellent	Good
	SAVUTE	Excellent	Excellent	Excellent	Excellent	Good	Good	Good	Good	Good	Good	Good	Good
	CHOBE	Fair	Fair	Fair	Good	Good	Excellent	Excellent	Excellent	Excellent	Excellent	Excellent	Good
	NXAI PAN	Excellent	Excellent	Excellent	Excellent	Good	Fair	Fair	Poor	Poor	Poor	Fair	Good
	MAKGADIKGADI	Excellent	Excellent	Excellent	Excellent	Good	Fair	Fair	Poor	Poor	Poor	Fair	Good
ZAMBIA	SOUTH LUANGWA (NORTHERN PART)	Closed	Closed	Closed	Closed	Closed	Good	Excellent	Excellent	Excellent	Excellent	Closed	Closed
	SOUTH LUANGWA (CENTRAL)]	Fair	Fair	Fair	Good	Good	Good	Excellent	Excellent	Excellent	Excellent	Good	Good
	LOWER ZAMBEZI	Fair	Fair	Fair	Fair	Good	Good	Excellent	Excellent	Excellent	Excellent	Good	Good
NAMIBIA	ETOSHA	Fair	Fair	Fair	Good	Good	Excellent	Excellent	Excellent	Excellent	Excellent	Good	Fair
SOUTH AFRICA	KRUGER	Poor	Poor	Poor	Fair	Fair	Good	Excellent	Excellent	Excellent	Excellent	Good	Fair
	PRIVATE RESERVES	Good	Good	Good	Good	Good	Excellent	Excellent	Excellent	Excellent	Excellent	Excellent	Good
	NATAL GAME RESERVES	Fair	Fair	Good	Good	Good	Good	Excellent	Excellent	Excellent	Excellent	Good	Fair

EcoMap

Of East, Central and Southern Africa

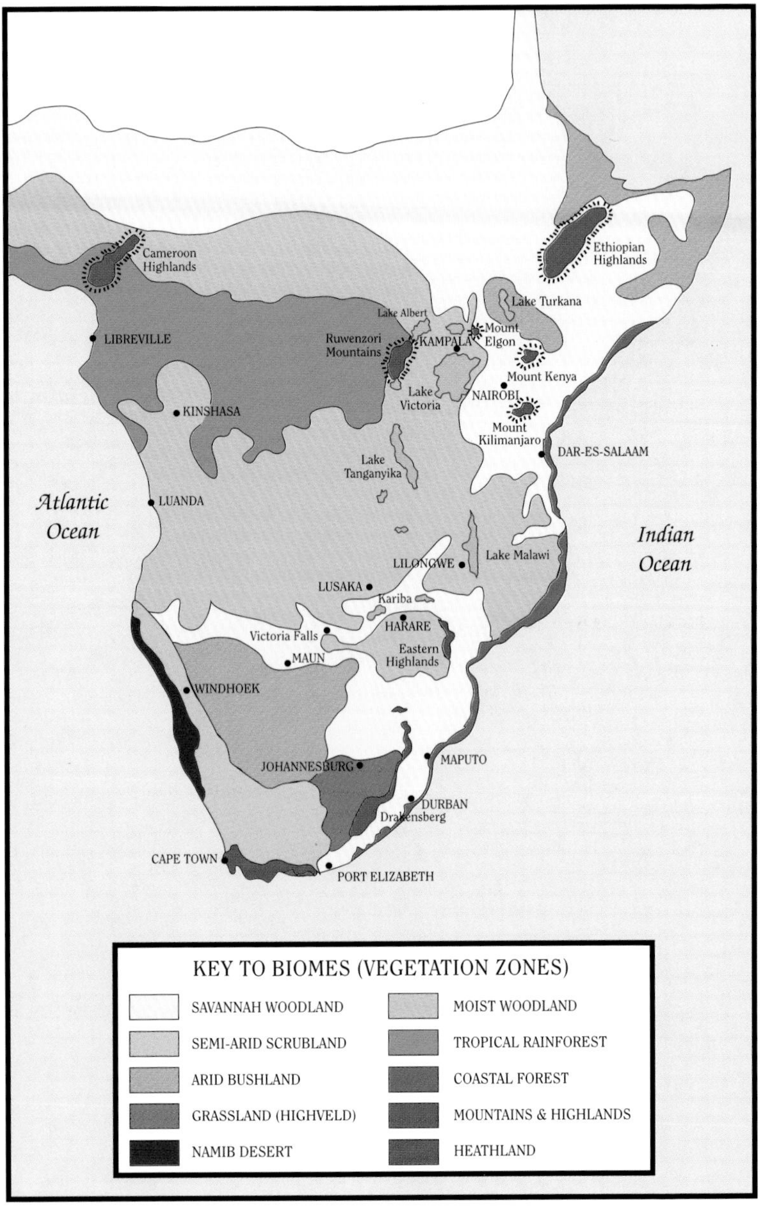

SAVANNAH WOODLAND

Generally from sea-level up to about 4,900 feet (1,500 m), with rainfall strongly seasonal. Characterized by relatively-short, widely-spaced, deciduous trees and extensive grass cover, this is the favored zone for most of Africa's larger mammals, including lion, giraffe, plain's zebra and common wildebeest. Typical trees include various species of thorny *Acacia* and *Combretum*, as well as baobab. Elephants, fire and herbivore feeding pressure can create and maintain areas of *derived grassland* – such as the Serengeti-Mara – within this zone.

Generally below 3,000 feet (1,000 m), with rainfall seasonal (summer) but sparse. Characterized by scattered thorny *Acacia* trees, grass cover may be sparse or extensive depending upon rainfall. Water-independent mammals such as oryx (gemsbok), springbok and brown hyena (Kalahari), gerenuk, Grevy's zebra and striped hyena (East Africa) are typical. Birds include sandgrouse, coursers, larks and social-weavers.

SEMI-ARID SCRUBLAND

ARID BUSHLAND

Generally below 3,300 feet (1,000 m), with rainfall extremely sparse. Characterized by low shrubs and bushes, including many succulent plants; grass cover is sparse to non-existent. Large mammals are very few, but numerous interesting arid-adapted birds and reptiles occur.

Generally above 4,900 feet (1,500 m), including foothills and slopes of some mountain ranges, with strongly seasonal (summer) rainfall. Characterized by dense grass cover, with woody-plant growth inhibited by winter frost and fires. Formerly supported large herds of black wildebeest and blesbok but now dominated by agriculture. Remaining marshes and wetlands support cranes, ducks and other waterfowl.

GRASSLAND (HIGHVELD)

Generally occurs above 3,300 feet (1,000 m), with rainfall seasonal. Characterized by fairly tall, closely-spaced, deciduous trees with little grass cover. This zone does not support great concentrations of large mammals, although elephant can be abundant and there are many endemic bird species. Typical trees include various species of *Brachystegia* and *Julbernadia*.

MOIST WOODLAND

From sea-level to slopes of mountains above 4,900 feet (1,500 m), with strongly seasonal (winter) rainfall. Characterized by fine- or leathery-leaved shrubs including *Protea* and *Erica*, as well as reed-like *Restios* and flowering bulbs; grass cover is sparse to non existent. Few large mammals occur naturally, but there are many endemic birds and reptiles. Plant diversity is astounding – this is one of the world's eight plant kingdoms.

HEATHLAND (FYNBOS)

At sea-level on Indian Ocean coast. Temperate forest in south (Tsitsikamma and Knysna), subtropical to tropical to the north with mangrove forests at large estuaries. Characterized by large to very large evergreen trees with interlocking crowns, and an understory of ferns and leafy shrubs. Large mammals are few, but include various duikers and monkeys. Typical birds include louries (turacos), flycatchers and thrushes.

COASTAL FOREST

Generally above 6,500 feet (2,000 m). Volcanic peaks in East Africa characterized by distinct bands of vegetation including bamboo, evergreen forest and heath; alpine peaks above 14,800 feet (4,500 m) snow-capped throughout the year. Southern ranges (Drakensberg and Eastern Highlands) are dominated by grasslands with scattered shrubs, with pockets of montane forest dominated by *Podocarpus* (small highland forests in Malawi and southern Cape too small to feature on map). Large mammals are few, but baboon, hyrax, duiker and bushpig are common; endangered mountain gorilla confined to Virunga Mountains and outlying Bwindi.

MOUNTAINS AND HIGHLANDS (AFRO MONTANE)

TROPICAL (LOWLAND) RAIN FOREST

Generally from sea-level to 1,000 feet (300 m) in and around the basin of the Congo (Zaire) River with abundant rainfall throughout the year (outlying, remnant patches of lowland forest exist in Uganda and western Kenya but are too small to show on the map). Characterized by very tall to massive evergreen trees with interlocking crowns which form a distinct canopy ecosystem. Understory includes ferns, ginger and lianas which twine up trees. Large mammals include elephant, chimpanzee, lowland gorilla, duikers, bongo and rarely seen okapi. Birdlife is abundant, but hard to see, including hornbills, turacos, trogons and woodpeckers. Hardwood trees at ever increasing risk to timber companies.

Lion cubs provide great entertainment on safari.

Mother cheetah and cub: Masai Mara National Reserve.

A tender moment between mother and child Masai giraffe.

Elephant babies are protected by adult members of the herd.

A family outing.

Taking a morning nap.

The black mane of this old male lion gives him a regal appearance.

A pair of bat-eared fox at their den.

Rare rhino and lion confrontation: Ngorongoro Crater.

Lions killing a buffalo: Chobe National Park.

Each of these Grevy's zebra has its own distinct stripes – as unique as fingerprints.

A majestic greater kudu bull.

Silverback mountain gorilla.

Juvenile mountain gorilla having breakfast, wild celery.

Typical buffet lunch served in the smaller safari lodges.

Blooming jacaranda in downtown Harare, Zimbabwe.

Mountain Village, Arusha.

Young Masai teenagers in traditional costume.

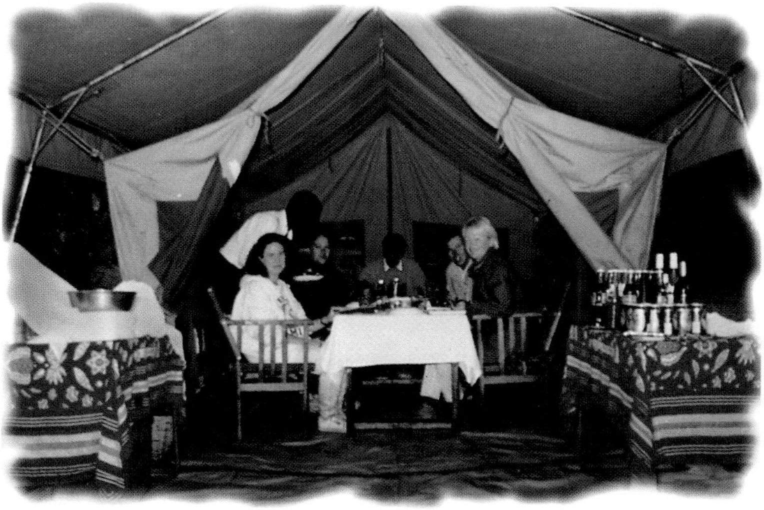

Mobile tented camp: dining tent.

Himba family, Kaokaland, Namibia.

Savuti Camp waterhole.

A visit by an elephant during a picnic lunch on safari.

A professional guide approaching an elephant; Mana Pools National Park.

A safari with a difference, on elephant-back through the Okavango Delta.

Cheetah mother on the lookout for prey.

Vervet monkeys at play.

A lioness resting up.

A common leopard pose, astride the lower branches of a spreading tree: Samburu National Reserve.

Great white egret, the largest of the egret family.

A pair of grey-hooded kingfishers.

Yellowbilled hornbill: Hwange National Park.

Whitefaced duck.

Sunset, Zambezi River.

Sunset, Hwange National Park.

Fish eagle feeding at sunset in the Okavango Delta.

An aerial view of the Okavango Delta, Botswana.

Victoria Falls on the Zimbabwe/Zambian border.

This sand dune, second highest in the world (1,000 feet/300 meters): Sossusvlei, Namibia.

Remote rustic bush camp, Damaraland, Namibia.

The annual migration, Masai Mara.

Red-billed oxpeckers enjoy a symbiotic relationship with a black rhino.

A breeding herd of elephant on the move.

A stunning scene in Etosha.

The night before...

...the morning after

A leopard moving her meal out of the reach of other predators.

Lion silhouette; Serengeti.

A battle of wills...they both wanted the sandbank, but the hippos won!

Sunrise at Mt. Kilimanjaro as seen from Amboseli National Park.

Elephant feeding on Acacia albida branches during the dry summer.

Wild dog: Hwange National Park.

An inquisitive lioness emerges from the bush.

Reflections of the pride.

Elephants after a midday drink at Etosha Pan, Namibia.

A close encounter on canoe safari along Mana Pools National Park, Zimbabwe.

DEMOCRATIC REPUBLIC OF THE CONGO

THE AQUATIC HIPPO

Amphibious, roly-poly hippos spend most of the day in the water, only courageous enough to show their unsightly bodies at night, when ambling off to graze.

Their webbed feet assist in both walking on the muddy riverbeds and swimming. They are nature's natural dredgers; they displace sand and silt in riverbeds and estuaries, which ensures a continuous flow of water. The paths which they stamp, while moving to and from rivers through the swamps, increase the flow of fresh water to the swamps.

Hippos make a noisy display by flapping their tails, which sends their organic dung flying into the water. This spreads organic nutrients for fish and is a natural fertilizer for plant life. Fish swim with the hippo and feed off algae growing on their skin.

Their barrel-like bodies have a natural buoyancy in the water, and only their noses, eyes and ears extend above the surface of the water. Hippos often stand on the bottom and let their front legs rise until their heads reach the surface.

When disturbed on land, they will run to water (the safe haven) and submerge, and they may hold their breath for up to six minutes. They close both their nostrils and ear flaps while underwater and, upon surfacing, will blow open their nostrils and twitch open their ear flaps. Babies are often seen gulping for air before disappearing underwater, to rest on their mothers' backs.

A content hippo is a grunting hippo; open, displayed jaws are a sign of aggression or annoyance. An even happier hippo is one who is able to feed his sweet tooth on fresh green grass at a bush camp or nearby sugarcane field!

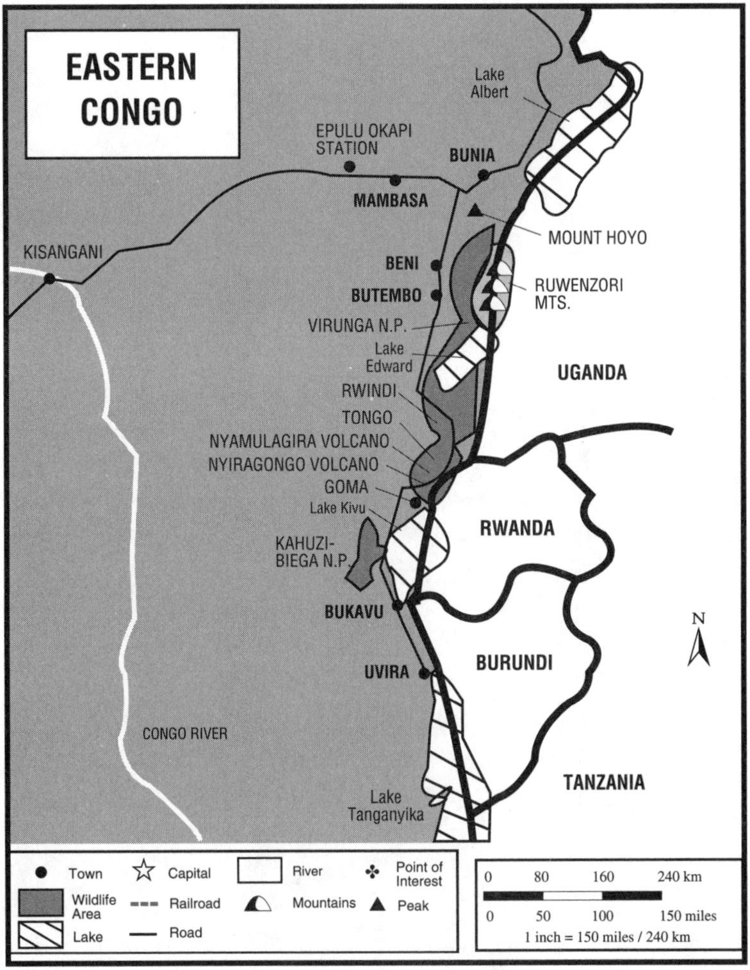

FACTS AT A GLANCE

AREA:	905,365 SQ. MI. / 2,344,885 SQ. KM.
APPROXIMATE SIZE:	U.S.A. EAST OF THE MISSISSIPPI RIVER OR TEN TIMES THE SIZE OF GREAT BRITAIN
POPULATION:	40 MILLION
CAPITAL:	KINSHASA (POP. EST. 3.5 MILLION)
OFFICIAL LANGUAGE:	FRENCH
NATIONAL LANGUAGE:	SWAHILI, TSHILUBA, KOKONGO, LINGALA

DEMOCRATIC REPUBLIC OF THE CONGO

The Democratic Republic of the Congo, formerly the Republic of Zaire, is the third largest country in Africa. The name Zaire came from the Kikongo word *nzadi*, meaning "river." The Congo River, the tenth longest river in the world, winds 2880 miles (4600 km) through the Congo basin, the world's second largest drainage basin (the Amazon is the largest), and finally empties into the Atlantic Ocean.

Of all the countries listed in this guide, the Congo is closest to "Tarzan's Africa." You can very easily imagine him swinging on a vine right in front of you as you travel through this country, visited more by adventurers than tourists.

Kivu Province, the most beautiful region of the Congo, holds the country's most exciting attractions. This province is situated along the western borders of Rwanda and Uganda in the region of the great lakes: Lakes Tanganyika, Kivu, Edward and Albert. This is an important agricultural area with large tobacco, coffee, tea and banana plantations. The only paved road in the Kivu Province runs from Goma to the Kabasha Escarpment.

Due to the altitude, the region has an agreeable Mediterranean-type climate. In general, the best time to visit the eastern Congo is during the dry seasons from December to February and mid-June to August.

Of the 200 or so tribal or ethnic groups in the Congo, four-fifths are Bantu. Physically, tribal groups range from the Tutsi, some of the tallest people on earth, to pygmies. About 80 percent of the population is Christian, with the balance having Muslim or traditional beliefs.

The Congo remained virtually unknown until Henry Morton Stanley traveled from East Africa to the mouth of the Congo River (1874–1877). Belgian King Leopold II claimed what became the Congo Free State as his personal property until he ceded it to Belgium in 1907, and it was renamed the Belgian Congo. Zaire achieved independence on June 30, 1960.

In 1997 President Mabutu Sese-Seko was overthrown, and Laurent Desire Kabila came to power and the country's name was changed from Zaire to the Democratic Republic of the Congo. As of this writing, the country is considered unsafe for travel. Please get a current update on the situation before traveling there. The accommodations listed may or may not be open, depending on the security in the region.

The Congo is a country of gigantic untapped resources. Fifty percent of the land is arable and scarcely 2 percent is under cultivation or used as pasture. The country holds 13 percent of the world's hydroelectric potential. Copper accounts for about half of the country's exports, followed by petroleum, diamonds and coffee.

WILDLIFE AND WILDLIFE AREAS

Eight reserves cover 15 percent of the country's area. Over 1000 species of birds have been recorded in the Congo, many in the Virunga National Park. In addition, the Congo is also a home of the rare okapi (antelope).

Like Uganda, gorillas are a major attraction in the Congo. Should the region stabilize, mountain gorillas may be visited in Virunga National Park and eastern lowland gorillas may be seen in Kahuzi-Biega National Park.

The Congo is the most difficult country covered in this book in which to travel. Those not willing to put up with delays and constant last-minute changes in their itineraries should look elsewhere for adventure.

THE NORTHEAST

GOMA

Goma is situated on the northern shores of Lake Kivu, one of the most beautiful lakes in Africa, with Mt. Nyiragongo (volcano) forming a dramatic backdrop to the north. It is the administrative center for Virunga National Park and Nyiragongo and Nyamulagira Volcanoes.

Three boats per week depart Goma for Bukavu across Lake Kivu.

ACCOMMODATIONS — TOURIST CLASS: * *Hotel Karibu* has rooms with ensuite facilities and is located six miles outside of Goma on Lake Kivu. * *Hotel des Grand Lacs* also has rooms with private facilities.

NORTH OF GOMA

On the drive from Goma northward one passes over the dramatic Kabasha Escarpment to Butembo. The route from the Kabasha Escarpment to Beni is one of the most beautiful in Africa and is properly named the "Beauty Route." The road passes through many picturesque villages, coffee, tea and banana plantations — the Africa that many of us have pictured in our minds.

VIRUNGA NATIONAL PARK (PARC NATIONAL DES VIRUNGA)

Virunga National Park, previously called Albert Park, is the oldest reserve in Africa and is the best game park in the Congo. Altitudes range from 3000 feet (915 m) on the grassy savannah to 16,794 feet (5120 m) in the Ruwenzori Mountains, resulting in a tremendous variety of topography, flora and fauna.

Virunga is about 185 miles (300 km) long and 25 miles (40 km) wide and is divided into several sections, each requiring separate entrance fees; from south to north: Nyiragongo and Nyamulagira Volcanoes, Tongo, Bukima (Rumangabo Station), Djomba Gorilla Sanctuary, Rwindi, the Ruwenzori Mountains, and Mt. Hoyo. Guides are compulsory and their services are included in the park entrance fees.

Unfortunately, as of this writing all of these areas within the park and the accommodations are closed to tourism. This situation will hopefully change for the better soon.

Volcanoes

The region around Goma is a highly volcanic area of constant activity. On my first visit here, I discovered that a new volcano had been born recently, and we hiked ten miles (16 km) into the bush to see it. In the event of an eruption, we camped uphill from the volcano, which was scarcely 300 feet (915 m) high, and watched the fabulous fireworks all night. For some unknown reason, a new volcano usually pops up in this active region about every other year. I just missed visiting another lava-filled caldera in 1984, which cooled a few weeks before my arrival.

In the southern part of the park near Goma lie the active volcanoes of Nyiragongo and Nyamulagira, which do not require technical mountaineering skills to climb. If the volcanoes are active at the time of your visit, you may want to spend a night near the crater rim to enjoy the remarkable fireworks display.

The best time to climb is December–January and June, when the weather is most clear. February, July and August are also good.

Nyiragongo

Nyiragongo (11,384 feet/3470 m) erupted in 1977, spewing out miles (kilometers) of molten lava which destroyed villages in its path. I visited the area three months later and could still feel the heat radiating from the newly hardened lava.

Nyiragongo can be climbed in one day if you begin climbing early in the morning. The guide and porter station is located at Kibati (6400 feet/1950 m), 8 miles (13 km) north of Goma on the Rutshuru road. Hike four to five hours through forest and Afro-alpine vegetation and past lava flows to the summit. Have lunch on the crater rim while watching sulfurous gases escape from the crater below. Allow two to three hours to return to Kibati before dark.

It is better to take two days for the climb, overnighting at a hut (in poor condition) about a 30-minute walk below the summit. At dawn the next morning, hike to the crater rim and enjoy breathtaking views of Lake Kivu, Goma and the surrounding countryside.

Nyamulagira

If you would like to see wildlife, this is the better of the two volcanoes to climb. An armed guide accompanies each group, and porters may be hired. With luck, you will see forest elephant, chimpanzees, buffalo and antelope.

Nyamulagira (10,023 feet/3055 m) is best climbed in three days. On the first day, hike about six hours through dense upland jungle, passing numerous lava flows to a basic lodge at 8200 feet (2500 m) altitude. Water is available at the lodge but must be purified.

On day two you reach the tree line after about an hour's hike and the crater rim about an hour after passing the tree line. The crater itself is about a mile and a half (2 km) in diameter. Within the crater is a blowhole with a huge 1300-foot- (400-m) diameter shaft. Descend into it and explore the crater, then return to the same lodge you slept in the night before. Hike down the mountain on the third day.

Nyamulagira is reached via Kakomero (5900 feet/1800 m), 24 miles (39 km) north of Goma.

ACCOMMODATIONS — CAMPING: Campsites are available at the Nyamulagira base camp.

Tongo

Located north of Goma about 9 miles (15 km) west of the main Goma/Rutshuru road is Tongo, presently the best place in the Congo to see chimpanzees.

A chimpanzee trek from Tongo Lodge can be arduous, often lasting five to eight hours. The land has been covered by lava flows (probably centuries old) from Mt. Nyamulagira, leaving the surface very rough and resulting in a lot of up-and-down hiking. Highland forest grew over the lava flows, camouflaging the rugged surface underneath, and requiring trekkers to watch nearly every step to prevent falling or twisting an ankle.

Chimps are often found; however, they often move away after a few minutes and trekkers must keep after them. Black and white colobus, red-tailed monkey and other primates may be seen. The park has an average altitude of about 3930 feet (1200 m).

ACCOMMODATIONS — CLASS C: * *Tongo Lodge*, located on a hill overlooking the forest where the trekking for chimps occurs, has several rooms with private facilities.

Bukima (Rumangabo Station)

The main attraction of Bukima is visiting mountain gorillas (*Gorilla gorilla beringei*). The Luawa and the Ndungutsi gorilla groups have about 65 members in total.

To reach Bukima from Uganda, drive from Ishasha to Rutshuru and turn off at the Park Headquarters at Rumangabo Station. From Rwanda, go north on the Goma/Rutshuru road to the turnoff. You then hike uphill for about 40 minutes to Bukima Lodge while porters carry your luggage. Trekkers usually spend the night and the following day hike for about 90 minutes through cultivated land and by small villages to the edge of the forest in which the gorillas live. From here gorillas may be found in less than an hour, or the search could take several hours.

For a description of gorillas and gorilla trekking in general, see "Bwindi Impenetrable Forest National Park" in the chapter on Uganda.

ACCOMMODATION — CLASS C: * *Bukima Lodge* is a small lodge (six beds) with shared facilities.

Djomba (Jomba) Gorilla Sanctuary

The Djomba Gorilla Sanctuary covers much of the Congo side of the Virunga Mountains, which are shared with Rwanda and Uganda.

Here, three groups of mountain gorillas have been habituated to man's presence. The Marcel (Rugabo) and Oscar (Rugenda) groups stay in the region, while the Ffeida Group sometimes crosses the Rwanda border. Marcel was killed, but the group still bears his name. Each group may be visited by up to six persons at a time. National Parks guides must accompany each group.

Djomba Camp is the base from which gorilla trekking begins. To reach Djomba (also spelled Jomba), drive about 40 miles (65 km) north from Goma past Nyiragongo and Nyamulagira volcanoes. Two miles before reaching Rutshuru, turn right and continue 19 miles (30 km) to Park

Headquarters. From there, visitors must hike for 30–45 minutes to Djomba Camp. Porters are available to carry luggage.

Trekkers may visit with the gorillas for about an hour, as in Uganda and Rwanda.

Buffalo and elephant are also present in the sanctuary, so keep an eye out for them.

ACCOMMODATION — CLASS C: * *Djomba Camp* has several cabins, each with two double rooms with private facilities and a shared sitting room with a fireplace.

CLASS F: A self-service hut with two bedrooms (six beds total) is available. Bring your own food.

CAMPING: Campsites are available.

Rwindi

Continuing north toward Rwindi are the **Rutshuru Waterfalls** and **Maji Ya Moto** hot-water springs, both near Rutshuru.

Rwindi is the chief game-viewing region of Virunga National Park and is predominantly composed of savannah plains and swamps,. Unfortunately, most of the wildlife here has either been poached or has crossed the border to Uganda.

The Kabasha Escarpment rises up to 6000 feet (1830 m) above the plains below and provides a dramatic backdrop. The fishing village of Vitshumbi, located on the southern shores of Lake Edward, is worth a stop.

The main road from Goma to Butembo passes right through the park.

The best time to visit is during the dry season. Roads and tracks are poor in the rainy season. Rwindi Lodge, Park Headquarters and camping sites are located at Rwindi, 81 miles (121 km) north of Goma.

ACCOMMODATION — CLASS D: * *Rwindi Lodge* has rondavels with private facilities (130 beds total) and a swimming pool.

CAMPING: Camping is allowed but not considered safe.

Ruwenzori Mountains

The third highest mountains in Africa (behind Mts. Kilimanjaro and Kenya), the "Mountains of the Moon" are the highest mountain chain on the continent. Permanently snow-covered at over 14,800 feet (4500 m), these jagged mountains are almost perpetually covered in mist. For a map of the Ruwenzoris, see "Ruwenzori National Park" in the chapter on Uganda.

The mountain chain is approximately 60 miles (100 km) long and 30 miles (50 km) wide, and the highest peak, Margherita, is 16,762 feet (5109 m) in altitude. A number of permanent glaciers and peaks challenge mountaineers. However, mountaineering skills are not needed for the hike itself — only for climbing the glaciers or peaks.

Unlike Mt. Kilimanjaro and many other mountains in east and central Africa, the Ruwenzoris are not volcanic in origin. The range forms part of the border with Uganda and can be climbed from either the Congo or Ugandan side. The trail on the Congo side of the Ruwenzoris is much steeper than the Ugandan side. Allow five days for the climb and longer if any peaks are to be attempted.

The vegetation zones one passes through on the Ruwenzoris are the most amazing I have seen in the world. Colorful mosses look solid, but when probed with a walking stick (or your foot) often prove to cover a tangle of roots more than 6 feet (2 m) deep. Several plants that are commonly small in other parts of the world grow to gigantic proportions.

The Butawu Route

The Butawu Route is the only route regularly used on the Congo side of the Ruwenzoris. All other routes are so overgrown with vegetation that they are virtually impossible to climb.

On the first day, it takes five to six hours of hiking from the Park Headquarters at Mutsora (5600 feet/1700 m) through small fields of bananas, coffee and other crops to reach Kalonge Hut (7015 feet/2135 m). The hut sleeps 16 persons, and there is room for tents nearby.

On the second day, one passes through areas with giant stinging nettles and bamboo forest over 100 feet (30 m) high. Soon you come to a resting spot where offerings are left for the mountain gods. Your guide will expect you to leave something, (i.e., a few coins).

At about 8500 feet (2600 m), the sides of the slick, muddy path become lined with spongy mosses and heather 25 feet (8 m) tall. After about five hours of hiking (actually the most difficult part of the climb), one reaches Mahangu Hut (10,860 feet/3310 m). The hut has room for 16 persons, and there is room for camping.

The third day, one finally hikes past the upper tree line at about 12,500 feet (3800 m) and enters a zone of giant groundsels over 16 feet (5 m) high and giant lobelia over 25 feet (8 m) high. Before completing the five-hour hike to Kiondo Hut (13,780 feet/4200 m), you hike along an open ridge with fabulous views of Lac Noir (Black Lake). Kiondo Hut has room for 12, and there is room for tents nearby.

On day four of the hike, the Butawu Route continues on to Wasuwameso Peak (14,600 feet/4450 m) for some fabulous views of Mt. Stanley. Climbers then return to Kiondo Hut and continue on down to Kalonge Hut for the night.

Alternatively, take a fabulous hike past Lac Vert (Green Lake) and Lac Gris (Grey Lake) to Moraine Hut (14,270 feet/4350 m) at the foot of the glaciers. The hike to Moraine Hut from Kiondo Hut takes about five hours round-trip and requires a short bit of easy rock climbing with fixed ropes. Then return to either Kiondo Hut or Mahangu Hut for the night.

If you hike to Moraine Hut, be sure to return to Kiondo Hut early. My guide insisted there was plenty of time to reach Moraine Hut and return to Kiondo Hut the afternoon of the third day. We were so late returning that we were forced to return in the dark. Had I not brought a flashlight, we might still be up there.

On the fifth day, return to Mutsora — hopefully for a hot bath and a soft bed!

Many hikers prefer camping at Grey Lake instead of using dilapidated Moraine Hut, which leaks. There is space for only one tent near Moraine Hut. Experienced mountaineers may press on to conquer the glaciers and peaks of the Ruwenzori from either location. Allow a minimum of six or seven days total for the climb if you wish to attempt any summits.

For information on climbing the summits and glaciers, I recommend the *East Africa International Mountain Guide* by Andrew Wielochowski (1986) and *Guide to the Ruwenzori* by Osmaston and Pasteur (1972), both published by West Col Productions in England.

The best time to climb is from December to February; June to August is also good. To reach the Ruwenzoris, travel north from Goma through Butembo, and just before Beni turn east 28 miles (45 km) to Mutwanga. Park Headquarters is at Mutsora, about 1.5 miles (2.5 km) from Mutwanga.

A guide is required and his fee is included in the park entrance fee; porters are available for a small fee. Both guides and porters expect cigarettes in addition to a tip. The guides know the path and where to find water en route — but little else. All guides speak French; an English-speaking guide may not be available. Guides who speak English tend to know only a few words.

Guides are not equipped for, or experienced in, glacier or rock climbing. Your group must be self-sufficient. There are no mountain rescue teams; bring a comprehensive medical kit.

Huts have fireplaces, bunk beds and wood stoves. Guides and porters love to smoke and often share the huts with you; consider bringing your own tent. Also, bring a warm sleeping bag, pad, food, fuel and enough water to last two days. Most of the windows are broken; you may wish to bring some plastic with which to cover them.

See "Mt. Kilimanjaro" in the chapter on Tanzania for a more extensive equipment checklist and other preparations. Mt. Kilimanjaro is higher, but the trail up the Ruwenzoris is much steeper, slicker and more difficult to negotiate.

ACCOMMODATION — TOURIST CLASS: See "Butembo" or "Beni" below.

CLASS F: Rooms are available at a basic lodge at Park Headquarters.

CAMPING: Camping is allowed at Park Headquarters.

Ishango

The Ishango region of Virunga National Park is situated at the northern end of Lake Edward. This seldom-visited region of the park is predominantly open savannah, similar to the Rwindi area and the southern shores of Lake Edward. Wildlife is also similar to what you find in the Rwindi region, except there are no elephant. Water birds are prolific, especially where the Semliki River leaves Lake Edward.

From Beni, travel east past the turnoff to the Ruwenzori Mountains and onward toward the Ugandan border to Kasindi. Then turn right (south) and continue to Ishango.

ACCOMMODATIONS: None.

CAMPING: Campsites are available.

Mt. Hoyo

Fifty-seven miles (92 km) north of Beni and 12 miles (19 km) south of Komanda, take the track to the east, uphill for 9 miles (15 km), to the colonial-style Mount Hoyo Lodge (Auberge du Mount Hoyo).

Halfway up this track, I came upon a line of millions of safari ants crossing the road. Thousands of ants had joined their legs and formed a "cocoon" across the road, protecting those that crossed beneath.

Mt. Hoyo has many attractions. The Cascades of Venus (l'Escaliers de Venus) is a stepped waterfall in a thick jungle setting of natural beauty. The cascades and the grottoes (caves) with stalagmites and stalactites can be easily visited in a half-day hike. Black and white colobus monkeys and chimpanzees may be seen in the forest.

A very interesting excursion is to join a few Balese (pygmy) hunters on a mock antelope hunt. Groups of up to three visitors follow these hunters, armed with their bows and arrows, through thick jungle vegetation in search of game. The pygmies whistle to attract their "prey." Here, they proved the advantage of being small — effortlessly walking under vines and limbs, while I had to crawl on my hands and knees.

We feasted on honey which they fished from a beehive in a tree trunk with their arrows, and they enjoyed another delicacy — termites from a large mound.

A pygmy family in front of their hut near Mt. Hoyo.

Be sure to visit a pygmy village while in the area. Villages along the main roads have become a bit "commercialized," so if you have time, have a guide take you to a village off the beaten track.

ACCOMMODATION — CLASS D: * *Mount Hoyo Lodge (Auberge du Mount Hoyo)* has rooms with private facilities and good views of the jungle below.

CAMPING: Campsites with basic shower and toilet facilities are available.

LOYA RIVER

The Loya River crosses the main road a few miles south of the turnoff to Mt. Hoyo. Take a ride in a piroque (dugout canoe) through the thick green Ituri Forest, past artificial dams created for fishing, and thick jungle. The Loya River flows into the Ituri River, which travels deep into the Ituri Forest.

Visit a pygmy village before returning. Be sure to bring a gift (i.e., pens or tobacco), especially if you wish to take pictures.

BUTEMBO

This busy town with a population of over 100,000 is situated in the highlands along the "Beauty Route" just north of the equator, about halfway between Goma and Bunia. Many banana, coffee and tea plantations are in the area. Travelers driving from Rwindi often spend the night here before continuing on to Mt. Hoyo or the Ruwenzori Mountains.

ACCOMMODATION — TOURIST CLASS: * *Auberge* has rooms with private facilities. * *Kikyo Hotel* has rooms with private facilities.

EPULU OKAPI STATION

At the Okapi Station at Epulu, you may see the rare okapi antelope (30 left at present) roaming several large pens set in natural surroundings. In addition, 14 primate species have been seen in the forests near Epulu.

An interesting excursion for the adventurous is to go hunting with pygmies and camp in the forest for a night or two. The pygmies will build you a shelter for the night or you may bring a tent.

Pygmy villages seldom visited by overseas visitors may also be visited by hiking into the jungle with a guide.

The Epulu Okapi Station is situated on the banks of the Epulu River about a six- to seven-hour drive from Mt. Hoyo in the dry season (December–February and June–August), which is the best time to visit. Roads are often impassable in the rainy season. From Mt. Hoyo, drive north to Komanda, then west past Mambasa to Epulu. Alternatively, charter a plane to Mambasa and try to hire a vehicle for the 50-mile (80-km) drive to Epulu.

ACCOMMODATION — CLASS F: Three rondavels and a guest house (20 beds total) with an ablution block with toilets and showers (cold water only).

CAMPING: Campsites are available.

THE SOUTHEAST

KAHUZI-BIEGA NATIONAL PARK

This 2300-square-mile (5960-km^2) mountain sanctuary, located 17 miles (27 km) northwest of Bukavu, is dedicated to preserving the eastern lowland gorilla (*Gorilla gorilla graueri*). Searching for these magnificent rare and endangered animals is recommended only for travelers in fairly good physical condition.

The four groups of habituated gorillas have been named Maheshe, Mushamuka, Naninja and Mubalala. The search for these gorillas usually takes an hour or two of hiking to altitudes from 7000 to 8200 feet (2135 to 2500 m) through dense upland jungle and bamboo forests. However, it occasionally takes three or four hours to locate the gorillas. The park also includes swamp, woodland and extensive equatorial rain forest. The highest point in the park, Mt. Kahuzi (10,853 feet/3308 m), can be climbed in about six hours.

On my visit to the park, I was the only tourist there to search for gorillas. I was accompanied by a guide and several cutters wielding pangas. As our search progressed, we found lairs where gorillas had spent the previous night.

After four hours of following their trail and cutting our way through dense tropical foliage, we finally located them. The silverback (dominant male) was one of the largest I have seen — estimated by the guide to weigh over 400 pounds (180 kg). Hanging vines and branches that blocked our view were cut until the silverback pounded his chest and charged — stopping just short of us and establishing his well-earned territory. In the background, an adult female and her young offspring were curiously watching us.

Other wildlife present in the park includes elephant, giant forest hog, duiker, chimpanzee and colobus monkey.

The park is managed by the Frankfurt Zoological Society. At present, a limit of eight people may visit a gorilla group at one time. Children under 15 years of age are not allowed to visit the gorillas.

Daytime temperatures average 50–65°F (10–18°C), and yearly average rainfall is high — about 70 inches (1790 mm). The heaviest rainfall is in April and November. The best time to visit the park is in the dry season. Bring waterproof light hiking boots (you may have to wade through water), a sweater, waterproof cover jacket, lunch, snacks and a water bottle.

To reach the park, go north from Bukavu along the western side of Lake Kivu for 13 miles (21 km) to Miti, then turn left (west), traveling for four miles (6 km) to Station Tshivanga, the Park Headquarters.

As of this writing, the park is closed.

ACCOMMODATION — CLASS B: * *Mbayo Cottage* has seven rooms (doubles) and is located on a tea plantation 6 miles (10 km) from the park gate. Gorillas are sometimes seen on the plantation.

CAMPING: Campsites are available at Park Headquarters.

BUKAVU

Bukavu, the region's capital, is situated on the southern shores of Lake Kivu near the Rwanda border. Bukavu is the nearest city to Kahuzi-Biega National Park.

Boats for Goma depart Bukavu and cross beautiful Lake Kivu to Goma three times per week.

ACCOMMODATION — FIRST CLASS: * *Orchids Safari Club,* located on the shores of Lake Kivu, has 14 rooms (doubles) with ensuite facilities. Cruises on Lake Kivu are offered.

TOURIST CLASS: * *Riviera Hotel* has rooms with ensuite facilities.

CENTRAL AND WESTERN

CONGO RIVER

Exploring the Congo River by riverboat from Kinshasa to Kisangani is truly an adventure into the dark continent. The boat is slow, taking about 12 days upstream and 8 downstream for the 1000-mile (1600-km) voyage — if no complications arise. You may also cruise from Lisala to Kisangani; this trip takes three to five days.

The riverboat is actually a motor boat with several barges tied on, with a dining room and bar on each barge. Local tribesmen paddle out to meet the riverboat in their dugout canoes, latch hold, and sell monkeys, crocodiles, huge juicy pineapples and other tropical fruits. One passes through the "mainstream" of Congo life on this river.

Deluxe and first-class cabins are recommended for all but the most rugged of travelers. This riverboat is only for those with flexible schedules; it is not uncommon for it to be a week or more "off schedule."

KINSHASA

Situated in the western Congo near the mouth of the Congo River, Kinshasa is the country's capital. Points of interest include the Presidential Gardens and Zoo, the central market, and the National Academy of Fine Arts. Thieves Market is a good place to shop for malachite and wood carvings.

One of the most popular attractions in this city is the numerous live bands playing the music of the Congo in clubs. Congo music is extremely popular throughout most of sub-Sahara Africa.

The airport is 18 miles (29 km) from Kinshasa. More travelers reach the Eastern Congo from Nairobi (Kenya) or Entebbe (Uganda) than from Kinshasa.

ACCOMMODATION — DELUXE: * The *Inter-Continental Hotel* is centrally located near the World Trade Center and has 510 air-conditioned rooms with ensuite facilities, swimming pool, tennis courts, squash, health club, casino and disco.

FIRST CLASS: * *Hotel Le Memling* has 212 rooms with ensuite facilities.

BURUNDI

THE LIKABLE CHIMPANZEE

Chimpanzees resemble humans in many physical, as well as behavioral, aspects. As humans, we are fascinated by these similarities and love to compare the familiar actions of chimpanzees to our own.

Chimpanzees begin their day with an early morning snack followed for a couple of hours by more selective feeding. They use twigs as tools (like we use knives and forks) to find food, to locate termites in decaying wood or as wooden hammers to crack nuts, and they use leaves as spoons to gather water or honey from within tree trunks. Chimpanzees are also known to eat meat.

During their parents' midday rest, youngsters engage in many "human" play activities. They use their five-digit hands to play tug-of-war with plants and roots, to climb trees and to play with ball-shaped objects (e.g., wild fruits).

They beat their chests when excited and often disturb their parents with squabbling, screeches and screams. As chimpanzees are naturally inquisitive creatures, they show their curiosity and indecisive nature by scratching their heads or continuing to feed and pretending not to notice. They will wield a stick to defend themselves, and others, if attacked.

At dusk they build their nests in the higher branches of trees, 19–60 feet (6–18 m) above the ground. They often sleep on their backs, hands behind their heads, or on their sides with their knees drawn up to their bodies in the fetal position.

BURUNDI

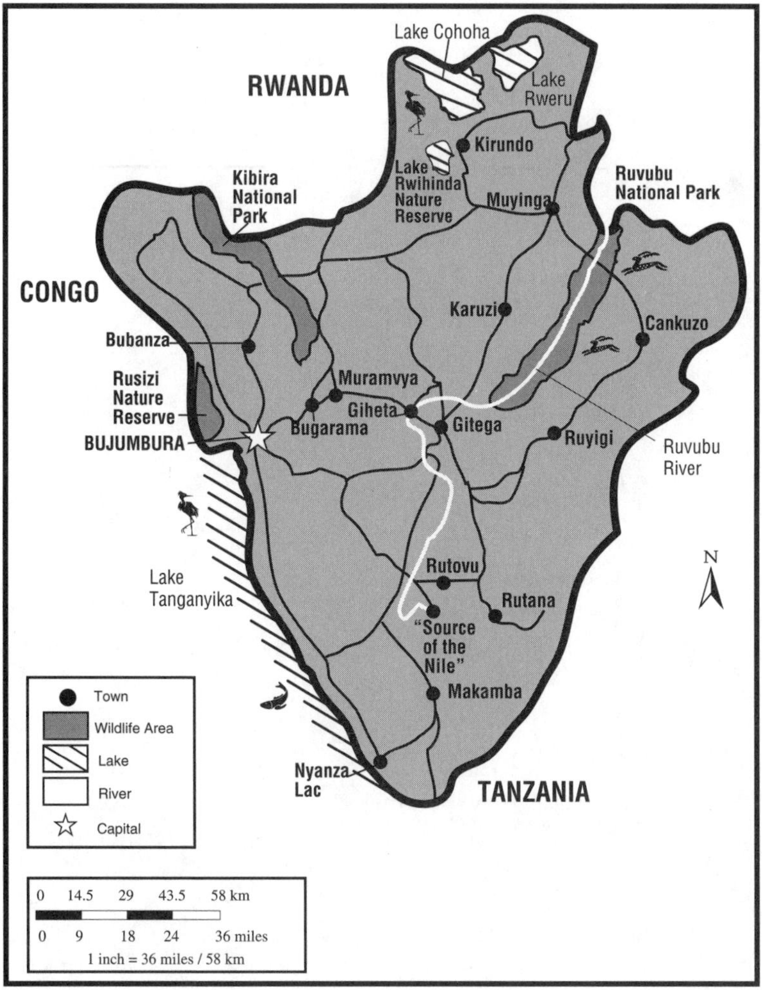

FACTS AT A GLANCE

AREA:	10,747 SQ. MI. / 27,834 SQ. KM.
APPROXIMATE SIZE:	VERMONT OR BELGIUM
POPULATION:	7 MILLION
CAPITAL:	BUJUMBURA (POP. EST. 400,000)
OFFICIAL LANGUAGE:	KIRUNDI AND FRENCH

BURUNDI

Burundi is one of the poorest and most densely populated countries in Africa. There are, however, some attractions that warrant a short visit, especially for the prolific bird life, chimpanzees and other primates.

Burundi is a hilly country with altitudes ranging from 2600 to 9000 feet (790 to 2745 m). The weather in Bujumbura and along the shores of Lake Tanganyika is warm and humid, with average temperatures ranging from 64 to 89°F (218 to 32°C); frost sometimes occurs at night in the highlands. Dry seasons are June–September and December–January; the principal rainy season is February-May.

The three major ethnic groups in the country are the Hutu, Tutsi and Twa (pygmy). Hutus are primarily farmers and comprise more than half the population; their Bantu-speaking ancestors came to Burundi over 800 years ago. The Tutsi are a pastoral tribe and comprise less than a quarter of the population; they came to the region a few hundred years after the Hutus. The pygmy (Twa), who were the original inhabitants, presently comprise less than two percent of the population.

For centuries, the region that is now Burundi had a feudal social structure headed by a king. Although Europeans explored the region as early as 1858, Burundi did not come under European administration until it became part of German West Africa in the 1890s.

In 1916, Belgian troops occupied the country and the League of Nations mandated it to Belgium as part of the Territory of Ruanda-Urundi in 1923. Ruanda-Urundi became a U.N. Trust Territory under the administration of Belgium after World War II, and in 1962 became the independent country of Burundi.

As of this writing, it is still not considered safe to travel in this country, due to the fighting between the Hutu and Tutsi tribes. Please get a current update on the situation before traveling there. The accommodations listed may or may not be open, depending on the security in the region.

French and Kirundi are the official languages, and Swahili is also spoken. At the top hotels, restaurants and shops, some English-speaking staff are usually available to assist travelers; otherwise, very little English is spoken in the country. Most of the people are Catholic.

There are only two large cities in the country — Bujumbura and Gitega. Over 90 percent of the population are subsistence farmers. Burundi's major exports include coffee, tea, cotton and food crops, with coffee providing 80–90 percent of the country's foreign exchange earnings.

WILDLIFE AND WILDLIFE AREAS

The National Institute for the Conservation of Nature (INCN) has created several parks and nature reserves. Most of the parks and reserves lack access roads, camping sites and other facilities. Hunting is forbidden throughout the country.

Burundi's premier wildlife attraction is chimpanzees, along with crested mangabeys and red colobus monkeys. Other wildlife includes buffalo, several species of antelope, hyena, serval, wildcats, monkeys, baboons, a wide variety of bird life and over 400 species of fish in Lake Tanganyika, more than almost any other body of water in the world. Hippo and crocs are present in Lake Tanganyika and the Rusizi and Ruvubu Rivers.

The combination of varying altitude and water creates a wide range of microclimates, giving rise to a great variety of flora.

RUSIZI NATURE RESERVE (RESERVE GEREE DE LA RUSIZI)

Entrances to this 35-square-mile (90-km^2) reserve are located 9–16 miles (15–23 km) northwest of Bujumbura. The park has hippo, crocs, and a variety of bird life.

KIBIRA NATIONAL PARK (PARC NATIONAL DE LA KIBIRA)

Kibira National Park and the Kibira Forest are the best areas in Burundi to look for chimpanzees, red colobus monkeys and crested mangabeys. This 155-square-mile (400-km^2) park is situated 30 miles (48 km) or more to the north and northeast of Bujumbura and has a network of over 100 miles (160 km) of tracks (poor roads).

RUVUBU NATIONAL PARK (PARC NATIONAL DE LA RUVUBU)

Ruvubu National Park is 193 square miles (500 km^2) in size and covers a strip of land from 1 to 6 miles (1.5 to 10 km) wide along both sides of the Ruvubu River in eastern Burundi. Wildlife in the Ruvubu basin and Parc National de la Ruvubu includes hippo, crocs, buffalo, leopard, antelope, monkeys and some lion. More than 425 bird species have been recorded. The closest road access to the park is 134 miles (216 km) from Bujumbura. The park has about 30 miles (50 km) of tracks. Accommodation is available in a newly erected camp.

LAKE RWIHINDA NATURE RESERVE (RESERVE NATURELLE GEREE DU LAC RWIHINDA)

The Lake Rwihinda Nature Reserve and the other lakes in the northern part of the country, located approximately 125 miles (202 km) from Bujumbura, are called the "Lakes of the Birds" and include Lakes Cohoha, Rweru, Kanzigiri and Gacamirinda; they are a bird-watcher's paradise. These lakes can be explored by canoe.

BUJUMBURA

Founded in 1896 by the Germans, Bujumbura is the capital city, major port and commercial center of Burundi. The city has excellent French and Greek restaurants. A fun restaurant and bar on Lake Tanganyika is Cercle Nautique, which also offers sailing, boating and fishing and has an abundance of hippos for entertainment. There is a public beach called

Martial Eagle

Kakaga near Club du Lac Tanganyika (beware of crocodiles and hippos).

The ethnological **Musée Vivant** has a traditional Burundian village and daily traditional drum shows. The **Parc du Reptiles** is next door. The **Musée du Géologie du Burundi** has a good fossil collection. Jane Goodall has recently opened a chimpanzee orphanage which is open to the public.

ACCOMMODATION — DELUXE: * *Novotel* has 114 air-conditioned rooms with ensuite facilities, a swimming pool, video and tennis courts. * *Méridien Source du Nil* has 117 air-conditioned rooms with ensuite facilities, a swimming pool and all the usual amenities of Méridien hotels.

FIRST CLASS: * *Club du Lac Tanganyika*, situated just outside of town on Lake Tanganyika, has a swimming pool and air-conditioned rooms with ensuite facilities.

TOURIST CLASS: * *Hotel Burundi-Palace* has 29 rooms with ensuite facilities.

INLAND

The people outside Bujumbura seldom see tourists. Try to visit a village on market day to get a feeling of daily life in Burundi.

En route to Gitega, one passes **Muramvya**, the ancient city of the king and royal capital, and an active market at **Bugarama**.

Gitega, the former colonial capital, is situated on the central plateau in the middle of the country and is the second largest city. Sights include the National Museum, fine arts school, and beer market.

The artistic center of **Giheta**, 7 miles (11 km) from Gitega, sells wood carvings, leather goods, baskets and ceramics. The southernmost possible source of the Nile is 4 miles (6 km) from the village of **Rutovu** and about 60 miles (97 km) from Gitega.

SOUTHERN AFRICA

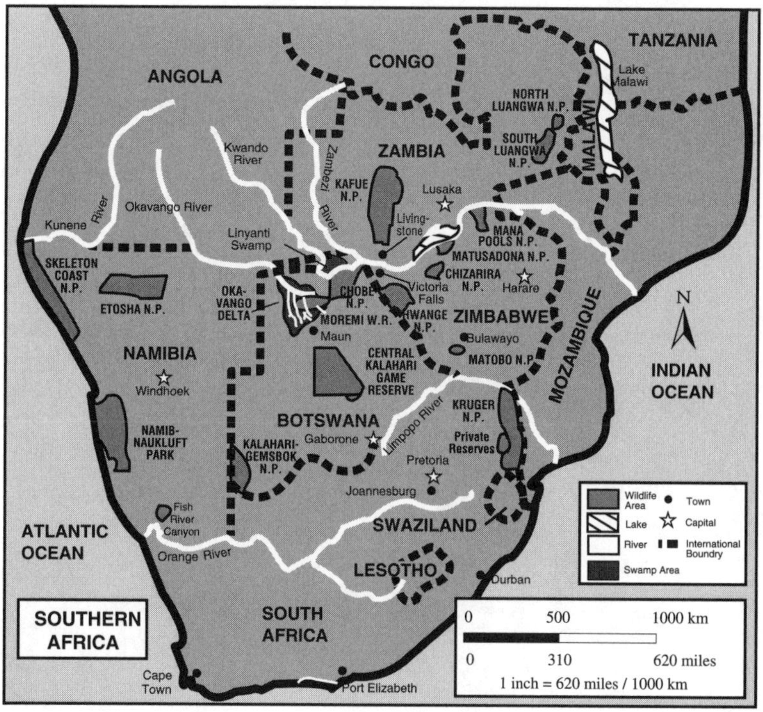

ZIMBABWE

THE ENDANGERED BLACK RHINO

This poor-sighted, bad-tempered mammal has been under intense poaching in the last few years due to the high price its hair-like horn fetches in the Yemen and Far East markets. The horn is used for dagger handles, which are a sign of wealth in Yemen, and for "medicinal" purposes in the Far East. To encourage its preservation, several programs have evolved in addition to working to lower demand.

Programs to dehorn rhinos have been conducted in some reserves to deter poaching, as the "value" of the rhino to poachers is its horn. However, there have been reports that poachers shoot the dehorned rhino as well. But since the rhinos' horns are used for defense, studies are being conducted to determine how the dehorning affects their behavior.

National parks have also employed antipoaching teams to patrol the parks, resulting in some protection to the rhino and the arrest of suspected poachers within the parks. Rhinos are creatures of habit; they return to the same drinking holes every day and can therefore be easily found by poachers.

So as not to be detected, black rhino may visit their drinking holes at night. This pattern of night drinking can interfere with their much-loved midday mud-wallow, where they will lie down in the mud to cool off.

In order to better protect the black rhino from poachers, many have been relocated into newly created IPZs (Intensive Protection Zones) within some national parks and in some private reserves which currently hold a large percentage of the existing population.

The relocation process involves tracking the animals for a distance and darting them with a sedative. Rhinos usually have the noisy red- or yellow-billed oxpeckers acting as their sentries — warning them of human approach. This makes it difficult for the darter to get close enough to shoot. Once under sedation, the rhinos are moved to their new (hopefully safer) homes.

Black rhino are exciting to track and, with luck, may be found on a morning's walk in certain reserves. Since the rhino has no natural enemy, there is no reason he should not survive if left alone by man.

ZIMBABWE

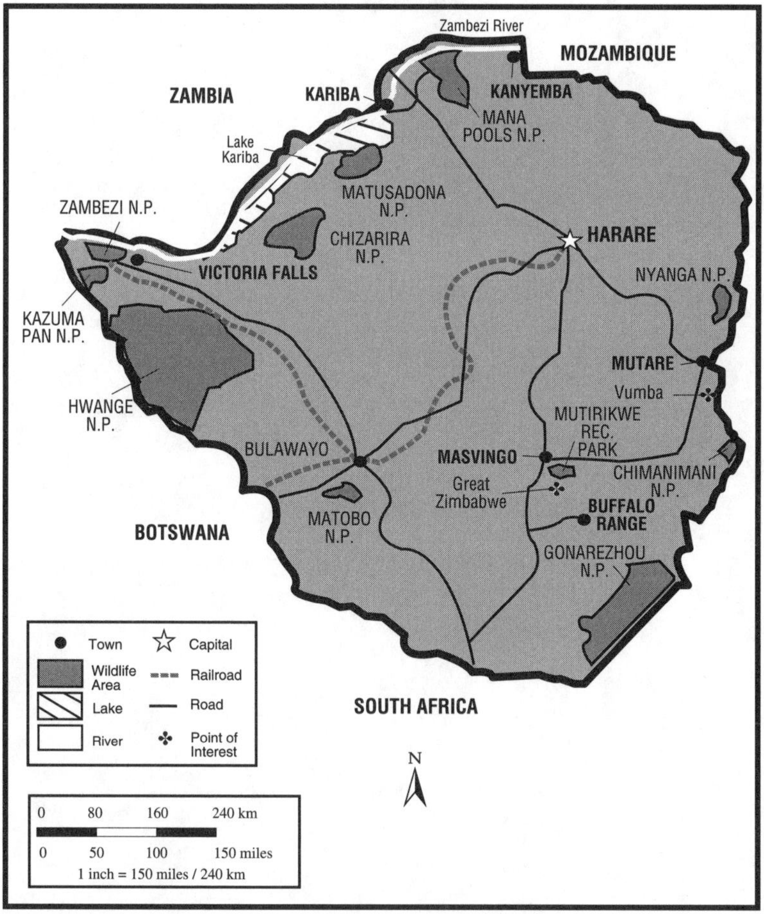

FACTS AT A GLANCE

AREA:	150,872 SQ. MI. / 390,759 SQ. KM.
APPROXIMATE SIZE:	CALIFORNIA OR ONE AND A HALF TIMES THE SIZE OF GREAT BRITAIN
POPULATION:	10.5 MILLION
CAPITAL:	HARARE (POP. EST. 1.5 MILLION)
OFFICIAL LANGUAGE:	ENGLISH
	OTHER:SHONA AND NDEBELE

ZIMBABWE

Thought by some to be the land of King Solomon's mines, Zimbabwe (previously called Rhodesia) is a country blessed with good farmland, mineral wealth, beautiful and varied landscapes, and excellent game parks.

Most of Zimbabwe consists of a central plateau 3000–4000 feet (915–1220 m) above sea level. The highveld, or high plateau, stretches from southwest to northeast from 4000 to 5000 feet (1220 to 1525 m) with a mountainous region along the eastern border from 6000 to 8000 feet (1830 to 2440 m) in altitude.

The Zambezi River runs along the northern border and the Limpopo River along the southern border. The Zambezi Valley is an extension of the Great Rift Valley. The southern edge of the Zambezi Valley is formed by the Zimbabwean Escarpment. The Zambian Escarpment, situated north of the Zambezi River, forms the northern edge of the Zambezi Valley.

The climate is moderate, and seasons are reversed from the northern hemisphere. Winter days (May–August) are generally dry and sunny with day temperatures averaging 59–68°F (15–20°C). Summer daytime temperatures average 77–86°F (25–30°C), with October being the hottest month. The rainy season is December–March.

The major ethnic groups are the Mashona and Ndebele. About 50 percent of the population is syncretic (part Christian and part traditional beliefs), 25 percent Christian, 24 percent traditional and 1 percent Hindu and Muslim. Twenty-five percent of the population lives in urban areas, with half of that 25 percent residing in the cities of Harare and nearby Chitungwiza alone. English is understood by a majority of the population.

In the first century, the region was inhabited by hunters related to the bushmen. Cecil Rhodes and the British South Africa Company took control in 1890, and the area was named Southern Rhodesia, which became a British colony in 1923. Unilateral declaration of independence from Britain was declared by Prime Minister Ian Smith and the white minority on November 11, 1965. Zimbabwe officially became independent on April 18, 1980, with Robert Mugabe as president.

Zimbabwe has one of the most widely diversified economies in Africa, consisting of industry, mining and agriculture (in which it is self-sufficient). Main foreign exchange earners are tobacco, minerals, agriculture and tourism.

WILDLIFE AND WILDLIFE AREAS

Adventurers wishing to do more than view wildlife from a vehicle should seriously consider a safari in this country. Zimbabwe offers the greatest variety of methods of wildlife viewing in Africa, including day and night game drives in open vehicles, boat game drives, walking, canoeing, kayaking and travel by houseboat.

Zimbabwe has excellent and well-maintained parks and reserves. The country's three premier reserves, which also rate among the best reserves in Africa, are Hwange, Mana Pools and Matusadona National Parks.

Hwange National Park is famous for its huge elephant population (over 25,000) and numerous large pans. Matusadona National Park, located along the southern shores of beautiful Lake Kariba, has an enormous buffalo population and a large population of elephant and other species. Mana Pools on the Zambezi River has one of the highest concentrations of wildlife of any park on the continent during the dry season.

Many of the safari camps are able to offer very personalized service because they cater to only 6 to 16 guests. Accommodations and food are excellent.

Instead of driving to the reserves, many people fly to the parks, taking advantage of scheduled daily flights connecting Kariba, Victoria Falls, Hwange, Bulawayo and Harare. There are also a number of deluxe, first-class and participation group or private mobile tented safaris available, where guests are driven from park to park or do some driving and some flying.

Game viewing is by open landrover, and walking is allowed with a licensed professional guide who carries a high-caliber rifle at all times. Night game drives are conducted in some areas adjacent to the reserves.

THE WEST

VICTORIA FALLS NATIONAL PARK

Dr. David Livingstone became the first white man to see Victoria Falls on November 16, 1855, and named them after his queen. In his journal he wrote, "Scenes so lovely must have been gazed upon by angels in flight."

Victoria Falls is approximately 5600 feet (1700 m) wide, twice the height of Niagara Falls, and one and one-half times as wide. It is divided into five separate waterfalls: Devil's Cataract, Main Falls, Horseshoe Falls, Rainbow Falls and Eastern Cataract, ranging in height from 200 to 355 feet (61 to 108 m).

Peak floodwaters usually occur around mid-April when 150 million gallons (625 million liters) per minute crash onto the rocks below, spraying water up to 1650 feet (500 m) in the air. At this time (March–April) so much water is falling that the spray makes it difficult to see the falls. May–February is actually a better time to see them, keeping in mind that they are spectacular any time of the year.

Victoria Falls and the Zambezi River form the border between Zambia and Zimbabwe. The banks of the 1675-mile- (2700-km) long Zambezi River, the fourth largest river in Africa and the only major river in Africa to flow into the Indian Ocean, are lined with thick riverine forest.

A rainbow over the falls can often be seen during the day and a lunar rainbow within a two- to four-night period over a full moon.

Fortunately, the area around the falls has not been commercialized, and there are unobstructed views from many vantage points connected by paved paths. An entry fee is required. Be prepared to get wet as you walk through a luxuriant rain forest surrounding the falls, a result of the continuous spray. A path called the Chain Walk descends from near Livingstone's statue into the gorge of the Devil's Cataract, providing an excellent vantage point.

The falls can also be viewed from Zambia. Zambian visas for day visits are generally available at the border for most nationalities. Generally speaking, the falls are more impressive on the Zimbabwean side.

The Zambezi Nature Sanctuary has crocodiles up to 14 feet (4.3 m) in length and weighing close to 1000 pounds (450 kg). The **Craft Village** in the middle of town has living quarters and other structures representing traditional Zimbabwean life of the country's major tribes, and features the best African dance show in town. **Tribal dancing** may also be seen at the Boma Restaurant at Victoria Falls Safari Lodge or at Elephant Hills Hotel. **Big Tree** is a giant baobab over 50 feet (15 m) in circumference, 65 feet (20 m) high and 1000–1500 years old.

Sundowner cruises operate above the falls, where hippo may be spotted and elephant and other wildlife may be seen coming to the shore to drink.

The "**Flight of Angels**," a flight over the falls by helicopter (best choice) or in a small plane, is highly recommended to acquire a feeling for the true majesty of the falls. Game-viewing flights upstream from the falls along the Zambezi River and over Victoria Falls National Park are also available. It is best to reserve seats in advance.

One of the world's highest commercially run **bungee jumps** is operated on the bridge crossing the Zambezi River. After falling over 300 feet (100 m), a member of the bungee staff is lowered to the jumper and connects a cable to his harness. The jumper is winched into the upright position and then winched back up onto the bridge.

Canoeing and kayaking safaris are a great way to explore the upper Zambezi from near Kazungula to just above Victoria Falls. Adventurers pass numerous hippo, crocs, elephant and other wildlife as they paddle two-man kayaks or canoes on safaris ranging from a half-day to four days in length. No previous kayaking or canoeing experience is necessary. Accommodation is in tents with separate bush shower and toilet facilities.

Half-day, full-day and overnight **horseback safaris** around the Victoria Falls area are an interesting way to view game. Morning and afternoon **elephant back safaris** (African elephants) are offered on a wildlife estate 15 miles (25 km) from Victoria Falls.

White-Water Rafting

The upper Zambezi River offers one of the most exciting (if not *the* most exciting) **white-water rafting** trips in the world. Numerous fifth-class rapids (the highest class runable) make this one of the most challenging rivers on earth.

One-, two-, three- and seven-day trips are operated on the Zambezi River below Victoria Falls from the Zambian and/or Zimbabwean side of the Zambezi River. No experience is required; just hang on and enjoy the ride!

The one-day trip is rated as the wildest commercially run one-day trip in the world. For many travelers, this trip is a highlight of their safari.

"Flight of the Angels" over Victoria Falls.

Around 8:30 a.m. rafters walk down into the gorge to the river's edge where the rafting safari begins. Rafts with up to eight paddlers, or up to eight riders and one oarsperson, disappear from sight as they drop into deep holes and crash into waves over 12 feet (3.5 m) high, being further dwarfed by sheer cliffs which often rise hundreds of feet on both sides of the canyon.

Each group is usually accompanied by a professional kayaker who helps "rescue" those who have fallen out of the rafts.

At the end of the trip, rafters have to climb back out of the gorge to the top of the escarpment, about 700 feet (213 m) above. For most people, this is the most difficult part of the excursion.

For the one-day trip I would suggest you wear a swimsuit and take a hat, sunglasses with something to tie them onto yourself, a short-sleeve shirt, sunscreen and tennis shoes (tackies) or Tevas (a type of sandal). For longer trips, obtain a checklist from your tour operator.

One-day trips are offered year-round. Longer rafting safaris (two to seven days) are usually run August–December. Rafters must be 16 years of age or older to participate.

Victoria Falls Safari Lodge.

Hippo and crocs are seen from the second day onward on multiday trips. Klipspringer and other wildlife can be seen on the banks, especially during the dry season. Camp is made on sandy riverbanks, and all meals are prepared by the staff. These multiday trips are not for those who wish to be pampered. There are no facilities en route.

Plans are under way to build a dam to relieve some pressure off the Kariba Dam downstream. Such a dam would flood the gorge and make these river trips a thing of the past. Go now while there are still rapids to run!

ACCOMMODATION: The *Victoria Falls Hotel, Makasa Sun* and *Ilala* have the advantage of being located nearest to the falls. As the falls area has become quite noisy with helicopter and small aircraft flying overhead during daylight hours, the other properties listed have the advantage of being in more peaceful settings.

DELUXE: * *Victoria Falls Hotel* has maintained much of its colonial elegance with its colonial architecture, spacious terraces and colorful gardens, and is only a ten-minute walk from the falls. The hotel has recently undergone a massive renovation project and is looking superb, with 188 air-conditioned rooms and suites with ensuite facilities, swimming pool, tennis courts and conference facilities. From the hotel you can see the bridge and the Zambezi gorge. * *Victoria Falls Safari Lodge,* located a five minute drive from the falls, has 72 stylishly decorated air-conditioned rooms and suites with ensuite facilities and a swimming pool. The lodge is built under thatch and overlooks a floodlit water hole where wildlife may be seen coming to drink. A complementary hourly shuttle service is available to Victoria Falls town.* *Elephant Hills Intercontinental* overlooks the Zambezi River a few miles upstream from Victoria Falls. The hotel has 276 rooms and suites with facilities ensuite, an exotic swimming pool, squash courts, tennis courts, an 18-hole championship golf course, casino, three restaurants and a conference center.

FIRST CLASS: * *Ilala Lodge,* a small 32-room thatched lodge with ensuite facilities and a swimming pool, is located close to the falls. * *Makasa Sun Hotel* is situated adjacent to the Victoria Falls Hotel, with 97 air-conditioned rooms and suites with ensuite facilities and a casino, swimming pool and tennis courts.

TOURIST CLASS: * *Sprayview Hotel* is a newly renovated budget hotel with rooms with ensuite facilities located a little more than a mile (2 km) from the falls. * *Rainbow Hotel* is located near Victoria Falls village and has 48 air-conditioned rooms with private facilities and a swimming pool. * The *A'Zambezi River Lodge,* one of the largest buildings under traditional thatch on the continent, is located 1.5 miles (2.5 km) from town on the banks of the Zambezi River. The lodge has a swimming pool and 83 air-conditioned rooms with ensuite facilities.

CLASS F & CAMPING: * *Victoria Falls Rest and Caravan Park* has small hostel, camping and caravan sites.

ACCOMMODATION NEAR VICTORIA FALLS — CLASS A: * *Elephant Camp,* located on a private wildlife estate 15 miles (25 km) from Victoria Falls, offers morning and afternoon elephant back riding (African elephants) and game drives. A maximum of eight guests are accommodated in four thatched cottages with ensuite facilities. **Sekuti's Drift* is a colonial-style ten-room lodge situated on top of a hill 9 miles (15 km) from Victoria Falls. * *Masuwe Lodge* is a 20-bed tented lodge located 4 miles (7 km) from Victoria Falls on a private game concession which adjoins Zambezi National Park. * *Matetsi Safari Camp* and * *Matetsi Water Lodge* are situated on a private game reserve about a 45-minute drive from Victoria Falls. Matetsi Water Lodge has three riverside camps, each with six air-conditioned ensuite rooms and a private splash pool. Matetsi Safari Camp consists of a tented camp with 12 air-conditioned luxury tents. Day and night game drives, walks, boat cruises and canoeing are offered. * *Imbabala Camp,* located on private land on the banks of the Zambezi River only a mile (2 km) from the Botswana border, has nine chalets (doubles) with ensuite facilities and a swimming pool. Day and night game drives by vehicle, boat game drives and fishing are offered.

CLASS A/B: **Gorges Lodge,* located 15 miles (24 km) from Victoria Falls, overlooks the Zambezi Gorge and has six single- and four double-story rooms with ensuite facilities and a swimming pool.

CLASS D: See "Zambezi National Park."

ZAMBEZI NATIONAL PARK

Victoria Falls National Park includes Victoria Falls as well as 216-square-mile (560-km^2) Zambezi National Park. The park is located west of the falls and extends for 25 miles (40 km) along the Zambezi River.

Zambezi National Park is well known for its abundance of sable antelope. Among other species are elephant, zebra, eland, buffalo, giraffe, lion, kudu and waterbuck.

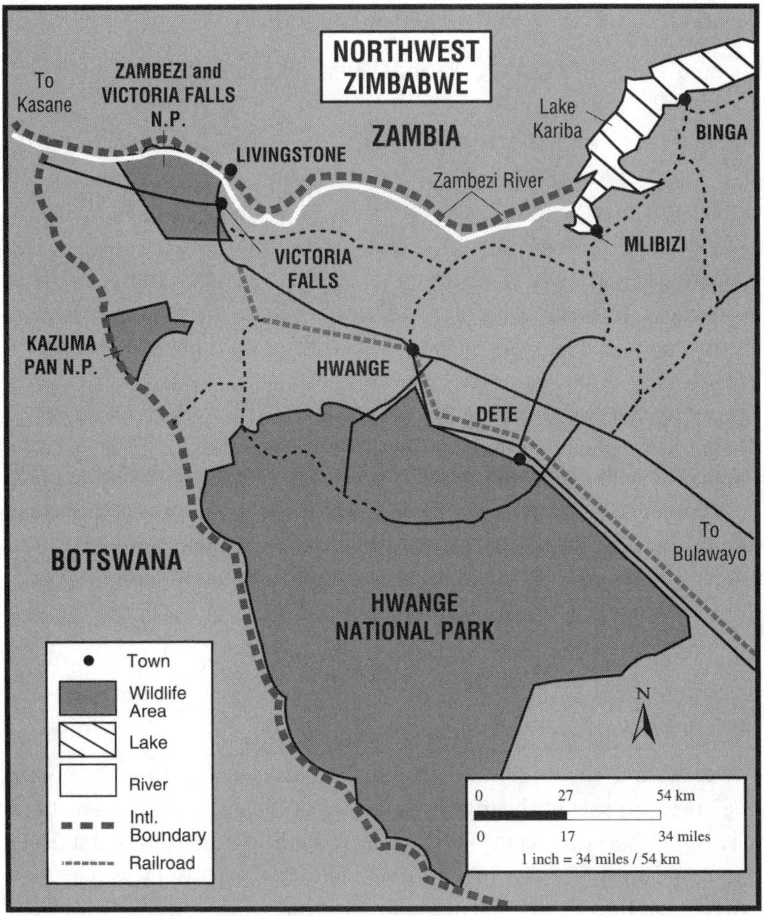

Day game drives, walks, canoeing and kayaking are offered from Victoria Falls. Fishing for tigerfish, tilapia and giant vundu (giant catfish) is very good. There are 30 sites along the river for picnicking and fishing (beware of crocodiles). Since the game reserve does not have all-weather roads, parts of it are usually closed during the rains from November 1 to May 1.

ACCOMMODATION — CLASS D: * *Zambezi National Park Lodges,* scenically situated on the banks of the Zambezi, consist of 15 self-service lodges, each catering to a maximum of six people.

KAZUMA PAN NATIONAL PARK

Located north of Hwange National Park in the Matetsi Safari Area, Kazuma Pan National Park is a small park (121 square miles/313 km^2) that has a series of pans that flood in the rainy season. The eastern part of the park is wooded, with more water and a greater variety and concentration of wildlife than the western side of the park, which is predominantly grasslands. Lion and cheetah may be seen. The park is open to campers who are self-contained. Walking is allowed with a professionally licensed guide. As there are no facilities, visitors generally stay in mobile tented camps with their own private guides.

HWANGE NATIONAL PARK

Hwange (previously called Wankie), Zimbabwe's largest national park, is famous for its large herds of elephant. Other predominant species include buffalo, giraffe, zebra, wildebeest, lion, wild dog and bat-eared fox. This is one of the best parks on the continent to see sable antelope.

Hwange is slightly larger than the state of Connecticut, covering 5656 square miles (14,651 km^2). The park is located in the northwest corner of the country just west of the main road between Bulawayo and Victoria Falls. Hwange boasts over 100 species of mammals and 400 species of birds.

The park ranges from semidesert in the south to a plateau in the north. The northern part of Hwange is mudstone and basalt, and the southern part is Kalahari sand veld. The park has an average altitude of 3300 feet (1000 m). Winter nights can drop to below freezing, and summer days can be over 100°F (38°C), while average temperatures range from 65 to 83°F (18 to 28°C).

There are no rivers and only a few streams in the north of the park, but boreholes (wells) provide sources of water year-round for wildlife. During the dry season, these permanent water holes (pans) provide an excellent stage for guests to view wildlife performing day-to-day scenes of survival.

Generally, there are no seasonal animal migrations. The best time to see wildlife is during the dry season, from July to October, when the game concentrates near permanent water. Game viewing is good in May, June and November, and fair December through April. During the rainy season from January to March, game is widely dispersed in the mopane woodland.

The wilderness area of Hwange in the southeastern part of the park is excellent for seeing a great variety of game and is much less crowded than the "Main Camp" area.

Wildlife commonly seen include elephant, giraffe, zebra, greater kudu, impala, buffalo, sable antelope, wildebeest, tsessebe, black-backed jackal, lion and hyena. On a recent visit in May, we saw sable antelope, lion, giraffe, hyena, buffalo, elephant, wildebeest, zebra and about a dozen bat-eared fox. On another visit we saw a very large full-maned male lion guarding a buffalo kill while a jackal darted in and out, snatching morsels as dozens of vultures waited their turn.

Another time we sat in a tree hide by a water hole and watched over 30 giraffe come to drink. From a ground-level hide we watched as a herd of over 70 eland passed within 65 feet (30 m) and 10 buffalo came within 30 feet (9 m) of us.

Moonlight game viewing occurs from one or two nights before and after a full moon, when park staff escort guests to the Nyamandhlovu (meaning "meat of the elephant") Platform near Main Camp. Morning walks with a national park game scout may be available. Camps that have professional guides on staff may also offer walks in certain regions of the park.

The area around Sinamatella Camp in the northern part of the park is good for spotting kudu, elephant, giraffe, impala, hippo, klipspringer, warthog, lion, hyena and leopard. The Bumbusi Ruins, the third largest ancient stone buildings in Zimbabwe, are located behind Bumbusi Camp, 15 miles (24 km) northwest of Sinamatella Camp.

The northwestern part of the park near Robins Camp has a large lion population. Other species often seen include impala (which attract the lion), buffalo, kudu, sable antelope, roan antelope, waterbuck, elephant, giraffe, reedbuck, tsessebe, lion, side-striped jackal, cheetah and hyena.

Hwange has 300 miles (480 km) of roads, some of which are closed during the rainy season. All-weather roads run through most of the park. Some roads near the main camp are tarmac, which detracts a bit from the feeling of being in the bush.

Vehicles must keep to the roads, and visitors are not allowed to leave their vehicles unless escorted by a licensed professional guide, or at hides, game-viewing platforms or at fenced-in picnic sites. Open vehicles are allowed for licensed tour operators only.

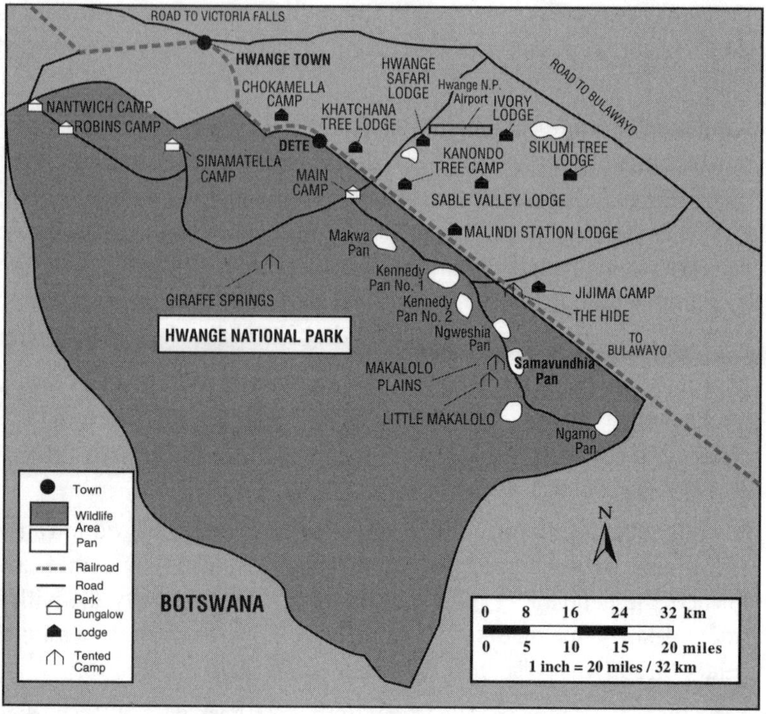

Airstrips for small aircraft are available at Makalolo, Giraffe Springs and at Main Camp; large and small aircraft may land at Hwange Airport. The closest rail station is Dete Station, 15 miles (24 km) from Main Camp.

Luxury, first-class and participation mobile tented camp safaris to the northern part of the park are also available.

ACCOMMODATIONS: *Makalolo Plains* and *Little Makalolo* are located in one exclusive area deep within the park, a 15-minute flight from Hwange airport. Only guests of these two camps are allowed in this region of the park. *Giraffe Springs Camp* is also located in another exclusive area. The *Hide* and *Jijima Camp* are located on private reserves; guests enter the park through the Kennedy Pan entrance. *Sable Valley Lodge, Sikumi Tree Lodge, Khatshana Tree Lodge, Ivory Lodge* and *Hwange Safari Lodge* are all located in 60,000-acre (24,000-hectare) Dete Vlei (private reserve) bordering Hwange National

Makalolo Plains Camp.

Park, a 30–60-minute drive from Hwange National Park; guests of these camps and *Kanondo Tree Camp* enter the park through the Main Gate.

CLASS A: * *Makalolo Plains Tented Camp* and * *Little Makalolo* (Class A/B) are situated in the Makalolo Wilderness Area, a remote region of the park in which only guests of these camps are allowed, guaranteeing exclusivity. * *Makalolo Plains* has luxury tents (16 beds) with ensuite facilities, set on raised wooden platforms, and a plunge pool. * *Little Makalolo* has five luxury tents (ten beds) with ensuite facilities. The camps offer day game drives and walks. * *Giraffe Springs Camp*, located in its own private concession area within the park, has eight luxury tents with ensuite facilities and a swimming pool. * *The Hide* is a 16-bed luxury tented camp only a ten-minute drive from the Kennedy Pan entrance to the park. The large "Manyara" tents have ensuite facilities and the camp overlooks a water hole. Day game drives are offered in the park; walks and night drives are offered on the private concession. * *Jijima Camp* is a luxury tented camp (16 beds) with ensuite facilities situated on a private reserve about a 35-minute drive from the Kennedy Pan entrance to the park.

CLASS A/B: * *Sable Valley Lodge* overlooks a water hole and accommodates up to 30 guests in luxury thatched lodges with ensuite facilities. Day game drives and walks are offered. * *Sikumi Tree Lodge* has

14 thatched tree houses (42 beds) set in acacia trees, all with private facilities, and a swimming pool. Activities include day game drives and walks. * *Khatshana Tree Lodge* has six tree houses with ensuite facilities, overlooking a water hole.

CLASS B: * *Kanondo Tree Camp* accommodates a maximum of 12 guests in tree houses with ensuite facilities. * *Malindi Station Lodge* is set on a private estate adjacent to the park. Accommodations consist of three vintage train carriages (11 beds) and a plunge pool. * *Detema Lodge* has nine tree houses and four family rooms with ensuite facilities and a swimming pool. Day and night game drives and walks are offered. * *Ivory Lodge,* located an hour's drive from the park, consists of ten tree houses with ensuite facilities and a swimming pool. * *Chokamella Camp* has ten brick chalets under thatch with private facilities and a small swimming pool. * *Hwange Safari Lodge* has 100 double rooms with private facilities and a swimming pool, conference center and elevated game-viewing platform with a bar.

CLASS D, F & CAMPING: There are seven National Park camps — *Main Camp, Sinamatella Camp, Robins Camp, Bumbusi Camp, Lukosi Camp, Deka Camp* and *Nantwich Camp* — all of which have lodge accommodation. Some rooms have ensuite facilities. Ablution blocks are available for campers and for people in rooms without ensuite facilities.

THE NORTH

KARIBA (TOWN)

Kariba is the major gateway to both Matusadona and Mana Pools National Parks. Many people fly here from Harare, Victoria Falls or Hwange and are then transferred by aircraft, boat or vehicle to their respective camps. This is a good place to meet Zimbabweans on vacation.

Kariba Dam, one of the largest in Africa, is a short distance from town. Water sports (beware of crocodile and hippo) and cruises on the lake are available.

ACCOMMODATION — FIRST CLASS: * *Caribbea Bay Resort*, located on the shores of Lake Kariba, is a Sardinian-style resort with 81 rooms (some air-conditioned) with ensuite facilities, two swimming pools, a popular poolside bar and a casino.

ACCOMMODATION — TOURIST CLASS: * *Cutty Sark Hotel* has 65 air-conditioned rooms with facilities ensuite and a swimming pool. * *Lakeview Inn* has 30 air-conditioned rooms with ensuite facilities and a swimming pool overlooking Lake Kariba. * *Kariba Breezes Hotel* has air-conditioned rooms with ensuite facilities and a swimming pool and marina.

CAMPING: * *M.O.T.H. Campsite* is located just below the Lakeview Inn.

LAKE KARIBA

Sunsets over the waters of island-dotted Lake Kariba are rated among the most spectacular in the world. One of the largest man-made lakes on earth, covering over 1970 square miles (5100 km^2), it, was formed in 1958 by damming the Zambezi River. The lake is 175 miles (280 km) long and up to 20 miles (32 km) in width and is surrounded, for the most part, by untouched wilderness.

When the dam was completed and the waters in the valley began to rise, animals were forced to higher ground, which quickly became islands soon to be submerged under the new lake. To save these helpless animals, Operation Noah was organized by Rupert Fothergill. Over 5000 animals, including 35 different mammal species, numerous elephant and 44 black rhino, were rescued and released in what are now Matusadona National Park and the Chete Safari Area.

Lights from commercial kapenta fishing boats are often seen on the lake at night. Fishing is excellent for tigerfish, giant vundu, bream, chessa and nkupi. October is the optimum month for tigerfishing and November–April for bream. Bird life, especially waterfowl, is prolific.

Sunset on Lake Kariba–nesting darters and cormorants

The Lake Kariba Ferry usually takes 22 hours to cruise from Mlibizi to Kariba Town. If you are thinking of taking a vehicle through Zimbabwe from Victoria Falls to Kariba, this ferry will save you over 775 miles (1250 km) of driving.

MATUSADONA NATIONAL PARK

Situated on the southern shore of Lake Kariba and bounded on the east by the dramatic Sanyati Gorge and the west by the Umi River, this scenic 543-square-mile (1407-km^2) park has an abundance of elephant, lion, kudu, impala and buffalo — especially along the shoreline in the dry season (May–October). Other game includes sable antelope, roan antelope and waterbuck. Cheetah have been recently introduced into the area. Black rhino may be seen on walks, and leopard are occasionally spotted.

Game viewing by boat near shore is a real attraction, and walking safaris are popular. Fishing is excellent, but beware of crocodiles. Private mobile tented safaris with professional guides are another great way to experience the bush. Motor yachts complete with captain, staff and professional guide provide private parties great freedom and comfort in exploring the region.

A private mobile tented camp can be your base from which to walk in Matusadona.

Walking Safaris

Three-day first-class walking safaris along the Matusadona foreshore offer a great adventure in a remote area of the park.

Up to seven guests along with their armed, professional guide begin walking from camp in the early morning, often arriving at their next camp in time for lunch. Afternoons are spent walking in the region or game viewing by open vehicle. Some of the routes traversed are along game corridors with a great abundance of wildlife.

Accommodations are in stand-up size, insect-proof tents with comfortable beds and one or two separate bush shower and bush toilet tents for the group, depending on the group size. The camp is full service; everything is taken care of by the cook and camp attendants. As the trip is landrover backed, you carry only a water bottle and your camera on your walks.

ACCOMMODATION — CLASS A: * *Matusadona Water Lodge*, located in a secluded area of the lake within the park, has four floating houseboats (eight beds) with facilities ensuite, moored near the central dining houseboat. Game walks, canoeing, vehicle game drives and sunset boat cruises are offered. * *Water Wilderness*, situated

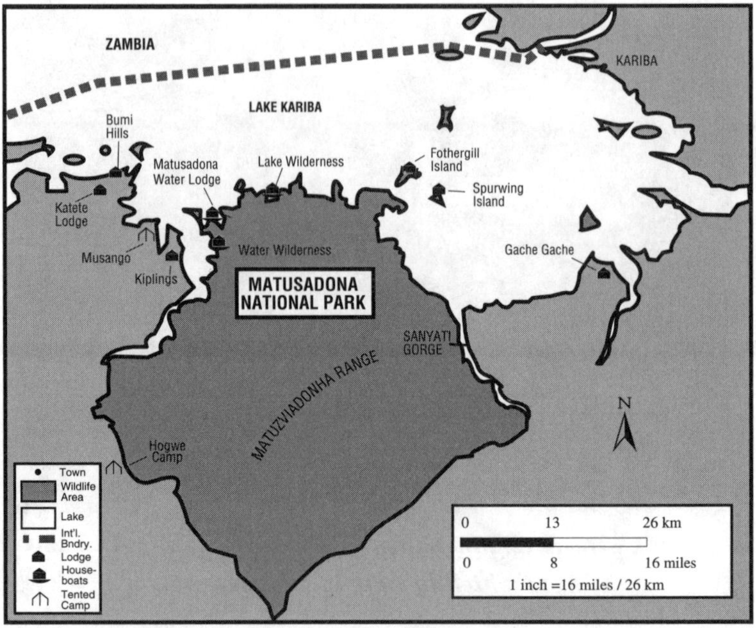

in an isolated area of the lake within the park, consists of four houseboats (eight beds) with ensuite facilities, moored near the dining houseboat. Game drives by boat and morning walks are conducted. * *Musango* is a 12-bed tented camp with ensuite facilities. Walks, vehicle and boat game drives, and canoeing are offered. * *Kiplings Lodge*, located at the mouth of the Ume River on the lake, has ten rooms with ensuite facilities and a plunge pool. Day game drives, walks, canoeing, boat game drives and fishing are offered. * *Katete Lodge*, set on a hill west of the park, has 17 rooms with ensuite facilities and a swimming pool. Day and night vehicle game drives in a private wilderness area, boat game drives, walks and village visits are offered. * *Bumi Hills Lodge*, located on the western outskirts of the park on a hill overlooking the lake, has 20 well-appointed luxury rooms with ensuite facilities and a swimming pool. Walks, day and night game drives by vehicle in a private wilderness area, game drives by boat, fishing and village visits are offered.

Matusadona Water Lodge.

CLASS A/B: * *Fothergill Island Safari Camp* has 15 A-frame thatched lodges (32 beds) with facilities ensuite and a swimming pool. Game viewing on foot, by boat and by vehicle as well as fishing are offered. Due to the fluctuating water level of Lake Kariba, Fothergill is usually connected to the mainland by a peninsula. * *Gache Gache*, situated on Lake Kariba an hour east of Matusadona by boat, has 10 thatched lodges (20 beds) with ensuite facilities and a swimming pool. Game drives by boat and vehicle as well as walks in a private wilderness area are offered.

CLASS B: * *Hogwe*, situated west of the park in the Matusadona Mountains, caters to a maximum of seven guests in tents with adjacent private bush shower and flush toilets. Walking, especially tracking rhino, is the main activity. Limited game drives and visits to remote villages are offered. * *Kiangwe Tented Camp* is a six-bed camp located at the tip of Spurwing Island, with ensuite flush toilets and bush showers. Walks and vehicle and boat game drives are offered. * *Spurwing Island* is a 40-bed camp with tents, cabins and thatched chalets with private facilities and a swimming pool. Walks, game drives by vehicle and by boat, and fishing are offered.

CLASS C: * *Lake Wilderness* has two houseboats with shared facilities, accommodating up to eight guests each, and a few smaller houseboats (doubles). Walks and game viewing by both boat and vehicle are offered.

CLASS D: The National Park has three self-service camps — *Ume, Mbalabala* and *Muuyu*; each camp may be booked by one party only.

CAMPING: The two National Park Campsites, *Tashinga* and *Sanyati*, have ablution blocks.

MANA POOLS NATIONAL PARK

During the dry season, Mana Pools National Park has one of the highest concentrations of wildlife on the continent. The park is situated on the southern side of the Lower Zambezi River downstream (northeast) of Lake Kariba.

This 845-square-mile (2190-km^2) park is uniquely characterized by fertile river terraces reaching from the slow-moving Zambezi River inland for several miles. Small ponds and pools such as Chine Pools and Long Pool were formed as the river's course slowly drifted northward. Reeds, sandbanks and huge mahogany and acacia trees near the river give way to dense mopane woodland to the park's southern boundary along the steep Zambezi Escarpment.

Mana Pools National Park covers part of the Middle Zambezi Valley, which is home for 12,000 elephant and 16,000 buffalo (with herds of over 500 each).

Species commonly seen in the park include elephant, buffalo, waterbuck, kudu, zebra, eland, impala, bushbuck, lion and crocodile. Large pods of hippo are often seen lying on the sandbanks soaking up the morning sun. Occasionally spotted are wild dog, leopard, jackal, hyena and the rare nyala. Large varieties of both woodland and water birds are present.

Canoe Safaris

For the adventurous traveler, this is one of the best ways to experience the African bush and is one of my favorite safaris on the entire continent. In fact, a canoe safari along Mana Pools National Park is *the* highlight for almost everyone who does a canoe trip as part of their safari.

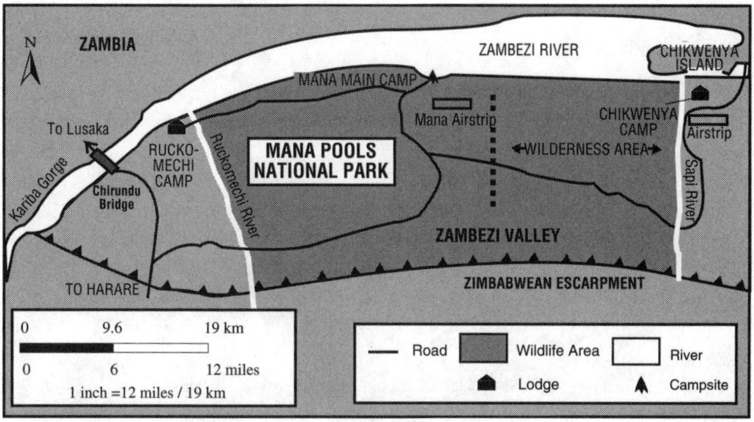

Traveling silently by canoe, you can paddle closely to wildlife which has come to drink along the shore. Most importantly, *you* actively participate in the adventure!

Canoe safaris are available, lasting from three to nine days, covering different stretches of the river and operated from Kariba Dam downstream for up to 159 miles (255 km) past Mana Pools National Park to Kanyemba near the Mozambique border. Only one canoe group of a maximum of seven to nine guests is generally allowed on any stretch of the river at one time.

The river is divided into four canoeing segments: (1) from below Kariba Dam through the Kariba Gorge to Chirundu, (2) from Chirundu to the border of Mana Pools, (3) along Mana Pools National Park and (4) downstream (east) of the park through the rugged Mupata Gorge to Kanyemba. The section along Mana Pools National Park is the best section for wildlife viewing. In addition, no motorized boats are allowed on the Zimbabwe side of this stretch of the river, making it all the more attractive.

Two different "levels" of canoe safaris are available:

(1) Budget (participation) canoe safaris do not have a support vehicle on land. Camping is often done on islands in the Zambezi where there are no facilities. Participants sleep in sleeping bags in small pup tents or under mosquito nets, and everyone pitches their own tents and helps with the chores. Walking inland is limited to 50 m (yards) from the riverbank.

(2) First-class (full-service) canoe safaris are led by a professional guide licensed to escort you on walks. These safaris have a cook and camp

First class canoe safari experience.

attendants taking care of all the chores, allowing guests to spend all their time exploring the area and enjoying the bush. This is by far the best option as it allows you to canoe, go on game drives by vehicle and walk. Guests are accommodated in comfortable tents (large enough in which to stand) with cots with mattresses, sheets and blankets. Bush shower tents and toilet tents are set up for the group.

On the second day of a recent first-class canoe safari, we pulled onto the riverbank for lunch. As we started walking up the bank, we were greeted by a young bull elephant coming down for a drink. He trumpeted, kicked dirt and shook his head a number of times before he backed off enough to let us by.

Later, as we were having lunch, another bull elephant paid us a visit, approaching within 15 feet (4.5 m) of us. That's close when the elephant is almost 10 feet (3 m) in height at the shoulder! As we were about to return to the canoes, the bull elephant that had almost kept us from coming ashore earlier apparently decided he wanted a mud bath, and completely covered our canoes with mud in the process. Our guide approached him from the riverbank above to try to persuade him to leave, and the elephant responded by using the tip of his trunk to throw a large blob of mud, just missing our guide by inches!

On a previous canoe safari along Mana Pools, I came the closest I have ever come to elephant. As we canoed past two large bull elephant walking along the river's edge, our guide instructed us to pull into shore about 50 yards (50 m)downstream of them. The larger of the elephants continued walking toward us, eating apple ring acacia (*Acacia albida*) pods that had fallen from trees along the river.

Our guide and I crouched silently behind our canoe, with the rest of the group doing the same behind us. The elephant came closer and closer and closer — until he was not more than *six feet (2m)* from us. One step more and he would have stepped into the canoe. What a thrill! Eventually, after having a drink, he turned around and walked back down the shoreline from whence he came.

Several times we saw elephant swimming from the mainland to islands in the Zambezi in search of food. We also saw hundreds of hippo, buffalo, waterbuck and impala and countless elephant, crocodile, lion and many other species.

On another canoe safari, a huge elephant walked out into the river in front of us and completely submerged with the exception of its trunk waving in the air. When it came up, we were almost on top of it, and we paddled madly to get out of the way. When the elephant finally noticed us, it trumpeted loudly and began moving through the water toward us. Fortunately, he stopped after a few steps, and the mighty Zambezi moved us quickly downstream out of danger. What fun!

Although these canoe safaris are by no means marathons, participants must paddle their own canoes, which allows them to be more involved in the adventure. Your guide will instruct you on safety precautions to use on your canoe safari. Previous canoe experience is not necessary. However, spending at least a few hours in a canoe before your African safari will allow you to feel more comfortable canoeing in a foreign environment.

Walking Safaris

The eastern part of Mana Pools has been designated a wilderness area in which only walking and canoeing along its shores are allowed. There are no roads or other signs of man.

Recently we joined a three-night/four-day walking safari (full service) escorted by a professional licensed guide through the rich Mana Pools floodplains along the Zambezi River — an area teeming with wildlife. We encountered no one else during the entire four days. The only humans we saw were canoeists off in the distance paddling down the Zambezi River.

On the first day, we encountered a bull elephant that decided to mock charge us not once — but twice! On the first charge, it stopped about 30 feet (9 m) from us, and on the second charge — about 15 feet (4.5 m). Keep in mind that as long as you do what your guide says, there is little danger — only a big rush of adrenaline!

Shortly after the charge, we reached camp. Later, under a full moon, the same elephant approached our camp, and we walked out to meet it. The elephant trumpeted, then gave us a mock charge in the moonlight!

On the last day of the safari, we encountered so many breeding herds (females with their young) of elephant that we had to continuously backtrack and look for alternative paths between them in order to get to our pickup point.

As it was late in the dry season and food was scarce, most of the large elephant herds had broken into several small ones. Our guide climbed several termite mounds, scouting out the area. We even found ourselves walking through "adrenaline grass" — thick golden grass often over seven feet in height that is so thick you would almost bump into a buffalo or elephant before seeing it.

Events like this are why walking safaris, and safaris in general, are so popular — you never know what is going to happen next!

Walking safaris like this one may sound a bit risky. They are, however, quite safe — as long as the safari is conducted by a fully licensed professional guide. Just use common sense and enjoy the adventure.

The best time to visit the park for one of the finest exhibitions of wildlife on the continent is at the end of the dry season (August–October) when large numbers of elephant, buffalo, waterbuck and impala come to the river to drink and graze on the lush grasses along its banks. Game viewing is also very good in June–July. During the rainy season, most large land mammals move away from the river toward the escarpment.

As many roads within the park are closed during the rainy season from early November until the end of April, the camps are also closed during that period. Charter flights operate to two airstrips in the park. Petrol is not available in the park, and power boats are not allowed. Four-wheel-drive vehicles are recommended in the dry season and necessary in the rainy season.

ACCOMMODATION — CLASS A: * *Chikwenya Camp* is situated on the Zambezi River just outside the eastern border of the park. The camp has 8 thatched lodges (16 beds) with ensuite facilities and offers walking and game viewing by vehicle and by boat. * *Ruckomechi Camp,* just outside the western boundary of the park, has 10 comfortable chalets (20 beds) with ensuite facilities. Game drives, walks and canoeing are offered.

CLASS D & F: National Parks accommodations include *Musangu Lodge, Muchichiri Lodge* and *Vundu Camp*.

CAMPING: * *Nyamepi Camp* has 29 caravan/camping sites and ablution blocks with hot and cold water. The exclusive camps, which are limited to one group at a time, are *Mucheni Camp, Nkupe Camp, Ndungu Camp* and *Gwaya (Old Tree Lodge) Camp*.

CHIZARIRA NATIONAL PARK

This remote undeveloped park is situated on the Zambezi Escarpment overlooking the Zambezi Valley and the southern part of Lake Kariba. Chizarira covers 737 square miles (1910 km^2) of wild, untouched bush with plateaus, deep gorges, thick woodlands and riverbeds.

Chizarira is a park for the adventurer more interested in experiencing the wilderness than in seeing huge herds of animals. Walking is allowed if accompanied by a fully licensed guide; this is the best way to explore the park.

The best view of Lake Kariba and the Zambezi Valley is from Mucheni View Point. Roads are rough; a four-wheel-drive vehicle is recommended year-round and is necessary in the rainy season. Petrol is not available in the park. The park is a day's drive from Matusadona National Park. Easiest access is by charter aircraft.

ACCOMMODATION — CLASS A/B: * *Jedson's Camp,* a tented camp (12 beds) with ensuite facilities and a swimming pool, is located adjacent to the park. Game drives and walks are offered. * *Chizarira Lodge* has 8 thatched chalets (16 beds) with ensuite facilities and a swimming pool. Activities include game drives, walks and overnight walking trails.

CLASS F & CAMPING: There are three exclusive national park campsites, *Kasiswi Bush Camp, Mobola Bush Camp,* and *Busi Bush Camp*. Each limited to one party (maximum 12 persons).

HARARE

Formerly called Salisbury, Harare is the capital and largest city. It is one of the cleanest and most modern cities on the continent. Points of interest include the National Art Gallery, Botanical Garden, Houses of Parliament and the Tobacco Auction Floors (the largest in the world). Mbare Msike Market is good for shopping for curios from local vendors.

Harare is an excellent place to shop for Shona carvings made of wood and soapstone, silverwork and paintings.

A beautiful park adjacent to the Intercontinental Hotel features a large variety of brilliant flora. Harare Botanical Gardens has indigenous trees and herbs.

Harare's best restaurants include Tiffany's, L'Escargot, The Bagatelle, 22 Victoria Street, La Chandelle, Wombles, La Francais and The Bamboo Inn. Both Barker's Lodge and Imba Matombo Lodge have restaurants that are open to the public and serve excellent food.

A short drive from Harare are the Larvon Bird Gardens, Ewanrigg Botanical Gardens and Lake Chivero (McIlwaine) Game Park. In addition to being well stocked with wildlife, Imire Game Park has an animal orphanage and bushmen paintings on the property.

ACCOMMODATION — DELUXE: * *Barkers Lodge,* located 15 minutes from Harare in the suburb of Kambanji, has eight rooms with ensuite facilities, satellite television and a swimming pool, tennis court and excellent restaurant. * *Imba Matombo,* located a 15-minute drive from Harare in the suburb of Glen Lorne, accommodates guests in rooms in a large home and chalets (20 beds total) with ensuite facilities. The property has a tennis court, swimming pool and excellent restaurant. * *Wild Geese Lodge,* located near the Mazowe Valley on a farm a 20-minute drive from Harare, has nine thatched cottages with ensuite facilities and a swimming pool. Horseback riding is available on the estate, while golf,

Wild Geese Lodge.

tennis and lawn bowling are available at a nearby club. * *Thetford House*, a lovely colonial home with four guest rooms (some with private facilities) set in beautiful gardens and a swimming pool, is located in the Mazowe Valley, a 40-minute drive from Harare. Activities include visits to a dairy farm, tobacco farm, ostrich farm and Bushmen paintings. * *Landela Lodge,* located 20 minutes by road from the airport in the suburb of Ruwa, has ten rooms with ensuite facilities, a swimming pool, tennis court, horseback riding and temporary membership at the Ruwa Country Club (18-hole golf course) * *Meikles Hotel* has 269 rooms and suites with ensuite facilities, a swimming pool, sauna, gym and traditional old-world atmosphere. * *Sheraton Hotel* has 325 air-conditioned rooms and suites with ensuite facilities, a swimming pool, tennis courts, and a sauna and gym. **Crowne Plaza Monomatapa Hotel* has 214 air-conditioned rooms with ensuite facilities, a swimming pool and convention facilities.

FIRST CLASS: * *Holiday Inn* has 205 air-conditioned rooms with ensuite facilities and a swimming pool. * *Best*

Western Jameson Hotel has 128 air-conditioned rooms and suites with facilities ensuite and a swimming pool.

TOURIST CLASS: * *Bronte Hotel* has 140 rooms and a swimming pool. * *Cresta Lodge* has 173 rooms. * *Oasis Hotel* has 84 rooms (including 5 family rooms) and a swimming pool.

ACCOMMODATION NEAR HARARE — CLASS A: * *Pamuzinda Safari Lodge*, located 53 miles (85 km) from Harare, is a private game ranch with 12 luxury bungalows (doubles) and a swimming pool. Game drives are offered.

CLASS A/B: * *Mwanga Lodge*, located on a game ranch 27 miles northeast of Harare, has six A-frame thatched cottages nestled beneath a large granite outcrop. Activities include game drives and walks. * *Imire Game Ranch*, situated about a 90-minute drive from Harare near Marondera, offers game drives in open vehicles, walks and elephant back riding. The ranch has a large number of black rhino, and guests may feed the young ones if they wish. Accommodation is in comfortable rooms with ensuite facilities.

THE EAST

NYANGA NATIONAL PARK

Most of this beautifully forested and mountainous park lies above 6560 feet (2000 m), rising to 8504 feet (2592 m). Mt. Inyangani is the highest mountain in Zimbabwe. Trout fishing, horseback riding, hiking and golf are just a few of the many sports enjoyed in this refreshing environment. The park covers 127 square miles (330 km^2) and is located near the Mozambique border north of Mutare.

On a recent visit in May we had a great time picnicking at World's View, horseback riding through the pine forests and fishing for trout.

ACCOMMODATION — FIRST CLASS: * *Pine Tree Inn* is a small country inn; rooms have facilities ensuite. * *Troutbeck Inn* has 74 rooms with ensuite facilities and offers horseback riding, trout fishing, lawn bowling, squash, tennis and golf. * *Montclair Hotel* has rooms with private facilities and a golf course and casino.

CAMPING: Numerous camping and caravan sites are available.

VUMBA BOTANICAL GARDEN AND RESERVE

Located just south of Mutare, Vumba Botanical Garden is beautifully landscaped around a number of small streams. The garden also affords extensive views of Mozambique to the east.

The **Bunga Forest Botanical Reserve**, located adjacent to the botanical garden, has footpaths through unspoiled indigenous forests.

ACCOMMODATION — DELUXE: * *Leopard Rock Hotel* has 58 rooms with ensuite facilities, an 18-hole golf course, casino, swimming pool, tennis and squash courts. Horseback riding and fishing are available.

FIRST CLASS: * *Inn on the Vumba* has 20 bedrooms with ensuite facilities. * *White Horse Inn* is a small hotel (20 beds); rooms have private facilities.

CAMPING: Camp and caravan sites are available.

CHIMANIMANI NATIONAL PARK

This rugged, mountainous 66-square-mile (171-km^2) park with deep gorges and numerous streams includes most of the Chimanimani Mountain Range, which rises to 7995 feet (2437 m). This is an excellent park for hiking and backpacking. Eland, sable antelope and bushbuck are often seen. Birding is good in the forest areas of the gorges.

ACCOMMODATION NEAR THE PARK — TOURIST CLASS: * *Kiledo Lodge*, located 44 miles (70 km) from the park, has rooms with ensuite facilities and a swimming pool.

ACCOMMODATION — CLASS F: A mountain hut is available for refuge.

CAMPING: Camping is allowed in the park.

This 33-foot (10 m) high conical tower is part of the Great Zimbabwe Ruins.

THE SOUTHEAST

GREAT ZIMBABWE

These impressive stone ruins, located 11 miles (18 km) from Masvingo, look distinctly out of place in sub-Saharan Africa where almost all traditional structures have been built of mud, cow dung, straw and reeds. The origin of these ruins is still not understood.

In 1890, Fort Victoria (now Masvingo) became the first settlement of whites in what is now Zimbabwe. The settlers first discovered the Great Zimbabwe Ruins in 1888.

The city which these ruins represent was at its prime from the twelfth to fourteenth centuries. The Acropolis or Hill Complex, traditionally the King's residence, is situated high on a granite hill overlooking the Temple (a walled enclosure) and the less complete restoration of the Valley complex.

ACCOMMODATION — FIRST CLASS: * *Lodge of the Ancient City* has been attractively built in the style of the ruins. The lodge has 20 rooms with ensuite facilities and a swimming pool.

TOURIST CLASS: * *Great Zimbabwe Hotel* is a country hotel, located a few minutes' walk from the ruins, with a swimming pool and 47 rooms with private facilities.

MUTIRIKWE (KYLE) RECREATIONAL PARK

Located 20 miles (32 km) southwest of Masvingo, this 65-square-mile (169-km^2) park is a great place to go horseback riding among white rhino and a variety of other game. Pony trails are led by a park ranger into the fenced wildlife section of the park.

ACCOMMODATION — TOURIST CLASS: See "Great Zimbabwe."

CLASSES D & F: * *National Park lodges,* some with private facilities and others without, are available.

CAMPING: Camping and caravan sites with ablution blocks are located near the National Park office and at Sikato Bay Camp on the west bank of Lake Mutirikwe.

GONAREZHOU NATIONAL PARK

The second largest park in Zimbabwe, Gonarezhou borders the country of Mozambique in southeastern Zimbabwe and covers over 1950 square miles (5053 km^2) of bush.

Gonarezhou means "the place of many elephants" and is definitely elephant country. Other species commonly seen are lion, buffalo, zebra, giraffe and a variety of antelope species. Nyala are regularly seen in riverine areas. Rarely seen are roan antelope and Lichtenstein's hartebeest.

The park is off the beaten path and has only recently been opened to international tourists.

The park is divided into two regions, the Chipinda Pools section, which includes the Lundi and Sabi subregions, and the Mabalauta section. Game viewing is best in the Lundi subregion.

Gonarezhou is usually only open in the dry season, May 1 to October 31. Winter temperatures are mild; however, summer temperatures can exceed 104°F (40°C).

From Masvingo drive southwest to Chiredzi, then continue either 36 miles (58 km) to Chipinda Pools or 105 miles (170 km) to Mabalauta Camp. Four-wheel-drive vehicles are highly recommended. The nearest airstrip is Buffalo Range.

ACCOMMODATION — CLASS A/B: * *Chilo Gorge Safari Lodge*, set on the cliffs of the gorge overlooking the Save River, has 14 thatched lodges (doubles) with ensuite facilities. * *Mahenye Safari Lodge* is situated on the Save River bordering the reserve and consists of eight thatched lodges (doubles) with ensuite facilities.

CLASS F: * *Swimuwini*, which means "the place of baobabs," is located five miles from the Warden's Office and has three self-service chalets and an ablution block.

CAMPING: * *Chipinda Pools Camping and Caravan Site* and * *Chinguli* have ablution blocks. Seven remote campsites with basic facilities are also available. * *Mabalauta* has five camping/caravan sites.

ACCOMMODATION NEAR GONAREZHOU NATIONAL PARK — CLASS A: * *Nduna Lodge,* set on the 378-square-mile (980-km^2) Lone Star Reserve bordering Gonarezhou National Park, has six air-conditioned luxury stone and thatch chalets (doubles) with ensuite facilities and a swimming pool. The lodge is nestled in a rock amphitheater on the edge of a lake. Elephant, buffalo, lion, black rhino, leopard and a variety of antelope may be seen. Activities include day and night game drives, canoeing, walks and viewing bushman paintings. Easiest access is by private air charter. * *Senuko Lodge,* located in the Save Valley Conservancy approximately 44 miles (70 km) from Chiredzi, has eight chalets, with a unique open-front design with rolldown canvas screens, and ensuite facilities and a swimming pool. Day and night game drives, walks and visits to local villages are offered.

CLASS C: * *Tambuti Lodge,* located 6 miles (10 km) outside Chiredzi, has chalets with separate facilities.

BULAWAYO

Bulawayo is the second largest city in Zimbabwe and holds the National Museum and Railway Museum — both well worth a visit. Visitors to Matobo National Park fly in to Bulawayo Airport.

Chipangali Wildlife Orphanage, 15 miles (24 km) southwest of Bulawayo on the Esigodini/Beit Bridge road, cares for a variety of young animals, often including lion, leopard, genet, civet, elephant and chimpanzee.

ACCOMMODATION — FIRST CLASS: * *Induna Lodge* has three rooms (eight beds) with private a facilities, swimming pool, sauna, personalized service and excellent food. * *Churchill Arms Hotel* is a modern Tudor-style hotel with 50 rooms with ensuite facilities, located 4 miles (6 km) from the city center. * *Holiday Inn Bulawayo* is located in the center of town and has

172 air-conditioned rooms with private facilities. * *Nesbitt Castle*, built in 1906 by a professional castle builder from Scotland, has eight double rooms with private facilities and is located only a few miles/kilometers from the city.

STEAM TRAIN

A restored **Steam Train** (first class) runs from Bulawayo to Victoria Falls. The train stops at Hwange National Park for an afternoon of game viewing, and then travels through the night, arriving in Victoria Falls the following morning.

MATOBO (MATOPOS) NATIONAL PARK

Hundreds of kopjes supporting thousands of precariously balanced rocks give the 164-square-mile (424-km^2) Matobo National Park one of the most unusual landscapes in Africa. This highly underrated park is divided into two sections — a general recreational area, where pony trails are very popular, and a game reserve.

Matobo National Park has the highest concentration of black eagles in the world. Part of the park is an ITP and contains one of the highest concentrations of black and white rhino in Africa. Leopard are plentiful but are seldom seen. Other wildlife includes giraffe, zebra, civet, genet, black-backed and side-striped jackal, caracal and porcupine. Bird life includes purple-crested louries, crowned eagles, peregrine falcons and lannar falcons.

In addition to viewing game, on our most recent visit we took an hour-long morning African elephant back ride, and then visited a rural clinic, a primary school (the children sang beautifully) and an authentic African healer in her village.

On a previous visit, accompanied by a national park ranger in the game reserve, we walked near two white rhino and a baby which were eventually scared off when a herd of wildebeest stampeded nearby.

Cecil Rhodes was buried on a huge rock kopje called "View of the World" from which one has sensational panoramas of the rugged countryside, especially at sunrise.

Spectacular granite, balancing rocks and kopjes are found all over Matobo hills. These are called "mother and child".

The region has over 3000 rock paintings — more than any other place in Africa. Nswatugi Cave **rock paintings** include images of giraffe and antelope. For Bambata Cave rock paintings, allow one and one-half hours for the hike. White Rhino Shelter rock paintings are also worth a visit.

ACCOMMODATION — CLASS A/B: * *Amalinda Camp*, attractively built into enormous kopjes, has ten chalets with ensuite facilities. Activities include game drives, walks and horseback riding in the park and on the game ranch, elephant back riding, overnight stays in a local village, day visits to nearby villages and Bushmen paintings. The camp is located about a ten-minute drive from the park. * *Big Cave Lodge* has 6 chalets (12 beds) with ensuite facilities. Game drives, horseback riding within the reserve, visits to local villages and bushmen paintings are offered. * *Matobo Hills Lodge,* located in a beautiful

Amalinda lodge is beautifully nestled in the rocks.

A village setting in the Matobo Hills.

"amphitheater" of rock kopjes about a ten-minute drive from the park, has 17 thatched chalets (doubles) and a swimming pool creatively built into the rocks. Game drives, walks, horseback riding and visits to Bushmen paintings and local villages are offered.

ACCOMMODATION NEAR THE PARK — CLASS A/B: * *Malalangwe Lodge,* located on a 6300-acre (2500-hectare) ranch about an hour drive from the park, has 6 luxury chalets (14 beds) with ensuite facilities. Game drives, walks and hikes to bushman paintings on their private game farm as well as day trips to Matobo National Park are offered.

CAMPING: Camping and caravan sites with ablution blocks are available at *Maleme Dam* and *Toghwana Dam*.

CLASSES D & F: * *National Park* bungalows with and without ensuite facilities are available.

BOTSWANA

THE ELEPHANT'S TRUNK

Watching a herd of elephant using their multipurpose trunks can provide hours of rewarding entertainment. The trunk is a combination of upper lip and nose, with the nostrils beginning at the tip and running the entire length. The trunk possesses thousands of muscles, and the tip of the trunk is covered by tiny hairs.

The matriarchal elephant may hold up her trunk in the air to try to pick up the scent of a nearby elephant herd. When the two groups come together, the elephants may softly entwine their trunks, caress each other gently and place their trunks in each other's mouths as a greeting.

During feeding, an elephant's trunk will first touch the object and then will pluck leaves, tufts of grass and branches; shake fruit off trees; tug at roots;, or strip tree bark. Its feet gently nudge away the roots of stubborn grass before the trunk swishes and flaps the soil off the grass and delicately places the food in its small mouth for chewing.

Air is expelled through the trunk as a trumpet, and it may be used to chastise a playful calf, to greet another elephant or as a display of defense.

Young calves clumsily trip over their trunks, since they are too young to control the muscles. They also suck the tip like a thumb and, best of all, they use their trunks to enjoy daily visits to a water hole.

An elephant trunk holds about 7.3 quarts (7 liters) of water, and adults drink about 212 quarts (200 liters) of water per day. They also cool themselves by spraying a fine mist of water over their bodies. They finish with a dust bath, which they accomplish by sucking dust into their trunks and blowing it all over themselves.

Elephants are sometimes seen resting their trunks over the tip of one of their tusks; after all, those muscles have been put to hard work smelling, touching, feeding, drinking and communicating!

BOTSWANA

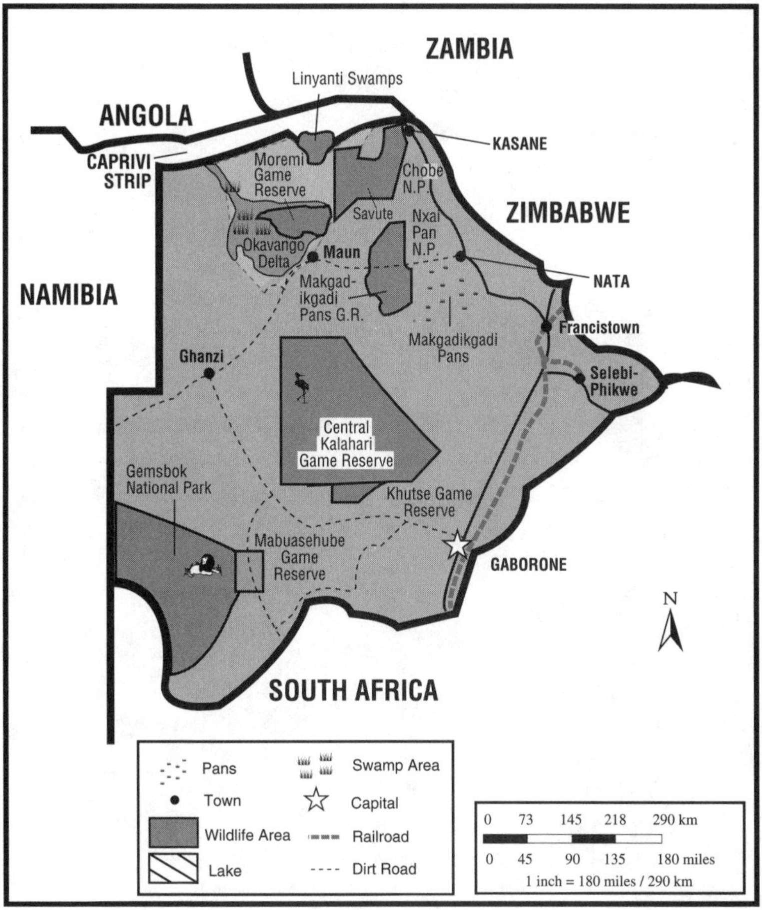

FACTS AT A GLANCE

AREA:	224,606 SQ. MI. / 581,730 SQ. KM.
APPROXIMATE SIZE:	TEXAS OR FRANCE
POPULATION:	1.45 MILLION
CAPITAL:	GABARONE (POP. EST. 190,000)
OFFICIAL LANGUAGE:	ENGLISH
NATIONAL LANGUAGE:	SETSWANA

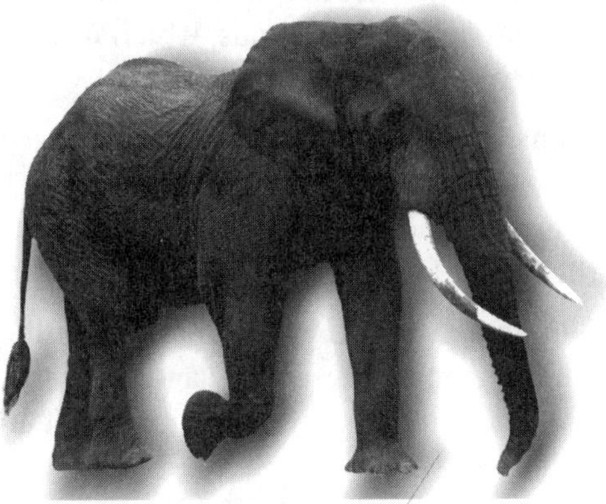

BOTSWANA

The best-selling book *The Cry of the Kalahari*, the hilarious feature films *The Gods Must Be Crazy (I and II),* feature stories in *National Geographic* and documentaries on television have assisted Botswana in gaining international recognition as a top safari destination.

More than four-fifths of the country is covered by the Kalahari sands, scrub savannah and grasslands. The land is basically flat with a mean elevation of 3280 feet (1000 m). Over 85 percent of the population is concentrated near the better water resources in the eastern part of the country.

The Kalahari Desert is not a barren desert of rolling sand dunes as one might imagine. It has scattered grasslands, bush, shrub and tree savannah, dry riverbeds and occasional rocky outcrops.

The "pula" is Botswana's unit of currency and also the Setswana word for rain, which is so critical to this country's wealth and survival. The rainy season is December–March, with the heaviest rains in January and February. Winter brings almost cloudless skies. January (summer) temperatures range from an average maximum of 92°F (33°C) to an average minimum of 64°F (18°C). July (winter) temperatures range from an average maximum of 72°F (22°C) to an average minimum of 42°F (6°C). Frost occasionally occurs in midwinter.

The San, Basarwa or bushmen were the first inhabitants of the area and may have come to southern Africa 30,000 years ago. Most of the estimated 60,000 bushmen live in what is now Botswana and Namibia. Their language uses "clicking" sounds, which distinguishes it from Bantu and most other languages in the world.

Traditionally, bushmen have been nomadic hunter-gatherers, but today only a few live this kind of existence in the Kalahari. Men hunt with poisoned arrows and spears while women use sticks to dig up roots and gather other food for the group.

Bushmen are unique in that they distribute wealth equally among the members of the group, share in the day-to-day aspects of life, and believe they are not superior to their environment and must live in harmony with it.

There are currently very few pure bushmen around, as most have interbred with other tribes and have all but ceased their nomadic existence.

The Sotho-Tswana group of people comprise well over half of the country's population and speak the Setswana language. The Batswana (citizens of Botswana) prefer to live in large, densely populated villages. Cattle are the most important sign of wealth and prestige. Ancestor worship was the chief form of religion until missionaries arrived in 1816 and converted large numbers of Batswana to Christianity.

Bechuanaland became a protectorate of the British Empire on September 30, 1885 and became the independent country of Botswana on September 30, 1966.

Today, very few of the people dress in their traditional costume except for special celebrations. However, for many Batswana, tribal customs are still important in day-to-day life. English is spoken by most of the people, and especially by the youth.

Botswana has a multiparty democracy and is one of the most economically successful and politically stable countries on the continent. Diamonds are Botswana's greatest foreign exchange earner, followed by cattle (there are three times as many cattle in Botswana as people), copper-nickel matte, and tourism.

WILDLIFE AND WILDLIFE AREAS

As far as wildlife is concerned, Botswana has been one of Africa's best-kept secrets. National parks and reserves cover 17 percent of the country's area — one of the highest percentages of any country in the world. In addition, another 22 percent of the country has been set aside as wildlife management areas.

Botswana's combination of great game, uncrowded reserves, excellent small camps (most cater to 20 or fewer guests) and the use of open vehicles for game viewing is difficult to beat.

The five main reserve areas most often visited by international tourists are all in northern Botswana. These are the Okavango Delta, Linyanti, Moremi Game Reserve, the Savute (southwestern part of Chobe National Park), and the Serondela/Chobe River region in the northeastern part of Chobe National Park near Kasane. The latter four are Botswana's best reserves for seeing big game.

As these five regions are distinct in character, a well-rounded wildlife safari to Botswana should include two to three days in each region (if time allows).

Chobe National Park, Moremi Game Reserve and Linyanti rank as three of the best wildlife areas in Africa. The Okavango Delta is the largest inland delta in the world. This "water in the desert" phenomenon has created a unique and fascinating ecosystem well worth exploring.

Generally speaking, game viewing for the Okavango Delta, Chobe, Moremi and Linyanti is best in the dry winter season (May–November) and fair during the hot, rainy season (December–February). Game viewing in March–April can be quite good.

In the dry season, wildlife is concentrated near the marshlands and along the rivers. After the first rains, much of the wildlife ventures far into the interior.

Calving season throughout the country is November–February, during the rainy season. Fishing for tigerfish, bream, barbel and pike is very good, especially September–December.

Other northern attractions include Nxai Pan National Park and Makgadikgadi Pans Game Reserve. Game viewing in Nxai Pan is best in the wet summer season (November–April), and Makgadikgadi Pans is best January–April. Reserves in the south are at times excellent but are seldom visited by international travelers.

Most camps are serviced by small aircraft, allowing visitors to minimize time spent on roads between reserves and maximize time viewing wildlife and a variety of other activities the country has to offer.

Game viewing by air is usually quite fruitful. On one flight from the Savute to the Okavango Delta, we spotted four large herds of elephant, among numerous other species. Most charter flights have weight limits of 25 pounds (12 kg) per person, so bring only what you need, packed in soft-sided bags only. Laundry service is available at all the better camps.

Group first-class (full-service) and budget (participatory) mobile tented safaris are less expensive per day than flying safaris and are another excellent way to experience the bush. Private and group luxury mobile tented camping is also available.

The Wildlife Department runs the parks. Driving in the parks is not allowed at night. Camping is allowed at designated spots. Some lodges and camps close January–February.

The are a number of private concessions surrounding the game reserves which offer night drives and off-road driving — activities not allowed in the reserves themselves. Only guests staying at the camps within each respective concession are allowed in these areas, guaranteeing exclusivity and no crowds. Game viewing in many of these concessions is as good or better than game viewing in the reserves themselves.

THE NORTH

MAUN

Maun is the safari center of the country's most important tourist region. Many travelers fly into Maun to join their safari. Others begin their safari at Victoria Falls (Zimbabwe) and end up in Maun.

Maps, books and souvenirs are available from shops a short walk from the airport.

ACCOMMODATION — FIRST CLASS: * *Riley's Hotel* is the best place to stay in Maun. The hotel has air-conditioned rooms with ensuite facilities and a popular bar and restaurant.

TOURIST CLASS: * *Island Safari Lodge* is located 9 miles (14 km) north of town on the western bank of the Thamalakane River and has brick and thatch bungalows with private facilities, campsites and a swimming pool, bar and restaurant. * *Crocodile Camp* is located on the banks of the Thamalakane River, 8 miles (12 km) north of Maun on a tarred road. Chalets with ensuite facilities and campsites are available.

THE OKAVANGO DELTA

The Okavango, the largest inland delta in the world, covers over 6000 square miles (15,000 km^2) and is in itself a unique and fascinating ecosystem. Instead of finding its way to the ocean as most rivers do, the Okavango River, which originates in the Angolan highlands, fans out into a vast system of thousands of waterways, separated by innumerable islands, to eventually disappear into the Kalahari sands.

The Okavango, an ornithologist's and botanist's dream come true, is beautifully presented in *Okavango: Sea of Land, Land of Water* (Struik Publishers) by Peter Johnson and Anthony Bannister, *Okavango: Jewel of the Kalahari* by Karen Ross (Macmillan Publishing) and *Okavango* by Frans Lanting.

Game viewing for the larger land mammal species should not be your main reason for visiting the Okavango. Big game exists in the delta, but is less commonly seen than in Chobe, Moremi or Linyanti. The main reason for visiting the Okavango should be to explore the wonder of this inland delta, to enjoy the primordial silence, the unusual flora, the bird life, hippo, crocs, and excellent fishing.

However, this is not to say that large land mammals are not encountered in the delta. Large herds of buffalo, as well as elephant, giraffe and a variety of antelope, are often seen; lion and other predators are occasionally encountered.

Crocodiles are most heavily concentrated in the larger waterways and in the northern part of the delta and the panhandle, where there is permanent deep water. However, crocs are found throughout the delta.

Mother Nature must have smiled on this region, for the delta waters are highest during the dry season, since it takes six months for the rainy season floodwaters to travel from their source in the Angolan highlands to the delta.

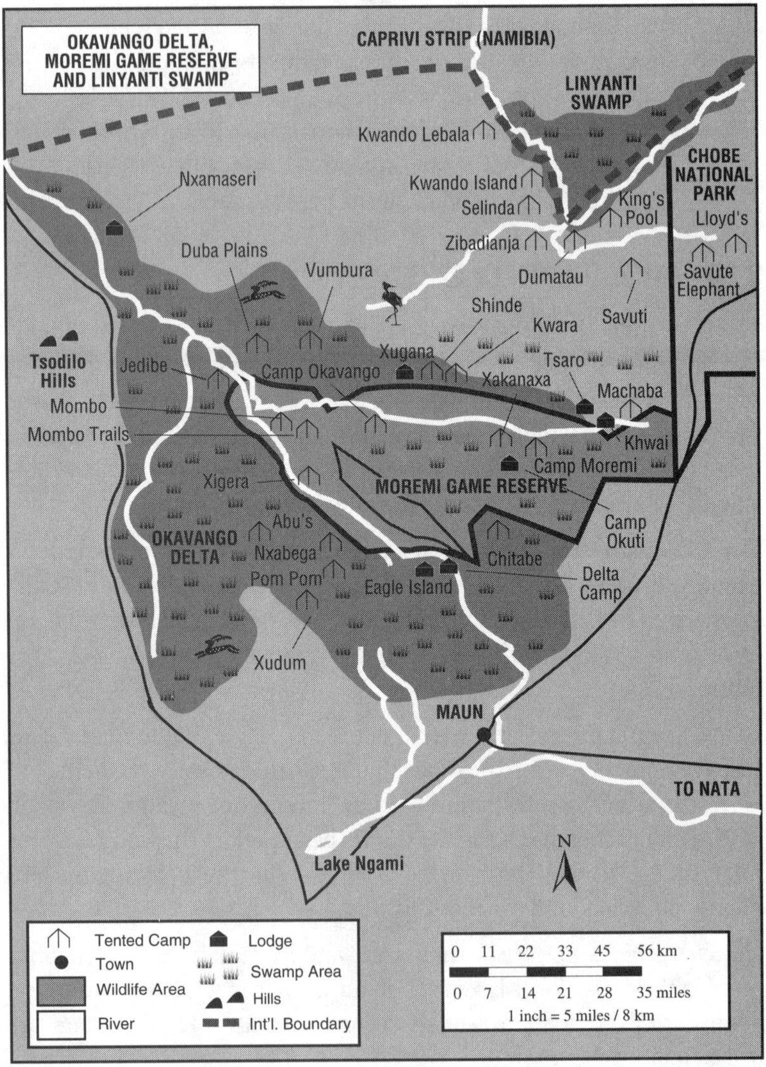

Most visitors reach the camps in the Okavango by small aircraft. Flying into the delta gives one an overall perspective of the region and is an adventure in itself. Game can be easily spotted and photographed from the air.

A 150-mile- (240-km) long buffalo fence has been constructed along the southern and western edges of the delta to keep cattle from the swamp. Therefore, little game is found on the Maun (southern) side of the fence.

Calling the Okavango a "swamp" is a misnomer, since the waters are very clear. This is mainly due to the fact that there is only about a 203-foot (63-m) drop in altitude over 150 miles (240 km) from the top to the bottom of the delta. The water flows gradually and therefore carries very little sediment. Many people drink directly from the delta waters. In addition, the larger stands of papyrus in the panhandle and in the north act as a large filtration plant, filtering out impurities and helping to keep the waters crystal clear. Little bilharzia exists in the area; the only real problem region is around Maun where the waters are stagnant.

Activities include mokoro and canoe excursions, boat and vehicle game drives, nature walks on islands, bird watching, and fishing on request. Motor boats allow you to visit more distant attractions and must be used where the water is too deep to pole a mokoro or canoe and for fishing. Where there is access by land, a four-wheel-drive vehicle is necessary.

An excellent way to experience the Okavango is by mokoro (dugout canoe). Traveling by mokoro allows you to become a part of the environment. Sitting inches from the waterline, thoughts of hippos or crocodiles overturning your boat cross your mind but soon pass with assurances from your guide and the peacefulness of this pristine environment.

Patterns of gold are created from the reflection of papyrus on the still waters of the narrow channels at early morning and late afternoon. You sometimes pass through channels that often appear to be narrower than the boat itself. Silence is broken only by the ngashi (boatman's pole) penetrating and leaving the water, by the cries of countless birds and by the movement of mostly unseen game along the delta's banks. Tiny frogs chime to some unknown melody. Sunsets with rosy pink clouds reflected in the waters are too beautiful for words. Life slows to a regenerative pace. This relaxed form of adventure and exploration is difficult to match anywhere in the world.

On one occasion, I tried poling our canoe across a small lagoon. My guide was right. It's definitely not as easy as it looks!

Guided excursions, ranging in length from a few hours to a full day, using mekoro (plural for mokoro), canoes or small motor boats, are offered by many camps in the delta. Canoes are larger and therefore a little more comfortable; mekoro harmonize better with the natural surroundings. In order to minimize the cutting of large trees in the delta, many camps are using fiberglass mekoros. Mokoro trips for two or more days, where you camp on remote islands in the delta, are possible when booked in advance.

Poling through the waterways and islands of the Okavango Delta by mokoro.

On a mokoro trip we spotted an elusive sitatunga running through the reeds. Sitatunga are shy, solitary antelope that are not often seen, and a real highlight if spotted.

The islands in the delta are thought to have been made over the eons by termite mounds. Because of the cement-like quality of termite mounds, these mounds are dug up and used to build airstrips and elevated paths in camps. Meanwhile, diamond prospectors inspect termite mounds closely. Since dirt is brought up from quite a depth, it provides them with easily accessible core samples.

Game viewing can be quite productive on island walks. On our last mokoro excursion we saw otter, impala, red lechwe, giraffe and Pel's fishing owl, along with other game.

The Okavango has possibly the highest concentration of fish eagles in the world. On numerous occasions our guide waved a fish in the air and called to a fish eagle perched high in a tree over a half-mile away, then tossed the fish into the water about 30 feet (9 m) from the boat. Like magic, the eagle dived down at full speed and plucked the fish from the water. You must be fast with a camera to catch that on film!

Other bird species we spotted on a recent visit included the coppery-tailed coucal, purple heron, striped kingfisher, Meyer's parrot, black-collared barbet, yellow-fronted tinker barbet, hamerkop, red-billed woodhoopoe, saddle-billed stork, Dickenson's kestrel, lesser spotted eagle, grey lourie, carmine bee-eater, slaty egret, little egret, reed

On elephant back – a unique safari in Botswana

cormorant, wattled crane, green-backed heron, goliath heron, blacksmith plover, pied kingfisher, yellow-billed kite, western banded snake eagle, African darter and African jacana.

Speeding along one afternoon in a small motorboat, we drove right by an 8-foot- (2.4-m) long crocodile. We went back for a closer look and discovered it was fast asleep. We maneuvered the boat within 5 feet (1.5 m) of it, and it still didn't wake up — and I'm glad it didn't!

Fishing in the Okavango is best in the northwestern part of the delta. The Okavango River above the delta is too heavily fished. The best time of the year for catching tigerfish is September–November. For barbel, the best time is the end of September through October when the barbel are running (migrating). Overall, the best time for fishing is September–December.

Horseback safaris, possibly the finest in Africa, last from two to ten days. From four to six hours a day are spent in the saddle. Afternoons are often spent walking, swimming, fishing or on mokoro trips. Only experienced riders are allowed, as they must be able to confidently canter along side herds of game including zebra, giraffe and antelope. Accommodations are usually in mobile tented camps.

An elephant back safari on an *African* elephant is a unique way of experiencing the bush. Guests fly to Abu's Camp to join Abu, the lead elephant, along with his family including Bennie, Cathy, Bibi, Lethaba and several youngsters, for a six-day safari.

Gameviewing at full canter.

If you wish to visit Tsodilo Hills (see below) to see the bushmen and rock paintings, consider making reservations in advance so you may fly there from your camp in the Okavango and spend a morning at the hills.

ACCOMMODATION — CLASS A: * *Vumbura Camp* is located in the northern part of the delta and has eight luxury tents with ensuite facilities. Day and night game viewing by vehicle, mokoro excursions, walks, boat game drives and fishing are offered. * *Xigeria Camp* is situated on a large island in the delta within Moremi Game Reserve. The camp has eight luxury tented rooms with ensuite facilities. Activities include mokoro rides, walks and game viewing by vehicle and by boat. * *Jedibe Island Camp,* located in the permanent waters of the delta, offers mokoro excursions, boat trips, walks on islands and fishing. Guests are accommodated in 8 large tents (16 beds) with ensuite facilities and a swimming pool. The camp also has a double-decker houseboat, ideal for cruising the waterways. * *Abu's Camp* is a ten-bed deluxe tented camp with ensuite bush toilet and shower. Elephant back safaris, mokoro rides, walks and game drives by vehicle are operated. * *Xudum Camp* is a 14-bed luxury tented camp with ensuite facilities. Day and night game drives, walks, horseback safaris and mokoro excursions are offered. * *Xugana Island Camp* has eight reed chalets built on stilts (16 beds) with

The lovely lounge area of Vumbura.

ensuite facilities and a swimming cage. Xugana offers boat rides, mokoro trips, walks and fishing.

CLASS A/B: * *Duba Plains* accommodates a maximum of ten guests in luxury tents with ensuite facilities and is located in a remote region of the delta. Game drives, walks and mokoro excursions (depending on the water level) are available. * *Camp Okavango* is a 22-bed tented camp in the eastern delta with private facilities located down a private walkway behind each tent. Activities include mokoro safaris, boat trips and walks. * *Shinde Island Camp* has 7 deluxe tents (14 beds,) with private facilities situated a few feet behind each tent, and a small swimming pool. Activities include mokoro trips, boat rides, fishing, walks and game drives. * *Pom Pom* has 7 deluxe tents (14 beds) overlooking a lagoon in the central delta, with ensuite facilities and a small swimming pool. Activities include game drives, walks and mokoro rides. * *Nxabega Okavango Safari Camp* has 9 tents (18 beds) with ensuite facilities. Activities include game drives, walks and mokoro rides. * *Eagle Island Camp at Xaxaba* is situated in the delta west of Chief's Island and has 11 reed and thatch chalets with ensuite facilities. Activities include mokoro rides, walks and sundowner cruises.

CLASS B: * *Nxamaseri Camp* is located in the panhandle of the delta and is one of the top fishing camps in the Okavango. Boat game drives are also offered. * *Delta Camp* has eight reed chalets with ensuite facilities. Walks and mokoro excursions are offered.

TSODILO HILLS

Over 2700 bushmen paintings are scattered through the rocky outcrops of Tsodilo Hills, one of the last places in Botswana where bushmen may be found. The largest of the four hills rises 1000 feet (305 m) above the surrounding plain. Archeological evidence indicates that these hills may have been inhabited as long as 30,000 years ago.

Located west of the Okavango Delta, Tsodilo Hills is accessible by a flight from Maun or from safari camps in northern Botswana or a very long and rough day's ride from Maun by four-wheel-drive vehicle. There are no facilities, so travelers must be totally self-sufficient. Unfortunately, this site has become touristic, so don't expect to see bushmen living as they did thousands of years ago. However, the rock paintings may be worth a visit. Please do not drink anything in the presence of bushmen — water is scarce.

ACCOMMODATION: None.

MOREMI GAME RESERVE

Moremi is the most diversified of all the Botswana parks in terms of wildlife and scenery, and many people feel it is the most beautiful. Located in the northeastern part of the Okavango Delta, Moremi contains over 1160 square miles (3000 km^2) of permanent swamps, islands, floodplains, forests and dry land. The park's boundaries have been recently extended to the west and northwest, significantly enlarging its size.

In the floodplains, reedbuck, common waterbuck, red lechwe, tsessebe, ostrich, sable and roan antelope, crocodile, hippo and otter can be found.

In the riparian forest, you may spot elephant, greater kudu, Southern giraffe, impala, buffalo and Burchell's zebra, along with such predators as lion, leopard, ratel (honey badger), spotted hyena and cheetah.

Black-backed and side-striped jackals are often seen in the riparian forest as well as in the floodplain. Seldom-seen species include pangolin, bat-eared fox, porcupine and hedgehog.

The reserve has a large wild dog population, as creatively presented in the book *Running Wild: Dispelling the Myths of the African Wild Dog* by John McNutt and Lesley Boggs, with photography by Helene Heldring and Dave Hamman (Russel Friedman Books).

Game viewing is excellent during the drier months of May–November. In parts of Moremi, game viewing is in fact good year-round.

On a morning game drive, we saw two herds of sable antelope, elephant, greater kudu, tsessebe, impala and Burchell's zebra. That evening we saw a variety of game, including leopard. On another game drive, we spotted seven lion, cheetah, bat-eared fox, and several species of antelope.

On our most recent visit we followed three cheetah on a late afternoon hunt, and the next morning found a mother leopard and her two cubs!

Elephant and buffalo are the only large animals that migrate. After the rains have begun, they move northward to the area between Moremi and the Kwando-Linyanti River systems. Other wildlife may move to the periphery of, or just outside, the reserve.

In the bush it is not always the larger animal, but more often the more aggressive one that gets his way. While on a game drive in Moremi we experienced a perfect example of this. A lone hippopotamus chased an entire herd of over 20 elephant out of "its" water hole. Astounding!

Moremi is an ornithologist's delight. Fish eagles, kingfishers and bee-eaters abound. Other birds commonly seen include parrots, shrikes, egrets, jacanas, pelicans, bateleur eagles, hornbills, herons, saddle-billed storks, yellow-billed oxpeckers, wattled cranes, reed cormorants, spur-winged geese, long-tailed shrikes and flocks of thousands of red-billed quelea which fly together in a sphere like a great spotted flying ball.

With the onset of the floods in May or June, waterfowl follow the progression of the floodwaters as they progress through the region.

The decked lounge/dining area of Mombo Camp.

Moremi is open year-round; however, some areas may be temporarily closed due to heavy rains or floods. Four-wheel-drive vehicles are necessary. The South Gate is about 62 miles (100 km) north of Maun.

ACCOMMODATION — CLASS A: * *Mombo Camp* is situated in the reserve near the northern tip of Chief's Island where the savannah meets the Okavango. Big game including lion, leopard, cheetah and African wild dog is plentiful in this concession area year-round. Accommodation is in 10 large tents with ensuite facilities (20 beds total) and a plunge pool. Activities include day and evening game drives (up to a half hour after sunset) and walks. * *Chitabe Camp*, located on a private concession surrounded by Moremi Game Reserve on three sides, has eight luxury tents set on wooden decks, with ensuite facilities. Day and night game drives, walks and mokoro excursions are offered. * *Tsaro Lodge,* located outside the reserve, offers accommodation in 8 thatched chalets (16 beds) with ensuite facilities and a swimming pool. Activities include game drives within the reserve and walks outside the reserve.

CLASS A/B: * *Mombo Trails Camp* is located within the reserve and caters to a maximum of eight guests in tents with ensuite facilities. Day and evening game drives (up to a half hour after sunset) and walks are offered. **Chitabe Trails* is an eight-bed tented camp with ensuite facilities, located on a private concession. Activities include day and night game drives, mokoro excursions and walks. * *Camp Moremi* is a 22-bed tented camp located within the reserve overlooking Xakanaxa Lagoon. Private facilities are situated a short walk down a secluded pathway behind each tent. Game drives are offered. * *Xakanaxa Camp* is a 22-bed tented camp with ensuite facilities located within the park, overlooking the Xakanaxa Lagoon. Game drives and boat trips are offered. * *Kwara Camp,* situated just north of the reserve, has 8 tents (16 beds) with ensuite facilities and offers day and night game drives, walks and mokoro rides. * *Machaba Camp* is located outside the reserve and has 7 large tents (14 beds) with ensuite facilities and a small swimming pool. The camp offers day and night game drives and walks outside the reserve.

CLASS B: * *Khwai River Lodge,* situated outside the reserve, has 12 brick and thatched bandas with ensuite facilities (26 beds) and a swimming pool. * *Camp Okuti,* located within the reserve, has brick and thatch chalets with separate facilities.

CAMPING: * *South Gate Campsite* is located just outside the South Gate and has toilet facilities only. * *Third Bridge* is Moremi's most popular campsite and can be very crowded in peak season. This camp has long-drop toilets only. Water is available from the river. Beware of lions. * *Xaxanaka* has no facilities. * *North Gate* campsite is situated just inside the reserve and has shower and toilet facilities and water.

LINYANTI SWAMPS

The Linyanti Swamps, situated northeast of the Okavango Delta and northwest of the Savute, is home to many crocodile, hippo, sitatunga, lechwe, elephant, buffalo, lion and spotted hyena. The Linyanti region is, in essence a mini "Okavango Delta" with lots of big game.

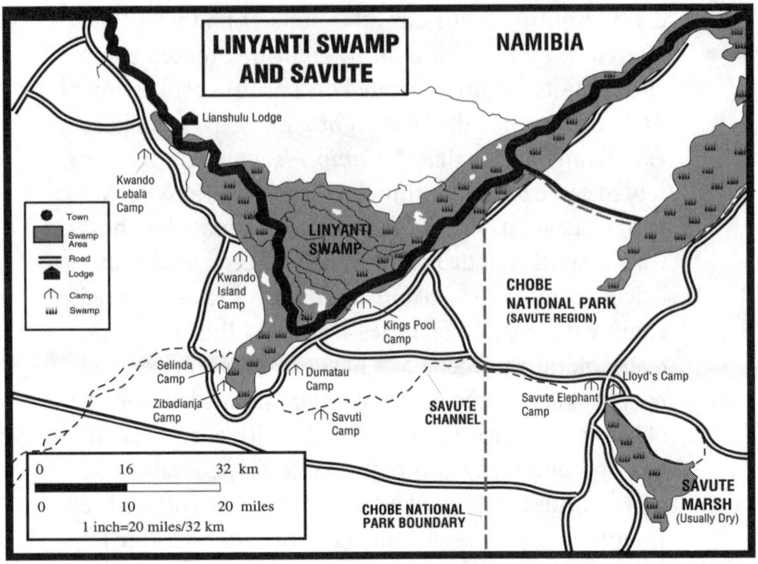

On our most recent visit we saw large herds of elephant, zebra, several prides of lion, buffalo and bat-eared fox, along with a variety of other game. While we stopped by a lagoon for a cool drink, we watched two elephant playing in the water with the sun setting behind them. On a night game drive we saw six wild dog on a greater kudu kill, a pride of 13 lion, leopard, serval, and a very vocal and aggressive confrontation between two adult female hyena and a sub-adult — the likes of which I have never seen!

The Kwando and Linyanti Rivers form the region's border with Namibia. The Kwando River flows southeast and then meets the end of the Great Rift Valley. This causes the river to flow northeast, and at this point its name changes to the Linyanti River and later to the Chobe River which eventually meets the Zambezi River.

This region is prolific in bird life. Big game is most concentrated in this region in the dry season (May–November).

ACCOMMODATION — CLASS A: * *Kings Pool Camp,* located on a large private concession and overlooking a lagoon, has ten luxury tents set on raised decks with ensuite facilities and a plunge pool. Day and night vehicle game drives, boat game drives on a double-decker

Elephant feeding in front of Kings Pool Camp.

houseboat and walks are offered. * *DumaTau* is a 16-bed tented camp with ensuite facilities and plunge pool overlooking an enormous lagoon. Day and night vehicle game drives, boat game drives and walks in this private concession are offered. * *Selinda Camp* is a 12-bed tented camp with private facilities set on a private concession. Activities include day and night game drives by vehicle, boat game drives (water levels permitting — usually July–October), morning walks and walking safaris lasting two to three days .

ACCOMMODATION — CLASS A/B: * *Zibadianja Camp*, located on the Selinda concession, is an exclusive six-bed camp with ensuite facilities. Day and night game drives and walks are offered. * *Kwando Lagoon Camp* has 6 tents (12 beds) under thatch with ensuite facilities. Day and night vehicle game drives, boat game drives, walks and fishing are offered. * *Kwando Lebala Camp* has 8 tents (16 beds) under thatch with ensuite facilities. Day and night vehicle game drives, walks, boat game drives and fishing are offered.

SAVUTE (CHOBE NATIONAL PARK)

The Savute is an arid region located in the southern part of Chobe National Park. The landscape ranges from sandveld to mopane forest, acacia savannah, marshlands to rocky outcrops. The Savute Channel connects the marshlands with the Kwando/Linyanti river waterways. However, the Savute River has not flowed since 1981, and the marshlands are currently dry.

Game-viewing opportunities here are usually excellent. The Savute, like the northern part of Chobe National Park, is known for its elephant. The area also contains zebra, eland, kudu, roan antelope, sable antelope, waterbuck, tsessebe, wildebeest, impala and many other members of the family of ungulates (hoofed mammals).

The predator population is also very large. The Savute is famous for its lions. Within a two-month period prior to a recent visit, lions had killed 19 giraffe in the area.

On one game drive, we parked within 15 feet (5 m) of a pride of nine lion and turned off the engine. I was sitting next to the driver in the open land cruiser. A very large male and a large female lion walked by within 5 feet (1.5 m) of us. They both stood taller than the driver and I were sitting. I simply held my breath and reminded myself that I was quite safe inside the vehicle!

Other predators include leopard, cheetah, wild dog, spotted hyena, black-backed jackal and bat-eared fox. Hyena have tremendous crushing power with their jaws; they have been known to chew hinges off of refrigerators in camps in the Savute in order to get at the food inside.

On another game drive we spotted impala, 5 greater kudu, warthog, elephant, 2 black-backed jackals, steenbok, about 50 tsessebe, a herd of blue wildebeest, *12* bat-eared fox, tawny eagle, yellow-billed hornbill and kori bustard. We followed vultures to a warthog kill where we found only the head remaining and a large male lion in the bush nearby.

Sometimes during the dry season 70–90 elephant gather at a water hole at once. They are usually lone males gathering together; females tend to stick close to permanent water.

On my last visit we saw a large breeding herd of about 80 elephant moving through the mopane woodland, and an incredible number of bataleur eagles and numerous vultures.

Game viewing is best from just after the first good rains (usually late November) through April. Game viewing from June to October is good, with bull elephant concentrated around the water holes; however, it is very dry and dusty.

Game viewing along the Savute Channel from the park's northern boundary to the Linyanti Swamps is best from May to November. Burchell's zebra migrate from the Mababe Depression, which is south of the Savute Marsh, northward to the Linyanti Swamps in May and return to the Mababe Depression in November.

A few bushmen paintings may be found in this region. Four-wheel-drive vehicles are necessary for the Savute.

ACCOMMODATION — CLASS A: * *Savuti Camp* is located on a private reserve overlooking the dry Savuti Channel and a water hole. The camp caters to a maximum of eight guests in luxury tents with ensuite facilities and a plunge pool. Day and night game drives, walks and game viewing from hides are offered. As this camp is located between Chobe National Park and the Linyanti Swamps, game viewing is excellent May–November. * *Savute Elephant Camp* is located within the park and has eight luxury tents with ensuite facilities. Only day game drives are offered.

CLASS B: * *Lloyd's Camp*, set on the banks of the dry Savute Channel within the park, is a 12-bed tented camp with shared facilities located near the tents. The camp offers day game drives and a hide overlooking a water hole.

CAMPING: A National Parks Campsite is located near Savute Elephant Camp. The site is very sandy and there is little shade. Toilet and shower facilities are not always operational.

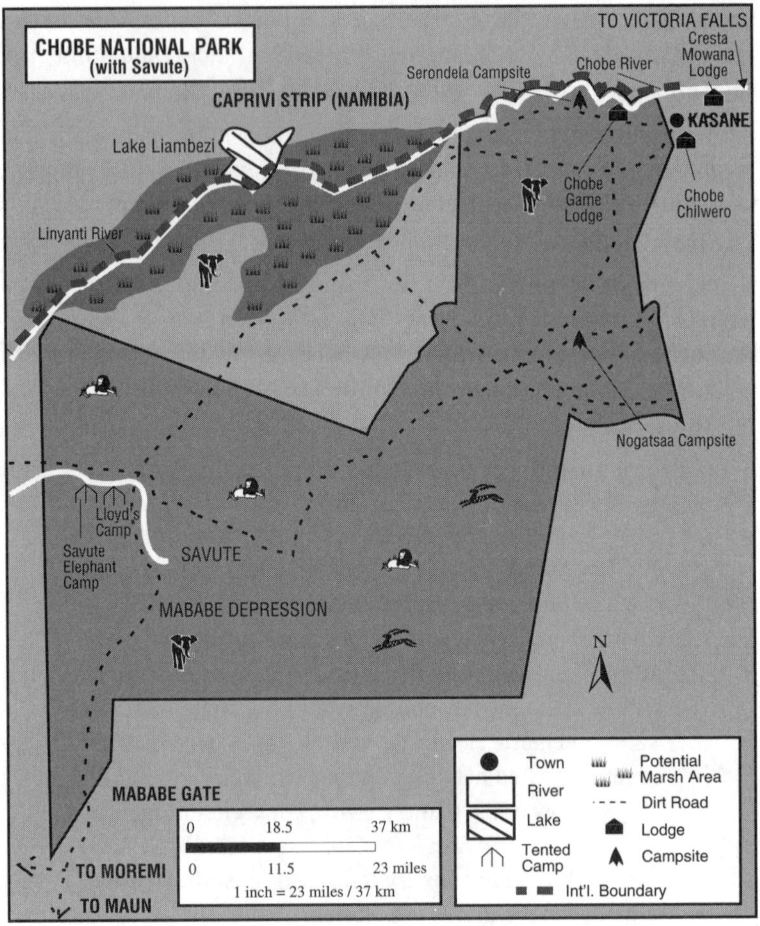

CHOBE NATIONAL PARK (CHOBE RIVER/SERONDELA REGION)

Famous for its large herds of elephant, Chobe National Park covers about 4250 square miles (11,000 km^2). The park is situated only about 50 miles (80 km) from Victoria Falls in Zimbabwe, with the Chobe River forming its northern and northwestern boundaries. Across the river is Namibia's Caprivi Strip. Bird life is prolific, especially in the riverine areas.

The four main regions of the park are Serondela in the northeast near Kasane, the Corridor around Ngwezumba and Nogatsaa, a portion of the Linyanti Swamps in the northwest, and the Savute (discussed above) in the west.

The Serondela region is famous for its huge elephant and buffalo populations, which number in the thousands. The elephant are some of the most vocal and active I've encountered on the continent, constantly trumpeting, making mock charges and sometimes sparring with each other. Great entertainment!

Game viewing by boat along the Chobe River can be spectacular, especially May–November in the dry season. Often large herds of elephant and a variety of other wildlife come down to the river to drink. On a recent visit we witnessed a herd of over 50 elephant swimming across the river at sunset. Mothers were assisting several babies in the herd to make it across. Once they reached the riverbank, the herd had a dust bath and wandered off into the bush.

You can get within close range of these animals by boat. Large monitor lizards are commonly seen.

Along the Chobe River between the Chobe Game Lodge and the village of Kasane, you are likely to see numerous hippo, red lechwe, common waterbuck, warthog and guinea fowl. Driving from the lodge toward Serondela Camp you can usually see giraffe, impala, zebra and occasionally kudu and Chobe bushbuck.

The hot and dry Corridor (Ngwezumba to Nogatsaa) is the only area in the country where oribi is found. Gemsbok, eland, ostrich and steenbok are sometimes seen. Prevalent species include giraffe, elephant, roan and sable antelope.

The Serondela or northern region is accessible by two-wheel-drive vehicles, while four-wheel-drive vehicles are necessary for the rest of the park.

This is the only reserve in Botswana that may be crowded.

ACCOMMODATION — NORTHERN CHOBE - CLASS A: * *Chobe Chilwero Camp* has eight chalets with ensuite facilities. The camp is located on an escarpment overlooking the park. Day game drives are made by vehicle and by boat. * *Chobe Game Lodge* is a beautifully decorated Moorish-style lodge with 96 beds set on the banks of the Chobe River within the park. The lodge has a large swimming pool and beautifully kept spacious grounds. All rooms have ensuite facilities, and four luxury suites have private swimming pools. Sundowner cruises and day game drives are offered.

CLASS A/B: * *Cresta Mowana Lodge* is located 5 miles (8 km) east of the park. All 112 rooms have ensuite facilities. Game drives by vehicle and by boat are offered.

CLASS C: * *Kubu Lodge* has wood and thatch chalets with ensuite facilities, a swimming pool and spacious lawns. It is a ten-minute drive from the Chobe National Park gate. * *Chobe Safari Lodge* has rooms and rondavels with private facilities, a swimming pool and boats for hire.

CAMPING: The public campsites at Serondela, Linyanti, Savute and Nogatsaa have toilets and showers, while the campsite at Tjinga only has a water tank. Serondela is often very crowded; it is accessible by two-wheel-drive vehicles and is close to Kasane.

KASANE

Kasane is a small town a few miles northeast of Chobe National Park about a two-hour drive from Victoria Falls (Zimbabwe). Many tourists are driven here from Victoria Falls, and after clearing customs at the border begin their Botswana safari. Kasane Enterprises has a small shop of quality souvenirs.

ACCOMMODATION — See "Chobe National Park" above.

CAMPING: Sites are available at * *Chobe Safari Lodge* and * *Kubu Lodge*.

NXAI PAN NATIONAL PARK

Nxai Pan National Park, well known for its huge giraffe and springbok population, covers over 810 square miles (2100 km^2) and is located north of the Maun-Nata road in Northern Botswana.

The Nxai Pan is a fossil lake bed about 15 square miles (40 km^2) in size; it is covered with grass during the rains. The landscape is dotted with trees. Kgama-Kgama Pan is second to Nxai Pan in size.

In addition to Southern giraffe, wildlife includes gemsbok, eland, greater kudu, blue wildebeest, red hartebeest, springbok, steenbok, brown and spotted hyena, cheetah and other predators. During the rains, elephant and buffalo may also be seen. After the first rains have fallen, game viewing can be good (i.e., December–April). Bird life is excellent during the rains.

Baines' Baobabs, situated in the park not far from the Maun-Nata road, were immortalized by the famous painter Thomas Baines in 1862. His painting, entitled "The Sleeping Five," is of the five baobabs, one of which is growing on its side. Seldom are baobab trees found growing so closely together. Baines' Baobabs were later painted by Prince Charles.

This park is seldom visited by international travelers as there are no permanent fully catered camps. A four-wheel-drive vehicle is necessary.

ACCOMMODATION: None.

CAMPING: There are two campsites, one of which has an ablution block. Water is usually available at both sites.

MAKGADIKGADI PANS GAME RESERVE

Makgadikgadi Pans Game Reserve includes a portion of the 4600-square-mile (12,000-km^2) Makgadikgadi Pans, which is the size of Portugal. The pans are nearly devoid of human habitation and give one a true feeling of isolation.

Once one of the world's largest prehistoric lakes, the Makgadikgadi Pans, is salt plains covered with grasslands and isolated "land islands" of vegetation, baobab and palm trees. Scattered Stone Age tools have been found. Engravings left by explorers David Livingstone and Frederick Courteny Selous in the trunks of ancient baobob trees mark their passage through the region so many years ago.

Makgadikgadi Pans.

The reserve itself covers about 1550 square miles (3900 km^2). It is located south of the Maun-Nata road in northern Botswana and borders Nxai Pan National Park to the north. Large herds of blue wildebeest, zebra, springbok, gemsbok and thousands of flamingos may be seen December–March. Other wildlife includes hyena, suricate and meerkat. A four-wheel-drive vehicle is highly recommended.

ACCOMMODATION: CLASS A/B: * *Jack's Camp* is a classic camp (12 beds) in the forties style, with large tents and ensuite bathrooms with flush toilets and bucket showers. Activities include day and night game drives, riding quad motorbikes on the pans, game walks with bushmen trackers and lectures by resident researchers. * *San Camp,* a 12-bed camp with bush toilets and bucket showers offers the same activities as Jack's Camp.

CAMPING: There are two camping areas with limited facilities. Travelers must be totally self-sufficient.

CENTRAL KALAHARI GAME RESERVE

This 20,000-square-mile (52,000-km^2) reserve, one of the largest reserves in the world, covers but a portion of the Kalahari Desert. There is an abundance of wildebeest, hartebeest, springbok, gemsbok, ostrich, eland, lion, cheetah and giraffe — especially in the rainy season (December–April). May and June may also be good months for game viewing.

ACCOMMODATION: None.

ACCOMMODATION IN THE KALAHARI WEST OF THE RESERVE: * *Kanana Camp,* located between the town of Ghanzi and the Namibian border, is one of Botswana's most remote camps. Guests spend time with bushmen who have settled in the region. Activities may include tracking gemsbok, hartebeest, springbok and other game and learning the medicinal value of indigenous plants and some of the bushmen's secrets of survival in the desert. This eight-bed camp has tents with ensuite facilities. Guests do not visit the Central Kalahari Game Reserve.

CAMPING: No facilities. Travelers must be self-sufficient and use four-wheel-drive vehicles.

KHUTSE GAME RESERVE

The Khutse Game Reserve shares its northern boundary with the Central Kalahari Game Reserve and is the closest reserve to Gaborone. Khutse covers 965 square miles (2500 km^2) of gently rolling savannah and pans (over 50) and is best known for its bird life.

Lion, leopard, cheetah and antelope adapted to an arid environment are present. However, wildlife is seasonal, depending on the rains. If there has been little rain, then game is usually scarce. The best time to visit is after the rainy season has begun, usually December–April.

Khutse is a five-hour drive (136 miles/220 km) from Gaborone via Molepolole. The route is not well sign-posted. Four-wheel-drive vehicles are essential.

ACCOMMODATION: None.

CAMPING: There is one public campsite with toilets. Water is available at the gate.

THE SOUTH

GABORONE

Gaborone, phonetically pronounced "Ghabarony," is the capital of Botswana. In the center of town is the main shopping and commercial center — the Mall. Other than some shopping, there is little of interest for the international traveler except for possibly the National Museum.

ACCOMMODATION — DELUXE: * *Grand Palm Hotel* has 152 air-conditioned rooms, three restaurants, outdoor heated pool, fitness center, lighted tennis courts and business center.

FIRST CLASS: * The *Gaborone Sun* is located 1.5 miles (2 km) from the city center. This 203-room, air-conditioned hotel has a swimming pool, tennis and squash courts and casino. * The *President Hotel* is an air-conditioned hotel centrally located in the Mall.

MABUASEHUBE GAME RESERVE

Mabuasehube is an extremely remote reserve in southwestern Botswana. Mabuasehube is about 695 square miles (1800 km^2) in size and shares its western border with Gemsbok National Park. The park has six large pans and sand dunes over 100 feet (30 m) high.

The best time to visit is during the rainy season (October–April) when an abundance of eland, hartebeest, gemsbok, wildebeest, springbok, lion and other predators are present.

Mabuasehube is 333 miles (533 km) from Gaborone. A four-wheel-drive vehicle is needed, and the drive takes at least 11 hours.

ACCOMMODATION: None.

CAMPING: No facilities. Water may be available at the Game Scouts Camp.

GEMSBOK NATIONAL PARK

Entry is only possible from the Republic of South Africa. See "Kalahari Gemsbok National Park" in the chapter on South Africa for details.

ZAMBIA

THE LONESOME LEOPARD

This shy, solitary, nocturnal, secretive creature is an independent animal that moves silently and, by its intelligence, can adapt to any environment. Its presence is widespread, but sightings are uncommon. However, there are ways of increasing your chances of seeing a leopard in the bush.

Leopards wake early in the morning, often with tails hanging from beneath the branches of trees. They often watch their prey before descending. They commence a short stalk, chase and pounce on their victims and, finally, give the death bite. Both their phenomenal neck and claw strength are used to drag their meal, step by step, back up the tree. Later in the morning, they find an open sunny spot on a rock outcrop to warm and groom themselves.

Leopards are natural swimmers and often supplement their diet with fish and other river species and may be seen taking a drink at a river in the late afternoon. If baboons are nearby, they will always reveal the leopard's presence. The elusive leopard never goes undetected by wary baboons in the trees above; they move through the branches chattering and barking, creating a noise loud enough to deter an attack.

It is not uncommon, however, for a leopard to initiate an attack on a baboon troop only to be attacked itself and driven up a tree. There, the leopard is chided by baboons above and below, and the great cat finds peace only when the baboons move off. Hyrax will also announce the presence of leopard hiding in rocky outcrops.

Two of the biggest thrills on a safari are to hear and recognize the sound of the leopard's sawing grunt in the dead of the night and to sight them on a game drive.

ZAMBIA

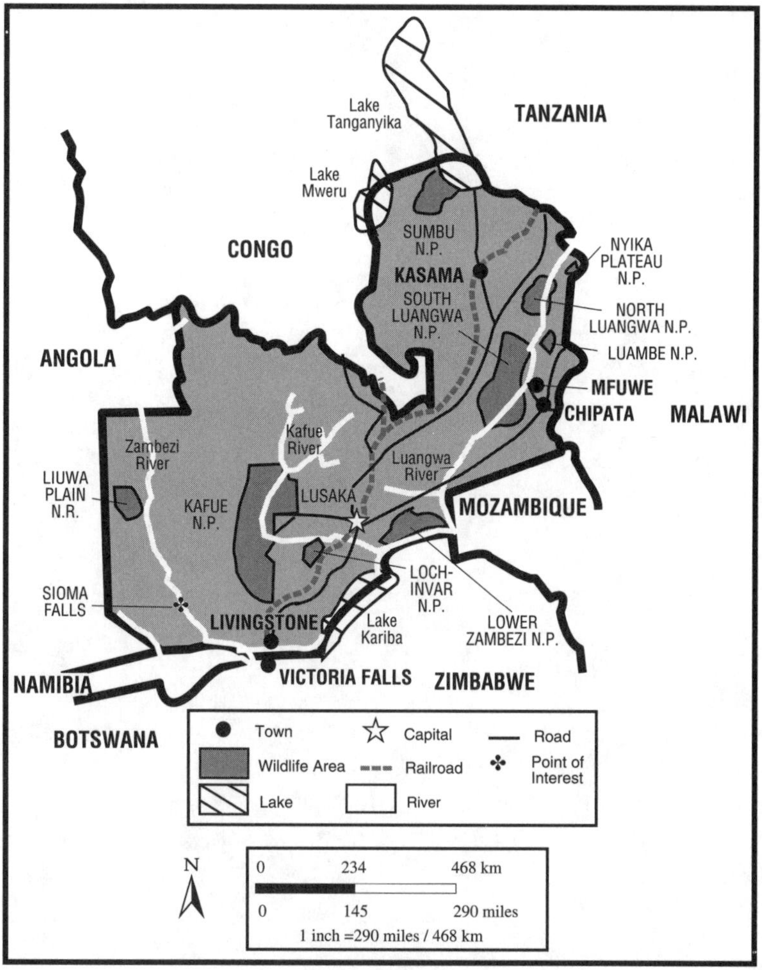

FACTS AT A GLANCE

AREA:	290,586 SQ. MI. / 752,614 SQ. KM.
APPROXIMATE SIZE:	LARGER THAN TEXAS OR FRANCE
POPULATION:	8.7 MILLION
CAPITAL:	LUSAKA (POP. EST. 1.5 MILLION)
OFFICIAL LANGUAGE:	ENGLISH

ZAMBIA

A country rich in wildlife, Zambia was named after the mighty Zambezi River which flows through southern Zambia. The Zambezi River is fed by its Kafue and Luangwa tributaries. The three great lakes of Bangweulu, Mweru and Tanganyika lie in northern Zambia, and Lake Kariba lies along the southeastern border adjacent to Zimbabwe.

The country is predominantly a high plateau ranging in altitude from 3000 to 5000 feet (915 to 1525 m), which is why it has a subtropical rather than a tropical climate. April–August is cool and dry, September–October is hot and dry, and November–March is warm and wet. Winter temperatures are as cool as 43°F (6°C) and summer temperatures exceed 100°F (38°C). The dry season, with clear sunny skies, is May–October.

The Zambian people are predominantly composed of Bantu tribal groups who practice a combination of traditional and Christian beliefs. English is the official language and is widely spoken. Seventy-three other languages and dialects are also spoken. In contrast to most African countries, over 40 percent of the population lives in urban areas, due mainly to the copper mining industry.

In 1888, Cecil Rhodes obtained mineral right concessions from the chiefs of what was proclaimed Northern Rhodesia, which came under British influence. In 1953, Northern Rhodesia, Southern Rhodesia and Nyasaland (now Malawi) were consolidated into the Federation of Rhodesia and Nyasaland. Northern Rhodesia seceded from the federation in 1963 and achieved its independence on October 24, 1964, as the Republic of Zambia.

Zambia's economy is based primarily on copper from the government-owned mines (currently being privatized) in the "copper belt" near the Congo border. The price and subsequent production of copper have declined since 1975; this has brought on hardship and forced the economy to diversify. More emphasis is now being placed on developing agriculture (exporting fruit, coffee, sugar) and the tourism industry as greater sources of foreign exchange.

Since the elections in 1991, Zambia has a multiparty political system.

WILDLIFE AND WILDLIFE AREAS

Zambia provides fabulous options for the wildlife adventurer, including both night and day game drives by open vehicle, walking safaris using remote bush camps, old-fashioned portered walking safaris like those undertaken by early explorers, mobile tented safaris, canoe safaris and white-water rafting.

Zambia boasts 19 gazetted national parks covering over 24,000 square miles (60,000 km^2), and with the 34 game management areas adjacent to the parks, Zambia has set aside 32 percent of its land for the preservation of wildlife. However, many national parks and reserves are not open to the general public.

Zambia's three major parks are South Luangwa National Park , Lower Zambezi National Park and Kafue National Park. South Luangwa is the most popular of the three, largely due to its concentration of elephant and other game.

Going on safari in Zambia is different. In Kenya and Tanzania, visitors are often rushed from park to park with only one or two nights in the same park. In Zambia, the emphasis is on experiencing the bush and wildlife by participating in walking safaris and night safaris (the biggest attractions) as well as day game drives in open vehicles and canoeing.

Zambia is excellent for walking safaris, which are operated primarily in South Luangwa, North Luangwa, Lower Zambezi and Kafue National Parks. Virtually all of the camps offer morning walks and day and night game-viewing drives.

Fishing is very good for tigerfish in Lake Kariba and the Zambezi River and for tigerfish, goliath tigerfish and lake salmon in Lake Tanganyika.

Visitors who have their own vehicles must be in the camps by nightfall and therefore cannot conduct night safaris on their own. Guests must not leave the roads in search of game or walk in the park without the company of an armed wildlife guard. I've been told that crocodiles in Zambia are responsible for more deaths than automobile accidents.

The best time to visit South Luangwa, Lower Zambezi and Kafue National Parks is June–October. Game viewing is fairly good in November, April and May in the eastern part of South Luangwa National Park near Mfuwe Airport, where camps are open year-round. December–March is the hot and humid rainy season when foliage becomes thicker, making wildlife more difficult to spot.

THE NORTH AND NORTHEAST

SOUTH LUANGWA NATIONAL PARK

The natural beauty, variety and concentration of wildlife make this huge 3494-square-mile (9050-km^2) park one of the finest in Africa. Game can be so prolific that Luangwa is called "The Crowded Valley"

South Luangwa is home to savannah, wetland and forest animals. The southern regions are predominantly woodland savannah with scattered grassy areas. Leopard, kudu and giraffe are numerous. To the north, the woodlands give way to scattered trees and open plains where wildebeest and other savannah animals dominate the scene.

Thornicroft's giraffe are indigenous to the park. Lion, hyena, buffalo, waterbuck, impala, kudu, puku, bushbuck and zebra are plentiful. Small herds of Cookson's wildebeest, unique to Luangwa, may be seen. Leopard are most commonly sighted July–October and are frequently seen on night game drives. We saw at least one on each night drive during my last visit.

Hippo and crocs abound in the muddy Luangwa River, a tributary of the Zambezi which runs along much of the park's eastern boundary and then traverses the southern part of the park.

Over 400 species of birds have been recorded, including sacred ibises, saddle-billed storks, yellow-billed storks, Egyptian geese, spur-winged geese, fish eagles, crowned cranes, carmine bee-eaters, kingfishers,

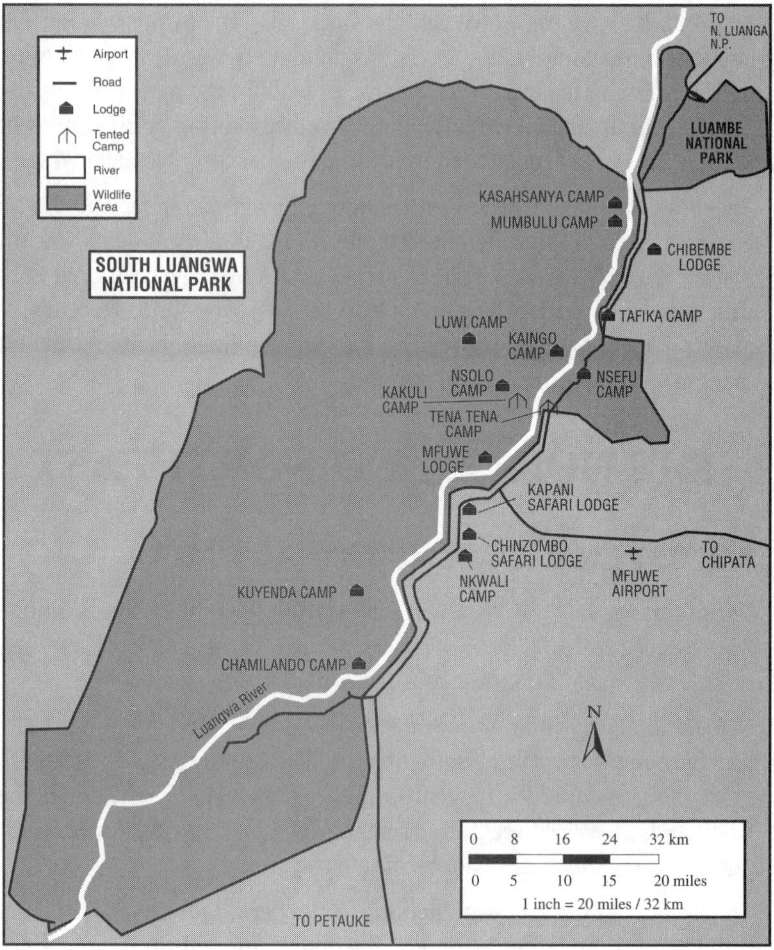

lilac-breasted rollers, bateleur eagles, Pel's fishing owl and long-tailed starlings. The best time for bird watching is November–April.

A real advantage of this great park is that visitors can experience day and night game drives in open vehicles as well as participate in walking safaris ranging in length from a few hours to three or more days.

In the central eastern part of the park, we saw lion, a pack of 21 African wild dogs, civet, buffalo, Cookson's wildebeest, common waterbuck, greater kudu, puku, impala, crocs, hippos mating and fighting, Thornicroft's giraffe, elephant, zebra, monitor lizard, warthog, and the ever-present baboons and vervet monkeys. Just before sunrise, elephant can sometimes be seen crossing the Luangwa River.

Driving from Mfuwe Airport to the north of the park, we sighted a spotted hyena, Cookson's wildebeest, impala and warthog. As we were sitting around the camp fire that night, we listened to baboon, hyena and hippo noises and watched honey badger (ratel) pass by within 20 feet (6 m) of us.

Night Game Drives

South Luangwa is one of the best parks in Africa for night drives. On a recent visit, the night game drive started out slowly until we almost ran over a lion lying in the middle of the road. What a shock! He was a member of a pride of seven that was hunting in thick bush. We followed them for a while until the driver was afraid that we might accidentally get caught in the middle of the hunt and become the hunted!

We then followed a leopard at close range (20 feet/6 m) which all but ignored our presence. We had quite a thrill when the leopard jumped high into a bush after two doves that must have been sleeping. Other sightings on the night game drives included spotted hyena, Pel's fishing owl, several more leopard and lion, and a number of genet and civet.

Wildlife seen on a one-week safari to South Luangwa included baboon, buffalo, bushbuck, civet, eland, elephant, large-spotted genet, Thornicroft's giraffe, hippo, honey badger, spotted hyena, impala, greater kudu, 4 leopard, over 20 lion, puku, vervet monkey, warthog, common waterbuck, African wild dog, gnu, Burchell's zebra, banded mongoose, white-tailed mongoose, crowned crane, African darter, fish eagle, goliath heron, marabou stork, sacred ibis, long-tailed glossy starling, brown snake eagle, a very large colony of storks nesting in three trees and many other birds.

There are few all-weather roads in the park north of Mfuwe, so most of the northern camps are closed from November 1 to June 1. In May and early June the grass is still high. The northern part of the park is usually closed December through May.

Guests of most camps usually have a game drive or walk in the early morning and in the afternoon take either a day game drive, departing about 3:30 p.m. and returning at dusk, or a late afternoon/night game drive, departing after 4:00 p.m. and returning around 8:00 p.m. Schedules will, of course, vary from camp to camp. Be sure to sign up for the option of your choice when checking in or as soon as possible thereafter.

Walking Safaris

Walking safaris are the highlight of many visitors' trips to Africa and are certainly one of my favorite ways of experiencing the bush. For those who would enjoy walking 3–7 miles (5–11 km) per day at a reasonable pace and wish to experience nature up close, walking safaris are highly recommended.

Walking safaris are only conducted from June to October during the dry season when the foliage has thinned out enough for safe walking. Walks may last from a few hours to five or more days. Guests are accompanied by a naturalist and an armed game scout from the national parks. Children under the age of 12 are not allowed on walks.

Most camps offer morning walks to their guests. Many camps have their own bush camps, catering to a maximum of six or seven guests, set in remote regions of the park in which walking is the main activity. However, bush camps are also excellent for those who do not want to do a lot of walking, but wish to simply relax and experience isolation in the bush.

Facilities in bush camps vary from comfortable chalets with ensuite facilities to simple huts with one shower and one long-drop toilet for the camp (see "Accommodations" below for details). From bush camps, groups of up to six or seven adults (depending on the camp) may participate in morning and afternoon walks. Some bush camps also offer day and night game drives.

Some camps offer programs where guests may walk from one bush camp to another. Your luggage is carried ahead to the next bush camp by vehicle or by porters who walk separately from the group. Guests usually carry only their cameras and a little water. The terrain is fairly flat, but often rugged. Food is prepared by a resident cook, and camps are stocked with cold drinks, wine and liquor. Huts are cleaned by the staff, and laundry service is available.

On the first morning of a four-day walking safari, we walked about two hours, and then our tea-bearer made hot tea. Our guide showed us how

Watching elephant from afoot.

to make fire with a piece of wood, a stick and dried elephant dung. On the walk he did an excellent job answering our endless questions about spoor (animal footprints and droppings) and flora and fauna of the bush.

After another one-and-one-half-hour walk, we reached our first camp. Scenically situated on the banks of the Luangwa River, there were more than 40 hippo in the water below and numerous crocs on the far shore.

After much-welcomed cold drinks, lunch and a short siesta, we regrouped at 3:30 p.m. for tea. At 4:00 p.m. we set off for another walk and returned just before dark (about 5:45 p.m.). After everyone had a hot shower, dinner was served. Then we sat around the camp fire, listening to the mysterious sounds of the night and gazing up at millions of stars.

Hippo, lion, hyena and elephant often came into camp at night. So, it's not a good idea to leave your hut after everyone has gone to bed.

One night we were awakened by an elephant silhouetted in the moonlight and standing next to our hut. One of the group took a flash photo and spooked it, and it ran out of camp. But I would have loved to have watched it longer, to have more fully experienced this encounter with the wildlife that is Africa.

Lion are sometimes encountered on walking safaris.

One afternoon as we were walking through an area with high golden grass I commented to our guide that a lion could be 20 feet (6 m) from the path and we might not see it. Just as the guide agreed with me, we turned around and there was a large female lion on the path not 50 feet (15 m) behind us. Once the lion knew we were all aware of her presence, she ran off. That was our first lion sighting!

The following morning we walked to our next bush camp, then had another walk in the afternoon. Two days later we returned to main camp, having seen numerous herds of impala, Burchell's zebra, puku, elephant and buffalo, along with Thornicroft's giraffe, baboon and lion. Most importantly, we felt a sense of accomplishment from experiencing the bush on more intimate terms, in the way that Livingstone, Stanley and other early African explorers confronted the challenge of the continent — on foot!

I suggest that you stay at least one or two additional nights in the park to go on day and night game drives by open vehicle; this will give you the opportunity to see many species that you might not have seen on your walking safari.

Mfuwe International Airport is about an hour flight from Lusaka. South Luangwa's main gate is 433 miles (700 km) from Lusaka; driving takes about ten hours and is not recommended. Some international visitors fly into Mfuwe from Lilongwe (Malawi) and Harare (Zimbabwe).

ACCOMMODATION IN *CENTRAL* SOUTH LUANGWA (usually open year-round) — CLASS A/B: * *Nkwali Camp*, sister camp to Tena Tena (see below), is situated just outside the park on the eastern banks of the Luangwa River near an elephant crossing point. The camp is open April–December and has 6 chalets (12 beds) with ensuite facilities. Day and night game drives and walks are offered. * *Kapani Safari Lodge* was operated by the late Norman Carr — the man who introduced walking safaris to Zambia. This camp has 8 chalets (16 beds) with ensuite facilities, a large swimming pool, and a library/video room where you can watch wildlife videos or even plug in your video recorder and view the footage shot during your safari. Kapani offers day and night game drives, walks, and visits to traditional villages and a crocodile farm. * *Chinzombo Safari Lodge* is located on the eastern bank of the Luangwa River across from the park. The camp has 9 chalets (18 beds) with ensuite facilities. Day and night game drives, morning walks and visits to local villages are offered. Chinzombo has two bush camps, * *Kuyenda Camp* and * *Chamilandu Camp* (Class B). Both have reed and grass huts (six beds) with ensuite facilities. Walks and game drives are offered, as are walks from one camp to the other. * *Mfuwe Lodge,* set on a picturesque lagoon, has 36 rooms with ensuite facilities and a swimming pool and offers day and night game drives. As of this writing, the lodge was being renovated, and when renovations are complete it is expected to have a Class A/B rating.

ACCOMMODATION IN *NORTHERN* SOUTH LUANGWA (usually open June–early November) — CLASS A: * *Tafika* has four thatched chalets (eight beds) with ensuite facilities. Day and night game drives, walks and microlight flights are offered. * *Tena Tena*, operated along with Nkwali Camp (see above) by Robin Pope, is

Tafika Camp's dining area.

located on the banks of the Luangwa River inside the park. Accommodations consist of 6 large tents (12 beds) under thatch, with ensuite facilities. Day and night game drives, morning walks and two different six-day mobile tented walking safaris are offered. * *Kaingo Camp* overlooks the Luangwa River and has four thatched chalets (eight beds) with ensuite facilities. Walks, day and night game drives, and photography from a hide are offered.

CLASS B: Kapani Lodge (see above) operates three bush camps in the Northern part of the park — Nsolo Camp, Luwi Camp and Kakuli Camp. Escorted walks may be taken from all three camps, and guests may walk from camp to camp. * *Nsolo Camp,* situated near a permanent water hole, caters to a maximum of six guests in four cottages with ensuite facilities. Walking safaris are the prime activity; game viewing from a hide overlooking a water hole and day and night game drives are also offered. * *Luwi Camp* has four bamboo huts with ensuite facilities accommodating a maximum of six guests. A large hippo pool is located nearby. Walking safaris are offered. * *Kakuli Camp,* set on a riverbank overlooking the confluence of the Luangwa and Luwi Rivers, accommodates a maximum of six guests in tents

Tena Tena tent.

with ensuite facilities. Day and night game drives as well as walks are offered. * *Nsefu Camp* is located near the Luangwa River a 60- to 90-minute drive from Mfuwe Airport. It has 6 brick and thatch rondavels (12 beds) with facilities ensuite. Day and night game drives and morning walks are offered. A water hole and hides are situated adjacent to the camp. * *Chibembe Lodge*, located just outside the park on the banks of the Luangwa River, has chalets with ensuite facilities (20 beds) and a swimming pool. Day and night game drives and morning walks are offered. This is also base camp for four-day walking safaris. Chibembe's two rustic bush camps, * *Kasansanya* and * *Mumbulu* (Class C), each have seven beds with a shared long-drop toilet and shower.

CAMPING: Camping is not allowed in the park except with a licensed tour operator.

NORTH LUANGWA NATIONAL PARK

As the name implies, this largely undeveloped 1780-square-mile (4636 km^2) park lies north of South Luangwa National Park in the upper Luangwa Valley.

Mark and Delia Owens, coauthors of *Eye of the Elephant* and *Cry of the Kalahari*, conducted wildlife research here and were successful in reducing poaching and creating an infrastructure to attract tourists.

The park lies between the 4600-foot- (1400-m) high Muchinga Escarpment on the west and the Luangwa River on the east, with altitudes ranging from 1640 to 3610 feet (500 to 1100 m). Vegetation includes miombo woodland, scrubland and riverine forest.

Wildlife includes lion, leopard, elephant, buffalo, zebra, eland, kudu, Cookson's wildebeest, impala, bushbuck, hippo, crocodile and a large population of spotted hyena. Nearly 400 species of birds have been recorded, including half-collared kingfisher, long-tailed wagtail, white-winged babbling starling, yellow-throated longclaw, black-backed barbet and white-breasted cuckoo shrike.

Walking is by far the primary activity, as there are very few roads.

This park is visited by very few tourists. It is in fact unlikely that you will encounter any other groups on your visit!

The rainy season is November–March. The best time to visit is July–October.

ACCOMMODATION — CLASS B/C: * *Mwaleshi Camp* is a rustic bush camp set on the banks of the Mwaleshi River with three chalets with separate facilities. Escorted walks in the bush are offered.

CLASS C: * *Buffalo Camp* is a rustic six-bed camp with separate facilities.

CAMPING: Campsites are not available.

LUAMBE NATIONAL PARK

This undeveloped, 99-square-mile (254-km^2) savannah and woodlands park is located just northeast of South Luangwa National Park. Luambe has many of the same species and features of South Luangwa National Park, but lacks tourist facilities to accommodate visitors.

ACCOMMODATION: None.

CAMPING: No camping sites available.

Mwaleshi Camp, North Luangwa.

NYIKA PLATEAU NATIONAL PARK

Located in northeast Zambia on the border with Malawi, this 31-square-mile (80-km^2) park includes the small Zambian portion of the Nyika Plateau. This is a good park to visit for a keen naturalist or anyone wishing to escape the summer heat of the valleys below. Due to the high altitude, night temperatures sometimes drop below freezing in May–September.

Montane grassland and relic montane forest dominate the scene. A great variety of orchid and butterfly species are present, along with Moloney's monkey, blue monkey, civet and a number of other small mammals. Leopard, serval, bushbuck, reedbuck, blue duiker and klipspringer are present but rarely seen. Several species of birds not found elsewhere in Zambia may be seen. The best time for bird watching is November–June.

ACCOMMODATION — See "Nyika National Park" in the chapter on Malawi.

SUMBU NATIONAL PARK

Sumbu National Park borders the huge inland sea of Lake Tanganyika in the extreme north of Zambia. Visitors come to this 780-square-mile (2020-km^2) park mainly for fishing and water sports. This part of Lake Tanganyika is reputedly bilharzia-free, but be sure to check the current status.

Forest and wetland wildlife species are plentiful. In fact, visitors are often accompanied to the sandy beaches by wildlife guards. Elephant, lion, buffalo, eland, puku, roan antelope, blue duiker and Sharpe's grysbok may be seen. The shoreline is inhabited by hippo, crocodile and water birds. Savannah dominates the park inland.

Day and night game drives in open vehicles, guided walks, and day and night game viewing by boat for crocodile are available.

Fishing for goliath tigerfish, vundu (giant catfish), lake salmon and Nile perch in Lake Tanganyika is excellent, especially December–April. The Zambia National Fishing Competition at Kasaba Bay is held every March or April, depending on the water level. Boats are available for hire.

ACCOMMODATION — CLASS C: * *Kasaba Bay Lodge* has 18 chalets (doubles) with ensuite facilities and a swimming pool, and is located a few hundred yards from the beach. The lodge offers fishing, game viewing and boating. * *Ndole Bay Lodge,* located just outside the park, has chalets (18 beds) with facilities ensuite; game viewing, fishing and boating are available.

* *Nkamba Bay Lodge,* located 15 miles (24 km) from Kasaba Bay in the park on a hill overlooking the beach, has ten chalets (doubles) with ensuite facilities. Activities include fishing, boating and game viewing.

THE SOUTH AND WEST

LUSAKA

Lusaka, the capital of Zambia, has little to offer the international tourist. Sights include the Luburma Market and Chief Mungule's Village. Wood carvings made by local craftsmen can be seen at Kabwata Cultural Center.

There is a duty-free shop in town that only takes foreign currency; this shop has liquor and other items you may be unable to find in other stores, since shopping is limited. The airport is 16 miles (26 km) from the city.

ACCOMMODATION — FIRST CLASS: * *Pamodzi Hotel* is a 480-bed air-conditioned hotel with facilities ensuite, a swimming pool and casino. * *Lusaka Inter-Continental Hotel* is an air-conditioned hotel with 402 rooms with facilities ensuite, 24-hour room service, three restaurants, a casino and a swimming pool. * *Holiday Inn Garden Court* is an air-conditioned 215-bed hotel with facilities ensuite, a casino and a swimming pool. * *Andrews Motel* is a 250-bed air-conditioned motel with a swimming pool.

ACCOMMODATION NEAR LUSAKA — CLASS A/B: **Lechwe Lodge* is located on a game sanctuary an hour's drive from the airport. The lodge, set on the banks of the Kafue River, has rooms (eight beds total) with ensuite facilities. Day trips to Lochinvar National Park may be arranged.

CLASS B: * *Lilayi Lodge,* a guest ranch located about a 40-minute drive from the airport, has six chalets with ensuite facilities. Game drives and walks are offered.

LOCHINVAR NATIONAL PARK

Lochinvar is a bird-watcher's paradise, with over 400 species recorded. In addition, the park is host to about 30,000 Kafue lechwe (their stronghold), 2000 blue wildebeest and 700 zebra. Greater kudu, buffalo, bushbuck, oribi, hippo, side-striped jackal, reedbuck and common waterbuck are also present.

Kafue lechwe are unique to the Kafue Flats and are related to the red lechwe of the Busanga Swamps of Kafue National Park.

Bird watching in this 153-square-mile (410-km^2) park is best February–March and also very good November–December and April–May. Water birds such as the wattled crane are especially abundant. Other bird species include fish eagles. The park also encompasses part of Chunga Lake, which is fished by villagers living outside the park boundaries.

The park is open year-round and is located 145 miles (235 km) southwest of Lusaka, 30 miles (50 km) northwest of Monze off the Lusaka–Livingstone road. A four-wheel-drive vehicle may be necessary in the rainy season.

ACCOMMODATION NEAR THE PARK — CLASS A/B: **Lechwe Lodge,* located on a game sanctuary along the banks of the Kafue River, has rooms (eight beds total) with ensuite facilities. Day trips to the park may be arranged.

ACCOMMODATION — CLASS D: **Lochinvar Lodge* has a 20-bed capacity with ensuite facilities.

KAFUE NATIONAL PARK

Kafue National Park, one of the largest in Africa, covers 8687 square miles (22,400 km^2), making it two and one-half times the size of South Luangwa National Park and half the size of Switzerland.

Kafue has the largest number of different antelope species of any park in Africa. Many of the species, such as greater kudu and sable antelope, are said to be substantially larger than elsewhere in the country. However, game is more difficult to see here than in South Luangwa, since the wildlife is not as habituated to human presence and much of Kafue, especially the southern area, is clothed with a double-canopy forest.

The southern and central parts are open all year while the northern area is only open during the dry season (June–October/November). Game is especially difficult to spot in the rainy season.

Game drives in this park are sometimes a combination of riding in a vehicle and walking, according to the wishes of the group.

On daylight game drives in the south of the park, we found elephant, impala, warthog, hippo, sable antelope, Burchell's zebra, wildebeest and buffalo. Night game drives produced sightings of impala, oribi, hundreds of spring hares, greater kudu, buffalo, serval, bushbuck, duiker, spotted hyena, Burchell's zebra, elephant, Defassa waterbuck and bushbabies.

Lake Itezhi-Tezhi, formed as the result of a hydroelectric dam constructed at the southern end of the Kafue Flats, provides fishing, birdwatching and boating opportunities for visitors.

The Busanga Plains and marshes in the north have a greater number and variety of wildlife species. Wildlife is easier to spot here than in the dense woodland savannah in the south. This region is predominantly miombo forest giving way to savannah grasslands, along with rock hills, marshes and riverine forests. The Kafue River runs through the northern part of the park and along its east central border.

Large herds of red lechwe may be seen on the Busanga Plains. Sitatunga may be found in the Busanga Swamps on the northern border of the park. Lion are often seen on day and night game drives, while cheetah and leopard are occasionally encountered. Buffalo, elephant, puku, wildebeest, impala, roan antelope, sable antelope, kudu, Lichtenstein's hartebeest, waterbuck and hyena are also present. More than 400 species of birds have been recorded.

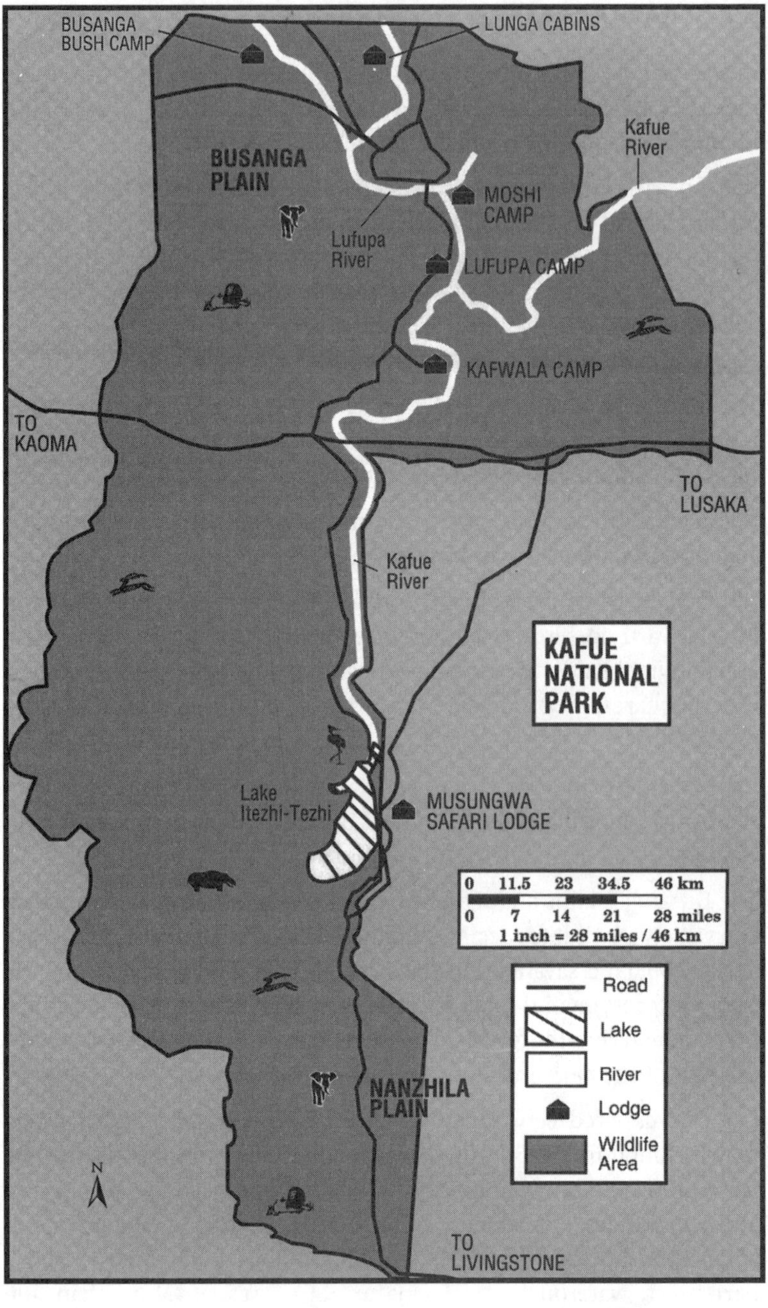
BUSANGA BUSH CAMP
LUNGA CABINS
Kafue River
BUSANGA PLAIN
MOSHI CAMP
Lufupa River
LUFUPA CAMP
KAFWALA CAMP
TO KAOMA
TO LUSAKA
Kafue River
KAFUE NATIONAL PARK
Lake Itezhi-Tezhi
MUSUNGWA SAFARI LODGE
0 11.5 23 34.5 46 km
0 7 14 21 28 miles
1 inch = 28 miles / 46 km
Road
Lake
River
Lodge
Wildlife Area
NANZHILA PLAIN
N
TO LIVINGSTONE

There is little to be seen on the four-hour, 170-mile (275-km) drive from Lusaka; scheduled group charter flights from Livingstone, Lusaka and Lower Zambezi National Park are available and are a better alternative. Mobile tented safaris are another way to explore the park.

ACCOMMODATION IN SOUTHERN KAFUE (open year-round) — CLASS B/C: * *Musungwa Safari Lodge* (46 beds) is located just outside the eastern boundary of the park. The lodge has a swimming pool, and most rooms have private facilities. Sunset cruises, river trips and game drives are offered.

ACCOMMODATION IN NORTHERN KAFUE (open June–October/November) — CLASS A: * *Lunga Cabins* has six thatched chalets with ensuite facilities. Day and night game drives, walks, boat game drives and canoeing are offered.

CLASS B: * *Busanga Bush Camp* has three thatched huts with ensuite facilities. Day and night game drives are offered.

CLASS C: * *Kafwala Camp* overlooks the Kafwala Rapids and has chalets (some with ensuite facilities). Day and night game drives are offered. * *Lufupa*, situated in the center of the northern region near the confluence of the Kafue and Lufupa Rivers, has chalets (some with ensuite facilities) and offers day and night game drives, fishing and game viewing by boat.

LIUWA PLAIN NATIONAL PARK

Located in southwestern Zambia, this remote 1413-square-mile (3660-km^2) park of open plains contains large numbers of wildebeest along with lion, hyena and spectacular numbers of migrating birds.

Wildlife, however, should be considered a plus and not the main reason for traveling to this seldom-visited park, which is more suited for bird watchers, for those looking to travel in a remote wilderness area, and to meet Africans who have had little contact with tourists.

ACCOMMODATION: As of this writing, a permanent camp is under construction. Mobile tented safaris are available.

SIOMA FALLS

Sioma Falls, located a six-hour drive and 185 miles (300 km) upstream (northwest) of Victoria Falls, is a magnificent series of six horseshoe-shaped falls stretching across the one-and-one-half-mile-wide Zambezi River. The best time to visit is July–January.

ACCOMMODATION — CLASS A/B: * *Maziba Bay Lodge* has six chalets with ensuite facilities and a swimming pool. Activities include fishing, white-water rafting, canoeing, game activities and microlighting.

MOSI-OA-TUNYA (VICTORIA FALLS) NATIONAL PARK

Called Mosi-oa-Tunya (the smoke that thunders), Victoria Falls should not be missed. Visitors may walk along the Knife Edge Bridge for a good view of the Eastern Cataract and Boiling Pot.

A **sunset cruise** is a very pleasant experience; hippo and crocodile are often seen. Fixed-wing aircraft flights over the falls are a great way to get a bird's-eye view of Victoria Falls.

Canoe safaris are conducted upstream of the falls. Fishing for tigerfish on the Zambezi River is best from June to October (September is best), before the rains muddy the water.

The falls are located about 3 miles (5 km) from Livingstone. See the chapter on Zimbabwe for a detailed description of the falls.

White-Water Rafting

The Zambezi River below Victoria Falls is one of the most exciting white-water rafting experiences in the world. Numerous fifth-class rapids (the highest class runable) make this one of the most challenging rivers on earth. One-, two-, three- and seven-day trips are operated on the Zambezi River below Victoria Falls from the Zambia and/or Zimbabwe side of the Zambezi River. See the description of white-water rafting in the "Victoria Falls" section of the chapter on Zimbabwe for further details.

ACCOMMODATION — See under "Livingstone" below.

Tongabezi Honeymoon House.

LIVINGSTONE

Livingstone is a small town of about 80,000 inhabitants, 5 miles (8 km) from the town of Victoria Falls. Driving from Lusaka takes five to six hours (295 miles/470 km) and flying takes a little over an hour.

The Livingstone Museum is the National Museum of Zambia and is renowned for its collection of Dr. Livingstone's memoirs. Other exhibits cover the art and culture of Zambia. The Maramba Cultural Center exhibits bandas from various districts in Zambia and presents colorful costumed performances by Zambian dancers. The Railway Museum has steam engines and trains from the late 1800s and 1900s.

Livingstone Zoological Park is a small fenced park near Livingstone covering 25 square miles (65 km^2). It is stocked with giraffe, buffalo, impala and other wildlife. The best time to visit is from June to October.

ACCOMMODATION — DELUXE: * *Mosi-oa-Tunya Inter-Continental Hotel,* a 200-bed hotel with air-conditioning, a swimming pool and three restaurants, is a five-minute walk from Victoria Falls.

TOURIST CLASS: * The *New Fairmount Hotel* has air-conditioned rooms (168 beds) with ensuite facilities and a swimming pool and casino. * *Rainbow Lodge* has traditionally styled rondavels and rooms (104 beds) and ensuite facilities.

ACCOMMODATION NEAR LIVINGSTONE — CLASS A: * *Tongabezi Camp*, situated on the Zambezi River 12 miles (20 km) upstream from Victoria Falls, is an exclusive 18-bed camp with five tents under thatch and four luxury chalets: Honeymoon House, Tree House, Bird House and Dog House. All units have ensuite facilities, and there is a swimming pool hewn out of rock. Canoeing, boat excursions, fishing, tennis, croquet and flights over the falls are offered. Tongabezi also operates * *Livingstone Island Camp* (Class C), a mobile tented fly–camp set on the edge of Victoria Falls in the midst of the thundering spray. The camp is open June–December.

CLASS B: * *Sindabezi Island Camp*, located on an exclusive island in the Zambezi River 2 miles (3 km) downstream from Tongabezi Camp, has four thatched cottages with ensuite bush (bucket) showers and flush toilets. * *Chindukwa Camp* is a small eight-bed camp located 16 miles (25 km) upstream from Livingstone. Activities include canoeing, horseback riding and walking. * *Thorn Tree Camp* is set on the banks of the Zambezi River 6 miles (10 km) from Victoria Falls. Accommodations are in tents under thatch with ensuite facilities.

LAKE KARIBA

Lake Kariba is one of the largest man-made lakes in the world — 180 miles (290 km) long and up to 20 miles (32 km) wide (see "Lake Kariba" in the chapter on Zimbabwe for full details). The Zimbabwe (southern) side of the lake is currently more developed than the Zambia (northern) side of the lake. Canoe safaris are offered downstream of Kariba Dam through the Kariba Gorge.

SIAVONGA

Siavonga is a small village situated on Lake Kariba just west of Lake Kariba Dam.

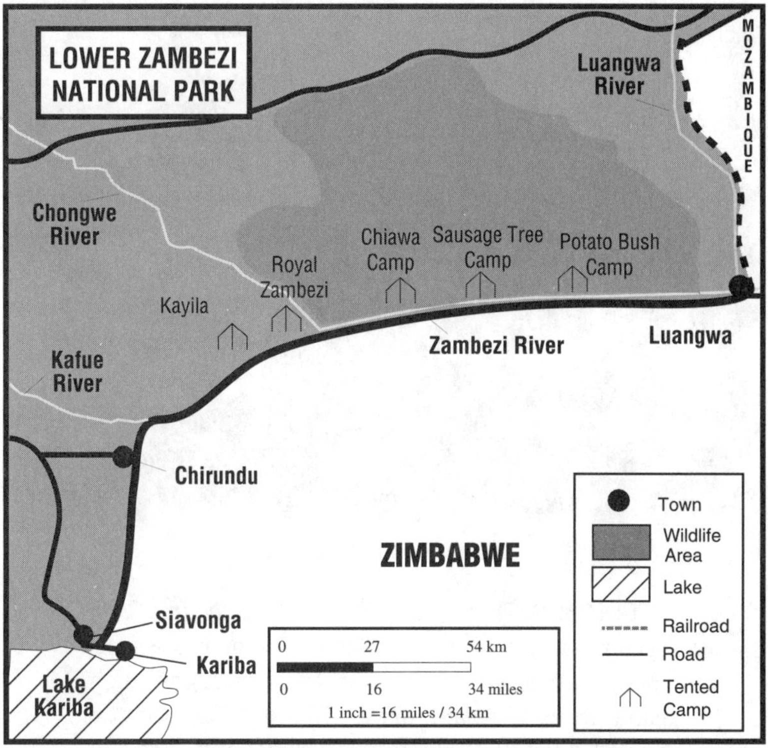

ACCOMMODATION — TOURIST CLASS: * *Manchinchi Bay Lodge* is a 50-bed lodge with air-conditioned rooms and a swimming pool. Boating and fishing are offered.

LOWER ZAMBEZI NATIONAL PARK

Located along the Zambezi River across from Mana Pools National Park (Zimbabwe), the Lower Zambezi National Park extends 75 miles (120 km) along the Zambezi River between the Chongwe River on the west and nearly to the Luangwa River to the East, and approximately 20 miles (35 km) inland.

A major attraction is canoe safaris on the Zambezi River. On most canoe safaris, guests overnight in comfortable permanent camps with ensuite facilities.

Walks, day and night game drives, and boat game drives are also offered. Elephant, buffalo, lion and a variety of antelope are often seen.

Sausage Tree Camp.

ACCOMMODATION — CLASS A/B: * *Sausage Tree Camp* accommodates up to 12 guests in large oval-shaped marquee-style tents with ensuite facilities. Day and night game drives, boat game drives, fishing and canoeing are offered. * *Potato Camp,* located downstream from Sausage Tree Camp, has four large tents with ensuite facilities. Day and night game drives, boat game drives, canoeing and fishing are offered. Full-day canoe safaris are available from Sausage Tree Camp to Potato Camp. * *Chiawa Camp,* a tented camp (16 beds) situated on the banks of the Zambezi River, has tents under thatch and facilities ensuite. Day and night vehicle game drives, boat game drives, canoeing and walking are offered.

ACCOMMODATION NEAR THE PARK — CLASS A/B: * *Kayila Lodge,* situated on a private game sanctuary near the park on the banks of the Zambezi River, has stone and thatch chalets with ensuite facilities. Day and night game drives, walks, canoeing and fishing are offered. * *Royal Zambezi Lodge,* located 6 miles (10 km) from the park, is a tented camp (12 beds) with ensuite facilities. Game drives into the park are offered.

MALAWI

HORSE-LIKE ANTELOPE – ROAN AND SABLE

Sable antelope are majestic animals — with their long scimitar-like horns. Males with their dark glossy black coats with a long upstanding mane look far classier than their cousin the roan antelope. Roan have shorter horns, large floppy ears and are dun colored and rather reminiscent of an odd-looking donkey.

Sable antelope like deciduous broad-leaved woodlands, especially open miombo (*brachystegia*) woodlands with good grass cover, and also frequent mopane woodlands. Roan antelope prefer thinly treed areas and open grassed savannah.

Exclusively African, these antelope share a common ancestry with gazelles and goats and, like them, are adapted to dry conditions. They are grazers with molars well adapted to grinding hard grasses. They are specialists in exploiting zones with an impoverished flora and fauna, preferring areas where there are few competitors and few predators.

They develop attachments to large home ranges and get to know these areas intimately. During the dry season, these antelope may move out of their wooded and grassland areas to valley bottoms or riverine grasslands where water is more readily available.

Sable herds of up to 30 females and youngsters are controlled by an old cow, but during the rut, a bull dominates the herd and defends it aggressively from other males. Roan are not territorial, and in the breeding season a dominant bull maintains access to a female herd by defending it from intruders.

Both species of antelope have single calves. Young animals are exceptionally social, spending much of their time cavorting, running about and mock fighting. Adult antelope are unusual in that the horns of females are as long as males. This enables females to resist attempts by males to limit their movements or threaten their youngsters.

MALAWI

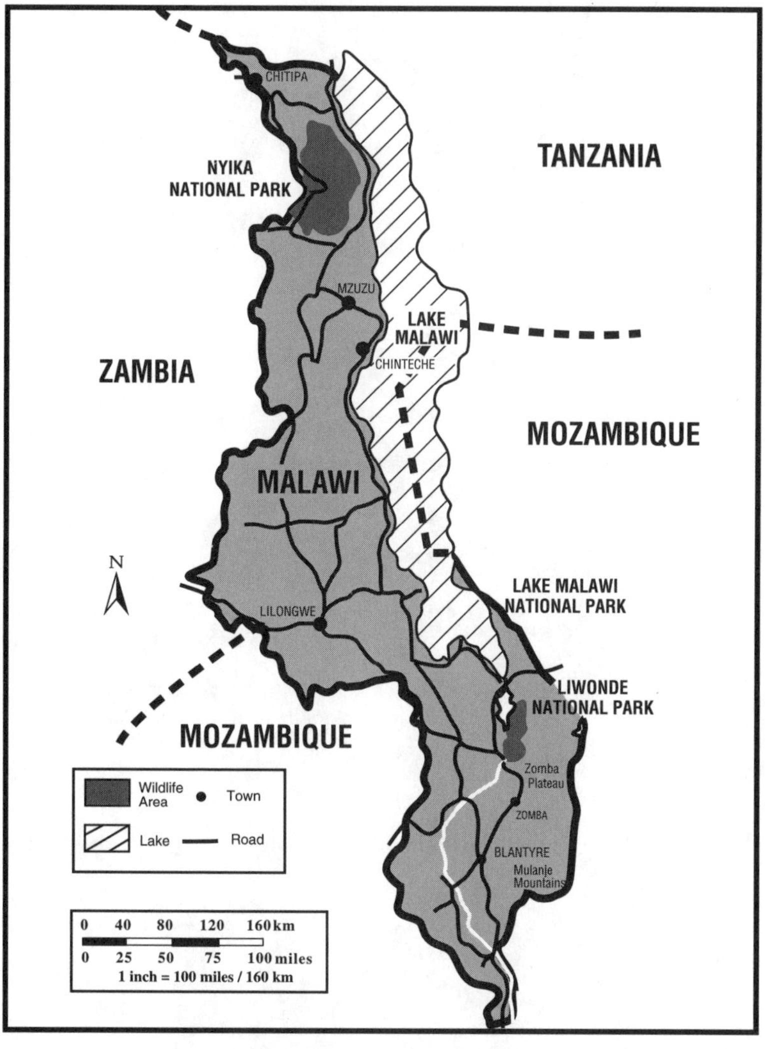

FACTS AT A GLANCE

AREA:	45,560 SQ. MI. / 118,000 SQ. KM.
APPROXIMATE SIZE:	ONE SIXTH THE SIZE OF TEXAS
POPULATION:	10 MILLION
CAPITAL:	LILONGWE (POP. EST. 350,000)
OFFICIAL LANGUAGE:	ENGLISH
NATIONAL LANGUAGE:	CHICHEWA

MALAWI

Malawi, the "warm heart of Africa," is a beautiful country with a variety of wildlife and cultural and holiday attractions of interest to the international traveler.

Geographically the country is dominated by Lake Malawi, which stretches along the spine of the country. It is often referred to as the calendar lake as its surface dimensions are 365 miles (568 km) long and 52 miles (84 km) wide at its widest point.

This freshwater lake, the southernmost in the Rift Valley chain, is the third largest in Africa. It is also one of the deepest of the Great Rift Valley lakes, over 2296 feet (700 m) deep, with its deepest point 755 feet (230 m) below sea level. Lake Malawi has over 400 species of freshwater fish and the largest number of cichlid fish species in the world.

Malawi is bordered by Zambia to the west, Tanzania to the north and Mozambique to the east and south. From north to south Malawi is about 560 miles (900 km) long. The dominant geographical features in the south of the country are the Shire River and the high plateau of Dedza, Zomba and the Kirk Mountain Range, reaching an altitude from 5050 feet (1540 m) to 8000 feet (2440 m) above sea level.

As a whole, the country ranges in altitude from 121 feet (37 m) in the lower Shire Valley in the south to a height of 9847 feet (3002 m) at Mt. Mulanje, also in the south. The northern lakeshore coastal area and adjacent low country rises steeply to the west with several areas, the

Misuku Hills, the Nyika plateau (Nganda point being the highest peak on the plateau at 8551 feet/2607 m) and the Viphya plateau, dominating the areas of higher ground. The dominant vegetation of Malawi is brachystegia or miombo woodlands.

Malawi has a tropical climate with a rainy season extending from November to March in the South and November to April in the North. Its climate is influenced locally by the lake and by altitude. A curious weather effect, known as *chiperoni* — low clouds, condensation and a light drizzle precipitated by a high-pressure system in Mozambique forces moist cool air over higher ground — is a frequent occurrence during the dry season. Temperatures vary considerably, from a maximum of 104°F (40°C) in the low-lying Shire Valley (pronounced shirry) to below freezing on the plateaus, where frost may occur.

In the early fifteenth century, the area was inhabited by the Maravi people (the derivation of the word "Malawi"), who moved in from the west of the continent around the twelfth century. Arab slave traders were well established in the area by 1870 and were handling more than 20,000 slaves per year. David Livingstone first visited the area in 1859, and on his subsequent visits brought many British missionaries.

Nyasaland became a protectorate of the British Empire in 1891 and in 1953 joined the Federation of Northern (now Zambia) and Southern (now Zimbabwe) Rhodesia. Malawi became independent in 1964.

Chichewa is the national language, but English is the official language and is widely spoken. The most popular beer is Carlsberg, brewed according to Danish traditions. Do try the local wine Mlunguzi, but don't be surprised if it is not quite up to your taste — it certainly has never seen a grape. Also try some Malawi Gin, and do not miss out on Malawian cashew nuts, peanut butter and Mulanje Gold, an admirable substitute for Kahlua.

The country's economy is based on agriculture; 90 percent of its population is rural and agriculture accounts for 40 percent of the gross domestic product and 90 percent of its export revenues. Almost 70 percent of agricultural produce comes from smallholder farmers, with the principal crops being maize, tobacco, tea, sugarcane, groundnuts and coffee. With a population in excess of ten million, almost every available piece of arable land is cultivated.

WILDLIFE AND WILDLIFE AREAS

Great importance has been attached to the protection of Malawi's natural heritage, and this is reflected in the number of national parks and reserves within the country. Despite the burdens of overpopulation, almost 20 percent of Malawi's land area is set aside as either national park, game reserve or forest reserve.

Malawi's primary wildlife attractions are Liwonde National Park, Nyika National Park and Lake Malawi itself. Zambia is an excellent country to combine with Malawi, as South Luangwa National Park (Zambia) is easily accessible by air from Lilongwe.

LILONGWE

Lilongwe became the capital in 1975. Zomba, the old administrative capital, is still the venue of parliamentary debates.

While you are here, you will hear people talk of the "**Old Town**" and the "**New Town**." They are exactly that — the Old Town with its hustle and bustle, markets and buildings close together, and the New Town (also known as the "Garden City"), with its modern architecture, open pedestrian precincts and parklands.

A visit to the **market** in the Old Town is a worthwhile experience. Here one can buy anything from live chickens to used motor car parts. The air is high with the aroma of dried fish, spices and fresh vegetables.

The Lilongwe **Nature Sanctuary**, located between the old and new towns, is a good place for seeing small mammals such as porcupine, civet and vervet monkeys and for spotting birds such as Peter's twinspot and perhaps African finfoot.

ACCOMMODATION — DELUXE: * *Capital Hotel* is located in the New Town, adjacent to the commercial and diplomatic areas. The hotel has 185 air-conditioned rooms with ensuite facilities, two restaurants and a swimming pool.

FIRST CLASS: * *Lilongwe Hotel,* situated on 3 acres of landscaped gardens in the heart of the Old Town, has 91 air-conditioned rooms with ensuite facilities, two restaurants and a swimming pool.

BLANTYRE

Blantyre, named after the birthplace of the great explorer David Livingstone, began as a mission station in 1876. Its position in the agriculturally rich highlands and more temperate climate made it attractive to the first commercial traders.

Today, Blantyre is the largest city in the country and is also the commercial and industrial centre of Malawi. Historical sites include the **Blantyre Mission**, the beautiful church of **St. Michaels and All Angels**, and the **Mandala House**, the oldest building in the country (erected in 1882). Blantyre's market is more modern and does not have quite the same appeal as that of Lilongwe.

For six months of each year (April–September), the nearby city of Limbe is a hive of activity as the **Tobacco Auction Floors** are opened to buyers from around the world. Those thinking of visiting the floors should call in advance.

ACCOMMODATION — DELUXE: * *Mt. Soche Hotel,* located very close to the city center, has 132 air-conditioned rooms with ensuite facilities, two restaurants and a swimming pool.

LAKE MALAWI

Lake Malawi is the country's largest tourist attraction and a seemingly endless supplier of protein in the form of fish to the local people. *Chambo*, a sought after tilapia (freshwater bream), is a good eating fish.

On the lake you will see fishermen in their *bwatus* (dugout canoes) fishing either with nets or with lines. Sometimes at night you will see the twinkling of lights on the lake from bwatus and boats with small outboard motors.

The mostly clear waters of the lake make this an inviting environment for recreational activities. The southern lakeshore hotels are best equipped in this regard, and board sailing, water skiing, sailing, snorkeling and scuba diving are all available.

Malawi offers some of the best inland sailing in Africa. Although rough waters can suddenly develop with the onset of strong winds, there are no tides or currents in the lake. The prevailing wind is southeasterly and the lake is at its calmest from April to November.

Livingstonia Beach Hotel.

LAKE MALAWI NATIONAL PARK

Lake Malawi National Park is the first national park to give protection to freshwater life of a deep-water Rift Valley lake. The 34-square-mile (88-km^2) park is located in the southern part of the lake and includes 12 islands and most of the Nankhumba Peninsula.

Its crystal clear waters and myriad colorful cichlid fish darting amongst the rocky shoreline entice one to don a mask and snorkel and join the fish in their daily activities. Day excursions to the park can be arranged from Nkopola and Club Makokola lodges.

Wildlife that may be seen includes bushbuck, klipspringer, crocs and hippos. Bird life includes fish eagles, trumpeter hornbill, white-breasted cuckoo-shrike, crowned and black eagles, golden-backed pytilia and mocking chat.

ACCOMMODATION ON THE SOUTHERN LAKESHORE — DELUXE: **Livingstonia Beach Hotel*, one of the finest hotels in Malawi, has 18 rooms and 8 rondavels, all fan-cooled, with ensuite facilities and a restaurant and swimming pool. Sailboards, kayaks and boats are available for hire.

FIRST CLASS: * *Club Makokola,* set on a sand beach on the shores of Lake Malawi near Nkopola Lodge, has cottages and 68 rooms with ensuite facilities, a swimming pool, tennis courts, squash court and a conference center. * *Nkopola Lodge* is set on a hillside on the shore of Lake Malawi about 12 miles (20 km) north of the town of Mangochi. The lodge has 55 air-conditioned rooms with facilities ensuite and a restaurant.

ACCOMMODATION ON THE NORTHERN LAKESHORE — FIRST CLASS: * *Chintheche Inn,* ideally located on a quiet part of the northern lakeshore, has ten fan-cooled rooms with ensuite facilities and a restaurant. Bird life of note in this area includes palmnut vulture, green coucal, moustached warbler, Gunning's robin narina trogon and purple-banded sunbird.

LIWONDE NATIONAL PARK

Established in 1973, the 212-square-mile (548-km^2) Liwonde National Park was created to protect the important riverine vegetation and mopane woodland of the upper Shire Valley and is now Malawi's showpiece park.

A major feature of the park is the Shire River, which provides one of the last refuges in the country for hippo and Nile crocodile. The river flows out of Lake Malawi and forms the western boundary of the park. It forges its way southward over tumultuous rapids and falls to join the Zambezi River beyond Malawi's borders.

A recent cooperative project between the South African National Parks Board and the Government of Malawi helped fence the park to prevent poaching, restock it with species that were previously present in the region, and assisted in the construction of overnight accommodations suitable for tourists.

In Liwonde you have a good chance of seeing good numbers of impala, sable antelope, common waterbuck, warthog, hippo, elephant and crocodile. Predators like hyena and lion occur in small numbers.

This is a birder's paradise with over 400 species having been recorded. Boehm's bee-eater, Lilian's lovebird, brown-breasted barbet, Pel's fishing owl, white-backed night heron and marsh tchagra are a few of the species seen.

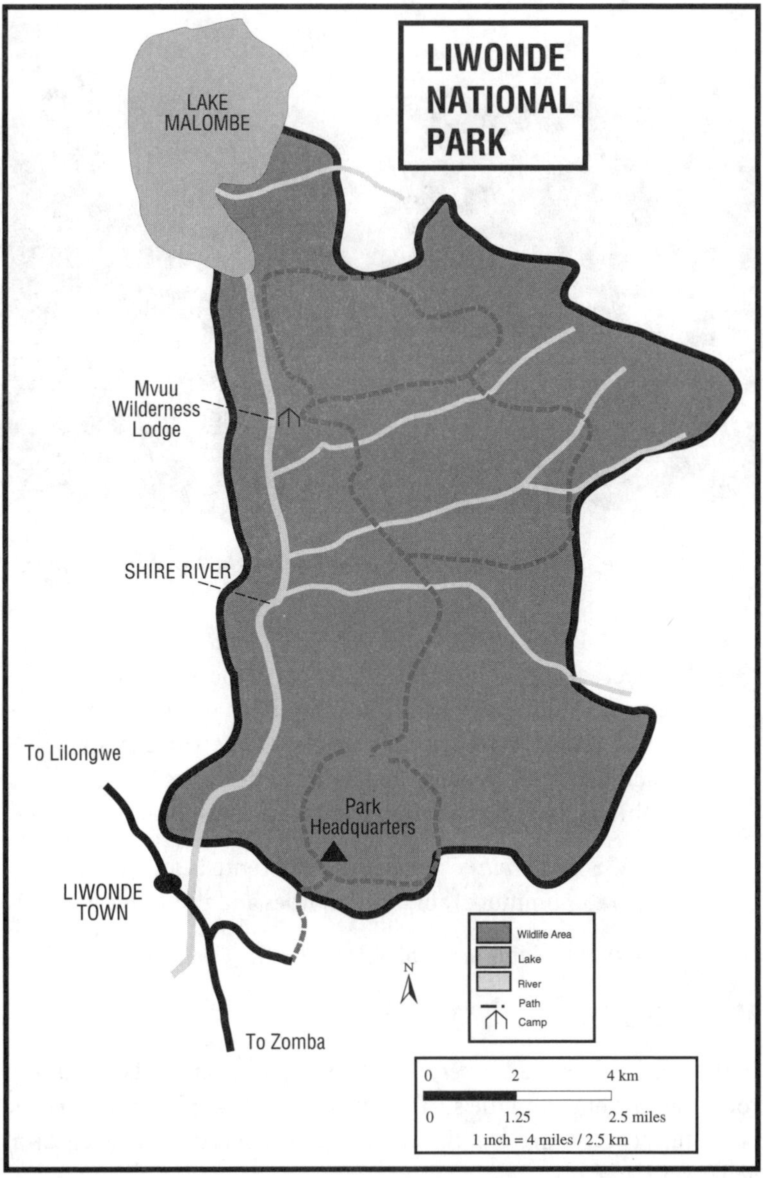

The best time for game viewing is during the dry season, May–October. Birding is best November–April, but is indeed very good year-round.

Liwonde lies 75 miles (120 km) from Blantyre and 152 miles (245 km) from Lilongwe, via the town of Liwonde.

Mvuu Lodge, seen from a boat game drive on the Shire River.

ACCOMMODATION — CLASS A: * *Mvuu Wilderness Lodge,* set on a quiet backwater area of the Shire River, has splendid views of this mighty river from its bar/dining deck. The lodge has five luxury tents with ensuite facilities, and offers day and night game drives in open vehicles, boat game drives and escorted walks.

CLASS D: * *Mvuu Camp* is a 20-bed tented camp with separate communal ablution facilities and a restaurant.

CAMPING: Sites are available.

MULANJE

In the southeast of the country lies Mt. Mulanje, an impressive hunk of rock that juts out from the surrounding featureless plains. This is one of the finest scenic areas in the country. Sapitwa is the highest peak at 9847 feet (3002 m).

There are a number of forestry rest huts on the plateau, and there are trails leading from hut to hut. A number of footpaths lead up to the massif from its base, the most popular being that from Likhabula on the west side of the mountain. A Forestry Rest House at the foot serves as

Guest House with Mt. Mulanje in background.

a base camp, and from here you can organize your climb. Porters may be hired to carry your gear as you must take all your supplies with you. The path is quite steep in places.

Mulanje is home to the Mulanje cedar, which is said to be one of the world's finest softwoods. Because the plateau is inaccessible by vehicle, all sawn and felled trees are carried off the plateau on the heads or shoulders of people who carry wood for a living.

Mulanje is a flower-lover's paradise. A variety of soil types have resulted in a range of habitats from evergreen rain forests with begonias on the sides of the plateau to heathlike grasslands covered in ericas and giant lobelias at higher altitudes. *Helichrysum* daisies dominate the landscape in the spring, as do a number of species of iris and brilliantly colored red-hot pokers. Two interesting birds seen here are the cholo alethe and the yellow-streaked bulbul.

Unfortunately, most game animals have been eliminated, but Mulanje can be very rewarding for botanists and birders.

The mountain is subject to extremes of climate, so if you are planning to walk on Mulanje, it is best to avoid the rainy season, January–April. Daytime temperatures May–August (the southern winter) are cool, with the likelihood of heavy mists in the mornings and the possibility of some frost at night. Between August and November it can get quite hot. Thunderstorms occur November–April.

ACCOMMODATION — CLASS F: * *Forestry Rest House* at Likhabula provides bedding. Forestry huts on the plateau have wooden bunks; bring all necessary equipment.

ACCOMMODATION NEAR MULANJE — CLASS C: * *Chawani Bungalow,* located on the Satemwa Tea Estate below Thyolo Mountain, has four rooms with separate facilities. Bring your own food and drink, and the cottage attendants will prepare your meals.

ZOMBA PLATEAU

The Zomba Plateau, decreed a forest reserve in 1913, rises 3300 feet (1000 m) above the surrounding plains. Although much of the plateau is covered in commercially planted Mexican pine (for the timber and wood pulp industries), the forest reserve protects some patches of exquisite indigenous forest and some extensive grasslands.

A series of walking trails meander about the plateau. The less energetic can drive, although some roads may become impassable during the wet season. The highest point on Zomba is Chiradzulu at 6835 feet (2084 m), and the climatic extremes are very similar to those on Mt. Mulanje. A narrow one-way road leads to the top of the plateau from the town of Zomba, and another takes you down.

Clear, cool mountain streams drain the plateau. Trout fishing in these streams and dams on the plateau is a popular pastime. Indeed, Malawi's only fish-fly-making factory is found in Zomba, home to the University of Malawi and one-time capital of the country. Fishing licenses are required and can be obtained from the Ku-Chawe Inn.

ACCOMMODATION — DELUXE: * *Ku-Chawe Inn,* located on the top of the Zomba Plateau, has 40 air-conditioned rooms with ensuite facilities and a restaurant.

CLASS D: Self-service cottages are available.

CAMPING: Forestry campsites area available.

Nyika Plateau.

NYIKA NATIONAL PARK

The Nyika Plateau is a wild, remote and spectacular area of rolling montane grasslands interspersed with pockets of evergreen forest.

The upland area of the Nyika (which means "wilderness" in the local Tumbuka language) Plateau was designated as Malawi's first national park in 1966. An important extension to the park, effectively doubling its size, was gazetted in 1976. Today it is the country's largest park, with a total area of 1210 square miles (3134 km^2).

Game on the plateau is plentiful, with reedbuck, common duiker and roan antelope the dominant animals, along with eland and Burchell's zebra. Leopard and bushpig are often seen on evening drives.

The flower-filled rolling grasslands of the Nyika are home to wattled crane, Denham's bustard, churring and black-lored cisticolas, common quail, rufous-naped lark, red-tufted malachite sunbird and mountain nightjar. The evergreen forest pockets, often beginning in valley heads and following drainage lines, are sanctuary to the large checkered elephant shrew, bushpig and forest duiker, along with a number of forest-dwelling birds such as moustached green tinkerbird, Fuelleborn's boubou, Sharpe's akalat, olive-flanked alethe, scaly francolin, Malawi batis, white-tailed flycatcher and bar-tailed trogon.

The best time to visit the park for botanists (for wildflowers and orchids) is September–January. For birders, September–March is best, although the heavy rains in January–April can restrict access to the park as well as one's activities in the park. Wildlife viewing is good throughout the year.

Horseback-Riding Safaris

Horseback safaris, ranging from day rides to three- to ten-day overnight trails for a maximum of six guests, are a great way to see the park. The horses are thoroughbred, part thoroughbred or cross breeds, and all between 14 and 17 hands in height. Tack is western McClellan for comfortable riding over long distances.

Overnight trails are supported by pack horses or by vehicle, depending on the size of the group and length of the safari. The camp is full service and is set up in advance of the guests' arrival. Riders sleep in stand-up-size tents, with a separate shower tent and long-drop toilet for the group. Meals are served in the dining tent or under the stars, depending on the weather. Riders are met in Mzuzu and transferred by road to Chelinda, where the horses are stabled.

A network of dirt roads meanders across the plateau. Access to the park is via Thazima Gate, 34 miles (55 km) from Rumphi and 81 miles (130 km) from Mzuzu. From Thazima Gate it is about 37 miles (59 km) to the Malawian Parks Board Camp of Chelinda.

ACCOMMODATION — CLASS C & D: * *Chelinda Rest Camp*, the Malawi Parks Rest Camp, has four two-bedroom cottages with private facilities and kitchen and 12 twin-bedded rooms with shared facilities. Bring your own food and drink, and cottage attendants will prepare your meals as requested.

CAMPING: A campsite with pre-erected tents and limited ablution facilities is available. You may also bring your own tent.

NAMIBIA

THE HEAT-ADAPTED GEMSBOK

Gemsbok normally inhabit arid regions and the key to their survival is their ability to survive without drinking much water. Also, various heat-resistant methods help the gemsbok exist in a dry environment.

They have splendid grey, white and black colorations, and their black face markings and dark leg and underpart markings may deflect heat and light away from their bodies. In extremely hot areas, gemsbok will use any form of shade. When none can be found, they are known to dig a small area in the sand and lie down to reduce the amount of hide exposed to the sun. If subjected to intense heat during the heat of the day, they increase their body temperature by several degrees, thereby not using up precious body water in the form of perspiration or panting (evaporation). They will then slowly lower their temperature by radiation during the cooler desert nights.

The gemsbok, for an animal of its size, has a lower than normal body metabolism which means that it requires less water. It has an extensive network of blood vessels close to surface of the nose which cools the blood flowing through the vessels by inhaled and exhaled air, thereby lowering the temperature of the blood returning to the brain. Its highly efficient kidneys are able to conserve valuable moisture as waste products pass as only a few drops of concentrated urine.

Gemsbok have also adapted amazing digging techniques to find bulbs, roots and underground plants–including cucumber and Tsamma melon –to obtain much needed moisture. Their stomachs have a high moisture content (80%), and bushmen are known to squeeze and strain gembok stomach contents for the water.

NAMIBIA

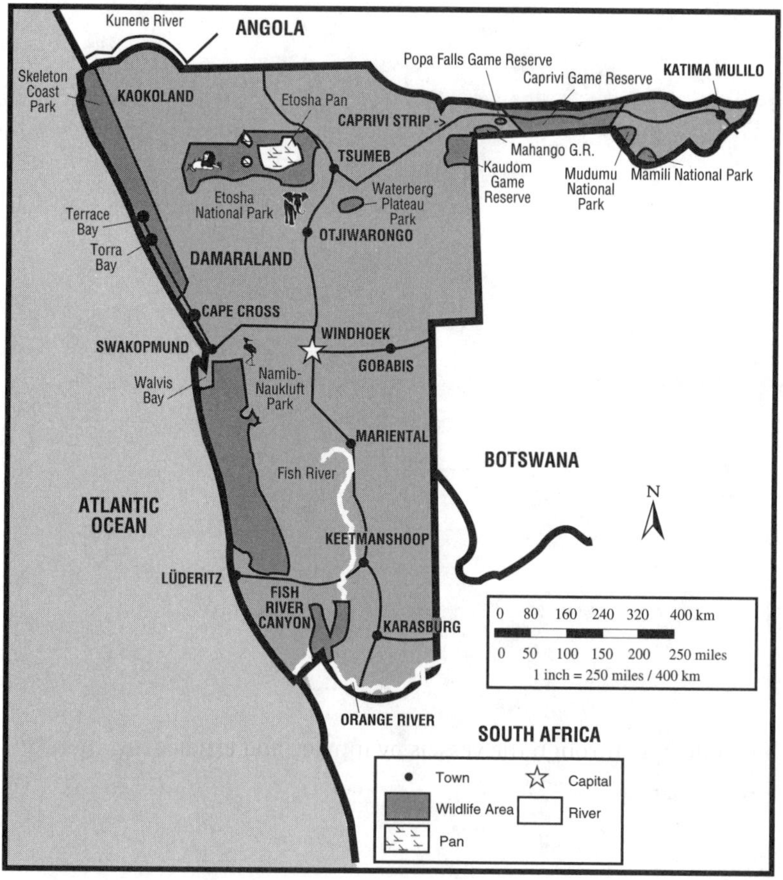

FACTS AT A GLANCE

AREA:	318,250 SQ. MI. / 824,268 SQ. KM.
APPROXIMATE SIZE:	TEXAS + OKLAHOMA OR ONE AND A HALF TIMES THE SIZE OF FRANCE
POPULATION:	1.5 MILLION
CAPITAL:	WINDHOEK (POP. EST. 170,000)
OFFICIAL LANGUAGE:	ENGLISH

NAMIBIA

In addition to wildlife, Namibia has some of the most spectacular desert ecosystems in the world. It is famous for its stark beauty and diversity of tribes, and is a geologist's and naturalist's paradise.

Namibia has a subtropical climate. Inland summer (October–April) days are warm to hot with cool nights. Summer is the rainy season, with most rainfall occurring in the north and northeast.

Namibia is one of the world's most sparsely populated countries. Its population is 86 percent black, 7 percent white and 7 percent colored (of mixed descent). Most people live in the northern part of the country where there is more water. Herero women, colorfully dressed in red and black, continue to wear conservative, impractical and extremely hot attire fashioned for them by puritanical nineteenth century missionaries who wished to cover the savage breast.

In 1884 much of the coast became German Southwest Africa until 1915 when South Africa took control during World War I. The Union of South Africa received a mandate by the League of Nations over the region in 1920; the United Nations retracted the mandate in 1966 and renamed the country Namibia. The country became independent on March 21, 1990.

Namibia is the world's largest producer of diamonds and has the world's second largest uranium mine. Tsumeb is the only known mine which has produced over 200 different minerals.

WILDLIFE AND WILDLIFE AREAS

Etosha National Park is Namibia's premier reserve for wildlife and is one of the best reserves in Africa. Skeleton Coast Park and Namib-Naukluft Park have small concentrations of wildlife in fascinating desert environments with spectacular scenery. Several new reserves have been created fairly recently in the Caprivi Strip "panhandle."

May–November is the best time to visit the game parks and the central and northern regions. From May to August (winter) days are warm with clear skies and nights are cold. From September to November days are hot and nights are cool.

Open-sided game-viewing vehicles registered to a few select tour operators are allowed in Etosha National Park. Open-sided vehicles are allowed in all other parks. Walking is allowed in all parks and reserves except Etosha. Walking is not, however, recommended unless accompanied by an experienced guide. The parks are well organized and the facilities clean.

THE NORTH

WINDHOEK

Windhoek is the capital and administrative, commercial and educational center of Namibia, situated in the center of the country at 5410 feet (1650 m) above sea level.

Sights include the two Windhoek castles (Schwerinsburg and Sanderburg) built between 1913 and 1918 and the State Museum at the Alte Feste (Old Fort).

ACCOMMODATION — DELUXE: * *Windhoek Country Club Resort and Casino* has 151 air conditioned rooms with ensuite facilities, tennis courts, an 18-hole golf course and a swimming pool.

FIRST CLASS: * *Kalahari Sands Hotel and Casino,* located in the center of town, has 185 air-conditioned rooms and suites with ensuite facilities, a rooftop swimming pool and a fitness center. * *Hotel Safari* and *Safari Court*, located 2 miles (3 km) out of town, has 452 air-conditioned rooms with ensuite facilities, a swimming pool and free transport to and from Windhoek. * *Heinitzburg Hotel* is an old castle with 11 air-conditioned rooms with ensuite facilities.

TOURIST CLASS: * *Villa Verdi*, a small guest lodge located a few minutes walk from downtown, has ten rooms with ensuite facilities and a swimming pool. * *Pension Kleines Heim* has 13 rooms with ensuite facilities. * *Hotel Thüringerhof* has 42 air-conditioned rooms with ensuite facilities and a beer garden. * *Continental Hotel* has 70 air-conditioned rooms, most with ensuite facilities, and a popular nightclub and disco.

CAMPING: * *Arebush*, located about 2.5 miles (4 km) from the city center, has campsites and budget self-catering chalets. * *Daan Viljoen Game Park*, 17 miles (27 km) from Windhoek, has campsites available.

ETOSHA NATIONAL PARK

Etosha is one of Africa's greatest parks in both size and variety of wildlife species. The park covers 8598 square miles (22,270 km^2) in the northern part of the country and lies 3280–4920 feet (1000–1500 m) above sea level.

The park is mainly mixed scrub, mopane savannah and dry woodland surrounding the huge Etosha (Salt) Pan. The pan is a silvery-white shallow depression, dry except during the rainy season. Mirages and dust devils play across what was once a lake fed by a river that long ago changed course. Along the edge of the pan are springs that attract wildlife during the dry winter season.

The eastern areas of the park experience the most rainfall and have denser bush than the northwestern region, which is mainly open grasslands. About 40 water holes spread out along 500 miles (800 km) of roads provide many vantage points from which to watch game.

One of the many herds of elephant at one of the many water holes.

Etosha is famous for its huge elephant population which is most visible July to September in the center of the park. Large numbers of elephant may also be seen in May, June and October. When the rains begin in January, some elephant herds migrate north to Angola and west to Kaokoland and begin returning in March. Large populations of zebra, blue wildebeest, springbok and gemsbok migrate westward from the Namutoni area in October–November to the west and northwest of Okaukuejo Camp where they stay until around March–May. From June to August they migrate eastward again past Okaukuejo and Halali Camps to the Namutoni plains where there is water year-round. The calving season (which attracts predators) for a number of antelope species is November–April. The park is totally fenced, although this does not always stop the elephant from going where they please.

Lion are commonly seen, and zebra are often sighted way out on the barren pan where lions have no cover from which to launch an attack. Black-faced impala and Damara dikdik, one of Africa's smallest antelopes, are two distinctive species of this area. Rhino occur throughout the park. Leopard are seen fairly often.

During one visit, we spotted black rhino, elephant, lion, red hartebeest, greater kudu, giraffe, gemsbok, zebra, blue wildebeest, springbok,

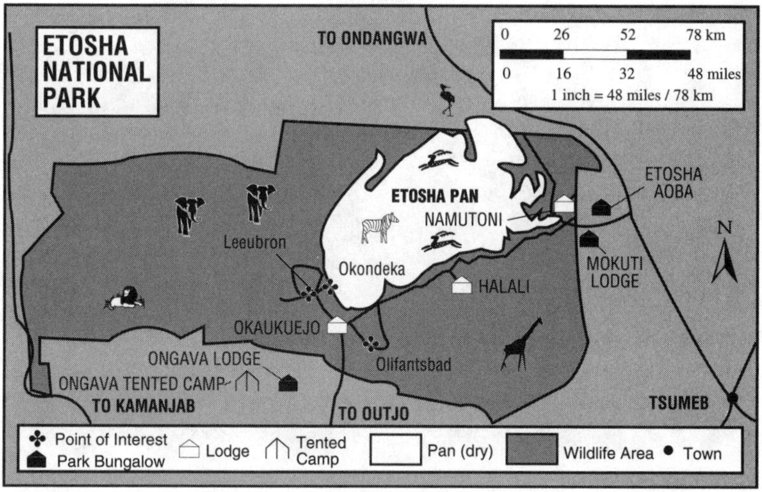

black-faced impala, black-backed jackal, honey badger, warthog and mongoose. Other wildlife in the park includes brown hyena, spotted hyena, caracal, African wildcat, leopard, cheetah, aardwolf, silver fox, bat-eared fox, eland, roan antelope and grey duiker.

Bird life is prolific, with over 325 species recorded, particularly on the Etosha Pan during the summer rainy season from mid-January to March. However, a diverse range of bird species can be seen year-round. Kites, pelicans, greater and lesser flamingos, and marabou storks migrate seasonally. Other species commonly sighted include kori bustard, guinea fowl, francolin, ostrich, turtle dove, lilac-breasted roller, Namaqua sand grouse and crimson-breasted shrike.

Roads run along the eastern, southern and western borders of the Etosha Pan. The area around Namutoni Camp in the eastern part of the park receives more rain than the other region of the park. Eland, kudu and Damara dikdik are often seen in the area. A good spot to see elephant is at Olifantsbad, a water hole between Halali and Okaukuejo Camps.

At the floodlit water hole at Okaukuejo Camp we witnessed an hour-long standoff between a black rhino and two elephants over control of the water hole. A lioness also came for a drink. The flatulence of the elephants was almost deafening!

Ongava Lodge, located adjacent to Etosha.

From Okaukuejo one can drive along the southwestern edge of the pan to Okondeka and west to the Haunted Forest, a dense concentration of eerie-looking African moringa trees. I wouldn't want to walk through this forest at night!

ACCOMMODATION — CLASS A: * *Ongava Lodge*, situated on a 135-square-mile (350-km^2) private reserve along the southern boundary of Etosha near Andersson Gate, has ten luxury air-conditioned rock and thatch chalets with ensuite facilities and a swimming pool. * *Ongava Tented Camp*, also located on the reserve, has five large tents with ensuite facilities and a private water hole. Both Ongava Lodge and Ongava Tented Camp offer day and night game drives and walks on the reserve, day game drives in open-sided vehicles into Etosha and day excursions by air charter to Epupa Falls.

CLASS A/B: * *Etosha Aoba Lodge* accommodates up to 20 guests in thatched cottages with ensuite facilities and is located 7 miles (12 km) from the Van Lindequist Gate (near Namutoni Camp). * *Mokuti*

Okaukuejo Camp.

Lodge, located 500 yards (500 m) from the Van Lindequist Gate, has 96 air-conditioned thatched bungalows with ensuite facilities, a swimming pool and an air strip.

CLASS C & D: There are three National Park camps: *Namutoni, Halali* and *Okaukuejo*. All three camps have lodge accommodations, caravan and camping sites, swimming pool, floodlit water hole, restaurant, store, petrol station and landing strip. The camps are fenced for the visitors' protection. * *Namutoni Camp*, situated 7 miles (11 km) from the Van Lindequist Gate, features an attractive fortress built in 1903 and converted to hotel rooms, many of which have private facilities. * *Halali Camp*, the most modern of the camps, lies halfway between Namutoni and Okaukuejo Camps at the foot of a dolomite hill. Some rooms have private facilities. * *Okaukuejo Camp*, situated 11 miles (18 km) from the Andersson Gate entrance, has chalets with private facilities.

Giraffe at home in Damaraland.

DAMARALAND

Damaraland is a large region with many attractions and is located east of Skeleton Coast National Park. This is an arid mountainous region of spectacular rugged scenery. Damara herders can be seen throughout this region.

The **Brandberg** is a massive mountain covering an area 19 x14 miles (23 x 30 km) and rises 6500 feet (1980 m) above the surrounding plains to 8440 feet (2573 m) above sea level. Its special attraction is that it harbors thousands of rock paintings, including one of the most famous in the region — "The White Lady."

Twyfelfontein has rock engravings of wildlife, including rhino, elephant and giraffe, which are considered to be some of the best on the continent. The **Petrified Forest** has many broken petrified tree trunks up to about 100 feet (30 m) in length. Welwitschia plants may also be seen here. **Burnt Mountain**, a colorful mountain composed of many shades of purple and red, glows as if on fire when it is struck by the rays of the setting sun.

Wildlife is sparse and should be considered a bonus. However, many consider the search for wildlife which has adapted to a near-waterless environment well worth the effort. Wildlife includes desert elephant, desert black rhino, lion, desert-dwelling giraffe and Hartmann's mountain zebra. Wildlife migrates east and west along the dry riverbeds in search of food and water.

The best time to visit is May–December.

ACCOMMODATION — CLASS B: * *Damaraland Camp*, a 16-bed tented camp with ensuite facilities, rock pool and airstrip, is situated in the Huab River valley where desert-adapted elephants are often seen. Activities consist of guided walks and nature drives in open vehicles. Twyfelfontein Rock Paintings are located nearby.

CLASS B/C: * *Etendeka Mountain Camp* is a tented camp (16 beds) with communal showers and flush toilets. Exploring the region by open four-wheel-drive vehicle and walks is offered. * *Palmwag Lodge* has two- and four-bed thatched bungalows (24 beds) with a swimming pool. Activities include hiking and guided tours.

CLASS D: * *Khorixas Rest Camp* has rondavels with ensuite facilities.

CAMPING: * *Khorixas Rest Camp* and *Palmwag Rest Camp* have campsites with an ablution block. Campsites with shower and toilet facilities are also available at Aba Huab River near Twyfelfontein.

KAOKOLAND

This is a region of rugged mountain ranges interspersed with wide valleys bordered on the west by Skeleton Coast National Park. Wildlife is sparse but includes elephant, giraffe, oryx, ostrich and some black rhino and lion. Himba tribes may be seen in the region.

If you wish to visit a Himba village, it is customary to wait a distance from the village until someone comes and invites you in. If you come across a village that is deserted, please do not take anything that you may find lying around. Due to their nomadic lifestyle, the Himba often leave possessions behind as they know they will return.

Epupa Falls, Kunene River.

The best time to visit is May–December. A minimum of two fully self-contained four-wheel-drive vehicles per party is required, and a professional guide is highly recommended. There is no fuel in the western region.

ACCOMMODATION — CLASS B/C: * *Sesfontein Lodge* is an old fort that has been renovated.

CLASS C: * *Sierra Cafema* has six tents with ensuite facilities. Walks, nature drives, boat game drives and visits to local Himba tribes are offered. Access is by air charter or on a guided tour. * *Epupa Camp* has ten tents with shared facilities.

WATERBERG PLATEAU PARK

This 156-square-mile (400-km^2) park is the home of several scarce and endangered species, including black rhino, white rhino, roan antelope and sable antelope. Other species include brown hyena, eland, tsessebe, kudu, oryx, giraffe, impala, klipspringer and dikdik. Leopard are sometimes seen on the top of the plateau.

Waterberg Plateau Park also contains unique flora along with rock paintings and engravings. Three trails lead up to the top of the plateau, which rises over 820 feet (300 m) above the surrounding plains, and one runs across the top. Walking on the plateau is restricted to organized guided walking trails.

ACCOMMODATION — CLASS C & D: * *Bernarbe de la Bat Rest Camp* has a restaurant, swimming pool, and bungalows with and without ensuite facilities.

CAMPING: Campsites with an ablution block are available.

ACCOMMODATION NEAR WATERBERG — CLASS B: * *Okonjima Guest Farm* is family-run and located on a private game reserve. The farm is the home of the Africat Foundation, which is committed to saving cheetah, leopard and lion. Accommodations are in rooms with ensuite facilities. Activities include bird watching, walks and watching orphaned wild animals adopted by the family roam freely about the farm.

KAUDOM GAME RESERVE

Situated in the extreme northeast section of the country on the Botswana border, this 1480-square-mile (3800-km^2) park, composed primarily of Kalahari sand dunes and dry woodland savannah, is one of the most remote reserves in Namibia.

Mammal species include elephant, lion, leopard, side-striped jackal, African wild dog, giraffe, wildebeest, eland, kudu, roan antelope and sable antelope.

During the dry season (June–October), game viewing can be good, especially at springs and water holes lying along dry riverbeds which serve as "roads." However, wildlife is not nearly as concentrated as in Etosha National Park. Kaudom should primarily be visited by those seeking a wilderness experience in a reserve which they will most likely have to themselves. Bushmen are sometimes found in the region; however, they are seldom seen in traditional dress.

Access to the park is from Tsumkwe in the south or Katere in the north. A minimum of two four-wheel-drive vehicles is required per party visiting the reserve.

ACCOMMODATION — CLASS D: * *Sigaretti,* located in the south of the reserve, has three thatched huts with shared facilities. * *Kaudom,* situated in the north of the park, has two huts.

CAMPING: Campsites are available at *Sigaretti* and *Kaudom*.

THE CAPRIVI STRIP

The Caprivi Strip is the "panhandle" of Namibia, bordered by Angola and Zambia to the north and Botswana on the south.

Much of the wildlife in this region has been poached, especially during the conflict with Angola. However, wildlife populations are increasing, and the Caprivi is well worth a visit for anyone looking for a wilderness experience first, with wildlife as a bonus.

Mudumu National Park and Mamili National Park are similar to Botswana's Okavango Delta.

Access to the region is by scheduled flights to Katima Mulilo, private charter flights and by road.

MAHANGO GAME RESERVE

Mahango is a 96-square-mile (250-km^2) reserve of floodplain and lush vegetated savannah with baobab trees. The park is situated along the banks of the Kavango River and bordered by the Caprivi Game Reserve on the east.

Wildlife includes elephant, hippo, crocs, buffalo, waterbuck, lechwe, reedbuck, bushbuck, kudu, tsessebe, impala and the rare sitatunga. Bird life includes fish eagle, wattled crane, crowned crane and African skimmer. Four-wheel-drive vehicles are required to explore the most remote regions of the park, but two-wheel drive vehicles may be used on the main route.

ACCOMMODATION AND CAMPING: None.

ACCOMMODATION AND CAMPING NEAR MAHANGO: See "Popa Falls" below.

POPA FALLS GAME RESERVE

This small park features rapids (more so than "falls") of the Kavango River, which has numerous hippo and crocs. This is a good base from which to explore the Mahango Game Reserve and Caprivi Game Reserve.

ACCOMMODATION — CLASS C: * *Ndhovu Lodge* has tents with ensuite facilities. Boats are available for hire.

CLASS D: * *Popa Falls Government Camp,* located about 10 miles (16 km) north of the Mahango Game Reserve entrance, has thatched bungalows and ablution facilities.

CAMPING: Campsites with ablution facilities are available.

CAPRIVI GAME RESERVE

Wildlife in this park includes elephant, buffalo, hippo, crocs, roan antelope, sable antelope and plenty of waterfowl.

An all-weather gravel road runs through the park. Travelers are not allowed to leave the main road without permission. Four-wheel-drive vehicles are necessary off the main road.

ACCOMMODATION: None.

CLASS D: See "Popa Falls" above.

CAMPING: Campsites with no facilities are available.

MUDUMU NATIONAL PARK

This newly proclaimed park of floodplains, islands and bush is similar to the Okavango Delta (Botswana), but with not quite as much game. The Kwando River runs along the park's western border. On a recent visit, while on walks we encountered elephant, impala and a number of other species. Other wildlife includes lion, hippo, crocs, roan antelope and sitatunga.

Game viewing by open vehicle and walks is allowed. Four-wheel-drive vehicles are recommended.

ACCOMMODATION — CLASS A/B: * *Lianshulu Lodge* is located on the banks of the Kwando River and has eight thatched chalets (doubles) with ensuite facilities and a swimming pool. Activities include game drives, walks, game viewing by boat, sunset cruises on a double-decker barge and excursions to Mamili National Park. Access is by scheduled flights to Mpacha, air charter and by road.

MAMILI NATIONAL PARK

This newly proclaimed park is predominantly floodplain and has similar wildlife as Mudumu National Park. The Linyanti River flows along its southeastern border, which it shares with Botswana. Wildlife is increasing in this park quite rapidly, and plenty of game is seen on the Botswana side of the river.

ACCOMMODATION: None. See "Mudumu Reserve" above.

CAMPING: Campsites with no facilities are available.

THE COAST

The freezing Benguela Current of the Atlantic flows from Antarctica northward along the Namibian coastline and meets the hot, dry air of the Namib Desert, forming a thick fog bank which often penetrates inland up to 55 miles (90 km).

The best time to visit the coast for sunbathing, fishing and surfing is from December to February; June–July is cold with some rain.

SKELETON COAST PARK

Skeletons of shipwrecks and whales may be seen on the treacherous coast of this park which stretches along the seashore and covers over 2000 square miles (5000 km^2) of wind-sculpted dunes, canyons and jagged peaks of the Namib.

Skeleton Coast by Amy Schoeman (Southern Book Publishers) is a superb pictorial and factual representation of this fascinating region.

Fog penetrates inland for over 20 miles (32 km) almost every day and often lingers until the desert sun burns it off at 9:00–10:00 a.m. When the wind blows from the east, there is instant sunshine.

The park is divided into southern and northern sections. The southern section is more accessible and lies between the Ugab and Hoanib Rivers. Permits and reservations (paid in advance) must be made with the Directorate of Tourism and Resorts for stays at either Torra Bay or Terrace Bay.

The northern part of the park has been designated as wilderness area and can only be visited with fly-in safaris.

The northern region has many unusual and fascinating attractions. One such attraction is the **Cape Frio Seal Colony**, which has grown to about 40,000 seals.

A walk down the **roaring dunes** will give you the surprise of your life. Suddenly everyone is looking up to spot the B-52 bomber that must be overhead. Apparently the sand is just the right diameter and consistency to create a loud noise when millions of its granules slide down the steep dune. Incredible!

Driving through Hoarusib Canyon, one witnesses striking contrasts of dark-green grasses against verdite canyon walls and near-vertical white dunes.

Big game is scarce, but includes black rhino, desert elephant, leopard and baboon. Brown hyena are plentiful but rarely seen. Black-backed jackal, springbok and gemsbok are often sighted.

The east wind brings detritus (small bits of plant matter) providing much-needed compost for plants and food for lizards and beetles. The west wind brings moisture on which most life depends in this desert, which is almost completely devoid of water. The ancient "fossil" plant, *Welwitschia mirabilis*, is also found in the region.

ACCOMMODATION — SOUTHERN SKELETON COAST — CLASS D: * *Terrace Bay* is open year-round and offers full board and lodging in basic bungalows with private facilities. There is a landing strip for light aircraft.

CAMPING: * *Torra Bay* has campsites and caravan sites and is open only over the holidays (December 1 to January 31). You must be self-contained as supplies are not readily available.

ACCOMMODATION NEAR THE SKELETON COAST — CLASS C: * *Kuidas Camp, Purros Camp* and *Kunene Camp* accommodate guests in basic igloo huts with ensuite chemical toilets and separate bucket showers. Guests normally fly from camp to camp and go on walks and nature drives from the camps.

SWAKOPMUND

The resort town of Swakopmund, located on the coast and surrounded by the Namib Desert, has many fine examples of German colonial architecture.

Some travelers base themselves here and take day trips to Namib-Naukluft National Park, Walvis Bay and the Cape Cross Seal Reserve.

ACCOMMODATION — FIRST CLASS: * *Swakopmund Hotel & Entertainment Centre,* built around the original colonial railway station, has 92 rooms with ensuite facilities, a swimming pool, tennis courts and a gym. Guests have use of the Rossmund Golf Course, one of only four desert golf courses in the world. * The *Hansa Hotel* is an attractive hotel with 34 rooms with ensuite facilities.

TOURIST CLASS: * The *Strand Hotel* is located on the beachfront and has 42 rooms with private facilities. * *Hotel Schweizerhaus* has 24 rooms (some with seaview) with ensuite facilities.

CAPE CROSS SEAL RESERVE

Cape Cross Seal Reserve, home of over 100,000 seals, is open daily from 10:00 a.m. to 5:00 p.m.

THE SOUTH

NAMIB-NAUKLUFT PARK

The consolidation of the Namib Desert Park and the Naukluft Mountain Zebra Park along with the incorporation of other lands, including most of what was called "Diamond Area #2", created the largest park in Namibia and one of the largest in the world. Namib-Naukluft Park covers 19,215 square miles (49,768 km^2) of desert savannah grasslands, gypsum and quartz plains, granite mountains, an estuarine lagoon, a canyon and huge drifting apricot-colored dunes.

The Kuiseb River runs through the center of the park from east to west and acts as a natural boundary separating the northern grayish-white gravel plains from the southern deserts.

Herds of mountain zebra, gemsbok, springbok and flocks of ostrich roam the region.

Many small, fascinating creatures have uniquely adapted to this environment and help make this one of the most interesting deserts in the world. The dunes are home to numerous unique creatures such as the translucent Palmato gecko, the shovel-nosed lizard and the Namib golden mole.

The five main regions of the park are the Namib, Sandvis, Naukluft, Sesriem and Sossusvlei areas.

The **Namib** may well be the world's oldest desert. The welwitschia flats region lies on a dirt road about 22 miles (35 km) north of the Swakopmund-Windhoek road and is the best area to see the prehistoric *Welwitschia mirabilis* plants. Actually classified as trees, many welwitschia are thousands of years old and are perfect examples of adaptation to an extremely hostile environment. The water holes at Hotsas and Ganab are good locations to spot game; Ganab and Aruvlei are known for mountain zebra.

If you plan to deviate from the main road through the park, a permit is required and is obtainable weekdays only at the Environment and Tourism Office in Swakopmund, Windhoek or Sesriem.

The **Sandvis** area includes Sandwich Harbour, 26 miles (42 km) south of Walvis Bay, and is accessible only by four-wheel-drive vehicles. Fresh water seeps from under the dunes into the saltwater lagoon, resulting in a unique environment. Bird watching is excellent September–March.

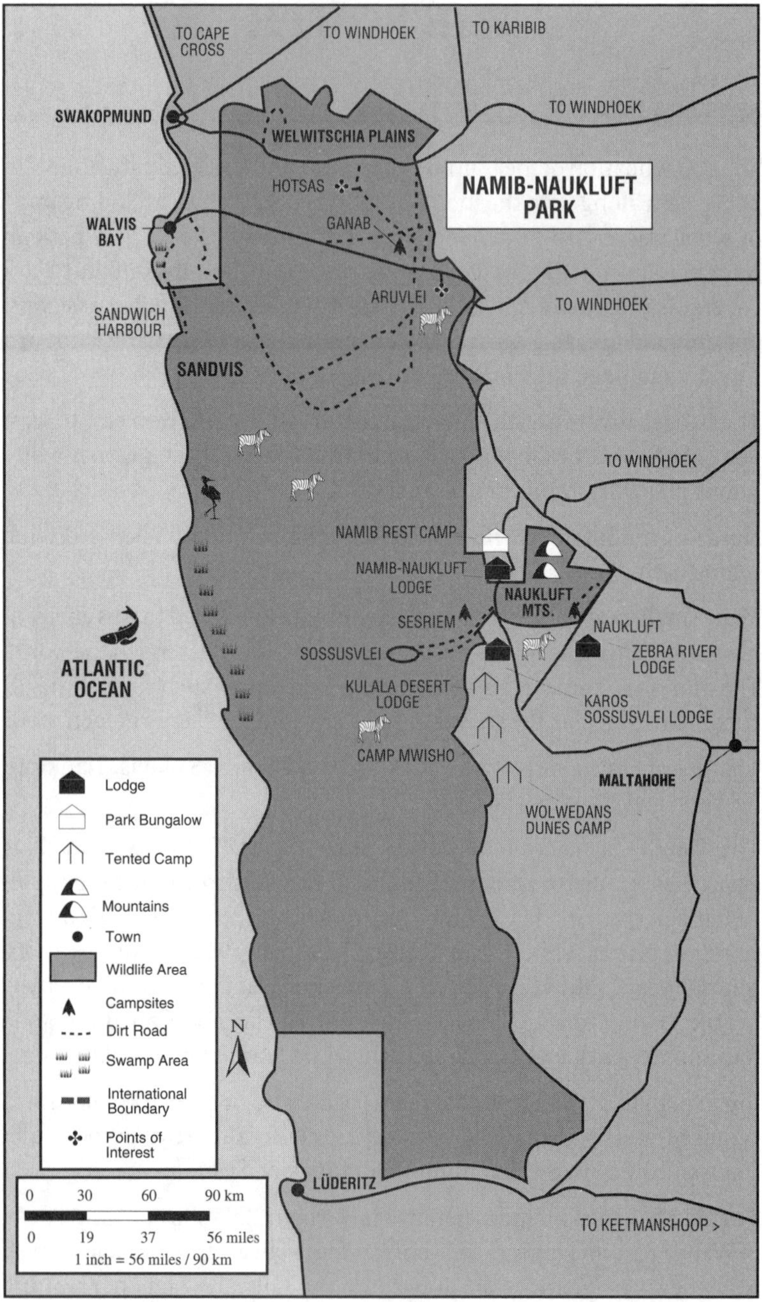
TO CAPE CROSS
TO WINDHOEK
TO KARIBIB
SWAKOPMUND
TO WINDHOEK
WELWITSCHIA PLAINS
HOTSAS
NAMIB-NAUKLUFT PARK
WALVIS BAY
GANAB
ARUVLEI
TO WINDHOEK
SANDWICH HARBOUR
SANDVIS
TO WINDHOEK
NAMIB REST CAMP
NAMIB-NAUKLUFT LODGE
NAUKLUFT MTS.
SESRIEM
NAUKLUFT
ZEBRA RIVER LODGE
ATLANTIC OCEAN
SOSSUSVLEI
KULALA DESERT LODGE
KAROS SOSSUSVLEI LODGE
CAMP MWISHO
MALTAHOHE
WOLWEDANS DUNES CAMP
Lodge
Park Bungalow
Tented Camp
Mountains
Town
Wildlife Area
Campsites
Dirt Road
Swamp Area
International Boundary
Points of Interest
N
LÜDERITZ
0 30 60 90 km
0 19 37 56 miles
1 inch = 56 miles / 90 km
TO KEETMANSHOOP >

Many* Welwitschia mirabilis *trees common in Namib-Naukluft National Park are more than 2,000 years old.

Only day trips are allowed to the harbor. Permits are required and may be obtained from the Ministry of Environment and Tourism or from service stations in Walvis Bay.

The **Naukluft** region is an important watershed characterized by dolomitic mountains over 6445 feet (1965 m) in height with massive picturesque rock formations and thickly foliated riverbeds. Large numbers of mountain zebra, along with springbok, kudu, klipspringer, rock rabbit, baboon and black eagles are frequently sighted. Also present are cheetah and leopard.

There are several hiking trails from which to choose. One of the more interesting trails is the Naukluft Trail, 10.5 miles (17 km) in length, requiring six to seven hours of hiking. A 75-mile (120-km) trail which takes eight days may also be hiked April–October with prior permission.

Sesriem Canyon is about 0.6 mile (1 km) long and is as narrow as 6 feet (2 m) wide with walls about 100 feet (30 m) high. In some places the canyon takes on a cave- or tunnel-like appearance.

Sossusvlei has the highest sand dunes in the world, exceeding 1000 feet (300 m). The base of the second highest sand dune in the world can be fairly closely approached by vehicle.

The hike along the knife-edge rim to the top is strenuous, requiring 60–90 minutes of taking two steps up and sliding one step down. The view from the top into other valleys and of the mountains beyond is marvelous. Even up here, colorful beetles, ants and other desert critters roam about.

Driving back to camp from Sossusvlei, a gemsbok ran full speed beside our vehicle for several minutes, proving the strength and resiliency of these majestic animals.

Sunrise on these magnificent and colorful dunes is spectacular.

Ballooning safaris are offered by one company and can be booked from Camp Mwisho, Kulala Desert Lodge or Karos Sossusvlei Lodge.

In order to help preserve the delicate ecosystem at Sossusvlei, permits must be obtained from the Ministry of Environment and Tourism Office in Windhoek prior to arriving at Sesriem. Only 150 vehicles are permitted entry per day in three time slots: sunrise–10:00 a.m., 10:00 a.m.–2:00 p.m. and 2:00 p.m.–4:00 p.m.

At Sossusvlei camping is not allowed and there are no accommodations.

ACCOMMODATION — CLASS A/B: * *Kulala Desert Lodge*, situated on the boundary of Sossusvlei, is a 24-bed tented camp with ensuite facilities. A rooftop sleeping area allows one to enjoy a night under the spectacular desert sky. Activities include drives into the desert, waking trails, horseback riding and visits to bushman painting sites. * *Karos Sossusvlei Lodge*, located in the Sesriem area about 37 miles (60 km) from Sossusvlei, has 45 rooms with ensuite facilities.

Wolwedans Dune Camp.

CLASS B: * *Wolwedans Dune Camp*, set on the 463-square-mile (1200-km^2) Namib Rand Game Ranch, has six igloo tents with ensuite facilities. Activities include desert drives, game viewing and walking trails. * *Camp Mwisho* has three large tents with ensuite facilities and a small swimming pool. Balloon safaris over the Namib Desert, followed by a champagne breakfast, and day and night nature drives are offered. * *Namib-Naukluft Lodge* is a 14-room lodge with ensuite facilities and a swimming pool. * *Zebra River Lodge* is located in the Tsaris Mountains and has five rooms with ensuite facilities. Swimming, nature drives and hikes to five natural springs are offered on the farm.

CLASS C: * *Namib Rest Camp,* located about 37 miles (60 km) from Sesriem, has five bungalows and four double rooms with ensuite facilities and a swimming pool.

CAMPING: * *Namib Campsites* have no firewood or water. * *Naukluft Campsites* have water, charcoal and ablution facilities. * *Sesriem Campsite* has two ablution blocks with hot and cold water and a swimming pool. Firewood and fuel are available.

FISH RIVER CANYON

Second in size only to the Grand Canyon, Fish River Canyon is 100 miles (161 km) in length, up to 17 miles (27 km) in width and up to 1800 feet (550 m) deep. The Fish River cuts its way through the canyon to the Orange River, which empties into the Atlantic Ocean.

The vegetation and wildlife are very interesting. Many red aloes make the area appear like one imagines the planet Mars. Baboons, mountain zebra, rock rabbit, ground squirrel and klipspringer are often seen, while kudu and leopard remain elusive. The river water is cold and deep enough in areas to swim.

There is a well-marked path into the canyon in the north of the park where the four-day hike begins. For those hiking into the canyon for the day, allow 45–60 minutes down, and 90 minutes back up. Permission to walk down to the canyon floor must first be obtained from the ranger at Hobas.

The main hiking trail is 53 miles (86 km) in length and is open May–August. The going is tough since much of the walking is on the sandy, rock-strewn floor. No facilities exist en route, so this hike is not for the tenderfoot. Water is readily available (bring purification tablets) from the many pools that join to become a river during the rainy summers. Hot sulfur springs are located about halfway through the hike.

A maximum group of 40 people is allowed per day. Permits must be obtained in advance from the Directorate of Tourism and Resorts. A medical certificate of fitness is also required.

ACCOMMODATION — CLASS C: * *Canyon Lodge*, located 12 miles (20 km) from the main viewpoint, has 20 thatched bungalows with ensuite facilities. The original farmhouse, built in 1910, serves as the restaurant. * *Canyon Nature Park*, situated on the lip of the Fish River Canyon, has igloo tents (16 beds) with shared facilities. * *Ai-Ais Hot Springs*, located at the southern end of the canyon at the end of the hiking trail, has rooms with private facilities, refrigerators and hot plates, a large thermally heated swimming pool and mineral baths. Ai-Ais is open from the second Friday in March through the end of October.

CAMPING: * *Ai-Ais* campsites have hot showers. * *Hobas* campsite, located at the trailhead in the north of the park, has hot showers and a swimming pool.

SOUTH AFRICA

THE TERRITORIAL WHITE RHINO

The male white rhino maintains a territory, whereas the cow travels from territory to territory. Territorial bulls are the only bulls that will mate with a female within a marked territory, and they have devised several ways of marking and maintaining their distinct boundaries.

The bull paws the ground and scuffles the dust with his feet or scrapes the bushes or the bark of a tree with his horns. Then, curling his tail back over his rump, he sprays urine backwards between his legs on this mark so his scent impregnates it. Other bulls moving within the area will use the spot to urinate but will not spray-urinate because the area has already been reserved.

The territorial male also uses the same spot for defecating. These dung latrines are known as middens. Rhinos scrape their dung over the midden pile in a backwards motion with their feet, similar to the urination spraying.

Territories do overlap, however, and the territorial bull may be challenged by another bull looking for a new territory or following a female in estrus. If the territorial bull loses, he becomes a subordinate bull and moves out of the marked area to find a new one.

If a female in heat moves into a territory, the territorial bull tries to keep her by squealing and horn clashing and by physically preventing her from leaving.

When on conducted walks tracking rhino spoor, territorial markings are signs of a bull's presence, and these markings can indicate how recently rhino have moved through the area, which helps the guide interpret how long ago they may have passed.

SOUTH AFRICA

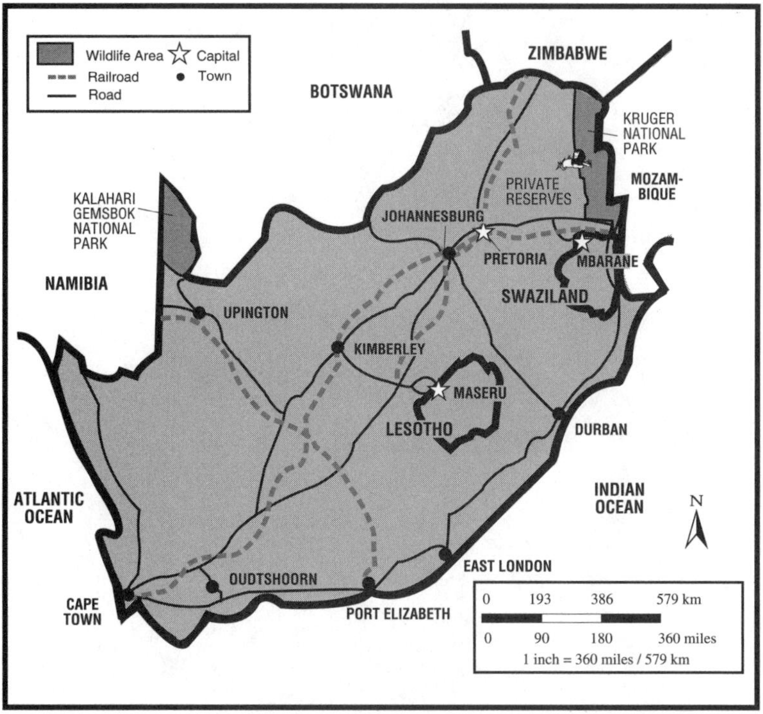

FACTS AT A GLANCE

AREA:	471,445 SQ. MI. / 1,221,037 SQ. KM.
APPROXIMATE SIZE:	THREE TIMES THE SIZE OF TEXAS OR FIVE TIMES THE SIZE OF GREAT BRITAIN
POPULATION:	40.5 MILLION
CAPITAL:	ADMINISTRATIVE: PRETORIA (POP. EST. 1.5 MILLION) LEGISLATIVE: CAPE TOWN (POP. EST. 2.5 MILLION) JUDICIAL: BLOEMFONTEIN (POP. EST. 310,000)
OFFICIAL LANGUAGES:	Afrikaans, English, isiNdebele, Sesotho sa Leboa, Sesotho, siSwati, Xitsonga, Setswana, Tshivenda, isiXhosa, and isiZulu.

SOUTH AFRICA

South Africa is a large country rich in natural beauty whose perceived size has been made to seem much larger by the media. Actually, it covers less than 3.8 percent of the continent.

Seventy percent of the total population belongs to four ethnic groups: Zulu (the largest), Xhosa, Tswana and Bapedi. Fifteen percent of the population is white, of which 60 percent is Afrikaner. English and Afrikaans are spoken throughout the country.

In 1488 Portuguese navigator Bartholomew Dias discovered the Cape of Good Hope. The first Dutch settlers arrived in 1652 and the first British settlers in 1820. To escape British rule, Boer (which means farmer) Voortrekkers (forward marchers) moved from Cape Town to the north and east, establishing the independent republic of Transvaal and Orange Free State.

Two very big economic breakthroughs were the discovery of diamonds in 1869 and, even more importantly, the discovery of gold in Transvaal shortly thereafter. Conflict between the British and Boers resulted in the Anglo-Boer War from 1899 until British victory in 1902.

In 1910 the Union of South Africa was formed and remained a member of the British Commonwealth until May 31, 1961, when the Republic of South Africa was formed outside the British Commonwealth. On April 27, 1994, a national election open to all races was held and was won by Nelson Mandela. Since that time, tourism to South Africa has increased dramatically.

WILDLIFE AND WILDLIFE AREAS

Kruger National Park and Kalahari Gemsbok National Park are the largest reserves of South Africa. Several private reserves adjacent to Kruger National Park offer the best options for international visitors, providing excellent accommodations, day and night game drives in open vehicles and walks. In Kwa-Zulu Natal there are several small reserves, including Itala, Ndumo, Hluhluwe Umfolozi and Mkuze, each with its own character.

The parks, reserves and sanctuaries in South Africa are very well organized and maintained, and in many ways are similar to those in North America. Most campsites have ablution blocks with running hot and cold water, and many sites have laundromats.

Generally speaking, the major roads in the parks are tarred and the minor roads are constructed of good quality gravel, allowing for comfortable riding. In the national parks, tourists must stay in their vehicles except where specifically permitted and cannot leave the roads in search of game. Open vehicles are not allowed, and roof hatches on vehicles must remain closed.

GAUTENG

JOHANNESBURG

Johannesburg began as a mining town when the largest deposits of gold in the world were discovered in the Witwatersrand in 1886. One-third of the gold mined in the world since the Middle Ages has come from the Witwatersrand field.

This "City of Gold" is now the country's largest commercial center and city and the main gateway for overseas visitors. The city itself has a population of approximately two million, while the total urban area including Soweto has a population of approximately four million. Attractions include the Africana Museum, the Gold Mine Museum and Gold Reef City, a reconstruction of Johannesburg at the turn of the century.

ACCOMMODATION — DELUXE: * *The Michelangelo*, located on Sandton Square, has 242 rooms with ensuite facilities, restaurants, a heated swimming pool, steam bath, fitness center, business center and direct access to one of South Africa's best malls. * *The Grace*, located in Rosebank, has 75 rooms with ensuite facilities and a swimming pool and business center. * *The Westcliff Hotel,* located in the suburb of Westcliff Ridge, has 120 rooms and suites with ensuite facilities, a business center and a swimming pool. Some of the suites have private swimming pools. * *Sandton Sun and Towers* is located 10 miles (16 km) from Johannesburg adjacent to one of the country's finest shopping malls. The hotel has 334 air-conditioned rooms with ensuite facilities and refrigerators; there is also a health club, swimming pool and five restaurants. * *Park Hyatt Johannesburg,* located in the suburb of Rosebank, has 239 rooms and suites with ensuite facilities, a heated swimming pool, sauna, steam rooms and a gymnasium.

FIRST CLASS: * *Villa Via Sandton* has two-bedroom suites, each with two ensuite bathrooms and a full kitchen, and a swimming pool. * *Balalaika Hotel,* located in Sandton, has 60 rooms with ensuite facilities. * *Sandton Holiday Inn* has 249 rooms with ensuite facilities. * *Holiday Inn Johannesburg International* has 362 air-conditioned rooms with ensuite facilities and a swimming pool.

TOURIST CLASS: * *Holiday Inn Garden Court,* located less than a mile from Johannesburg International Airport, has 238 air-conditioned rooms with facilities ensuite, a swimming pool and a sauna. * *City Lodges* have simple rooms with ensuite facilities.

ACCOMMODATION NEAR JOHANNESBURG — DELUXE: * *Mount Grace Country House Hotel,* located just an hour's drive from Johannesburg, has 60 rooms with ensuite facilities, swimming pools, a tennis court, lawn bowling, a croquet lawn and a walking trail.

FIRST CLASS: * *Lesedi Cultural Village,* located north of Johannesburg, has traditional villages with Xhosa, Zulu, Sotho and Pedi families whom guests may visit. Guests are accommodated in 16 rooms with ensuite facilities.

PRETORIA

Pretoria is an attractive city and the administrative capital of South Africa. Points of interest include Paul Kruger's house, Voortrekker Monument, Union Buildings, the State Opera House and Church Square.

ACCOMMODATION — DELUXE: * *Kloof House,* located in the suburb of Waterkloof, has seven rooms with ensuite or private facilities. * *Centurion Lake Hotel,* located outside Pretoria on a lake, has rooms with ensuite facilities.

FIRST CLASS: * *The Victoria Hotel,* a small old-world hotel located near the railroad station, has rooms with ensuite facilities. * *Villa Via* is an all-suite hotel with ensuite facilities and a swimming pool.

TOURIST CLASS: * *Holiday Inn Garden Court* has 238 rooms and suites with ensuite facilities and a swimming pool.

THE BLUE TRAIN

The world-renowned luxurious Blue Train offers an experience that has all but disappeared in modern times. The train is promoted as "A Five-Star Hotel on Wheels," and that it is.

Two identical Blue Trains were built in South Africa and put into service in 1972. One of the trains has been completely refurbished and offers deluxe and luxury suites, both of which have individual air-conditioning controls, television, radio and ensuite bathrooms with shower or bathtub. The luxury compartments also contain CD and video players. The train has 18 carriages and accommodates 84 passengers, with 34 staff to take care of them.

Five-star meals are served in the beautifully appointed dining car with its exquisite table settings. Most passengers dress elegantly for dinner, although this is not required.

The train runs overnight from Cape Town to Johannesburg and Pretoria, and vice versa, year-round and monthly to Victoria Falls. Book well in advance as reservations are often difficult to obtain.

ROVOS RAIL

Rovos Rail has two restored luxury steam trains with sleeping coaches, a dining car and an observation car. There are two different sizes of suites, deluxe and royal, both of which have ensuite facilities.

On our journey from Pretoria west to Kruger National Park, we enjoyed the scenery en route, along with quality wines and five-star dining.

You have the choice of a two-night trip from Pretoria to Cape Town with a stop in the old mining town of Kimberley; a two-night trip from Pretoria to Victoria Falls (Zimbabwe); an overnight trip from Pretoria to Komatipoort (near Kruger National Park); overnight trip along the Garden Route from Cape Town to Knysna via George; an occasional four-night safari from Pretoria to Kimberley, Upington, Windhoek and Swakopmund (Namibia); and an occasional 11-night safari from Cape Town to Dar es Salaam (Tanzania) and vice versa.

MPUMALANGA

KRUGER AND THE PRIVATE RESERVES

The most popular area in the country for wildlife safaris for international visitors is the private reserves that lie along Kruger National Park's western border, possibly followed by Kruger National Park itself.

There is a tremendous difference in the variety and quality of experience between visiting Kruger National Park versus visiting the adjacent private reserves. In Kruger, which has over 500,000 tourists each year, only closed vehicles are allowed, and off-road driving is not allowed. Night game drives can only be conducted by park rangers in large park vehicles; night drives in private vehicles are not allowed. Facilities are fair.

In the adjacent private reserves, day and night game viewing is conducted in open vehicles, walking is allowed and facilities are excellent. In other words, visitors have a greater opportunity to experience the bush in the private reserves than in Kruger. However, a safari to Kruger National Park using national park camps is less expensive than a safari of the same length in the private reserves.

The best game viewing for this region is May–October, during the sunny, dry winter season when the grass has been grazed down and the deciduous plants have lost their leaves. Calving season is in early spring (September–October) for most game species.

Winter days are usually warm, with an average maximum temperature of 73°F (23°C) and clear skies. Late afternoons are cool, while temperatures at night and in the early morning sometimes drop below freezing. From October to February there are light rains, with December, January and February receiving the heaviest downpours. Temperatures from October to February sometimes rise to over 104°F (40°C). March and April are cooler as the rains begin to diminish.

The best time to look for over 450 bird species in this region is October–March — just the opposite of the best game-viewing periods. However, bird watching is good year-round since less than half the bird population is composed of seasonal migrants.

To get to the area from Johannesburg, many people take about an hour flight to Skukuza, Hoedspruit or an air charter directly to their camp. Alternatively, the drive from Johannesburg to Kruger (Skukuza) is about 250 miles (400 km) northeast on tarred roads and takes five to six hours.

KRUGER NATIONAL PARK

Kruger is the largest South African park and has more species of wildlife than any other game sanctuary in Africa — 130 species of mammals, 114 species of reptiles, 48 species of fish, 33 species of amphibians and 468 species of birds.

The park is home to large populations of elephant (over 8000), buffalo (over 25,000), Burchell's zebra (over 25,000), greater kudu, giraffe, impala, white rhino, black rhino, hippopotamus, lion, leopard, cheetah, wild dog and spotted hyena, among others.

Kruger's 7523 square miles (19,485 km^2) make it nearly the size of the state of Massachusetts. The park is 55 miles wide at its widest point and 220 miles (355 km) long. It had been totally fenced until fairly recently, when the fences separating the park and the Timbavati and Sabi Sand Reserves were taken down, effectively increasing the size of the reserve by 15 percent and allowing the wildlife greater freedom of movement. However, the annual winter migration routes of antelope, zebra and various other species in search of water and better grazing are still cut off by fences. Several hundred windmills and artificial water holes have been constructed to provide the water so desperately needed in the dry season.

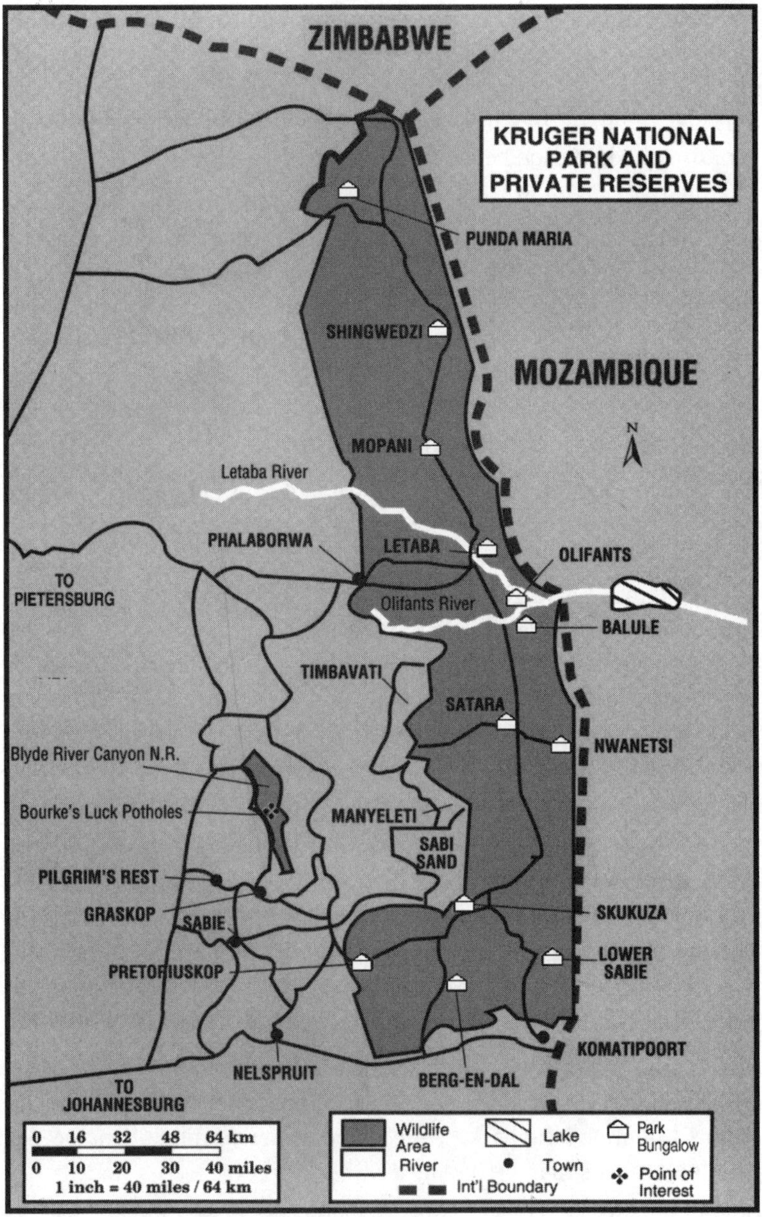
ZIMBABWE
KRUGER NATIONAL PARK AND PRIVATE RESERVES
PUNDA MARIA
SHINGWEDZI
MOZAMBIQUE
N
MOPANI
Letaba River
PHALABORWA
LETABA
OLIFANTS
TO PIETERSBURG
Olifants River
BALULE
TIMBAVATI
SATARA
NWANETSI
Blyde River Canyon N.R.
Bourke's Luck Potholes
MANYELETI
SABI SAND
PILGRIM'S REST
GRASKOP
SABIE
SKUKUZA
PRETORIUSKOP
LOWER SABIE
KOMATIPOORT
NELSPRUIT
BERG-EN-DAL
TO JOHANNESBURG
0 16 32 48 64 km
0 10 20 30 40 miles
1 inch = 40 miles / 64 km
Wildlife Area
River
Lake
Town
Int'l Boundary
Park Bungalow
Point of Interest

The park can be divided into three major regions: northern, central/southeastern and southwestern. Altitude varies from 650 feet (200 m) in the east to 2950 feet (900 m) at Pretoriuskop in the southwest. Summer temperatures may exceed 105°F (41°C), while winter temperatures seldom drop below freezing.

The northern region from the Letaba River to the Limpopo River is the driest. Mopane trees dominate the landscape, with the unique baobab (upside-down) trees becoming increasingly numerous toward Pafuri and the Limpopo River. From Letaba to Punda Maria is the best region for spotting elephant, tsessebe, sable and roan antelope. Elephant prefer this area since it is less developed than the other regions, making it easier to congregate away from roads and traffic, and mopane trees (their preferred source of food) are prevalent.

The central/southeastern region is situated south of Letaba to Orpen Gate and also includes the eastern part of the park from Satara southward, covering Nwanedzi, Lower Sabie and Crocodile Bridge. Grassy plains and scattered knobthorn, leadwood, and marula trees dominate the landscape. Lion inhabit most areas of the park but are most prevalent in this region, where there is also an abundance of zebra and wildebeest — their favorite prey. Cheetah and black-backed jackal are best spotted on the plains. Wild dogs are mainly scattered through flatter areas, with possibly a better chance of finding them in the Letaba–Malopene River area and northwest of Malelane.

The southwestern part of the park, including a wide strip along the western boundary from Skukuza to Orpen Gate, is more densely forested with thorny thickets, knobthorn, marula and red bush-willow. This is the most difficult region in which to spot game — especially during the rainy season. Many of the park's 600 white rhino prefer this area.

Black rhino are scattered throughout the southern and central areas, often feeding on low-lying acacia trees. Leopard are rarely seen. Buffalo roam throughout the park, while hippo prefer to inhabit the deeper parts of Kruger's many rivers by day.

During school holidays and long weekends, the number of day visitors to the park is limited and accommodations are almost impossible to obtain, so be sure to reserve in advance.

ACCOMMODATION — CLASS B/C, C, D & CAMPING: There are 16 *National Park Rest Camps* that offer a wide range of accommodations including cottages with ensuite facilities, thatched huts with or without private facilities and campsites. The larger rest camps have licensed restaurants. Many of the cottages and huts have cooking facilities and refrigerators.

ACCOMMODATION NEAR KRUGER NATIONAL PARK — CLASS A/B: * *Malelane Intercontinental*, located near Kruger's southernmost gate, has 102 chalets and suites with ensuite facilities, overlooking several water holes.

FIRST CLASS: * *Pine Lake Inn*, located in White River, a short drive from Kruger, has comfortable rooms with private facilities.

THE PRIVATE RESERVES

Along the western border of Kruger lie a number of privately owned wildlife reserves. These reserves are associations of ranchers who have fenced the western boundary of their reserves but have not placed fences between their individual properties, allowing game to roam throughout the reserves and Kruger National Park. The private reserves, in general, have exceptionally high standards of accommodation, food and service.

A very important advantage private reserves have over national parks is that private reserves use open vehicles, which give not only a better view but also a much better feel of the bush. At most reserves, a game tracker sits on the hood or the back of each vehicle. Drivers are in radio contact with each other, greatly increasing the chances of finding those species that guests want to see most.

Vehicles may leave the road to pursue game through the bush. Night drives, which are only allowed in national park vehicles in Kruger, provide an opportunity to spot game rarely seen during the day. Walking safaris with an armed tracker are available.

White rhinos are predominantly grazers. Their square-shaped lips facilitate this feeding habit.

ACCOMMODATION — SABI SAND PRIVATE GAME RESERVE: Sabi-Sand Private Game Reserve is situated to the north and northwest of Skukuza and includes Mala Mala (Mala Mala, Kirkman's and Harry's camps), Singita (Boulders and Ebony camps) Londolozi (Main, Tree and Bush camps), Ulusaba (Rock and Safari Lodge) and Djuma, Inyati, Indube and Sabi Sabi (Bush, River and Selati lodges and Mandleve Treehouse) reserves. All of the camps offer day and night game drives and walks. Many guests fly to Skukuza and are transferred to their respective camps. Others fly by private charter, drive or travel by tour bus to the camp of their choice.

CLASS A: * *Mala Mala* Game Reserve, the largest of the private reserves adjacent to Kruger National Park, has two "class A" camps – Mala Mala Main Camp and Kirkman's. * *Mala Mala* Main Camp is a very luxurious camp with 25 air-conditioned thatched rondavels (each with two ensuite "his" and "hers" bathrooms) and a

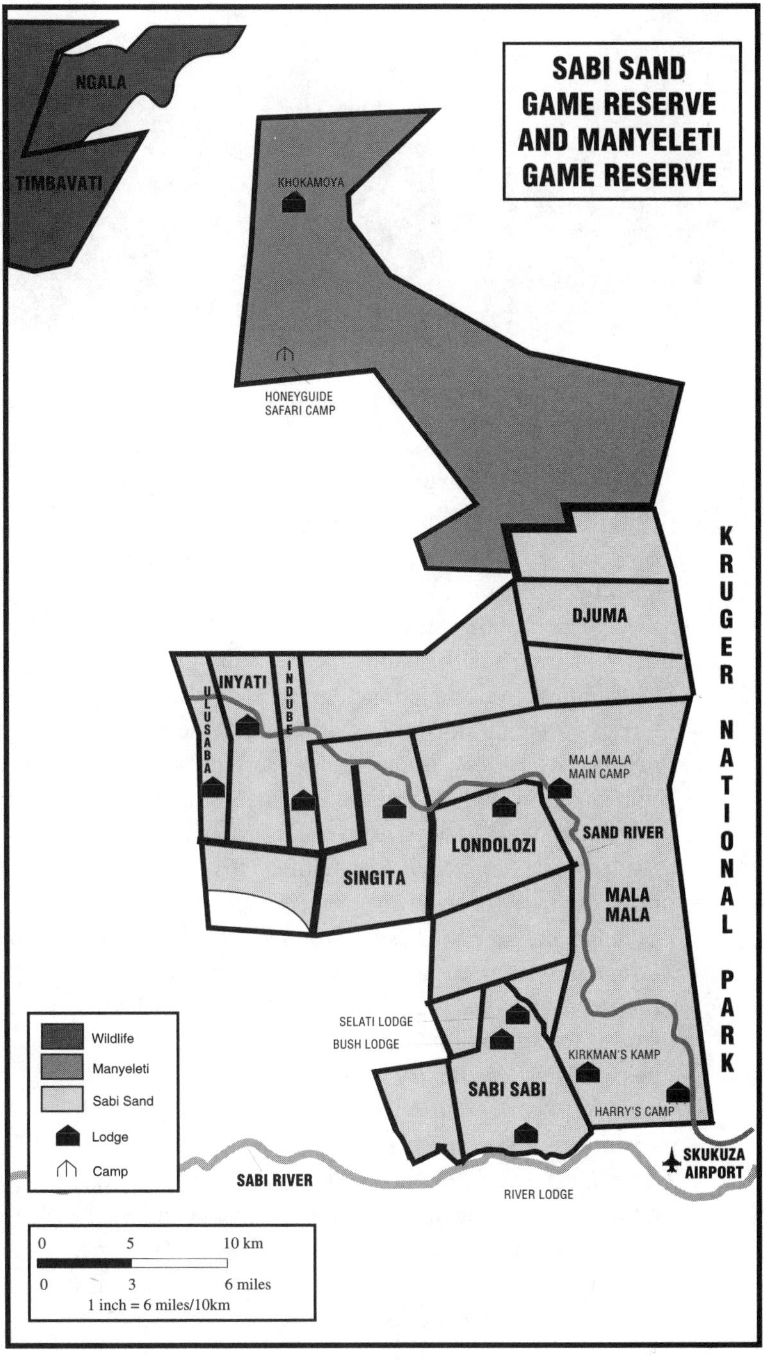
SABI SAND
GAME RESERVE
AND MANYELETI
GAME RESERVE
NGALA
TIMBAVATI
KHOKAMOYA
HONEYGUIDE
SAFARI CAMP
DJUMA
KRUGER NATIONAL PARK
INYATI
ULUSABA
INDUBE
MALA MALA
MAIN CAMP
SAND RIVER
LONDOLOZI
SINGITA
MALA
MALA
SELATI LODGE
BUSH LODGE
KIRKMAN'S KAMP
SABI SABI
HARRY'S CAMP
SKUKUZA
AIRPORT
SABI RIVER
RIVER LODGE
Wildlife
Manyeleti
Sabi Sand
Lodge
Camp
0
5
10 km
0
3
6 miles
1 inch = 6 miles/10km

Kirkman's Kamp main lodge.

swimming pool. In 1997 the camp was voted the "Best Hotel in the World" by *Travel & Leisure Magazine*. * *Kirkman's Kamp* has ten air-conditioned rooms with ensuite facilities and a swimming pool. Kirkman's Cottage, located 300 yards (300 m) from Kirkman's Kamp, has four rooms with ensuite facilities and its own private dining room and lounge. * *Singita Boulders Lodge* has six air-conditioned suites with ensuite facilities and fireplaces. * *Singita Ebony Lodge* has eight air-conditioned rooms with fireplaces and ensuite facilities. * *Londolozi* Game Reserve has three "class A" camps, Tree Camp, Bush Camp and Main Camp. * *Tree Camp*, the most exclusive of the three properties, is built around a giant ebony tree and has four rooms (doubles). * *Bush Camp* has eight rock bungalows. * *Londolozi Main Camp* accommodates 24 guests in rondavels and luxury suites. Rooms in all three camps have ensuite facilities. * *Sabi Sabi Bush Lodge* overlooks a water hole and has 22 air-conditioned rooms and five suites with ensuite facilities and a swimming pool. * *Sabi Sabi River Lodge,* overlooking the Sabi River, has 21 air-conditioned rooms and one suite with ensuite facilities and a swimming pool. * *Ulusaba Rock Lodge*, located on a hill 800 feet (244 m) above the reserve, has rooms with ensuite facilities and a rock pool.

CLASS A/B: * *Harry's Camp* has seven air-conditioned thatched rondavels with ensuite facilities and swimming pool. * *Indube Game Lodge* has nine air-conditioned chalets with ensuite facilities and a swimming pool. * *Inyati Game Lodge* has nine thatched chalets (doubles) with ensuite facilities and a swimming pool. * *Mandleve Treehouse Suite* (Sabi Sabi), located on the banks of the Sabi River, has two bedrooms with private facilities. * *Selati Lodge* (Sabi Sabi) has eight chalets with ensuite facilities and a swimming pool.

CLASS B: * *Djuma* has seven chalets with ensuite facilities and a swimming pool. * *Ulusaba Safari Lodge* is a rustic lodge with ten rooms with facilities ensuite.

ACCOMMODATION – MANYELETI GAME RESERVE: Guests fly to Hoedspruit or by charter aircraft directly to their respective camps.

CLASS A/B: * *Khoka Moya* has ten wood and thatch chalets with facilities ensuite. Day and night game drives and walks are offered. * *Honeyguide Safari Camp* caters to a maximum of 24 guests in tents with ensuite facilities. Daily walking trails and night game drives are offered.

ACCOMMODATION – TIMBAVATI GAME RESERVE: Guests of the camps listed below fly to Hoedspruit or by charter aircraft directly to their respective camps. Day and night game drives and walks are offered.

CLASS A/B: * *Kings Camp* has nine air-conditioned thatched bungalows with ensuite facilities accommodating up to 24 guests and a swimming pool. * *M'Bali* has eight tents under thatch with ensuite facilities. * *Motswari* has 15 rondavels with ensuite facilities and a swimming pool. * *Tanda Tula* Bush Camp has 12 tents with ensuite facilities. * *Ngala* has 20 air-conditioned cottages and one suite with ensuite facilities and a swimming pool.

Tanda Tula Bush Camp.

BLYDE RIVER CANYON, PILGRIM'S REST AND BOURKE'S LUCK POTHOLES

West of Kruger National Park and the private reserves, in the Drakensberg Mountains, lie a number of areas of natural beauty.

Blyde River Canyon is an impressive red sandstone gorge rising over half a mile above the river below. The "Three Rondavels" — peaks shaped like traditional African huts — may be seen from here.

Pilgrim's Rest is an attractively restored gold mining town where you can try your luck at panning gold.

Bourke's Luck Potholes, situated at the confluence of the Treur and Blyde rivers, are deep colorful cylindrical holes naturally formed by erosion.

ACCOMMODATION IN THE REGION — DELUXE: * *Blue Mountain Lodge* (White River), located on a 500-acre (200-hectare) estate, has 13 suites with ensuite facilities and a swimming pool. Activities include walking, bass fishing and bird watching. * *Cybele Forest Lodge* (White River) is a lovely lodge with rooms and

The Coach House.

cottages with facilities ensuite and a swimming pool. * *The Coach House* (Tzaneen) has 42 rooms with ensuite facilities and a swimming pool.

FIRST CLASS: * *Mount Sheba* (Pilgrim's Rest) has 25 rooms with ensuite facilities and a swimming pool.

ACCOMMODATION BETWEEN THE REGION AND JOHANNESBURG — DELUXE: * *Mount Anderson Ranch* is an exclusive 20,000-acre (8000-hectare) property with three rooms in a large ranch house with ensuite facilities. Trout fishing, horseback riding, nature drives and walks are offered. * *Walkersons,* located in the highlands of the Eastern Transvaal, has cottages with ensuite facilities and a beautiful stone and thatch manor house. * *Critchley Hackle* is a rustic stone-built complex with ensuite facilities.

NORTHWEST PROVINCE

PILANESBERG NATURE RESERVE

This relatively small 212-square-mile (550-km^2) reserve is located within a 17-mile- (27 km) wide volcanic bowl which rises over the surrounding plains. Pilanesberg has a variety of wildlife including black rhino, white rhino, elephant, lion, giraffe, hippo, eland, gemsbok, sable antelope, tsessebe, red hartebeest, leopard and cheetah. Over 300 species of birds have been recorded.

ACCOMMODATION — CLASS A: * *Kwa Maritane* has comfortable cabanas with ensuite facilities and a swimming pool. * *Tshukudu* has chalets with ensuite facilities.

CLASS C & D: * *Kololo,* * *Mankwe,* * *Manyane* and * *Metswedi* camps provide basic tented accommodation.

CAMPING: * *Manyane Caravan and Camping Site* has campsites and ablution facilities.

SUN CITY

Sun City is a premier entertainment vacation complex with Las Vegas–style floor shows, casinos, golf, tennis and a variety of water sports. Sun City is a two-hour drive (116 miles/187 km) or a short flight from Johannesburg. Excursions to Pilanesberg Nature Reserve are offered by some of the hotels.

ACCOMMODATION — DELUXE: * *The Palace Hotel of the Lost City* has been constructed as a royal residence from an ancient civilization and is set in 62 acres (25 hectares) of lush gardens. This lavish property has 338 rooms with ensuite facilities, a pool with 6-foot (2-m) surfing waves, water chutes, and several restaurants and bars. * *The Cascades,* landscaped with lush gardens, waterfalls and a swimming pool, has 245 rooms with facilities ensuite.

The Palace Hotel of the Lost City, Sun City.

FIRST CLASS: * *Sun City Hotel* has 340 rooms with ensuite facilities and a swimming pool. * *Sun City Cabanas* has 284 cabanas with facilities ensuite.

THE CAPE PROVINCE

KALAHARI GEMSBOK NATIONAL PARK

Located in the northwest corner of South Africa and sharing borders with Namibia and with Gemsbok National Park in Botswana, this 3703-square-mile (9591-km^2) park is predominantly semidesert and part desert. Scattered thorn trees and grasses lie between red Kalahari sand dunes. Bushmen inhabited the area as much as 25,000 years ago.

The park features large herds of blue wildebeest, eland, springbok and the stately gemsbok with their long, straight spear-like horns. Also present are red hartebeest, duiker, steenbok, Kalahari lion, cheetah, brown hyena and wild dog.

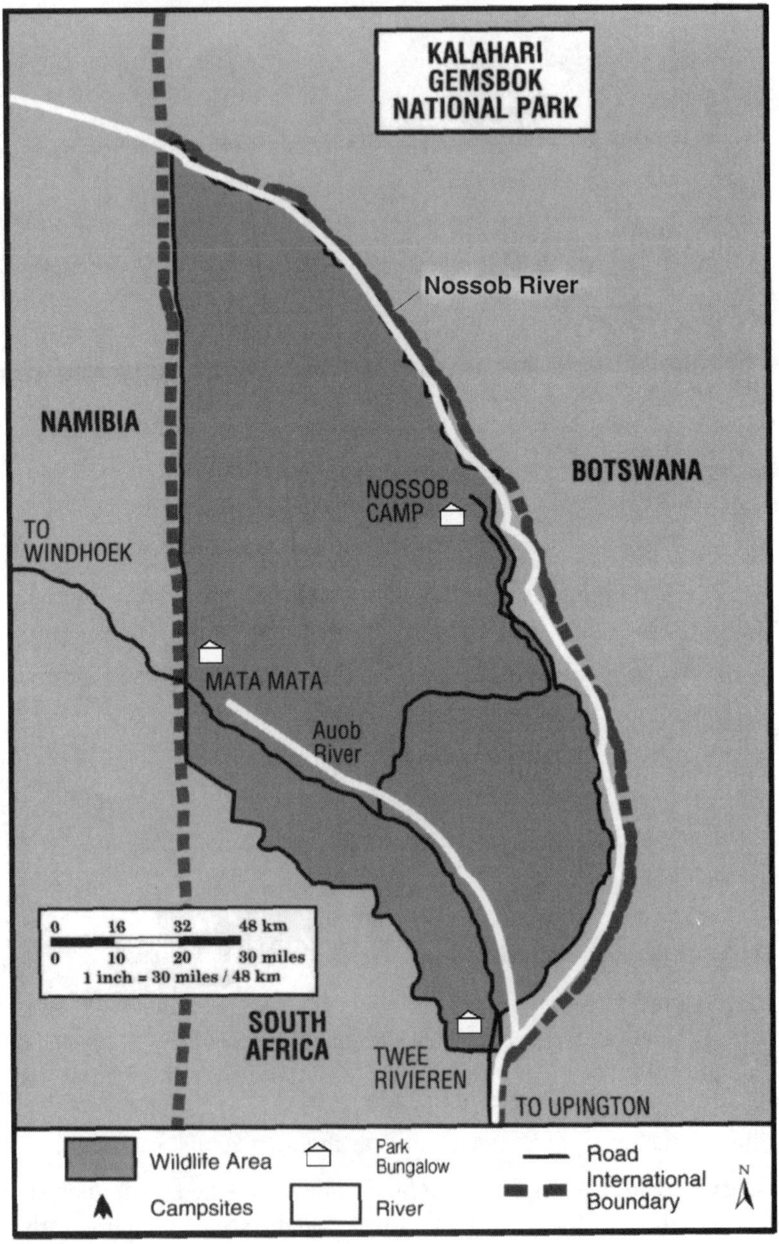
KALAHARI
GEMSBOK
NATIONAL PARK
Nossob River
NAMIBIA
BOTSWANA
NOSSOB
CAMP
TO
WINDHOEK
MATA MATA
Auob
River
0 16 32 48 km
0 10 20 30 miles
1 inch = 30 miles / 48 km
SOUTH
AFRICA
TWEE
RIVIEREN
TO UPINGTON
Wildlife Area
Park
Bungalow
Road
International
Boundary
Campsites
River
N

Summer temperatures can exceed 104°F (40°C). Winter days are pleasant, but temperatures can drop below freezing at night. Wells provide water for the animals which have adapted to desert conditions by eating plants with high water content, such as wild cucumber and tsamma melon.

The southern entrance to the park is about 255 miles (411 km) north of Upington.

ACCOMMODATION — CLASS C/D: There are three rest camps with self-contained cottages with kitchens, huts with and without bathrooms, camping sites, stores, petrol and diesel. * *Twee Revieren* is located at the southern entrance to the park. The camp has a restaurant, swimming pool and a landing strip for small aircraft. * *Nossob* is located in the northeastern part of the park near the Botswana border. The camp has an information center about the plant and animal life in the park and a has landing strip for small aircraft. * *Mata Mata* is located on the western border of the park.

ACCOMMODATION NEAR THE PARK — CLASS B & C: * *Molopo Kalahari Lodge,* located 37 miles (60 km) from the park, has ten air-conditioned rondavels with ensuite facilities and five chalets with separate facilities.

ACCOMMODATION IN THE KALAHARI DESERT — CLASS A: * *Tswalu Lodge,* located on the Tswalu Private Desert Reserve, is the largest privately owned game reserve in South Africa, covering 290 square miles (750 km^2). Up to 22 guests are accommodated in luxury desert suites with ensuite facilities and double fireplaces. Guests may go on day and night game drives, track desert rhino or just relax around the swimming pool. Visits to the sable antelope breeding program can be arranged. The reserve is located west of Kuruman. Transfers are available from Kimberley or Upington; quickest access is by air charter.

The big hole at Kimberley.

KIMBERLEY

Kimberley is the "diamond city," where one of the world's biggest diamond strikes occurred in 1868. Visit the open air museum and the "Big Hole," where over three tons of diamonds were removed from the largest hole dug by man on earth.

ACCOMMODATION — TOURIST CLASS: * *Holiday Inn Garden Court* has 114 rooms with facilities ensuite and a swimming pool.

CAPE TOWN

Sir Francis Drake once said of the Cape Town area: "The fairest cape we saw in the whole circumference of the globe." Today, Cape Town is thought by many well-traveled people to be one of the most beautiful settings in the world. The Cape reminds me of the California coast — stark, natural beauty and a laid-back atmosphere.

The **Cableway** (or three-hour hike) up **Table Mountain** with breathtaking views is a must. The new cable car can take 65 passengers at a time and does a full rotation on the way up. A new restaurant has been built on the top of the mountain. Bring warm clothing since it is usually much cooler and windier on top than below.

An afternoon **Champagne Cruise** past islands with hundreds of seals, rocky cliffs and sandy beaches allows a delightful perspective of the area.

The **Victoria and Alfred Waterfront** has a variety of shops, historical buildings, museums, waterfront walks, restaurants, nightclubs including a Hard Rock Cafe, luxury hotels, a brewery, theater, boat trips, helicopter rides and the **Two Oceans Aquarium**, which exhibits species from both the Atlantic and the Indian oceans.

Tours to **Robben Island**, where Nelson Mandela was held as a political prisoner for so many years, depart from the Victoria and Alfred Harbor. The boat transfer to the island takes about 45 minutes. An hour tour of the island includes a visit to Mandela's cell, a stone quarry, an old village and a drive around the island, where you may see jackass penguins and have great views of the city.

The one-day drive down the Cape Peninsula to the **Cape of Good Hope Nature Reserve** and **Cape Point** is one of the finest drives on the continent. The reserve has lovely picnic sites and a population of bontebok, as well as other species, and a variety of beautiful wildflowers. Some people say this is where the Atlantic meets the Indian Ocean, while others say it is at Cape Agulhas, the southernmost point of Africa. On our recent visit, we saw bontebok, ostrich and baboons at the ocean's edge eating mussels picked off the rocks.

Whale watching in Table Bay, Hout Bay and False Bay is good July–August and best September–October.

Sea Point is bustling with nightlife, with many distinctive restaurants, bistros and bars. **Kirstenbosch National Botanical Gardens**, one of the finest gardens in the world, has 9000 of the 21,000 flowering plants of southern Africa. A glass-house conservatory housing succulent plants from all over southern Africa, including a baobab tree, has recently been added.

A more active way to discover the area is by **kayaking** in single or double kayaks. Trips around Cape Point, from Table Bay to Clifton, in Hout Bay, in the Langebaan Lagoon and at Rietvlei (for bird watching) are available. **Horseback riding** on beaches at Hout Bay or

Miles Nolting's first encounter with Jackass penguins.

on the beaches, dunes and lagoons at Noordhoek Valley is another great option.

Some of the finer restaurants include Buitenverwachting and Cape Malay Kitchen (Constantia); Blue Danube (Tamboerskloof); Quay 4, Quay West and Atlantic Grill (Victoria and Alfred Waterfront); Panama Jacks (Town Harbour); Leinster Hall (Gardens); Blues (Camps Bay); Brass Bell (Kalk Bay); and La Perla (Sea Point). The Wooden Bridge, situated across Table Bay, is exceptionally nice in summer; guests may watch the sun set behind Table Mountain.

February–March is the best time to visit the Cape, as there is very little wind; October–January is warm and windy, and May–August is rainy and cool. However, this is one of the most beautiful cities in the world to visit any time of the year.

ACCOMMODATION — DELUXE: * *Table Bay* is a new 330-room hotel located in the Victoria and Alfred Waterfront, with ensuite facilities, with satellite television, a restaurant, conference facilities and a swimming pool, spa and health club. * *Mount Nelson* is an old-world British hotel set on seven landscaped acres. The hotel is situated near the base of Table Mountain and has

Table Bay Hotel and the Victoria and the Alfred Waterfont in the foreground, with Table Mountain behind.

rooms with facilities ensuite and a swimming pool. * *Cape Grace* is an elegant new hotel also located in the Victoria and Alfred Waterfront, with 104 rooms and suites with ensuite facilities, a restaurant and a swimming pool. * *Cape Sun* is a downtown business hotel with a great view of the harbor; it has 362 rooms with facilities ensuite and a pool, health club and gym.

FIRST CLASS: * *Villa Via Granger Bay,* located a few minutes' walk or water taxi ride to the Victoria and Alfred Waterfront, has 187 rooms with ensuite facilities, two restaurants and a pool in the hotel section. In the "all-suite" building there is a swimming pool and one-, two- and three-bedroom suites each with ensuite facilities, lounge, fully equipped kitchen and dining room. * *Victoria and Alfred Hotel,* located in the Victoria and Alfred Waterfront, has 68 air-conditioned rooms with ensuite facilities.

TOURIST CLASS: * *Portswood Hotel,* located a five-minute walk to the Victoria and Alfred Waterfront, has 104 air-conditioned rooms with ensuite facilities.

* *Holiday Inn Garden Court–St. George's,* located in the center of the business district, has 137 rooms with private facilities and a swimming pool.

ACCOMMODATION IN THE CAPE AREA — DELUXE: * *Ellerman House* is a grand old home with ten suites with ensuite facilities and a swimming pool, gym and steam bath. * *The Cellars-Hohenhort Hotel* is comprised of two luxury country houses with a swimming pool and is situated in the beautiful Constantia Valley, a 15-minute drive from Cape Town. All 38 rooms and 15 suites have ensuite facilities. * *Bay Hotel,* located on the beach at Camps Bay, a ten-minute drive out of Cape Town, has 70 rooms and suites with ensuite facilities and a swimming pool. * *The Lord Charles Hotel,* located in Somerset West, has 196 rooms with ensuite facilities.

FIRST CLASS: * *Peninsula Hotel,* located in Sea Point facing the Atlantic Ocean, has 112 suites with one to three bedrooms and two swimming pools. * *Constantia Uitsig* is a 200-acre (80-hectare) private wine farm with garden cottages (24 beds) with ensuite bathrooms, two restaurants and a swimming pool. * *Greenways,* located near Kirstenbosch Botanical Gardens, is a magnificent mansion with eight rooms and six suites with ensuite facilities, a swimming pool and a croquet lawn. * *The Palm House* is an elegant guest house with 11 rooms with ensuite facilities.

SCUBA DIVING IN THE SOUTHERN CAPE

The world's two great oceans, the cold south Atlantic and the warm Indio-Pacific, rub brawny shoulders along the southernmost curve of Africa. This contrast of temperatures produces two extremes in underwater habitats and at least three unique opportunities for the adventurous diver: the Southern Cape, Southern Natal Coast (Durban area) and Northern Natal Coast (near Sodwana Bay).

For those seeking the ultimate underwater thrill, the Southern Cape offers the magnificent cold-water predator — the *great white shark.* South Africa is one of the few places in the world where divers can encounter this formidable creature from the safety of a shark cage. The great white shark is a protected species in South Africa and reaches heroic proportions in these rich waters.

Great white shark dives are a specialized activity. These trips are sole-purpose adventures and are only conducted when individuals or small groups request them. The dives are boat-based, and the sharks are lured into range by chumming and baiting the area.

The best time of the year to dive with them is February–October. Visibility ranges from 10 to 100 feet, (3 to 30 m) and water temperatures range from 50 to 70°F (10 to 21°C).

The best place to dive with great white sharks is near Dyer Island off Gansbaai, about a two hour drive from Cape Town.

Diving facilities, equipment and training in South Africa have been modeled after the American system and modified to suit local conditions and are excellent.

THE WINELANDS: STELLENBOSCH, PAARL AND FRANSCHOEK

There are four popular wine routes through the beautiful wine country northeast of Cape Town. The Stellenbosch Route covers 55 private cellars and cooperative wineries, including the Bergkelder, Blaauwklippen and Delheim, and the Van Ryn Brandy Cellar. The Paarl Route covers 26 cooperative wineries and estates, including Nederburg Estate and KWV Cooperative. The Franschoek Route covers 24 cooperative wineries and private wine estates, including Bellingham and Boschendal. The Worcester Route has 20 cooperative wineries and estates.

There are a number of excellent restaurants in the region, including 96 Winery Road, Boschendal, Bosman's and La Petite Ferme.

ACCOMMODATION — DELUXE: * *Grand Roche,* a luxury estate hotel located in Paarl, has 35 rooms and suites with ensuite facilities and a swimming pool, fitness center and tennis courts. * *Le Quartier Francais,* located in Franschoek, has 15 rooms and two suites with ensuite facilities and a swimming pool. * *Roggeland Country House* is a stately Cape

Roggeland Country House, Paarl.

Dutch farmhouse located near Paarl, with ten bedrooms with ensuite facilities and a swimming pool.

FIRST CLASS: * *D'Ouwe Werf*, located in Stellenbosch, is a beautiful old inn with 25 rooms with ensuite facilities, tennis courts and a swimming pool. * *La Provence*, a quaint country inn situated in the middle of the Franschoek Valley, has rooms with facilities ensuite, a restaurant and a swimming pool. * *Auberge Rozendal Wine Farm Country House*, a 140-year-old homestead located near Stellenbosch, has Victorian-style cottages with ensuite facilities and a swimming pool. Horseback riding is available. * *Mountain Shadows*, a lovely Cape Dutch manor house situated near Paarl, has ten rooms with facilities ensuite.

WEST COAST NATIONAL PARK

West Coast National Park covers 107 square miles (276 km^2) and includes the Langebaan Lagoon, several islands and coastal areas. Langebaan Lagoon, a wetland of internationally recognized importance, often has populations of over 50,000 birds comprised of 23 resident species. Over 250 different species have been recorded.

Bird hides allow close viewing of the thousands of waders that migrate here in the summer months.

During spring, the land is in full flower. The **Postberg Nature Reserve** section of the park is open for visitors to enjoy from mid-August until the end of September. Bontebok, Cape Mountain zebra, eland and Cape grysbok can be seen. A special bird is the black harrier. At Geelbek is a historic farm and national monument with a country-style restaurant. It also serves as National Park Headquaters.

ACCOMMODATION — TOURIST CLASS: * *Farmhouse Guest House*, located in Langebaan, has ten rooms with ensuite facilities.

THE CEDARBERG

This is a rugged, mountainous 502-square-mile (1300-km^2) wilderness area dotted with interesting rock formations created by erosion, waterfalls, clear mountain pools, rock paintings and beautiful fynbos flora.

This is a fabulous area (along with Namaqualand to the north) in which to see millions of flowers blooming in the spring and is part of the "Wildflower Route." The best time to see wildflowers in the Cedarberg is August to early September.

There are over 250 marked hiking trails in the Cedarberg.

From the Cedarberg consider taking a day trip to Lamberts Bay to visit the gannet colony and see the whales in season.

ACCOMMODATION — CLASS A: * *Bushmanskloof Lodge*, located on the 2900-acre (7300-hectare) Bushmanskloof Game Reserve, has ten rooms with ensuite facilities and a swimming pool and sauna. Wildlife on the reserve includes bontebok, red hartebeest, black wildebeest, Cape Mountain and Burchell's zebra, eland and springbok. Activities include walks through the Cedarberg, game drives and visits to some of the 125 San bushmen painting sites on the reserve.

Ride an ostrich at Oudtshoorn.

THE GARDEN ROUTE

One of the most beautiful drives on the continent, the Garden Route is lined with Indian Ocean coastal scenery, beautiful beaches, lakes, forests and mountains with small country hotel accommodations and large resort hotels.

The Garden Route runs between Mossel Bay (east of Cape Town) and Storms River (west of Port Elizabeth).

A number of tours and self-drive options are available from Cape Town to Port Elizabeth (or vice versa) for a minimum of two nights/three days. These programs visit a variety of areas and attractions. The **coastal route** from Cape Town passes through the winelands, Hermanus, Mossel Bay and the coastal areas of Wilderness, Knysna and Plettenberg Bay to Port Elizabeth. The **mountainous route** from Cape Town passes through the winelands, Caledon, Swellendam, over magnificent Tradoun Pass to Barrydale and Calitzdorp, and then to Oudtshoorn. Continue over the Outeniqua Mountains to Wilderness and through the coastal areas to Port Elizabeth. The **northern route** from Cape Town passes through the winelands, Matjiesfontein, and Prince Albert to Oudtshoorn. From there you can join the coastal areas route to Port Elizabeth.

Departing Cape Town, the better way to begin the **coastal route** is to drive to Somerset West, turn towards the coast at The Strand and continue along False Bay passing Gordons Bay, Betty's Bay (where there is a mainland colony of Jackass penguins) and onward to Hermanus. The road down to the coast yields fine views of the rugged coastline. The southernmost vineyards in Africa are located nearby.

Southern Right whales usually start arriving in Walker Bay (Hermanus) in June or July and usually depart by December, with the peak season being August/September. The best time for whale watching in general along the Garden Route is August and September.

You may continue to **Cape Agulhas**, the southernmost tip of Africa, where the Atlantic and Indian oceans meet, and to **Waenhuiskrans** (Arniston), a 200-year-old fishing village. An interesting day visit from Arniston is the **De Hoop Nature Reserve** which is pristine reserve with magnificent, unspoilt beaches. It is the breeding ground of the African black oystercatcher and has a colony of Cape vultures. Other species seen include bontebok, eland and Cape zebra.

Continue to the town of **Mossel Bay** and then drive north to **Oudtshoorn** where you can ride an ostrich — or at least watch them race — and tour an ostrich farm. Located about 16 miles (26 km) north of Oudtshoorn are the **Cango Caves**, the largest limestone caves in Africa, with colorful stalactites and stalagmites.

Return to the coast via **George**, an old-world town with oak-tree-lined streets set at the foot of the Outeniqua Mountains. A narrow-gauge steam train may be taken in the morning from George across the Knysna Lagoon to Knysna and back to George that same afternoon.

Continue east to the **Wilderness Area**, which encompasses a number of interlinking lakes, onward to **Knysna**, a small coastal town with a beautiful lagoon excellent for boating. The Knysna Forest and the Tsitsikamma Forest together form South Africa's largest indigenous high forest.

Further east lies **Plettenberg Bay**, the Garden Route's most sophisticated resort area. Nearby is **Tsitsikamma National Park** — a lushly vegetated 50-mile (80-km) strip along the coast. Wildlife includes the Cape clawless otter, grysbok, bushbuck and blue duiker. Over 275 species of birds have been recorded. The park has hiking trails, including the famous Otter Trail, and underwater trails for both snorkelers and scuba divers.

The northern route passes the Paarl winelands area through a portion of the Great Karoo (semidesert) to **Matjiesfontein**, a charming little town where the buildings and railway station have been preserved in their original Victorian style. From here the route runs southeast through Prince Albert to Oudtshoorn, where it meets the southern route.

From Plettenberg Bay you may continue to St. Francis Bay, Jeffrey's Bay (famous for surfing) and to **Port Elizabeth**.

ACCOMMODATION — SOUTHWEST TO NORTHEAST:

HERMANUS — TOURIST CLASS: * *Beach House,* located in Kleinmond, near Hermanus between Cape Town and Mossel Bay, has 197 rooms and suites with ensuite facilities. * *Sandbaii,* located in Hermanus overlooks the ocean and has 10 rooms with ensuite facilities.

WAENHUISKRANS — FIRST CLASS: * *The Arniston* has 29 rooms with ensuite facilities and a swimming pool. Whales are often seen May–October.

SWELLENDAM — FIRST CLASS: * *Klippe Rivier Homestead* is a Cape Dutch homestead in which the old wine house and stables have been converted into six luxury bedrooms and one honeymoon cottage with ensuite facilities.

OUDTSHOORN — FIRST CLASS: * *Rosenhof Country Lodge* has 12 rooms with ensuite facilities and a swimming pool. TOURIST CLASS: * *De Opstal Farm,* a working ostrich farm located between Oudtshoorn and the Cango Caves, has air-conditioned rooms with ensuite facilities and a swimming pool. * *Queens Hotel* has 40 ensuite rooms and is located in downtown Oudtshoorn.

PRINCE ALBERT — TOURIST CLASS: * *The Swartberg Hotel,* located north of Oudtshoorn, is a charming 20-room hotel with facilities ensuite.

GEORGE — DELUXE: * *The Fancourt Hotel & Country Club Estate* is an elegant hotel (a national monument) with 37 rooms and suites with ensuite facilities, a championship 36-hole golf course, a swimming pool, tennis and a spa.

FIRST CLASS: * *Hoogekraal Country House,* an eighteenth century coastal estate, has ten rooms with facilities ensuite.

WILDERNESS — FIRST CLASS: * *Wilderness Hotel* is situated close to the ocean and the lagoon and has 160 rooms with ensuite facilities.

TOURIST CLASS: * *Holiday Inn Garden Court* has 148 rooms with facilities ensuite.

KNYSNA — DELUXE: * *St. James Club* is located on the shores of the Knysna Lagoon, with 11 suites with ensuite facilities, a swimming pool and floodlit tennis courts.

FIRST CLASS: * *Belvidere Manor* has guest cottages with ensuite facilities. * *Ai Due Camini Guest House,* located on the eastern head of Knysna Lagoon, has five bedrooms with facilities ensuite and a swimming pool.

TOURIST CLASS: * *Yellowwood Lodge,* a restored Victorian house, has ten rooms with ensuite facilities. * *Point Lodge,* set on the water's edge, has seven rooms with facilities ensuite and a swimming pool. * *Brenton-on-Sea,* located in the secluded Brenton Cliffs area, has rooms with ensuite facilities.

PLETTENBERG BAY — DELUXE: * *The Plettenberg,* formerly a magnificent nineteenth century mansion, has elegant rooms and suites with ensuite facilities. * *Hunter's Country House* has ten elegantly decorated thatched cottages with ensuite facilities.

FIRST CLASS: * *Beacon Isle,* located on a peninsula jutting into the sea, has 192 rooms and 8 suites with facilities ensuite, a swimming pool and a tennis court. Water skiing, scuba diving, deep-sea fishing and sailing are offered.

TOURIST CLASS: * *Formosa Inn,* an old established coach house, has 38 garden chalets with ensuite facilities. * *Country Crescent Hotel,* located just outside of Plettenberg Bay, has 26 rooms with facilities ensuite and a swimming pool.

STORMS RIVER — TOURIST CLASS: * *Tsitsikamma Forest Inn* has 34 Swiss-style chalets with facilities ensuite.

ST. FRANCIS BAY — FIRST CLASS: * *Jyllinge Lodge,* located on the beach in a charming coastal resort town, has eight rooms with facilities ensuite.

PORT ELIZABETH — DELUXE: * *Hacklewood Hill Country House,* built in 1898, is an elegant residence with eight rooms with ensuite facilities, a swimming pool and tennis courts.

FIRST CLASS: * *Marine Hotel,* located near the beach, has 69 rooms with ensuite facilities and a swimming pool.

TOURIST CLASS: * *Edward Hotel,* a historical landmark, has 95 rooms with facilities ensuite and a swimming pool. * *Kings Beach Holiday Inn Garden Court* has 232 rooms with ensuite facilities and a swimming pool.

MATJIESFONTEIN (NORTHERN ROUTE) — TOURIST CLASS: * *The Lord Milner* is located just off the Cape Town–Johannesburg road (N1).

SHAMWARI PRIVATE GAME RESERVE

Shamwari is a 35,000-acre (14,000-hectare) private game reserve located 47 miles (75 km) northeast of Port Elizabeth.

Wildlife on the reserve includes white rhino, black rhino, elephant, buffalo, lion, hippo and 17 species of antelope. Day and night game drives and walks are offered.

ACCOMMODATION — CLASS A: * *Long Lee Manor* is an Edwardian mansion with 18 air-conditioned rooms with private balconies and ensuite facilities. * *Shamwari Lodge* has six air-conditioned rooms with ensuite facilities. * *Carn Ingly* and * *Highfield* are two restored settlers homes, each with three rooms with ensuite facilities.

KWA-ZULU NATAL

Kwa-Zulu Natal is located in eastern South Africa along the Indian Ocean. The Drakensberg Mountains rise to 11,420 feet (3482 m) and run roughly north and south along its western border, which it shares with Lesotho.

Kwazulu-Natal is the home of the Zulu and a large variety of wildlife concentrated in several small yet interesting reserves.

DURBAN

The largest city in Kwazulu-Natal, Durban has a beachfront called **The Golden Mile** with amusement parks, amphitheater, colorful markets and aquarium (Sea World). Rickshaw pullers in traditional Zulu costume are available along the beachfront. The Victoria Market and Grey Street Mosque are evidence of the strong Indian influence in this area.

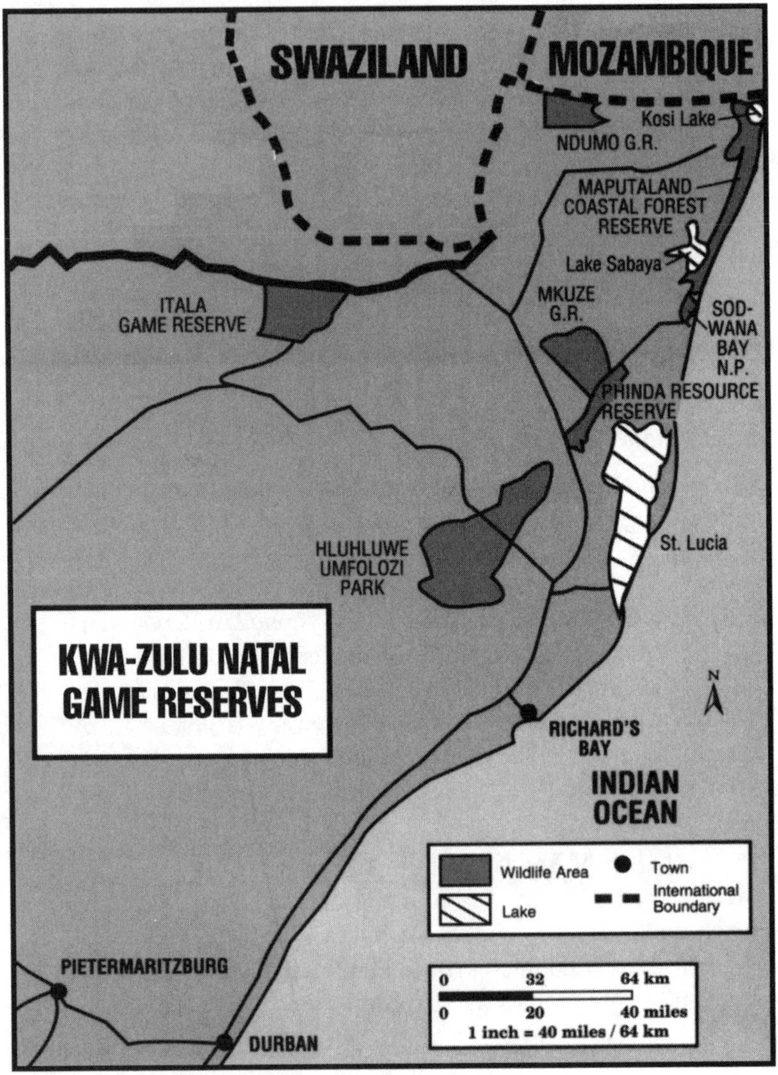

ACCOMMODATION — DELUXE: * *Karos Edward Hotel,* an elegant hotel with old-world charm located on the beachfront, has 101 rooms with ensuite facilities and a swimming pool. * *The Royal Hotel,* located in the city center, has 250 rooms and 22 suites with ensuite facilities, and swimming pool.

FIRST CLASS: * *Holiday Inn Crown Plaza* has 450 rooms and suites with ensuite facilities and two swimming pools.

TOURIST CLASS: * *Marine Parade Holiday Inn* has 336 rooms and suites with ensuite facilities and a swimming pool. * *Holiday Inn Garden Court* has 270 rooms and suites with facilities ensuite and a swimming pool.

ACCOMMODATION NEAR DURBAN (UMHLANGA ROCKS) — DELUXE: * *Beverly Hills* is located north of Durban on the beach and has 91 rooms with ensuite facilities and a swimming pool. * *Shorten's Country House,* an old colonial homestead built in 1905, is located a 20-minute drive from Durban and has chalets with ensuite facilities, an 18-hole golf course, squash and tennis courts and bowling greens.

TOURIST CLASS: * *The Oyster Box* is on the beach, with 206 rooms with facilities ensuite and a swimming pool.

ZULULAND

This is a land of scenic hills and valleys dotted with KwaZulu homesteads — many with traditional beehive huts. Zululand has the largest concentration of wildlife conservation areas and game ranches in the country.

ACCOMMODATION — CLASS B: * *Simunye Pioneer Settlement,* located between Durban and Hluhluwe Umfolozi Park, allows guests to experience contemporary Zulu culture. Accommodations are rock chalets built into the side of a cliff, with facilities ensuite, and a rock pool. There is no electricity; lighting is supplied by lamps and candles. Guests may learn to drive a single-horse ox cart or horseback ride in the valley.

HLUHLUWE UMFOLOZI PARK

The Hluhluwe and Umfolozi Reserves, the oldest reserves in Africa (proclaimed in 1895), were recently combined to form Hluhluwe Umfolozi Park — now the third largest reserve in South Africa. As there are no roads directly connecting Hluhluwe and Umfolozi, each section of the park must be visited separately. The best time to visit is during the dry winter months (May–September). Game drives by open vehicle and walks with national park guides are available.

The **Umfolozi** section of the park is located about 165 miles (265 km) north of Durban. This 185-square-mile (478-km^2) reserve of open grassland and savannah woodland is best known for having the world's largest concentration of white rhino — approximately 1900.

Other species include black rhino, elephant, nyala, kudu, waterbuck, zebra, wildebeest, buffalo, giraffe, black-back jackal, lion and cheetah. Over 400 species of birds have been recorded.

The 90 square miles (231 km^2) of grassland, forest and woodland of the **Hluhluwe** section of the park is host to a variety of wildlife including large numbers of white rhino, along with black rhino, elephant, buffalo, Southern giraffe, wildebeest, Burchell's zebra, kudu, lion, cheetah, Samango monkeys, hippo and crocs. This is one of the best parks in Africa to see nyala. Over 425 bird species have been recorded.

On a recent visit we spotted over 20 white rhino, 12 nyala and Southern giraffe, along with buffalo and grey duiker, among other species.

The Hluhluwe section of the park is located about 18 miles (29 km) from St. Lucia and 175 miles (282 km) from Durban. The park contains walking trails.

ACCOMMODATION IN THE UMFOLOZI SECTION — CLASS C & D: * The park has self-service chalets, huts and bush camps with ablution blocks.

ACCOMMODATION IN THE HLUHLUWE SECTION — CLASS B: * *Hilltop Camp,* an attractive new camp run by the park, has chalets with ensuite facilities and a restaurant.

CLASS C & D: The park has cottages with private facilities and self-service huts with ablution blocks. A small self-service bush camp with an ablution block is also available.

CAMPING: None.

ACCOMMODATION NEAR THE PARK — FIRST CLASS: * *Zululand Tree Lodge*, located on the Ubizane Game Reserve near the Hluhluwe entrance, has 24 fan-cooled tree-house-style chalets with ensuite facilities and a swimming pool. Game drives to Hluhluwe Umfolozi and Mkuzi Game Reserves, walks, horseback riding, local community visits and cruises on Lake St. Lucia are offered.

ITALA GAME RESERVE

This scenic 116-square-mile (300-km^2) reserve consists of open savannah, deep valleys, granite outcrops and rivers.

The reserve has a high concentration of a variety of wildlife, including black rhino, white rhino, giraffe, eland, kudu, tsessebe, waterbuck and cheetah. Over 300 bird species have been recorded, including birds of prey such as martial eagles, black eagles, Wahlberg's eagles and snake eagles. On a recent visit we went on a walk and were able to approach giraffe and white rhino very closely.

Game drives in open vehicles, wilderness trails and guided day walks are available. The park is located in northern Natal just south of the Pongola River.

ACCOMMODATION — CLASS B: * *Ntshondwe Camp* has 39 thatched chalets with ensuite facilities, overlooking a water hole.

CLASS D: A small self-service bush camp with separate facilities is available.

CAMPING: Campsites with ablution blocks are available.

ACCOMMODATION NEAR ITALA — CLASS B: * *Fugitives' Drift Lodge* consists of five "colonial-style" cottages with ensuite facilities. Most people who stay here are interested in tours of the Aglo/Zulu battlefields.

PHINDA RESOURCE RESERVE

Privately owned Phinda Resource Reserve covers 58 square miles (150 km^2) of riverine woodland, open savannah, flat acacia bushvelt and hilly terrain. Wildlife includes Southern giraffe, hippo, elephant, lion, white rhino, zebra, wildebeest, nyala and greater kudu, among other species.

View across Mkuze, after a morning walk.

Day and night game drives, walks, canoeing and boat trips are offered.

ACCOMMODATION — CLASS A: * *Phinda Vlei Lodge* has six suites each with their own plunge pool and ensuite facilities. * *Phinda Forest Lodge* has 16 glass chalets with ensuite facilities and overhead fans and a swimming pool. * *Phinda Mountain Lodge* has four spacious chalets and 17 suites with ensuite facilities and overhead fans and a swimming pool.

MKUZE GAME RESERVE

This 131-square-mile (340-km^2) park has a diversity of vegetation including riverine forest, savannah woodland and forests of large sycamore fig trees. Wildlife includes leopard, side-striped jackal, white rhino, black rhino, eland, kudu, nyala, bushbuck, reedbuck, klipspringer, hippo, crocs and a variety of aquatic birds.

CLASS C & D: * *National Park* bungalows, an eight-bed bush camp with facilities ensuite, and huts with ablution blocks.

ST. LUCIA AND MAPUTALAND MARINE RESERVES

These two reserves combined form Africa's largest marine reserve, covering 342 square miles (885 km^2). The reserve runs along the coastline from 0.6 mile (1 km) south of Cape Vidal to the Mozambique border and 3.5 miles (5.6 km) out into the Indian Ocean.

Several species of turtles, including loggerhead turtles and the endangered leatherback turtle, lay their eggs on the northern beaches. St. Lucia includes the southernmost coral reefs in the world and is the only breeding spot for pink-backed pelicans in South Africa. Flamingos migrate to the reserve. Boat tours are available from St. Lucia.

CLASS D: * *National Parks* huts and log cabins with ablution blocks are available.

CAMPING: Campsites are available.

MAPUTALAND COASTAL FOREST RESERVE

The Maputaland Coastal Forest Reserve is a remote reserve containing very possibly the highest forested sand dunes in the world. No construction is allowed on the ocean side of these huge dunes, making this one of the most beautiful and pristine beaches in Africa.

Wildlife includes large spotted genet, water mongoose, hippos and turtles (in season). During our visit we saw a variety of bird life including scarlet-chested sunbirds and dusky flycatchers. KwaZulu locals are often seen collecting mussels and catching reef fish in the reserve.

Beach walking, snorkeling, surf casting and fly-fishing, and exploring the unique flora and bird life of this region are the main activities. **Black Rock**, a large sandstone protrusion into the Indian Ocean about 4 miles (6.7 km) from Rocktail Bay, is one of the few places in the world where pelagics may be caught, fishing from shore. **Lala Neck**, located south of Rocktail Bay, is very good for snorkeling. **Lake Sibaya**, the largest freshwater lake in South Africa, is separated from the Indian Ocean only by the coastal dunes.

ACCOMMODATION — CLASS A/B: * *Rocktail Bay Lodge* has five attractive double-room wooden chalets (20 beds) with ensuite facilities and a swimming pool. Fishing, snorkeling, nature drives and excursions to Black Rock, Lala Neck and Lake Sabaya are offered.

Ndumo Wilderness Camp.

NDUMO GAME RESERVE

Located in northeastern Natal on the Mozambique border, this reserve is comprised of riverine floodplains and is called "the Little Okavango" (referring to the Okavango Delta, Botswana).

In spite of its small size (39 square miles/101 km^2), it is considered to be one of the finest reserves in Natal. There are no large herds of mammals here; however, riverine wildlife is superb. Wildlife includes hippo, crocs, nyala, bushbuck, red duiker, suni, black rhino and white rhino. Known as the "birding mecca" of South Africa, the reserve has recorded over 60 percent of the species found in the country.

ACCOMMODATION — CLASS A: * *Ndumo Wilderness Camp* has eight tents with ensuite facilities. Game drives and walks are offered.

CLASS D: * *National Parks* cottages with ablution facilities.

CAMPING: None.

SODWANA BAY NATIONAL PARK

Fishing (especially for marlin) and scuba diving are the main attractions of this 1.6-square-mile (4.1-km^2) reserve.

ACCOMMODATION — CLASS B/C: * *Sodwana Bay Lodge* has chalets with ensuite facilities and offers scuba diving and big-game fishing.

CAMPING: Campsites are available.

SCUBA DIVING – NATAL COAST

In the transition zone between Sodwana's coral and the Cape's kelp forests lie the city of Durban and the Southern Natal Coast. Aliwal Shoal, Lander's Reef and the *Produce* wreck are the diving focal points of the region.

Escorted boat dives to these rocky reefs give one an opportunity to view a wide variety of southern Africa's marine animals, including potato bass (a large grouper), eels, rays, turtles and reef fish.

The best time to see Aliwal's famed "raggies" is June–July. A group of huge resident bridle bass (jewfish) and schools of dagger salmon make the nearby wreck of the *Produce* their home.

Diving is possible year-round, with the best conditions March–May. Water temperatures range from 65 to 72°F (18 to 22°C). Diving depths range from 30 to 120 feet (9 to 36 m).

Zululand's semitropical coast has South Africa's warmest and clearest waters — ideal for scuba diving. Escorted boat dives are offered from Sodwana Bay (see above).

Africa's most southern coral reefs are composed of hard and soft reefs. Named according to their distance from the Sodwana launch site, these reefs are called quarter-, two-, three-, four-, seven- and nine-mile (0.4-, 3.2-, 4.8-, 6.4-, 11.2- and 14.5-km) reefs. The reefs are home to many species of colorful Indian Ocean tropical fish, rock cods (groupers), kingfish (a large jack), barracudas and moray eels. Dolphins are sometimes sighted on the way to dive sites, and humpback whales migrate through the area in February and September. "Raggies" (grey nurse sharks/sand tiger sharks) and whale sharks are sometimes seen by divers in January–February. Manta rays and pelagics are also part of the fish mix. Loggerhead, green and leatherback sea turtles use the undeveloped coastline for nesting December–March. Night drives and walks to see turtles nesting can be arranged.

Diving is possible year-round, with the best conditions in February–June. Visibility ranges from 20 to 100+ feet (6 to 30+ m), depending on sea conditions, with an average of 65 feet. Water temperature ranges from 70 to 80°F (21 to 27°C). Most diving is conducted from 25 to 125 feet (8 to 38 m) below the surface.

LESOTHO

THE WANDERING ELAND

Cow-like eland are very mobile animals within their chosen environment and have adapted their feeding habits accordingly. Food availability dictates where they move within their local area, whether nomadically or migrating between areas. For their size (5.5 feet/1.5 m shoulder height) and weight (many over 1500 pounds/680 kg), they are staggeringly good jumpers and will clear 7 feet (2 m) if a fence or other obstacle is in the way of their feeding path.

Eland browse during the winter months and have been known to eat 60 types of food plants, including 11 grasses. Feeding includes chewing twigs and branches (*mopane, combretum*, and *lonchocarpus*) up to two inches thick. They use their horns extensively to break the higher branches. They reach leaves (*grewia, mopane, syringa*), berries, flowering bushes (*tagestes* and *bidens*) and tasty fruit pods with their lips.

In the summer months, eland graze the new grass shoots to sustain their high-protein diet. In drier regions, they feed on the succulent branches, acacia leaves and roots to take in enough moisture, if water is not readily available. They also feed at night, when the grasses are laden with dew.

As they walk from feeding ground to feeding ground, eland make a distinct clicking sound caused either by their knees or tendons or the two toes of each hoof coming together as they are raised.

LESOTHO

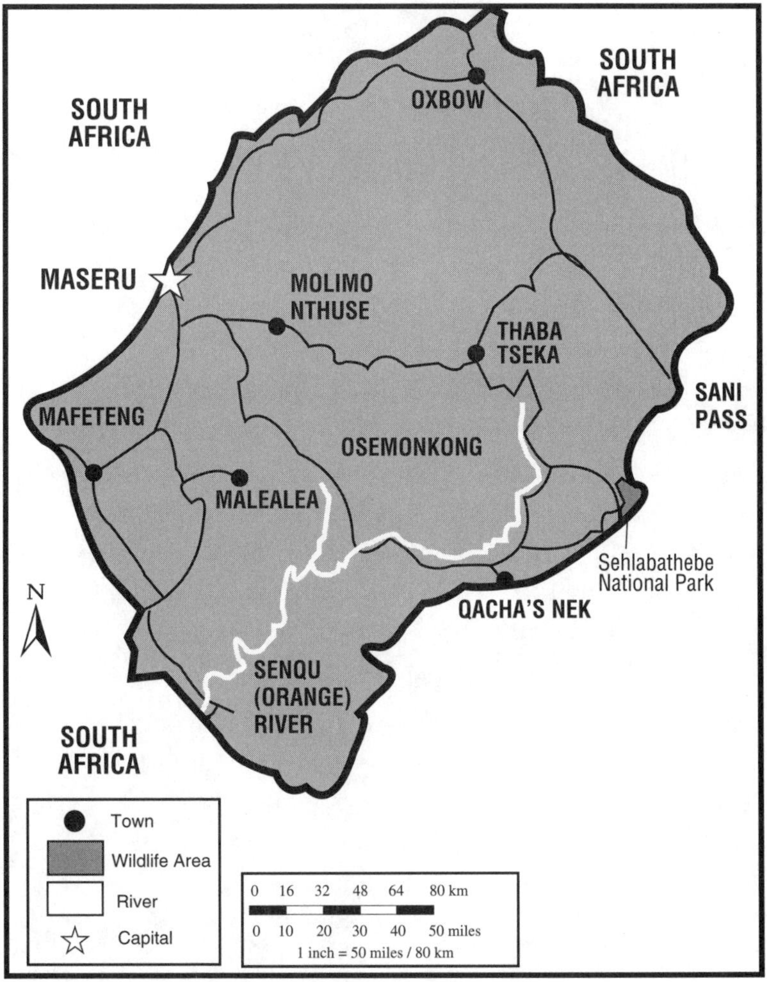

FACTS AT A GLANCE

AREA:	11,720 SQ. MI. / 30,355 SQ. KM.
APPROXIMATE SIZE:	MARYLAND OR BELGIUM
POPULATION:	1.94 MILLION
CAPITAL:	MASERU (POP. EST. 170,000 MILLION)
OFFICIAL LANGUAGE:	ENGLISH AND SESOTHO
	ENGLISH IS WIDELY SPOKEN

LESOTHO

Lesotho is a rugged country with spectacular mountain scenery which can best be explored on pony treks, hiking and camping in the remote regions of the country.

Called the "Kingdom in the Sky," Lesotho has the highest lowest altitude of any country in the world. In other words, Lesotho's lowest point (4530 feet/1380 m above sea level) is higher than the lowest point of any other country. Most of the country lies above 6000 feet (1830 m).

Lesotho is an "island" surrounded by the Republic of South Africa, which makes it one of only three countries in the world (including the Vatican and the Republic of San Marino) surrounded entirely by one other country.

The country is called Lesotho (pronounced *Lesutu*), an individual is called Mosotho and the people Basotho. Many men wear multicolored traditional blankets to keep them warm in the cool and often freezing air; they also wear the traditional conical basket hats.

The Basotho are the only Africans to adapt to below-freezing temperatures, which can drop to –8°F (–22°C). Snow can fall in the mountains any time of the year and in the lowlands between May and August. Summer temperatures seldom rise over 90°F (32°C). The rainy season is during the summer with 85 percent of the annual rainfall (about 28 inches/710 mm) occurring October–April, making many roads impassable.

The western part of the country is lowland, with altitudes of 5000–6000 feet (1525–1830 m). The eastern three-quarters of the country is highland, rising to 11,420 feet (3482 m) in the Drakensberg Mountain Range, bordering the Natal Province of South Africa.

Bushmen (Qhuaique) inhabited Basutoland (now Lesotho) until the end of the sixteenth century. For the following 300 years the area was inhabited by refugees from numerous tribal wars in the region; these refugees formed the Basotho tribal group.

Moshoeshoe I reigned from 1823 to 1870, and his kingdom was powerful enough to keep the warring Zulus at bay. Wars with South Africa from 1823 to 1868 resulted in the loss of much land, called "The Lost Territory." Lesotho asked to become a British protectorate to gain assistance in halting the encroachment of its lands by the Orange Free State (South Africa). Lesotho was a British protectorate from 1868 until its independence on October 4, 1966.

Lesotho has the highest literacy rate in Africa. Its economy is based on agriculture and earnings from laborers working in mines in South Africa. Light manufacturing and tourism are also important foreign exchange earners.

The mountains of Lesotho are southern Africa's most important watershed. The Highlands Water Project, a large project that involves selling water to South Africa, is under way and promises to provide Lesotho with much needed income.

The two best ways of seeing what this country has to offer are by pony trekking or a four-wheel-drive safari into its most remote regions.

WILDLIFE AND WILDLIFE AREAS

Sehlabathebe National Park, small by African standards, is Lesotho's premier wildlife reserve. The country is more often visited for its scenic beauty than wildlife, which should be considered a bonus.

Stopping at a village during a pony trek.

PONY TREKKING

Lesotho is one of the best countries in the world for pony trekking. The Basotho pony is the chief means of transportation in the mountainous two-thirds of this country and the best way to explore this land of few roads. Bridle paths crisscross the pristine landscape from one village or family settlement to the next.

The Basotho pony is the best pony in the world for mountain travel and was highly prized during wartime. It can easily climb and descend steep, rocky paths which other breeds of horses would not attempt. The riding style in Lesotho, as in most countries in Africa, is *English*.

PONY TREKKING FROM MOLIMO NTHUSE

Molimo Nthuse, located about an hour drive (34 miles/54 km) on a good tarred road from Maseru, is the center for pony trekking in this region. Escorted day trips to the refreshing rock pools of **Qiloane Falls** and other rides of up to seven days in length are offered. The ponies are well trained and a pleasure to ride.

Pony treks are conducted year-round — in "swimsuit" weather in the summer as well as in cold, snowy weather in winter. Remember, the seasons are reversed from the northern hemisphere!

Accommodation on overnight treks is in Basotho huts or camping (bring your own tent).

ACCOMMODATION — CLASS C: * *The Molimo Nthuse Lodge* offers 16 rooms with veranda and private facilities in a beautiful mountain setting.

PONY TREKKING FROM MALEALEA TO SEMONKONG

One of the most interesting pony treks in Lesotho (offered from September to April) is a four-day ride from Malealea in southwestern Lesotho to Semonkong and Maletsunyane Falls — the highest single-drop waterfall in southern Africa.

The pony trek begins after examining some interesting bushmen rock paintings and rock pools located near **Malealea**, about 50 miles (80 km) from Maseru. Riding east, the dark-blue skies are broken by high mountains in the distance. Basotho, wrapped in their traditional blankets and traveling on foot and by pony, offer friendly greetings and warm smiles. Riding in a cool breeze on a moonlit night in these remote mountains calms the soul and brings peace and harmony to one's spirit.

The nights are spent in traditional huts usually owned by the headman of the village, providing a firsthand knowledge of how the people live. Hikes to view **Ribaneng Falls** and **Ketane Falls** (495 feet/150 m) are made along the way.

The final destination is **Maletsunyane Falls**, a few miles and less than a half-hour ride from Semonkong. These impressive falls drop over 620 feet (190 m) in a majestic setting.

Semonkong is a dusty little town resembling America's "Wild, Wild West," with a general store, hitching posts, stables and horses providing the main means of transportation. Scheduled flights on Air Lesotho back to Maseru are available.

ACCOMMODATION — CLASS F: MALEALEA: * *Malealea Lodge* is a small self-service lodge with five bedrooms and six rondavels. Day pony treks are available. SEMONKONG: * *Mountain Delight Lodge* is a small self-service lodge with ten beds.

CAMPING: Campsites are available at *Fraser Lodge* (Semonkong).

THE MOUNTAIN ROAD

This route cuts through the center of Lesotho from west to east through spectacular mountain scenery to "the roof of Africa." From Maseru the road ascends over **Bushmen Pass** (Lekhalong la Baroa) to **Molimo Nthuse** ("God Help Me Pass"). Between December and March colorful scarlet and yellow red-hot pokers (flowers) may be seen in this area.

Continue to **Thaba Tseka**, where the good road ends and four-wheel drive is necessary to negotiate the tracks that pass small villages and isolated herd-boys. After **Sehonghong** the route descends into the **Orange (Senqu) River Canyon**, dotted with unusual rock formations, then climbs over **Matebeng Pass** (9670 feet/2948 m), which had snow, sleet and icicles during my visit in April, and onward to Sehlabathebe National Park.

SEHLABATHEBE NATIONAL PARK

Sehlabathebe has the highest sandstone formations (including arches) in southern Africa. This park, situated on a high plateau with small lakes, offers tremendous views of the Drakensberg Mountains and Natal. Sehlabathebe means "Plateau of the Shield" and has an average altitude of over 8000 feet (2440 m). Three peaks, called "The Three Bushmen" (Baroa-ba-Bararo), dominate the skyline.

This small 25-square-mile (65-km^2) fenced park has oribi, eland, reedbuck, wildebeest, baboon and abundant bird life, including the rare lammergeyer.

The best time to visit Sehlabathebe for game viewing, hiking and for some of the best freshwater fishing in southern Africa is November–March. Quickest access is by charter flight. Land access is by a 185-mile (300 km) drive across Lesotho from Maseru or from South Africa via Qacha's Nek, Sani Pass, or a five- to six-hour hike (or three- to- four-hour pony trek) of 15 miles (24 km) from Bushman's Nek Lodge.

ACCOMMODATION — CLASS D: * *Sehlabathebe Park Lodge* is a self-service lodge with four double rooms.

CLASS F: Dormitory accommodation is available.

CAMPING: Campsites are available near the lodge.

MASERU

This is the capital and largest city, located in the western lowlands. Sights include the Cathedral and the Royal Lesotho Carpet Factory. The tourist office is next to the Victoria Hotel.

Some interesting day excursions from Maseru include **Thaba-Bosiu** (The Mountain at Night), the table mountain fortress 19 miles (30 km) from Maseru where the Basotho fought off the Boers, and the **Ha Khotso** rock paintings, considered to be some of the finest in southern Africa, located 28 miles (45 km) from Maseru off the mountain road.

ACCOMMODATION — DELUXE: * *The Lesotho Sun* is situated on a hill overlooking Maseru, with 240 rooms with ensuite facilities, a swimming pool, tennis courts, health club, casino, tenpin bowling, several restaurants and conference facilities.

FIRST CLASS: * *Maseru Sun* has 112 rooms with ensuite facilities, tennis courts, a swimming pool, conference rooms and a casino.

SWAZILAND

THE MIGRATING ZEBRA

The zebras' regal black-and-white striped coats are a spectacle when they are assembled in herds during the annual dry season migration. As they go in search of a new water source, the gregarious behavior of male and female animals is interesting to observe.

The rich and polished stripes of a zebra give the impression of a healthy animal, plump with plenty of fat reserves. But they do not have ruminant stomachs, and they need to eat nearly double the amount of grass as, say, the wildebeest, to give them enough protein. Zebra are odd-toed ungulates, similar to the rhino, and they play an important role in the migratory herbivorous trail. Zebra graze the taller, upper parts of new grasses, while the wildebeest and other antelope species eat the shortened grasses.

Zebra breeding season is stimulated by the coming rains. Stallions test breeding female zebra for estrus by exhibiting flehmen. This is a characteristic act during which the male raises its head high, sniffs the female's urine and curls back its lips, assessing her reproductive status. The estrus filly is also a cause for fighting among the males; they rear, bare their teeth and bite each other, kicking and thumping their hooves.

Young foals are usually born as migration begins, their brown furry faces and wobbly legs a gorgeous sight to view as they hurry to keep up with the mares. The foaling season is timed to coincide with the new growth of food.

SWAZILAND

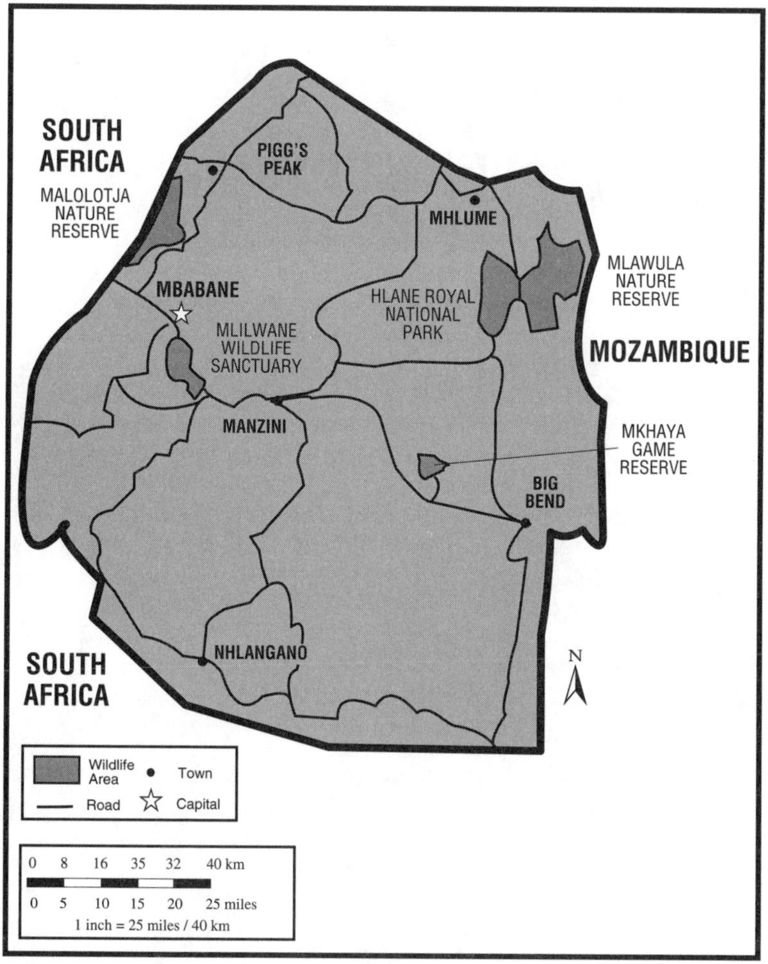

FACTS AT A GLANCE

AREA:	6,704 SQ. MI. / 17,364 SQ. KM.
APPROXIMATE SIZE:	NEW JERSEY OR WALES
POPULATION:	937,000 MILLION
CAPITAL:	MBABANE (POP. EST. 51,000)
OFFICIAL LANGUAGE:	ENGLISH AND SISWATI

SWAZILAND

The combination of friendly people, interesting culture, beautiful countryside and small game reserves makes Swaziland an attractive country to visit.

Swaziland, along with Lesotho and Morocco, is one of the last three remaining kingdoms in Africa. The country is deeply rooted in tradition — an important part of present-day life.

Although Swaziland is the second smallest country in Africa, within its boundaries lie every type of African terrain except desert. Swaziland has several small wildlife reserves, bushmen paintings, international-class resorts and superb scenery.

Unlike most African countries, Swaziland has never been a totally subject nation. Although the British administered the country for 66 years, the people have always been governed by their own rulers according to their own traditions.

Swaziland has an excellent climate; the higher altitudes have a near temperate climate, while the rest of the country has a subtropical climate. Summers (November–January) are rainy, hot and humid. Winters (May–July) are crisp and clear, with occasional frosts in the highveld (higher altitudes). July is usually windy and dusty.

Geographically, the country is divided into four belts of about the same width, running roughly north to south: the mountainous highveld in the west, the hilly middleveld, the Lubombo Plateau along the eastern border, and the lowveld bush.

Swaziland may have been inhabited by bushmen between the early Stone Age and fifteenth century. In the fifteenth century, descendants of the Nguni migrated to what is now Maputo, Mozambique, from the great lakes of Central Africa. About 1700, the Nkosi Dlamini settled within the present-day borders of Swaziland.

Mswati II was proclaimed king of the people of the Mswati in 1840, forming the seed of a Swazi nation. By this time, the kingdom had grown to twice its present size, and whites began to obtain valuable commercial and agricultural concessions.

Dual administration of the country by British and Boer (Transvaal) governments failed. The Boers took over from 1895 until the Anglo-Boer War broke out in 1899. Swaziland became a High Commission Territory under the British after the war in 1903.

In 1921, Sobhuza II became king and remained on the throne until his death in 1982, making him the longest ruling monarch in the world. This long reign gave his country a higher level of political stability than experienced by most of the world.

Only four rulers in modern times have reigned over 60 years: Queen Victoria of Great Britain, Louis XIV of France, Karl Friedrich the Grand Duke of Badan, and Sobhuza II.

Swaziland regained its independence on September 6, 1968, making it the last directly administered British colony in Africa. The Queen Regent, Indlovukazi, ruled after the death of Sobhuza, until Prince Makhosetive was crowned king in 1986. The mining of the highlands' (Ngwenya's) iron ore deposits began as early as 26,000 B.C. and continued until 1980, when supplies were exhausted. In the late 1800s, the Swazi gold rush centered around Pigg's Peak and Jeppe's Reef and lasted for 60 years.

The people are called Swazi(s), most of whom are subsistence farmers, following a mixture of Christian and indigenous beliefs. About 95 percent are of Swazi descent, with the rest of the population composed of Zulu, European, Mozambiquean and mulatto. Most live in scattered homesteads instead of concentrating themselves in villages and cities.

More than 15,000 Swazis work outside the country, primarily in South African gold and platinum mines. Much of Swazi tradition revolves around the raising of cattle.

The country's main crops are maize, sugar, citrus, cotton, pineapples and tobacco. Seventy-five percent of the population works in agriculture.

WILDLIFE AND WILDLIFE AREAS

Less than 100 years ago, Swaziland was abundant in most forms of wildlife. But much wildlife was exterminated by hunters in the years to follow. Conservation programs have revived this nation's wildlife heritage. Most of the indigenous mammal species have been reintroduced.

Swazi reserves are among the smallest on the continent, but for their size contain a great variety of species. The parks are ideal for horseback, bicycle or walking safaris, providing close contact with nature. Open vehicles are most often used.

The country is prolific in bird life, hosting more than 450 different species; these include such rarities as the bald ibis and blue crane. Other more common species include the glossy starling, lilac-breasted roller, hamerkop, sunbirds, kingfishers, geese and guinea fowl.

In the country's wide range of altitude grow over 6000 different species of flora, including 25 varieties of aloes and six species of cycads.

Cycads, often called "living fossils," are the oldest known seed-bearing plants in the world. According to carbon dating, these plants have changed very little during the last 50 million years and are presently protected by law.

THE NORTH

MALOLOTJA NATURE RESERVE

Malolotja Nature Reserve covers 70 square miles (180 km^2) of mountains and gorges harboring unique highveld flora and fauna. Rock faces, rapids, waterfalls, grasslands, impenetrable riverine forests and mountains rising to an altitude of 6025 feet (1837 m) provide scenic backdrops for game. Tree cycads over 20 feet (6 m) may be found in the valleys.

Malolotja Falls, with more than a 300-foot (100-m) drop, are the highest in the country. Wildlife includes oribi, vaal rhebok, klipspringer, impala, red duiker, reedbuck, white rhino, wildebeest, aardwolf, black-backed jackal, honey badger, serval and zebra. Over 150 species of birds have been sighted. There are bald ibis colonies and blue cranes in the park November–February. Flora characteristic only of this region of southern Africa include barberton, kaapsehoop and woolly cycads.

Ngwenya Mine may be the site of the world's earliest known mine, thought to have been worked as early as 26,000 B.C.

With limited roads, the park is best suited for walkers and backpackers. Wilderness trails one to seven days in length are well marked and require a permit; day trails may be used without a permit. Camping along the trail is only allowed at official sites; these sites have water but no facilities. Permits must be obtained for backpacking and for fishing at the Forbes Reef Dam and Upper Malolotja River from the tourist office.

The best time to visit is August–April; June–July is cold and windy. The main gate is located 22 miles (35 km) northwest of Mbabane on the road to Pigg's Peak.

ACCOMMODATION — CLASS C & D: * *National Park Cabins* have six fully furnished cabins, each with six beds, private facilities, crockery and cutlery. Bring your own food, bedclothes and towels.

CAMPING: Campsites with ablution blocks are available.

HLANE ROYAL NATIONAL PARK

Located in the northwestern corner of the country about 44 miles (70 km) from Manzini, this 115-square-mile (300-km^2) park is the largest in Swaziland and is composed of unspoiled acacia bushveld. Large herds congregate at the water holes during the dry winter months and disperse during the wet summer months.

Wildlife includes lion, cheetah, elephant, white rhino, black-backed jackal, spotted hyena, giraffe, kudu, blue wildebeest, waterbuck, steenbok and zebra. Some roads are impassable in the rainy season.

ACCOMMODATION — CLASS D: * *Bhubesi Rest Camp* has three self-service lodges (12 beds).

CLASS F: * *Ndlovu Rest Camp* has five rustic huts (20 beds) and an ablution block.

CAMPING: Camping is allowed.

MLAWULA NATURE RESERVE

Situated east of Hlane Royal National Park, Mlawula is a 70-square-mile (180-km^2) reserve composed of lowveld and Lubombo mountainside which support oribi, ostrich and red hartebeest, among other species.

ACCOMMODATION—CLASS F: Four self-catering tents.

CAMPING: Campsites are available.

MLILWANE WILDLIFE SANCTUARY

Located in the Ezulwini Valley, Mlilwane means "little fire," named for the lightning which often strikes a nearby hill where large deposits of iron ore exist. This 17-square-mile (45-km^2) game sanctuary has a variety of wildlife including giraffe, hippo, buffalo, zebra, crocodile, jackal, caracal cat, serval cat, civet, nyala, blue wildebeest, eland, kudu, waterbuck, blesbok, reedbuck, bushbuck, oribi, springbok, duiker and klipspringer.

The sanctuary is composed of middleveld and highveld with altitudes ranging from 2200 to 4750 feet (670 to 1450 m). It is located on an escarpment that was once a meeting point of westerly and easterly migrations of animals, which resulted in the congregation of a large number of wildlife species.

The northern limits of Mlilwane are marked by the twin peaks of "Sheba's Breasts." "Execution Rock" is another legendary peak where common criminals were supposedly pushed to their deaths.

Over 60 miles of gravel roads run throughout the sanctuary. Guided tours in open vehicles, on foot or on horseback can be arranged in advance at the Rest Camp. Horseback-riding safaris are conducted along bridle trails through the park. The best time to visit is the dry season, May–September.

ACCOMMODATION — DELUXE/FIRST AND TOURIST CLASS: See "Ezulwini Valley" below.

CLASS D: * *Mlilwane Rest Camp* has thatched wooden huts with ensuite facilities and traditional "beehive" huts and an ablution block. In the evenings traditional dancing may be seen.

CAMPING: Campsites are available.

EZULWINI VALLEY

The Ezulwini Valley, or "Place of Heaven," is the entertainment center of the country and is the most convenient area in which to stay when visiting the Mlilwane Wildlife Sanctuary.

ACCOMMODATION — DELUXE: * The *Royal Swazi Sun Hotel, Casino and Country Club*, situated on 100 acres (40 hectares), has 147 rooms with ensuite facilities, a swimming pool, a large alfresco spa, nearby mineral springs and sauna, casino, cinema, 18-hole championship golf course, horseback riding, tennis, squash, lawn bowling and a large convention center. Guests of the Ezulwini Sun and the Lugogo Sun may use the facilities of the more exclusive Royal Swazi Sun Hotel; a courtesy inter-hotel shuttle service is provided.

FIRST CLASS: * *Ezulwini Sun* has 120 air-conditioned rooms with private facilities, a swimming pool and tennis courts.

* *Lugogo Sun* has 202 air-conditioned rooms with ensuite facilities and a swimming pool.

LOBAMBA

Lobamba is the spiritual and legislative capital of the country. The Queen Mother's village is situated here. The King Sobhuza the Second Monument and National Museum, concentrating on Swazi culture and traditions, and the House of Parliament may be visited.

The country's two most important ceremonies are the Ncwala and Umhlanga, both of which take place at the Ludzidzini Royal Residence.

The most important of the two ceremonies is the **Ncwala** or First Fruit Ceremony, usually held in December and January; its exact date depends on the phases of the moon as analyzed by Swazi astrologers. The Ncwala symbolizes the religious spirit identifying the Swazi people with their king. The Ncwala is spread over about a three-week period and involves the entire Swazi nation.

The famous week-long Umhlanga (**Reed Dance**) is a colorful ceremony in which hundreds of Swazi maidens gather reeds and march with them to the Royal Residence at Ludzidzini, where the reeds are used to repair the windbreakers around the residence of the Queen Mother, Indlovukazi. The Umhlanga occurs in late August/early September.

Photographs of these two ceremonies may be taken only with permission from the Swaziland Information Services (P.O. Box 338, Mbabane, Swaziland, telephone: 011-268-4-2761).

PIGG'S PEAK

Pigg's Peak, located in one of the most scenic areas of the country, was named after William Pigg, who discovered gold there in January of 1884. Nearby is the country's most famous bushman painting, located at the **Nsangwini Shelter**. Ask the District Officer at Pigg's Peak to find a guide to take you there.

ACCOMMODATION — FIRST CLASS: * *Protea Pigg's Peak Hotel & Casino,* located 6 miles (10 km) north of Pigg's Peak, has 106 rooms with facilities ensuite, a swimming pool, gym, tennis and squash courts, cinema and casino.

THE SOUTH

MBABANE

Mbabane, the capital of Swaziland, is located in the mountainous highveld overlooking the Ezulwini Valley. Mbabane has a number of shops that sell local crafts. Most international visitors stay in Ezulwini Valley instead of Mbabane. The international airport (Matsapha) is located about 15 miles (24 km) from Mbabane, between Mbabane and the industrial city of Manzini.

NHLANGANO

Nhlangano means "The Meeting Place of the Kings" and commemorates the meeting between King Sobhuza II and King George VI in 1947. Nhlangano is located in the southwestern part of the country in an unspoiled mountainous area and is the burial place of many Swazi kings.

Mother and her foal.

ACCOMMODATION — FIRST CLASS: * The *Nhlangano Sun* is the best hotel in the area, with a casino, disco bar, swimming pool, tennis, and 47 comfortable chalet-type rooms with ensuite facilities. Golf, squash and lawn bowling are available at the nearby country club.

MKHAYA GAME RESERVE

Swaziland's official refuge for endangered species, Mkhaya covers 25 square miles (65 km^2) with sandveld savannah in the north and acacia-dominated savannah in the south. Altitude ranges from 600 to 1150 feet (1880 to 350 m). Winters are warm by day and cold at night; summers are hot, with temperatures exceeding 100°F (38°C).

Wildlife includes elephant, hippo, black and white rhino, zebra, roan antelope, sable antelope, buffalo, eland, wildebeest, waterbuck, kudu, tsessebe, reedbuck, red duiker, grey duiker, steenbok, ostrich, spotted hyena, black-backed and side-striped jackal and crocodile.

ACCOMMODATION — CLASS C: * *Stone Camp* has tents with ensuite facilities. Game drives in open landrovers, walks and white-water rafting are offered.

THE INDIAN OCEAN

MAURITIUS

THE EXTINCT DODO

"Dead as a dodo" is a popular saying, in memory of this island bird. The name "dodo" stems from Portuguese for "foolish" or "simple."

Mistakenly thought to be related to the swan, it belonged to the family that includes pigeons. Though it had small wings, it had no flight feathers and a large, fat body. The crop under its chin held stones, which broke up the nuts and grains of its diet.

Unable to fly, the dodo was doomed as game meat for visiting sailors, and dodos provided them a much sought after change of diet. And sadly, between Dutch settlers' domestic animals and the ships' rats, the dodos' one-egg nests were completely plundered — the dodo became nothing more than a legend.

MAURITIUS

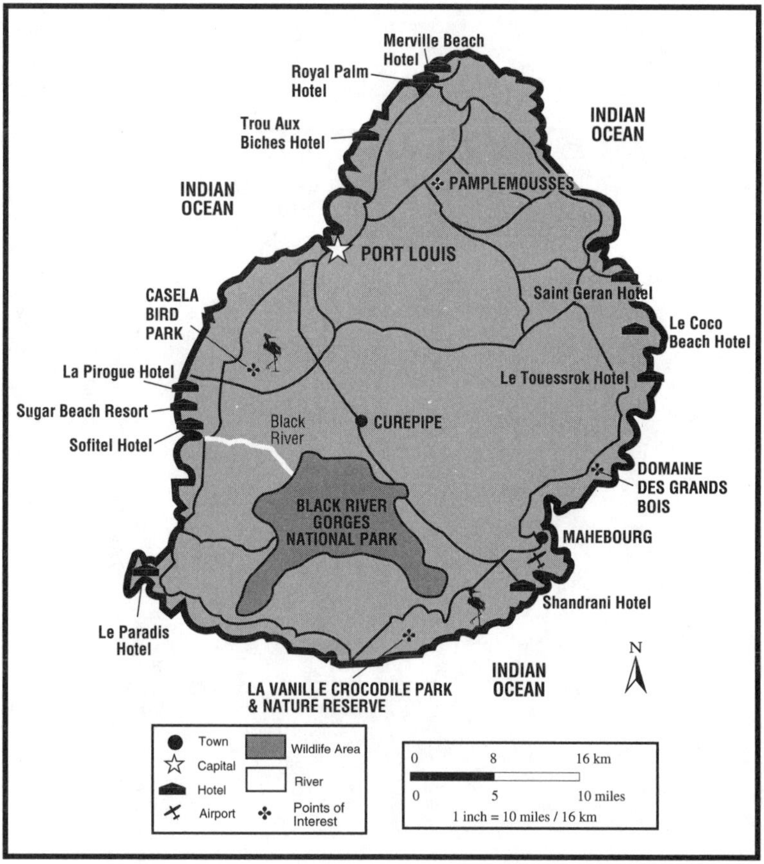

FACTS AT A GLANCE

AREA:	720 SQ. MI. / 1,865 SQ. KM.
APPROXIMATE SIZE:	RHODE ISLAND OR LUXEMBOURG
POPULATION:	1.1 MILLION
CAPITAL:	PORT LOUIS (POP. EST. 135,000)
OFFICIAL LANGUAGE:	ENGLISH, FRENCH AND CREOLE PREDOMINATE

MAURITIUS

If you have come part way around the world to visit Africa, you may wish to consider visiting Mauritius, which lies east of the coast of southern Africa.

Mauritius is a favorite destination for jet-setters, celebrities and royalty from around the world, many of whom rate this as one of the best getaways on earth. The combination of a cosmopolitan atmosphere, virgin-white beaches, crystal-clear waters, chic hotels and service to match and exquisite Creole, Indian, Chinese and European cuisine is difficult to beat.

This mountainous island paradise lies in the middle of the Indian Ocean in the tropics about 1200 miles (1935 km) east of Durban (South Africa), 1100 miles (1775 km) southeast of Mombasa (Kenya), 2900 miles (4675 km) southwest of Bombay (India) and 3700 miles (5970 km) west of Perth (Australia). Incorporating a visit to this remote island with a tour on the African mainland or an around-the-world vacation should be considered.

The most appropriate and frequently heard phrase on this island is "No Problem in Paradise." Unlike many "paradises," most of the people here have maintained their genuine and refreshing friendliness in the face of tourism.

This 720-square-mile (1865-km^2) island has a central plateau, with the south more mountainous than the north. Much of the lush vegetation has been converted into fields of sugarcane and other crops.

The population of just over one million consists of Indians, Creoles, French and Chinese. Hindu, Muslim, Christian and Chinese festivals occur with uncanny frequency. English is the official language and French is widely spoken, but most of the people prefer to speak Creole.

The island is known for the awkward dodo bird which, it is believed, lost its ability to fly because there were no predators from which it needed to escape. This evolutionary trait ironically contributed to its demise; the dodo was easily hunted to extinction during Dutch rule in the 1800s.

Creole cooking, which emphasizes the use of curries, fresh seafood and tropical fruits, is often served. Mauritian beer and rum are popular.

Mauritius has a tropical oceanic climate. The best time to visit this island paradise for a beach holiday is from September to mid-December and April to June, when the days are sunny and temperatures warm. From mid-December to March is the cyclone season, bringing occasional tropical rains. June-August (winter) nights are cool and the temperatures along the coastline pleasant.

The average daily maximum temperature in January is 86°F (30°C) and in July is 75°F (24°C). Surf temperatures inside the reefs near shore are around 74°F (23°C) in winter and 81°F (27°C) in summer.

The first known discovery of Mauritius was by colonizers from Iran in 975 A.D., but they chose not to settle. They moved on to what is now Mombasa and Pemba Island. Later, in the sixteenth century, the Portuguese used the island as a staging post along their trade route to India.

The Dutch came in 1598 led by Wybrandt van Warwyck, who named the island Mauritius after Prince Maurice of Nassau. However, the Dutch did not settle on the island until 1638. In 1710 they left the island to be replaced by the French in 1715; the French renamed it *Isle de France*. The island then became a "legal" haven for pirates who preyed on British cargo ships in time of war between Britain and France. In fact, this type of pirating was viewed by many as a respectable business.

After 95 years of French control and influence, the British took over in 1810. Slavery was abolished in 1835. As the emancipated slaves no longer wished to work on the sugar plantations, thousands of indentured Chinese and Indian workers were brought in to fill their places.

Mauritius became an independent member of the British Commonwealth in 1968. Mauritius has a parliamentary democracy, holding elections every five years. *Republic Day* was proclaimed on March 12, 1992.

Industrial products and sugar are the country's major exports.

SCUBA DIVING/SNORKELING

The 205-mile (330-km) coastline of Mauritius is almost completely surrounded by coral reefs, making this an excellent destination for snorkeling and scuba diving. You can dive on the colorful coral reefs and over 50 wrecks which harbor a great variety of sea life.

The best conditions for scuba diving and sailing are in October–March. Most of the larger beach hotels offer dive excursions and lessons and rent equipment.

Spearfishing while diving with an Aqua-lung is prohibited; spearfishing while snorkeling is allowed, but the catch cannot exceed ten fish per day.

BIG-GAME FISHING

Big-game fish, including blue marlin (plentiful), black marlin, yellowfin and skipjack tuna, jackfish, wahoo, barracuda, sea bass and many species of shark can be caught. Fishing is excellent only a few miles off shore; the ocean drops to over 2300 feet (700 m) in depth just one mile out!

The best fishing is from December to March and is sometimes good as late as May. An international fishing tournament is held every year in December.

The largest fleets of deep-sea fishing boats are based at the Centre de Pêche at Rivière Noire (Black River) and at the Organization de Pêche du Nord at Trou-aux-Biches. Boats can be hired through your hotel or travel agencies and should be booked well in advance during this season. Fishing in the lagoons during this same period is also very good.

WILDLIFE AND WILDLIFE AREAS

Mauritius' major wildlife attractions are found both on land and below the surface of the Indian Ocean.

BIRD LIFE

Mauritius has a number of endemic species of birds — birds which are found nowhere else in the world. Many ornithologists or keen birders wishing to add unique species to their lists will find the long journey to this island paradise well worthwhile.

The pic-pic is the only one of the nine known remaining endemic species on the island commonly seen. The pink pigeon is thought to be the rarest pigeon in the world. The Mauritius kestrel is one of the rarest birds in the world; only four were known to exist in 1974. Fortunately, due to conservation efforts, populations are increasing. The other endemic species include the flycatcher, parakeet, Mauritius fody, olive white-eye, the Merle and the cuckoo shrike.

About 45 species in total are found on the island. *Birds of Mauritius*, a book by Claude Michel, is available in Mauritius.

CASELA BIRD PARK

This peaceful 20-acre (8-hectare) park harbors over 140 varieties of birds from five continents, including the Mauritian pink pigeon.

BLACK RIVER GORGES NATIONAL PARK

Proclaimed as the country's first national park in 1994, this 25-square-mile (65-km^2) park covers 3.5 percent of the island and protects much of its remaining native forests. Nine endemic bird species including the pink pigeon and Mauritius kestrel are present.

The Black River Gorges are located in the highest mountain chain on the island and offer splendid views of the countryside. There are several scenic hiking trails including a 4-mile (7-km) hike to the Macchabee Forest and the 9-mile (15-km) hike through the gorges to the Black River.

DOMAINE DES GRAND BOIS

In this 2000-acre (800-hectare) forested park, located north of Mahebourg on the east coast, roam stags, deer, wild boar and monkeys.

LA VANILLE CROCODILE PARK AND NATURE RESERVE

Located in the south, this farm breeds Nile crocodiles brought from Madagascar. There is also a small zoo with wild animals found on Mauritius and a nature walk.

PORT LOUIS

Port Louis, the chief harbor and capital city, is partially surrounded by mountains and is multifaceted in character. The city has a large **market** where indigenous fruits and vegetables, pareos (colorful cloth wraps) and other clothing and souvenirs are sold. Just off the main square along Place d'Armes are some eighteenth century buildings, including the **Government House** and **Municipal Theatre**.

Chinatown is also worth a visit. The Chinese casino, L'Amicale de Port Louis, located on Royal Street, is popular. The season for horse racing at the Champ de Mars is from May to November.

CUREPIPE

Curepipe, a large town located on the central plateau, is a good place to shop and cool off from the warm coast. An extinct volcano, Trou aux Cerfs, may be visited nearby.

PAMPLEMOUSSES

The world-renowned botanical gardens of Pamplemousses have dozens of bizarre plants and trees including the talipot palm — at 60 years of age, it blooms for the first time then dies. Giant water lilies imported from Brazil are also found here.

TERRES DE COULEURS

The land takes on the colors of the rainbow (on sunny days) at Terres de Couleurs (the colored earth), located in the southwest in the mountains near Chamarel.

GRAND BASSIN

Grand Bassin is a lake in an extinct volcano; it is the holy lake of the Hindus, who celebrate the Maha Shivaratree, an exotic festival held yearly in February or March.

ACCOMMODATION – BEACH HOTELS

The beaches, water sports, fabulous holiday hotels and exquisite dining are by far the major attractions of the island.

Hotels are spread out, so visitors spend most of their time enjoying the many activities and sports their particular hotel has to offer. In many of the top hotels, most water and land sports, with the exception of scuba diving, horseback riding and big-game fishing, are free, including wind surfing, water skiing, sailing, snorkeling, volleyball, golf and tennis. Small sailboats are available at most resorts. Casinos are operated at the Saint Géran, La Pirogue, Le Paradis, Trou aux Biches and the Belle Mare Plage Hotel, as well as at the Casino of Domaine Les Pailles in Pailles, the Casino de Maurice in Curepipe and L'Amicale de Port Louis (the Chinese casino) in Port Louis.

If you wish to visit the island during the high season, December–February and July–August, I suggest you book your trip several months in advance. Demand for accommodation in the top hotels is high year-round.

DELUXE: * *Royal Palm Hotel* is an elegant 84-room deluxe hotel located on Grand Bay on the northwest tip of the island. This is a good place for couples looking for a quiet hotel. * *Le Saint Géran* is a hotel resort of the highest standard with an international flair unmatched in Mauritius. If you are going to see anyone famous while on this island, it will probably be here. Located on Pointe de Flacq on the east coast of the island, facilities include four restaurants, a casino, nine-hole golf course, sailing and scuba diving. All 175 rooms are air-conditioned with private facilities. * *Le Touessrok* is a splendid holiday hotel, situated on the east coast south of the Le Saint Géran at Trou d'Eau Douce. Facilities include two swimming pools, four restaurants, a disco, shops and a beauty parlor. What truly sets this resort apart from the rest is the pristine Ilot Mangenie, a private "Robinson Crusoe"–style island retreat. Guests have complimentary transfers to this

Le Touessrok Hotel, located at Trou d'eau Douce.

nearby island as well as to Ile de Cerfs — Le Touessrok's offshore water-sport playground, which also offers secluded coves for sunbathing. The hotel has 200 air-conditioned rooms, each with ensuite facilities, refrigerator and minibar. * *Le Paradis* is located in the southwest of the island on a lagoon at the foot of the dramatic Le Morne Mountain. The hotel has air-conditioned rooms with facilities ensuite, a swimming pool, a casino, a disco, nightly entertainment and a fleet of deep-sea fishing boats.

FIRST CLASS: * *Sugar Beach Resort* is a plantation-style resort set on the west coast of the island, with 16 villas and 238 rooms located in the Manor House — all air-conditioned with ensuite facilities. Guests may enjoy a variety of water sports and the island's largest landscaped swimming pool, and may also use the amenities of the nearby sister hotel, La Pirogue. * *La Pirogue* is located on a fine white beach at Flic-en-Flac on the island's west coast. Thatched cottages spread out from the main building with its distinctive sail-like roof. There is a casino, and all 246 rooms are air-conditioned with ensuite facilities. * *Trou aux Biches Hotel,* located

Sugar Beach Resort.

on Trou aux Biches on the northwest coast, has 208 air-conditioned rooms (410 beds) with ensuite facilities and offers the usual water sports, golf, tennis and has a dive center.

TOURIST CLASS: * *Le Coco Beach* is located on the east coast and has 337 air-conditioned rooms with ensuite facilities. Water sports and family entertainment activities are offered. * The *Merville Beach Hotel* is a comfortable hotel situated on Grand Bay near the northern tip of the island, with 170 air-conditioned rooms with private facilities, a swimming pool and the usual water sports. * *Shandrani Hotel* is conveniently located 4 miles (6 km) from the international airport on Blue Bay at the southeastern coast. This 186-room hotel has a fine beach, all the usual water sports and tennis. All rooms are air-conditioned with ensuite facilities. * *Sofitel*, located at Flic-en-Flac on the island's west coast, has 145 air-conditioned rooms with ensuite facilities, three restaurants, a piano bar and the usual water sports.

SEYCHELLES

ESMERALDA – THE GIANT ALDABRAN TORTOISE

Esmeralda has a safe haven on Bird Island, where he (yes, he) slowly ambles around the lodge, introducing himself to unsuspecting guests. Though the giant Aldabran tortoise (*Geochelone gigantea*) originated in the Aldabran islands, a small breeding colony was set up in the Seychelles islands to ensure its chance of survival.

The giant Aldabran tortoises can grow a carapace as long as 140 cm (56 inches), and in the instance of Esmeralda (believed to be the oldest in the world) can live to be over 150 years old. The tortoises found on mainland Africa are smaller than these island giants and are found mostly in tropical areas. They are primarily herbivores.

The raised shell of terrestrial tortoises probably evolved from the thinner shell of their aquatic ancestry for two reasons: as a defense against predators, who otherwise might well have been able to crush the reptile in their jaws, and to provide for increased lung capacity, since they have proportionately larger lungs than do turtles.

SEYCHELLES

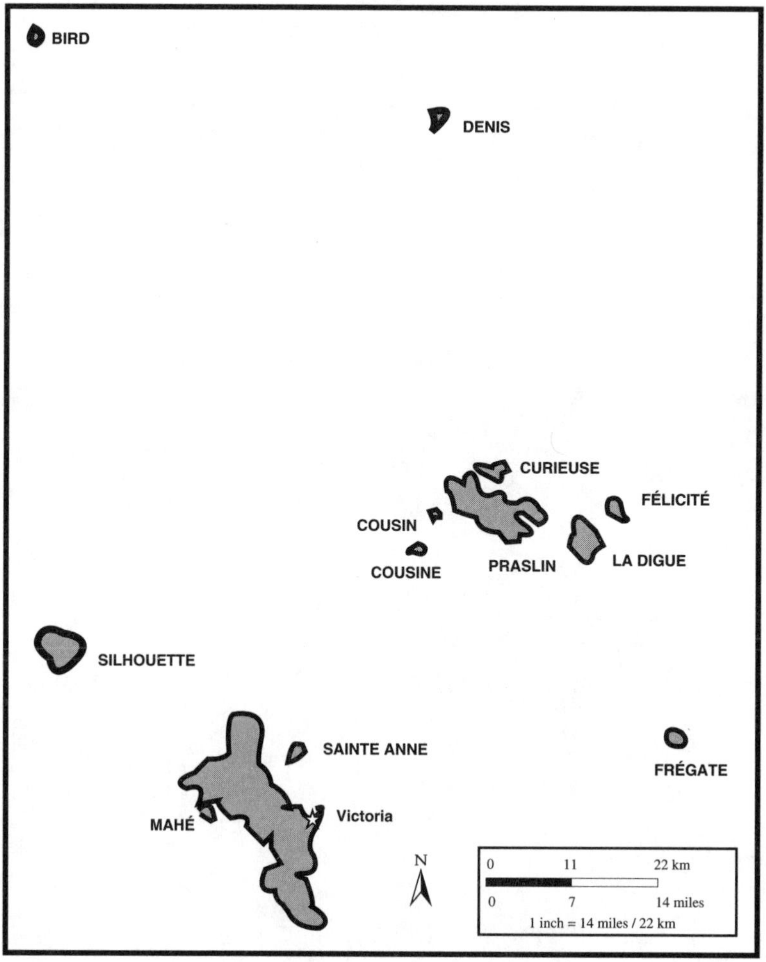

FACTS AT A GLANCE

AREA:	171 SQ. MI. / 443 SQ. KM.
APPROXIMATE SIZE:	1/7 THE SIZE OF RHODE ISLAND
POPULATION:	72,000
CAPITAL:	VICTORIA (POP. EST. 25,000)
OFFICIAL LANGUAGE:	CREOLE, ENGLISH AND FRENCH ARE WIDELY SPOKEN

SEYCHELLES

The Seychelles are unspoiled islands which have a charm all their own, complemented by the genuine friendliness of the people. The beauty and variety of the islands make the Seychelles an excellent add-on to any safari or a vacation in itself. Numerous scheduled flights make it easy to hop from island to island. The Seychelles are certainly a fabulous place for a honeymoon!

In order to help maintain the unspoiled nature of the islands, construction of new hotels (additional beds) is strictly limited.

The Seychelles is comprised of 115 islands spread over more than 155,000 square miles (400,000 km^2) in the Western Indian Ocean, situated northeast of Madagascar and approximately 1100 miles (1800 km) east of Kenya. Mahé, the largest of the islands, is located 5 degrees south of the equator.

Forty-one granitic and 74 coraline islands make up the Seychelles. The granitic group are rocky islands with peaks rising up to 2970 feet (905 m) with narrow coastal strips, and they include the "inner islands" of Mahé, Praslin and La Digue. Félicité and Frégate are all smaller granite islands which have only one lodge on each island.

Many of the islands in the coraline group, or "outer islands," are only about 3 feet (1 m) above sea level. Visitors should consider including at least one granite and one coral island in their stay.

The people of the Seychelles are a mixture of African, Malagasy and French cultures. About 90 percent of the population resides on Mahé, the largest island. About 89 percent of the population is Roman Catholic, 7 percent the Church of England, and the balance divided among Pentacostal, Seventh-Day Adventists, Jehovah's Witnesses, Hindus and Muslims.

Creole cuisine, a mixture of French, African, Chinese and English, is well worth sampling. The locally brewed beer, *Seybrew,* is quite good. Accommodations include comfortable hotels as well as less expensive *relais des iles* — small, simple hotels and guest houses, most with fewer than 15 rooms.

The Seychelles have a tropical oceanic climate with relatively consistent temperatures year-round. The "hot" season is December–May and has higher humidity and rainfall than the cooler dry season, June–November. The mean daily maximum temperature for Victoria (the capital) in January is 82°F (28°C) and in July is 81°F (27°C). The mean monthly rainfall in January is 15.2 inches (386 mm) and in July is 3.3 inches (84 mm). Cyclones are rare.

The Seychelles were probably discovered by Arab traders about 1000 years ago. Vasco de Gama touched on the islands in the 1500s. In 1756, the French were the first to colonize the islands, on which they established spice plantations. The English conquered the islands in 1794. Slavery was abolished in 1835. In 1902 the islands became a dependency of Mauritius and in 1903 became a British Crown Colony. Seychelles became independent in 1976. Tourism is the major foreign exchange earner.

WILDLIFE AND WILDLIFE AREAS

Like Mauritius, the islands' major wildlife attractions are their bird life and prolific marine life in the warm Indian Ocean waters. There are a number of marine parks and bird sanctuaries — which are protected by strict laws — giving nature a much better chance of surviving the influence of man.

There are seven established walking trails in the Seychelles — six on Mahé Island and one on La Digue Island. These walks offer great opportunities to enjoy the flora and fauna unique to these beautiful islands.

BIRD LIFE

The Seychelles are the "Galapagos" of the Indian Ocean. Many tropical species of birds are not afraid of man and can be approached from within a few feet (less than a meter). Colonies of over 200,000 sooty terns can be found nesting on some of the islands.

For keen twitchers (birders), these islands offer an opportunity to add several species to their lists. Two species found only in the Seychelles are the rare black parrot (found only on Praslin) and the Seychelles black paradise flycatcher (found only on La Digue). Other rarities include magpie robins and the Seychelles fodie.

MAHE ISLAND

Mahé is the largest (59 square miles/152 km^2) and most developed island, and it offers a variety of hotels and guest houses on many of its lovely beaches. Both the international airport and major harbor (Victoria) are on the island.

The interior of the island is mountainous, rising to 2668 feet (905 m) at Morne Seychelles. One of the most scenic drives on the island is from Victoria through the highlands, south of Morne Seychellois National Park, to Port Glaud, on the west coast. **Île Thérèse**, located off the west coast of Mahé, is an island home to a colony of giant tortoises.

There are 68 white sandy beaches, the most popular of which is **Beau Vallon Beach**, a 2-mile (3-km) crescent-shaped beach on the north-west coast. **Grand' Anse** is a good beach for surfing. **Anse Royale** is a 2-mile (3-km) beach protected by a coral reef and located on the southeast coast of the island. There is a better opportunity to find deserted or nearly deserted beaches in the less-developed south of the island than in the north.

Mahé has several hiking trails, including Victoria-Beau Vallon Bay-Victoria, The Trois Freres Trail through Morne Seychellois National Park to the summit, La Résèrve and Brulee through a palm forest, Danzil to the secluded beach Anse Major, Val Riche-Copolia through Morne Seychellois National Park, and the Tea Factory-Morne Blanc in Morne Seychellois National Park.

VICTORIA

Victoria is the capital city and the major port of the Seychelles. Places of interest include the **market**; the **Capuchin House**, which was built in colonial Portuguese style; the **State House**, which is a fine example of Seychelles architecture; the **Cathedral of the Immaculate Conception**; the **National Museum**; and the **Botanical Gardens**. The "Pirates Arms" is a popular bar.

MORNE SEYCHELLOIS NATIONAL PARK

This 11-square-mile (30-km^2) park covers much of northwest Mahé, with altitudes ranging from sea level to 2969 feet (905 m). There are hiking trails from Sans Souci Road to Copolia (1630 feet/497 m), Morne Blanc (2188 feet/667 m) and Trois Freres (2293 feet/699 m). Bird life includes the blue pigeon, Seychelles bulbul, Seychelles kestrel, cave swiftlet, sunbird and Seychelles white-eye.

Flora in the park includes five different species of palm trees, the vanilla orchid (*Vanilla phalaenopsis*), the extremely rare jellyfish tree (*Medusagyne oppositifolia*) and bwa-d-fer (*Vateria seychellarum*).

SAINTE ANNE MARINE NATIONAL PARK

Located east of Victoria, Sainte Anne Marine National Park includes six small islands and the waters surrounding them. Île Ronde (Round Island), Île au Cerf and Île Moyenne islands have lovely coral beds and are excellent for snorkeling or exploring in glass-bottom boats. Sainte Anne Island, which is closed to visitors, is the most important nesting site for hawksbill turtles among the granite islands.

ACCOMMODATION ON MAHÉ — DELUXE: * *Le Meridien Fisherman's Cove*, located on the southern end of Beau Vallon Bay, has 48 air-conditioned rooms with ensuite facilities, a swimming pool and tennis courts. * *The Plantation Club*, located on Baie Lazare in southwest Mahé, has 200 air-conditioned rooms with ensuite facilities, a swimming pool, tennis courts, casino and free water sports including snorkeling, wind surfing, canoeing, paddleboats and rowboats.

FIRST CLASS: * *Northholme Hotel,* located in the northwest on a rocky point overlooking a small sandy beach, has 19 air-conditioned rooms with ensuite facilities and a dive center. * *Sunset Beach Hotel,* situated on a rocky promontory overlooking a secluded beach near Beau Vallon Bay, has 25 air-conditioned rooms with ensuite facilities.

TOURIST CLASS: * *Coco D'Or Hotel,* located a three-minute walk from Beau Vallon Bay, has 12 simple air-conditioned rooms with ensuite facilities. * *Lazare Picault* overlooks Baie Lazare on the southwest coast and has 14 rooms with ensuite facilities.

PRASLIN ISLAND

Praslin, a granite island located 25 miles (40 km) northeast of Mahé, is the second largest island in the archipelago, covering 15 square miles (38 km^2).

The island is less mountainous than Mahé but still has hills over 1150 feet (350 m) high. Beaches are less crowded than on Mahé. **Côte d'Or** beach, located on the northeast coast, is considered to be one of the best beaches on the island.

VALLEE DE MAI NATIONAL PARK

The Vallée de Mai National Park contains over 4000 coco-de-mer palm trees that grow in excess of 100 feet (30 m) in height and have a unique double-lobed coconut in the shape of the female (human) pelvic region.

At 20 pounds (9 kg) this is considered to be the world's largest fruit and takes over ten years to ripen! Many myths and legends have arisen from the presence of this fruit, thought by some to be the "forbidden fruit" and the island the proverbial "Garden of Eden." Allow two or three hours for your visit, as this is a lovely park in which to walk.

The sale of the coco-de-mer (a unique souvenir, indeed) is strictly controlled, and it may be purchased at the park or from other shops on the island.

We were also amazed at the gigantic size of some of the palm fans and were lucky enough to spot the rare black parrot on our visit.

CURIEUSE MARINE NATIONAL PARK

Curieuse Marine National Park includes the waters between Curieuse Island and the northwestern coast of Praslin. The park covers 5 square miles (14 km^2) and reaches depths of 100 feet (30 m) A large colony of giant land tortoises is protected in Laraie Bay.

ACCOMMODATION ON PRASLIN — FIRST CLASS: * *L'Archipel* has 16 fan-cooled rooms with ensuite facilities. Water sports include wind surfing, canoeing and deep-sea fishing. * *La Résèrve,* located on Anse Petite Cour, has 4 air-conditioned suites and 34 fan-cooled rooms with ensuite facilities. * *Hotel Coco de Mer,* located on Anse Takamaka, has 40 air-conditioned rooms with ensuite facilities, a swimming pool, tennis and water sports, including wind surfing and canoeing. * *Praslin Beach Hotel,* located across the road from Côte d'Or beach, has 77 air-conditioned rooms with ensuite facilities, a swimming pool, dive center and water sports, including snorkeling and wind surfing.

TOURIST CLASS: * *Maison des Palmes,* located near the beach, has 24 fan-cooled thatched cottages with ensuite facilities, a swimming pool, tennis court and water sports, including wind surfing and sailing.

COUSINE ISLAND

Cousine, not to be confused with Cousin Island (below), is a privately owned 175-acre (70-hectare) island situated between Praslin and Mahé islands.

The island has large granitic outcrops, open plains and crystal clean sandy-white beaches with beautiful coral reefs just off shore. Wildlife above and below the sea is superb; many rare and endangered species such as brush warblers and giant tortoises may be found right on and around the island.

At certain times of the year, turtles come ashore during the day and night to lay their eggs. Over 200,000 nody terns plus a host of other interesting seabirds such as tropic birds and shearwaters roost and breed on the island.

Access to the island is by boat or helicopter.

ACCOMMODATION— FIRST CLASS: * *Cousine Island Lodge* caters to a maximin of eight guests in comfortable cottages with ensuite facilities. Resident scientists conducting research on the island act as your guides. No day-trippers are allowed here — guaranteeing an intimate meeting with nature for those guests wise enough to stay here. Activities include nature walks and lectures, beach walking, boating, fishing, snorkeling and scuba diving.

COUSIN ISLAND

Cousin Island, located 2 miles (3 km) from Praslin, was bought by the International Council for Bird Preservation with assistance from the World Wildlife Fund to establish a bird sanctuary, primarily to protect endangered species, including the Seychelles fody and Seychelles brush warbler. In April and May, thousands of seabirds can be seen nesting on the island.

The island can only be visited on Tuesdays, Thursdays and Fridays, with groups limited to 20 persons.

LA DIGUE ISLAND

La Digue is a granite island that has spectacular rock formations and secluded beaches. The best way to travel around this, the fourth largest island in the archipelago, is by foot, bicycle or ox cart. There are only a few vehicles on the island.

The highest point on this small 2 x 3-mile (3 x 5-km) island is 1092 feet (333 m). A lovely walking trail from La Passe to Grand' Anse can be completed on foot or by bicycle. We spent three days exploring the island by bicycle and on foot, and would have loved to have stayed longer.

The island is reached by a 30-minute boat ride from Praslin.

ACCOMMODATION — FIRST CLASS: * *La Digue Island Lodge,* located on the west coast, has 59 cottages (some air-conditioned) with ensuite facilities, a swimming pool, wind surfing, snorkeling and a dive center.

TOURIST CLASS: * *Le Patatran,* located on the northwest coast, has eight fan-cooled chalets with ensuite facilities.

Rock formations on a secluded beach, La Digue.

FELICITE ISLAND

Félicité is a small granite island with sandy white beaches, reached by a 30-minute boat ride from Praslin or La Digue. This is an exclusive island in that only one party of up to eight guests is accommodated at a time.

ACCOMMODATION — FIRST CLASS: * *Félicité Island* has two houses with air-conditioned rooms with private bathrooms.

BIRD ISLAND (ILE AUX VACHES)

Bird Island is a small coral island (1.5 x 0.5 miles/2.5 x 1 km) located about 60 miles (100 km) north of Mahé — about a 30-minute flight. A leisurely walk around this pristine island, stopping for an occasional swim and snorkel, takes about two to three hours.

During our visit, there were over 500,000 sooty terns nesting on the island, an event which usually occurs April–October. We also encountered "Esmeralda" — one of the largest giant tortoises in the world, thought to be over 150 years old.

ACCOMMODATION — TOURIST CLASS: * *Bird Island Lodge,* the only property on the island, has 25 fan-cooled bungalows with ensuite facilities. Snorkeling and big-game fishing are available.

DESROCHES ISLAND

Desroches, a coral island six miles long and one-half-mile wide (10 x 1 km), is the largest island in the Amirantes group. It is situated an hour by air from Mahé. This is an excellent island for those who enjoy water sports. Scuba diving is excellent.

ACCOMMODATION — DELUXE: * *Desroches Island Lodge,* the only lodge on the island, has 20 air-conditioned rooms with ensuite facilities. Water sports include hobie cat sailing, snorkeling, scuba diving, wind surfing and deep-sea fishing.

DENIS ISLAND

This small (350-acre/140-hectare) coral island is only 25 minutes by air, north of Mahé and is often thought of as the "perfect desert island." Denis is located on the edge of the Seychelles Bank where water depths quickly reach over 6500 feet (2000 m). Deep-sea fishing for barracuda, dog-tooth tuna, marlin and sailfish is excellent. There is only one exclusive (and expensive) lodge on the island.

ACCOMMODATION — TOURIST CLASS: * *Denis Island Lodge* has 24 large fan-cooled bungalows, with ensuite facilities, and excellent food. Water sports include wind surfing, snorkeling and deep-sea fishing.

FREGATE ISLAND

Frégate Island, historically a haven for pirates, is a granite island 1.5 miles long and a quarter-mile wide (2.5 x 0.4 km), situated about 20 minutes east of Mahé by air. The island has lovely beaches and a variety of flora and bird life, including the Seychelles magpie robin and Seychelles blue pigeon.

ACCOMMODATION — DELUXE: * *The Plantation House*, the only accommodation on the island, has air-conditioned villas with ensuite facilities.

SILHOUETTE ISLAND

Located 15 minutes northwest of Mahé by helicopter, this unspoiled granite island is the third largest island in the Seychelles and can be seen from the north coast of Mahé. Mountains rise to 2427 feet (740 m) on this thickly forested, round island which is approximately 3 miles (5 km) in diameter.

ACCOMMODATION — TOURIST CLASS: * *Silhouette Island Lodge*, the only lodge on the island, has 12 bungalows with ensuite facilities. Activities include nature walks, snorkeling and diving.

SAFARI PAGES

SAFARI PAGES

We have endeavored to make the information that follows as current as possible. However, Africa is undergoing constant change.

My reason for including the following information, much of which is likely to change, is to give you an idea of the right questions to ask — not to give you information that should be relied on as gospel. Wherever possible, a resource has been given to assist you in obtaining the most current information.

AIRPORT DEPARTURE TAXES

Call an airline servicing your destination or the tourist office, embassy or consulate of the country(ies) in question for current international and domestic airport taxes.

International airport departure taxes often must be paid in U.S. dollars or other hard currency, such as British pounds or German marks. Be sure to have the exact amount required — they will often not give change. Domestic airport departure taxes are usually payable in local currency.

At the time of this writing, international airport departure taxes for the countries in this guide are as follows: Botswana (included in your air ticket), Burundi (US $20.00), Kenya (US $20.00), Lesotho (10 rand/approx. US $3.00), Malawi (US $20.00), Mauritius (300 rupees/approx. US $15), Namibia (included in your air ticket), Rwanda (US $20.00), Seychelles (100 rupees/approx. US $20.00), South Africa (included in your air ticket), Swaziland (10 rand/approx. US $3.00), Tanzania (US $20.00), Uganda (none), Zambia (US $20.00) and Zimbabwe (US $20.00). Domestic departure taxes are usually under equivalent of US $5.00 and can generally be paid in local currency or are included in your air ticket.

BANKS

Barclays and Standard Chartered Banks are located in most of these countries.

BANKING HOURS

Banks are usually open Monday–Friday mornings and early afternoons, sometimes on Saturday mornings, and closed on Sundays and holidays. Most hotels, lodges and camps are licensed to exchange foreign currency. Quite often the best place to exchange money is at the airport upon arrival.

CREDIT CARDS

Major international credit cards are accepted by most top hotels, restaurants, lodges, permanent safari camps and shops. Visa and MasterCard are most widely accepted. American Express and Diner's Club are also accepted by most first-class hotels and many businesses.

CURRENCIES

The currencies used by the countries included in this guide are as follows:

Botswana (1 pula = 100 thebe)

Burundi (1 Burundi franc = 100 centimes)

Congo (1 Zaire = 100 makutas)

Kenya (1 Kenya shilling = 100 cents)

Lesotho (1 loti = 100 lisente)

Malawi (1 Kwacha = 100 tambala)

Mauritius (1 Mauritius rupee = 100 cents)

Namibia (1 Namibian dollar = 100 cents)

Rwanda (1 Rwanda franc = 100 centimes)

Seychelles (1 Seychelles rupee = 100 cents)

South Africa (1 rand = 100 cents)

Swaziland (1 lilangeni = 100 cents)

Tanzania (1 Tanzania shilling = 100 cents)

Uganda (1 Uganda shilling = 100 cents)

Zambia (1 kwacha = 100 ngwee)

Zimbabwe (1 Zimbabwe dollar = 100 cents)

The currencies of Namibia, Lesotho and Swaziland are on a par with the South African rand. The South African rand is widely accepted in Lesotho and Swaziland; however, the currencies of Namibia, Lesotho and Swaziland are not accepted in South Africa.

Current rates for many African countries can usually be found in the financial section of large newspapers and in periodicals such as *Newsweek* and on the internet.

CURRENCY RESTRICTIONS

Many African countries require visitors to complete currency declaration forms upon arrival; all foreign currency, travelers checks and other negotiable instruments must be recorded. These forms must be surrendered on departure.

When you leave the country, the amount of currency you have with you must equal the amount with which you entered the country less the amount exchanged and recorded on your currency declaration form.

For most countries in Africa, the maximum amount of local currency that may be imported or exported is strictly enforced. Check for current restrictions by contacting the tourist offices, embassies or consulates of the countries you wish to visit.

In some countries, it is difficult (if not impossible) to exchange unused local currency back to foreign exchange (i.e., U.S. dollars). Therefore, it is best not to exchange more than you feel you will need.

CUSTOMS

AUSTRALIAN CUSTOMS:

The Customs Information Center: (61 3) 1300 363263

Monday–Friday 8:30 a.m. to 5:00 p.m.

CANADIAN CUSTOMS:

For a brochure on current Canadian customs requirements, ask for the brochure *I Declare* from your local customs office, which will be listed in the telephone book under "Government of Canada, Customs and Excise."

NEW ZEALAND CUSTOMS:

One of the several customs offices is listed below. Contact the office for current information:

Box 29, 50 Anzac, Auckland; tel: (644) 748320

UNITED KINGDOM:

Contact the office below for current information:

HM Customs and Excise, Kent House, Upper Ground, London SE1 9PS

U.S. CUSTOMS:

For current information on products made from endangered species of wildlife that are not allowed to be imported, contact *Traffic* (U.S.A.), World Wildlife Fund, 1250 24th Street N.W., Washington, D.C. 20037, tel: (202) 293-4800 and ask for the leaflet "Buyer Beware" for current restrictions.

DIPLOMATIC REPRESENTATIVES OF AFRICAN COUNTRIES

IN AUSTRALIA:

Kenya: Tel: (61) 474788/474722/474688 or 474311
Sixth Floor, QBE Building, 33-35 Ainslie Ave., P.O. Box 1990, Canberra ACT 2601, Australia

Mauritius: Tel: (06) 281-1203 or (06) 282-4436
43, Hampton Circuit, Yarralumla, Canberra ACT 2600, Australia

Seychelles: Tel: (61) 2916570
Mr. Guy Robert, Hon. Consul General, 271 Canning Road, Les Murdie, Perth WA 6076

Zimbabwe: Tel: (61 6) 282700 or 286 2281 Fax: (61 6) 2901680
High Commissioner, 11 Culogoa Circuit, O'Malley, ACT 2606, Canberra

IN CANADA:

Burundi: Tel: (613) 236-8489/94
151 Slater St., No. 800, Ottawa, Ontario K1P 5H3, Canada

Congo: Tel: (613) 232-3983
18 Range Rd., Ottawa, Ontario K1N 8J3, Canada

Kenya: Tel: (613) 563-1773/4/5/6
Suite 600, 415 Laurier Ave. East, West Ottawa, Ontario K1N 6R4, Canada

Malawi: Tel: (613) 236 8931
7 Clemow Av., Ottawa, KIS2A9, Canada

Rwanda: Tel: (613) 722-5835
1221 Sherwood Dr., Ottawa, Ontario K1Y 3V1, Canada

South Africa: Tel: (613) 744 0330 Fax: (613) 741 1639
High Commission of the Republic of South Africa,
15 Sussex Drive, Ottawa, Ontario K1M 1M8

Swaziland: Tel: (613) 567-1480
130 Albert St., Suite 1204, Ottawa, Ontario K1P 5G4, Canada

Tanzania: Tel: (613) 232-1509/0 Fax: (613) 232 5184
50 Range Rd., Ottawa, Ontario K1N 8J4, Canada

Uganda: Tel: (613) 789-7797/8 Fax: (613) 789-8909
231 Coburg St., Ottawa, Ontario, K1N 8J2, Canada

Zimbabwe: Tel: (613) 237-4388/9 or 237 4484 Fax: (613) 563 8269
332 Somerset St. West, Ottawa, Ontario K2P 0J9, Canada

HIGH COMMISSIONS IN THE UNITED KINGDOM:

Botswana: Tel: (44 171) 499-0031 Fax: (44 171) 495 8595
6 Stratford Place, London W1N 9AE, England

Congo: Tel: (44 171) 235 6137 Fax: (44 171) 235 9048
26 Chesham, London SW1X 8HH, England

Kenya: Tel: (44 171) 63 62371/5 Fax: (44 171) 3236717
45 Portland Place, London W1N 4AS, England

Lesotho: Tel: (44 171) 235 5686 Fax: (44 171) 235 5023
E-mail: 106065.1632@compuserve.com
7 Chesam Place, Belgravia, London SW1 8HN, England

Malawi: Tel: (44 171) 491 4172 Fax: (44 171) 4919916
33 Grosvenor Street, London W1XODE, England

Mauritius: Tel: (44 171) 5810294/5
32/33 Elvaston Place, London SW 7, England

Namibia: Tel: (44 171) 636 6244 Fax: (44 171) 637 5694
6 Chandos Street, London W1M 0LQ, England

Seychelles: Tel: (44 171) 224 1660 Fax: (44 171) 487 5756
2nd floor, Eros House, 111 Baker St., London W1M 1FE, England

South African Consulate: Tel: (44 171) 930 4488
Fax: (44 171) 451 7284
South Africa House, Trafalgar Square, London WC2N 5DP, England
For visa, immigration, health info: Tel: (0891) 441 100, 39p–49p/min. Fax: (44 171) 451 7280

Swaziland: Tel: (44 171) 581 4976/7
58 Pont St., London SW1, England

Tanzania: Tel: (44 171) 499 8951
Fax: (44 171) 499 8954 or 491 9321
43 Hertford St., London W1Y 8DB, England

Uganda: Tel: (44 171) 839 5783 Fax: (44 171) 839 8925
66 Trafalgar Square, London WC 2N 5DX, England

Zambia: Tel: (44 171) 589 6655 Fax: (44 171) 581 1353
2 Palace Gage, Kensington, London W8 5NG, England

Zimbabwe: Tel: (44 171) 836 7755 Fax: (44 171) 379 1167
429 Strand, London WC 2R OSA, England

IN THE UNITED STATES:

Botswana: Tel: (202) 244 4990/1 Fax: (202) 244 4164
Suite 7M, 3400 International Dr. N.W., Washington, D.C. 20008

Burundi: Tel: (202) 342-2574
Suite 212, 2233 Wisconsin Ave. N.W., Washington, D.C. 20007

Congo: Tel: (202) 234-7690/1 Fax: (202) 686-3631
1800 New Hampshire N.W., Washington, D.C. 20009

Kenya: Tel: (202) 387-6101
2249 R St. N.W., Washington, D.C. 20008

Kenya Consulates:
9100 Wilshire Blvd., #111, Beverly Hills, CA 90212
Tel: (213) 274-6635
424 Madison Ave., New York, NY 10017
Tel: (212) 486-1300/3

Lesotho: Tel: (202) 797-5533 Fax: (202) 234-8815
E-mail: lesotho@afrika.com
2511 Massachusetts Ave. N.W., Washington, D.C. 20008

Malawi: Tel: (202) 797-1007 Fax: (202) 265-0976
2408 Massachusetts Ave., Washington, D.C. 20008

Mauritius: Tel: (202) 244-1491/2
Suite 134, 4301 Connecticut Ave. N.W., Washington, D.C. 20008

Namibia: Tel: (202) 986 0540 Fax: (202) 986 0443
1605 New Hampshire Ave. N.W., Washington D.C. 20009

Rwanda: Tel: (202) 232-2882/3/4
1714 New Hampshire Ave. N.W., Washington, D.C. 20009

Rwanda Consulate: Tel: (708) 439-9090
10 Gould Center, Suite 707, Rolling Meadows, IL 60008

Seychelles: Tel: (212) 687 9766/7 Fax: (212) 922 9177
Embassy of the Republic of the Seychelles and Tourist Office, Suite 900F, 820 Second Ave., New York, NY 10017

South Africa: Tel: (202) 232-4400
Fax: (202) 265-1607 or 232-3402
3051 Massachusetts Ave. N.W., Washington, D.C. 20008

South Africa Consulate: Tel: (213) 657-0200
50 N. La Cienega Blvd., Suite 300, Beverly Hills, CA 90211

Swaziland: Tel: (202) 362-6683 Fax: (202) 244 8059
E-mail: 73451.2752@compuserve.com
3400 International Dr. N.W., Suite 3M, Washington, D.C. 20008-3006

Tanzania: Tel: (202) 939-6125 Fax: (202) 797-7408
2139 R St. N.W., Washington, D.C. 20008

Uganda: Tel: (202) 726-0416 or 726-7100 Fax: (202) 7261727
In New York: (212) 949 0110
E-mail: ugembassy@aol.com
5911 16th St. N.W., Washington, D.C. 20011-2896

Zambia: Tel: (202) 265-9717/8/9 Fax: (202) 332-0826
2419 Massachusetts Ave. N.W., Washington, D.C. 20008

Zimbabwe: Tel: (202) 332-7100 Fax: (202) 483-9326
1608 New Hampshire Ave. N.W., Washington, D.C. 20009

MISSIONS TO THE UNITED NATIONS OR CONSULATES IN NEW YORK:

Botswana: Tel: (212) 889-2277
103 East 37th St., New York, NY 10016

Burundi: Tel: (212) 687-1180
336 East 45th St., New York, NY 10017

Congo: Tel: (212) 754-1966
77 Third Ave., 25th Floor, New York, NY 10017

Kenya: Tel: (212) 421-4740
424 Madison Ave., New York, NY 10017

Lesotho: Tel: (212) 661-1690 Fax: (212) 682-4388
204 East 39th St., New York, NY 10016

Mauritius: Tel: (212) 949-0190/1
211 East 43rd St., New York, NY 10017

Malawi: Tel: (212) 949-0180 Fax: (212) 599-5021
600 3rd Ave., New York, NY 10016

Rwanda: Tel: (212) 808-9330
336 East 45th Street, New York, NY 10016

Seychelles: Tel: (212) 687-9766
820 Second Ave., Suite 900-F, New York, NY 10017

South Africa: Tel: (212) 213-4880
333 East 38th St., New York, NY 10016

Swaziland: Tel: (212) 371-8910
866 United Nations Plaza, Suite 420,
New York, NY 10017

Tanzania: Tel: (212) 972-9160
205 East 42nd St., New York, NY 10017

Uganda: Tel: (212) 949-0110
Uganda House, 335 East 45th St., New York, NY 10017

Zambia: Tel: (212) 972-7200
800 Second Ave., New York, NY 10017

Zimbabwe: Tel: (212) 980-5984 or 980-9511 Fax: (212) 755-4188
128 East 56th St., New York, NY 10022

DIPLOMATIC REPRESENTATIVES IN AFRICA

AUSTRALIAN HIGH COMMISSIONS:

Kenya: Tel: (254 2) 334666/7
Development House, Moi Ave.,
P.O. Box 30360, Nairobi, Kenya

Mauritius: Tel: (230) 208 1700
Rogers House, John Kennedy St., Port Louis, Mauritius

South Africa: Tel: (27 12) 325 4315
Fourth Floor, Mutual and Federal Center, 220 Vermuelen St.,
Pretoria 0002, South Africa
Tel. (27 21) 232160
Tenth Floor, 1001 Colonial Mutual Bldg., 101 Adderby St.,
8001 Cape Town, South Africa

Tanzania: Seventh and Eighth Floors, NLC Investment Bldg.,
Independence Ave., P.O. Box 2969, Dar es Salaam, Tanzania

Zambia: Tel: (260 1) 229371
Ulendo House, P.O. Box 35395, Lusaka, Zambia

Zimbabwe: Tel: (263 4) 794591/4
Third Floor, Throgmorton House, Samora Machel Ave. & Julius
Nyerere Way, P.O. Box 907 (45341), Harare, Zimbabwe

CANADIAN HIGH COMMISSIONS:

Congo: Tel: (243 12) 21532 X2314 Fax: (243 12) 43805
C/O U.S. Embassy, Unit 31550, 310 Ave. Des Aviateurs,
Kinshasa, Congo.
Kenya: Tel: (254) 334033 214804 Fax: (254) 226987
Comcraft House, Haile Selassie Ave., P.O. Box 30481, Nairobi, Kenya

Mauritius: Tel: (230) 208-0821
c/o Blanche Birger Co., Ltd., Port Louis, Mauritius

Seychelles: Tel: (255 51) 20651 Fax: (255 51) 46005
38 Mirambo St., P.O. Box 1022, Dar es Salaam, Tanzania

South Africa: Tel: (27 12) 342 6923 Fax: (27 12) 342 3837
Private Bag X13, 1103 Arcadia St., Hatfield 0083,
Pretoria , South Africa

Tanzania: Tel: (255 51) 20651 Fax: (255 51) 46005
38 Mirambo St., P.O. Box 1022, Dar es Salaam, Tanzania

Uganda: Tel: (256 41) 258141 Fax: (256 41) 234518
P.O. Box 20115, 4 Ternan Ave., Nakasero, Kampala

Zambia: Tel: (260 1) 250 833 Fax: (260 1) 254 176
5199 United Nations Ave., P.O. Box 31313, Lusaka, Zambia

Zimbabwe: Tel: (263 4) 733 881/5 Fax: (263 4) 732 917
45 Baines Ave., P.O. Box 1430, Harare, Zimbabwe

UNITED KINGDOM HIGH COMMISSIONS:

Botswana: Tel: (267 31) 52841/2/3
Private Bag 0023, Gaborone, Botswana

Burundi: Tel: (257) 223711
British Liaison Office, 43 Ave. Bubanza, B.P. 1344, Bujumbura, Burundi. Permanent staff in Kinshasa, Zaire

Congo: Tel: (243 12) 34775/8
Avenue des Trois Z, B.P. 8049, Kinshasa, Gombe, Congo.

Kenya: Tel: (254 2) 335944 Fax: (254 2) 333196
Bruce House, Standard St., P.O. Box 30465, Nairobi, Kenya

Lesotho: Tel: (266) 313961 Fax: (266) 310120
P.O. Box MS 521, Maseru 100, Lesotho

Lesotho: Tel: (266) 313961 Fax: (266) 310120
P.O. Box MS 521, Maseru 100, Lesotho

Malawi: Tel: (265) 782400 Fax: (265) 782657
P.O. Box 30042, Lingadzi House, Lilongwe 3, Malawi

Mauritius: Tel: (230) 686-5795
King George V Ave., Floreal, P.O. Box 186, Curepipe, Mauritius

Namibia: Tel: (264 61) 223022 Fax: (264 61) 228895
British Liaison Office, 116A Lentwein St., P.O. Box 22202, 116 Robert Mugabee Ave., Windhoek, Namibia

Rwanda: Tel: (250) 75219
Honorary Consul, Ave. Paul VI, B.P. 351, Kigali, Rwanda
Permanent staff in Kinshasa, Congo

Seychelles: Tel: (248) 225 225/356 Fax: (248) 225 127
3rd Floor, Victoria House, P.O. Box 161, Victoria, Mahe, Seychelles

South Africa: Tel: (27 11) 331 9011/4
Consulate: Fifth Floor, Nedbank Mall, 145 Commissioner St., P.O. Box 10101, Johannesburg 2001, South Africa

Tel: (27 31) 305 2929/20
Tenth Floor, Fedlife House, 320 Smith St., P.O. Box 1404, Durban 4001, South Africa

Tel: (27 12) 433 121 Fax: (27 12) 433 207
255 Hill St., Arcadia, Pretoria 0002, South Africa

Tel: (27 21) 461 7220 Fax: (27 21) 461 0017
91 Parliament St., Cape Town 8001, South Africa

Swaziland: Tel: (268) 42581
Alister Miller St., Private Bag, Mbabane, Swaziland

Tanzania: Tel: (255 51) 46300/4 Fax: (255 51) 46301
Hifadhi House, Samora Ave., P.O. Box 9200, Dar es Salaam, Tanzania

Uganda: Tel: (256 41) 257054/9 and (256 41)257301/4
10-12 Parliament Ave., P.O. Box 7070, Kampala, Uganda

Zambia: Tel: (260 1) 251133 Fax: (260 1) 253798
15101 Ridgeway, Independence Ave., P.O. Box 50050, Lusaka, Zambia

Zimbabwe: Tel: (263 4) 793781 or 728716 Fax: (263 4) 728380
Stanley House, Jason Moyo Ave., P.O. Box 4490, Harare, Zimbabwe

UNITED STATES EMBASSIES:

Botswana: Tel: (267 31) 353982/3/4 Fax: (267 31) 356947
P.O. Box 90, Gaborone, Botswana

Burundi: Tel: (257) 223454
B.P. 1720, Ave. du Zaire, Bujumbura, Burundi

Congo: Tel: (243 12) 21532 or 21628 Fax: (243 12) 21534
B.P. 697, Unit 31550, 310 Ave. des Aviateurs, Kinshasa, Congo

Kenya: Tel: (254 2) 33441 or 334 141/7 Fax: (254 2) 340 838
Embassy Building, Haile Selassie & Moi Avenues, P.O. Box 30137, Unit 64100, Nairobi, Kenya

Lesotho: Tel: (266) 310116
P.O. Box MS 333, Maseru 100, Lesotho

Malawi: Tel: (265) 780 166 Fax: (265) 780 471
P.O. Box 30016, Area 40, FLAT18, Lilongwe 3, Malawi

Mauritius: Tel: (230) 208-2342
Rogers Bldg., Fourth Floor, John Kennedy St., Port Louis, Mauritius

Namibia: Tel: (264) 61 229791
Ausplan Bldg., 14 Lossen St., P.O. Box 9890, Private Bag 12029, Ausspannplatz, 14 Lossen St., Windhoek 9000, Namibia

Rwanda: Tel: (250) 205 755601/2/3
Blvd. de la Révolution, B.P. 28, Kigali, Rwanda

Seychelles: Tel: (248) 255 256 Fax: (248) 225 189
Victoria House, P.O. Box 251, Victoria, Mahe, Seychelles

South Africa: Tel: (27 12) 342 1048 Fax: (27 12) 342 2299
P.O. Box 9536, 877 Pretorius St., Pretoria, South Africa
Consulate: Tel: (27 11) 3311681
11th Floor, Kine Center, Commissioner & Kruis Streets., P.O. Box 2155, Johannesburg, South Africa

Swaziland: Tel: (268) 46441/2/3/4/5
Central Bank Bldg., Warner St., P.O. Box 199, Mbabane, Swaziland

Tanzania: Tel: (255 51) 66010/5 Fax: (255 51) 66701
36 Laibon Rd. (off Bagamoyo Rd.), P.O. Box 9123, Dar es Salaam, Tanzania

Uganda: Tel: (256 41) 259791/2/3/4/5 Fax: (25641) 259 794
P.O. Box 7007, Kampala, Uganda

Zambia: Tel: (260 1) 262 859 Fax: (260 1) 252 225
Independence & United National Aves., P.O. Box 31617, Lusaka, Zambia

Zimbabwe: Tel: (263 4) 14 794521 Fax: (263 4) 796480
172 Herbert Chitep o Ave., P.O. Box 3340, Harare, Zimbabwe

DUTY-FREE ALLOWANCES

Contact the nearest tourist office or embassy for current duty-free import allowances for the country(ies) which you intend to visit. The duty-free allowances vary; however, the following may be used as a *general* guideline: 1 liter (approximately 1 quart) (33.8 fluid ounces) of spirits, one carton (200) of cigarettes or 100 cigars.

ELECTRICITY

Electric current is 220–240 volt AC 50 Hz.

GETTING TO AFRICA

BY AIR:

Most travelers from North America flying to the countries listed in this guide must pass through Europe, with the exception of South African Airways which flies New York–Johannesburg and Miami–Cape Town–Johannesburg. Air fares and air routings to Africa are continuously changing. For special discount air fares, I suggest you call The Africa Adventure Company at 1-800-882-9453 (U.S.A. and Canada) or (954) 491-8877, fax (954) 491-9060, E-mail noltingaac@aol.com or visit the World Wide Web pages at http://www.africa-adventure.com.

BY ROAD:

From Egypt to Sudan and Ethiopia to Kenya and southward; trans-Sahara through Algeria, Niger, Nigeria or Chad, Cameroon, Central Africa Republic, Democratic Republic of the Congo, Rwanda and eastern and southern Africa. Allow several months as roads are very bad.

BY SHIP:

Some cruise ships stop along the coasts of Kenya, Tanzania and South Africa and at Mauritius and the Seychelles.

GETTING AROUND AFRICA

See each country's map for details on major roads, railroad lines and waterways.

BY AIR:

Capitals and major tourist centers are serviced by air. There is regularly scheduled air service to the following destinations within Africa:

Botswana: Gaborone, Maun, Francistown, Kasane and Selebi Phikwe.

Burundi: Bujumbura.

Congo: Goma, Bukavu, Kisangani, Lubumbashi and Kinshasa.

Kenya: Kisumu, Malindi, Mombasa, Lamu and Nairobi. Scheduled charter services are available to Amboseli, Masai Mara, Nanyuki and Samburu.

Lesotho: Maseru, Qacha's Nek, Semonkong, Thaba Tseka and other towns.

Malawi: Blantyre, Lilongwe, Mzuzu.

Mauritius: Port Louis, Rodrigues Island.

Namibia: Windhoek, Katima Mulilo, Keetmanshoop, Lüderitz, Swakopmund, Tsumeb and Mokuti (Etosha National Park).

Rwanda: Kigali.

Seychelles: Mahé, Praslin, Frégate, Bird, Denis and Desroches Islands

South Africa: Bloemfontein, Cape Town, Durban, Eastgate (Hoedspuit), East London, George, Johannesburg, Kimberley, Nelspruit, Port Elizabeth, Richards Bay, Skukuza, Umtata and Upington .

Tanzania: Kilimanjaro International, Dar es Salaam and Zanzibar.

Uganda: Entebbe.

Zambia: Chipata, Lusaka, Livingstone (Victoria Falls), Mfuwe (South Luangwa National Park), Kafue and Ndole.

Zimbabwe: Bulawayo, Harare, Hwange, Kariba and Victoria Falls.

BY ROAD:

Major roads are tarmac (paved) and are excellent in Namibia, South Africa and Zimbabwe. Most major roads are tarmac in fair condition in Botswana, Kenya, Malawi and Swaziland and poor in Tanzania, Rwanda, Uganda and Zambia. Burundi, Lesotho and the Congo have very few tarmac roads. Many dirt roads (except in Namibia) are difficult, and many are impassable in the rainy season (especially the Congo), often requiring four-wheel-drive vehicles.

Petrol and diesel are readily available in Botswana, Kenya, Lesotho, Malawi, Mauritius, Namibia, South Africa, Swaziland and Zimbabwe; may be difficult to obtain in Burundi, Rwanda, Tanzania and Zambia; and very difficult to obtain in the Congo.

Taxis are available in the larger cities and at international airports. **Service taxis** travel when all seats are taken and are an inexpensive but uncomfortable means of long-distance travel. **Local buses** are very crowded, uncomfortable and are recommended only for the hardiest of travelers. Pickup trucks (matatus in East Africa), often crammed with 20 passengers, luggage, produce, chickens, etc., are used throughout the continent. Be sure to agree on the price before setting off.

BY RAIL:

Trains in South Africa are excellent (especially the Blue Train and Rovos Rail). The steam train from Bulawayo to Victoria Falls is also good. The "Lunatic Express" from Nairobi to Mombasa in Kenya is fair. See the chapters on Kenya, South Africa and Zimbabwe for details.

Otherwise, train travel is slow and not recommended except for those on an extreme budget on long journeys. Train travel is possible from Arusha (Tanzania) through Zambia, Zimbabwe and Botswana to Cape Town, South Africa. Railway lines are depicted on the maps of each country in this guide.

BY BOAT:

Steamer service on Lake Tanganyika services Bujumbura (Burundi), Kigoma (Tanzania), Mpulungu (Zambia) and Kalemie (Congo) about once a week; steamers on Lake Victoria service Kisumu (Kenya), Musoma and Mwanza (Tanzania) and Kampala-Port Bell (Uganda); the Ilale and Mtendere steamers circumnavigate Lake Malawi.

HEALTH

Malarial risk exists in all countries covered except Lesotho, so be sure to take your malaria pills, as described before, during and after your trip. Contact your doctor, an immunologist and the Centers for Disease Control in Atlanta for the best prophylaxis for your itinerary. Use an insect repellent. Wear long-sleeve shirts and slacks for further protection, especially at sunset and during the evening.

Bilharzia is a disease that infests most lakes and rivers on the continent. Do not walk barefoot along the shore or wade or swim in a stream, river or lake unless you know for certain it is free of bilharzia. Bilharzia does not exist in salt water.

If you must get in the water, as with canoe or kayak safaris, do not get out of the canoe or kayak where there are reeds in the water. A species of snail is involved in the reproductive cycle of bilharzia; these snails are more often found near reeds and in slow-moving water. By following your guide's instructions, your risk of contracting the disease will be minimized. If you feel you may have contracted the disease, go to your doctor for a blood test. If diagnosed in its early stages, it is easily cured.

Tap water is safe in many of the larger cities. Wear a hat and bring sunblock to protect yourself from the tropical sun. Drink plenty of fluids and limit alcohol consumption at high altitudes.

For further information, obtain a copy of *Health Information for International Travel* from the U.S. Government Printing Office, Washington, D.C. 20402.

INSURANCE

Be sure your medical insurance covers you for the countries you plan to visit. Acquire additional insurance for emergency evacuation should your present policies not include it.

Travel insurance packages often include a combination of emergency evacuation, medical, baggage, and trip cancellation. We suggest that all travelers to Africa cover themselves fully with a reputable insurance package. The peace of mind afforded by such insurance far outweighs the cost. Ask your Africa travel specialist for information on relatively inexpensive group-rate insurance.

MAPS

Before going on safari, obtain good maps for each country you intend to visit. This will increase your awareness of the areas you want to see and enhance your enjoyment of the trip. For a free catalog of difficult-to-find country maps, regional maps and mountain maps, see the catalog at the end of the book or contact The Africa Adventure Company, P.O. Box 70067, Fort Lauderdale, FL 33307-0067, tel: (954) 491-8877 or 1-800-882-9453

It is best to purchase maps before arriving in Africa, as they are often not readily available.

METRIC SYSTEM OF WEIGHTS AND MEASURES

The metric system is used in Africa. The U.S. equivalents are listed in the conversion chart below.

To convert centigrade into degrees Fahrenheit, multiply centigrade by 1.8 and add 32.

To convert Fahrenheit into degrees centigrade, subtract 32 from Fahrenheit and divide by 1.8.

Measurements	Temperature	
1 inch - 2.54 centimeters (cm.)	-20° C. =	-4° F.
1 foot - 0.305 meters (m.)	-15° C. =	5° F.
1 mile - 1.6 kilometers (km.)	-10° C. =	14° F.
1 square mile - 2.59 sq.km.	-5° C. =	23° F.
1 quart liquid - 0.946 liter (l.)	0° C. =	32° F.
1 ounce - 28 grams (g.)	5° C. =	41° F.
1 pound - 0.454 kilograms (kg.)	10° C. =	50° F.
1 cm. - 0.39 inch	15° C. =	59° F.
1 m. - 3.28 feet	20° C. =	68° F.
1 km. - 0.62 miles	25° C. =	77° F.
1 sq. km. - 0.3861 sq. mile	30° C. =	86° F.
1 l. - 1.057 quarts	35° C. =	95° F.
1 g. - 0.035 ounce	40° C. =	104° F.
1 kg. - 2.2 pounds		

MONEY

One way to receive additional funds is to obtain additional travelers checks with your American Express or other credit card. Other options include having money sent by telegraph international money order (Western Union), telexed through a bank or sent via international courier (i.e., DHL). Do not count on finding ATM machines.

PASSPORT OFFICES

To obtain a passport in the United States, contact your local post office for the passport office nearest you. Then call the passport office to be sure you will have everything on hand which will be required.

SEMINARS ON AFRICA

The Africa Adventure Company
Tel: (954) 491-8877 or 1-800-882-9453 Fax: (954) 491-9060
P.O. Box 70067 Fort Lauderdale, FL 33307-0067
E-mail: noltingaac@aol.com
Visit the Web pages at http://www.africa-adventure.com
Seminars by Mark Nolting, author of this guide.

SHOPPING

If you like bartering, bring clothing (new denims and T-shirts are great) or pens to trade for souvenirs. This works particularly well at roadside stands and in small villages in East and Central Africa, although the villagers are becoming more discerning in their tastes.

The following are some ideas of what to shop for:

Botswana: Baskets and carvings are sold in Maun, Kasane and the Mall in Gaborone. Also consider pottery, tapestries and rugs. There are curio shops in many safari camps, hotels and lodges.

Burundi: Crafts available in numerous shops.

Congo: Wood carvings, malachite, copper goods, semiprecious stones and baskets.

Kenya: Makonde and Akomba ebony wood carvings, soapstone carvings, colorful kangas and kikois (cloth wraps). In Mombasa, Zanzibar chests, gold and silverwork, brasswork, Arab jewelry and antiques.

Lesotho: Basotho woven carpets are known worldwide, tapestry weaving and conical straw hats.

Malawi: Wood carvings, woven baskets.

Mauritius: Intricately detailed, handmade model sailing ships of camphor or teak, pareos (colorful light cotton wraps), knitwear, textiles, T-shirts, and Mauritian dolls.

Namibia: Semiprecious stones and jewelry, karakul wool products, wood carvings and beadwork.

Seychelles: Coco-de-mer, batik prints, spices for Creole cooking and locally produced jewelry, weaving and basketry.

South Africa: Diamonds, gold, wood carvings, dried flowers and wine.

Swaziland: Beautiful handwoven tapestries, baskets, earthenware and stoneware, and mouth-blown, handcrafted glass animals and tableware.

Tanzania: Makonde carvings, Meerschaum pipes and Tanzanite.

Uganda: Wood carvings.

Zambia: Wood carvings, statuettes, semiprecious stones and copper souvenirs.

Zimbabwe: Carvings of wood, stone and Zimbabwe's unique verdite, intricate baskets, ceramicware and crocheted garments.

SHOPPING HOURS

Shops are usually open Monday–Friday from 8:00/9:00 a.m. to 5:00/6:00 p.m. and 9:00 a.m. to 1:00 p.m. on Saturdays. Shops in the coastal cities of Kenya and Tanzania often close midday for siesta. Use the shopping hours given above as a general guideline; exact times can vary within the respective country.

THEFT

The number one rule in preventing theft on vacation is to leave all unnecessary valuables at home. What you must bring, lock in safety deposit boxes when not in use. Theft in Africa is generally no worse than in Europe or the United States. One difference is that Africans are poorer and will steal things that most American or European thieves would consider worthless. Be careful in all African cities and do not go walking around the streets at night.

TIME ZONES

EST+7/GMT+2
Botswana
Burundi
Congo (Eastern)
Lesotho
Malawi
Namibia (winter months there is daylight savings time + 1 hour)
Rwanda
South Africa
Swaziland
Zambia
Zimbabwe
EST+8/GMT+3
Kenya
Tanzania
Uganda
EST+9/GMT+4
Mauritius
Seychelles

TIPPING

A 10 percent tip is recommended at restaurants for good service where a service charge is not included in the bill. For advice on what tips are appropriate for guides, ask the Africa specialist booking your safari.

TOURIST INFORMATION

In addition to the addresses below, information may also be available through embassies or consulates of the countries in question. See **DIPLOMATIC REPRESENTATIVES** above.

OFFICES IN AFRICA:

Botswana: Tel: (267) 353024 or 313 314
Division of Tourism, Private Bag 0047, Gaborone, Botswana

Burundi: Tel: (257) 222023 and 222202
National Office of Tourism, Liberty Ave., P.O. Box 902, Bujumbura, Burundi

Congo: Tel: (243 12) 30070 or 30022
Office National du Tourisme, Ave. des Orangers 2A/2B, B.P. 9502, Kinshasa/Gombe, Congo
Office National du Tourisme, Blvd. Mobutu, B.P. 242, Goma, Congo
Also contact Sabena Airlines for information.

Kenya: Tel: (254 2) 330 820 Fax: (254 2) 217 604
Ministry of Tourism and Wildlife, Utalii House, P.O. Box 42013, Uhuru Hwy., Nairobi, Kenya

Lesotho: Tel: (266) 31 2896
National Tourist Board, P.O. Box 1378, Maseru 100, Lesotho

Malawi: Tel: (265) 621 923
P.O. Box 402, Blantyre, Malawi

Mauritius: Tel: (230) 208 6397 Fax: (230) 212 5142
Tourism Promotion Authority, 11th Floor, Air Mauritius Centre, John Kennedy St., Port Louis, Mauritius
http://www.mauritius.net

Namibia: Tel: (264 61) 284 2111 Fax: (264 61) 221 930
Ministry of Environment & Tourism, Private Bag 13346, Windhoek 9000, Namibia

Rwanda: Tel: (250) 76514/15
Office Rwandais du Tourisme et des Parcs Nationaux (ORTPN), B.P. 905, Kigali, Rwanda

Seychelles: Tel: (248) 225 313 Fax: (248) 224 035
P.O. Box 92, Independence House, Victoria, Mahe, Seychelles

South Africa: Tel: (27 12) 3470600 Fax: (27 12) 454 889 or 454 768
Tourism Board, Private Bag X164, 442 Rigel Ave. South, Erasmus Rand Pretoria 001, South Africa

Swaziland: Tel: (268) 42531
Government Tourist Office, Swazi Plaza, P.O. Box 338,
Mbabane, Swaziland

Tanzania: Tel: (255 51) 27671
Tanzania Tourist Board, P. O. Box 2485, Dar es Salaam, Tanzania

Uganda: Tel: (256 41) 232 971/2 Fax: (256 41) 241 247
Ministry of Tourism, Wildlife and Antiquities, P.O. Box 4241,
Parliament Ave., Kampala, Uganda

Uganda Tourist Board, P.O. Box 17211, Parliament Ave.,
Kampala, Uganda
http://www.tomco.net/njssemwog/utb/utb.htm

Zambia: Tel: (260 1) 229 087/790 Fax: (260 1) 225 174
Century House, Cairo Road, P.O. Box 30017, Lusaka, Zambia

Tourist Centre: Tel: (260 3) 321 404/5 Fax: (2603) 321487
Mosi-oa-Tunya Road, P.O. Box 60342, Livingstone, Zambia

Zanzibar: Tel: (255 54) 32344
Tanzania Friendship Tourist Bureau, P.O. Box 216,
Zanzibar, Tanzania

Zimbabwe: Tel: (263 4) 793 666/7/8/9 or 706 571 Fax: (263 4) 793 669
Tourist Development Corporation (ZTDC), P.O. Box CY286,
Causeway, Harare, Zimbabwe

OFFICES IN AUSTRALIA:

South Africa: Tel: (61 2) 231 6166
AMEV-UDC House, 115 Pitt St., Sydney, NSW 2001

Uganda: Tel: (61 075) 880 411
33 Scarborough St., Southport, Queensland 4215

Zambia: Tel: (61 2) 299 5300 Fax: (61 2) 290 2665
C/O Obitair International Pty. Ltd., Levelio, 36 Clarence St.,
Level 10, Sydney, NSW 2000

OFFICES IN CANADA:

South Africa:
Suite 1001, 20 Eglington Ave. West, Toronto, Ontario, M4R 1K8
Tel: (416) 283 0563 Fax: (416) 283 5465
Suite 205, 4117 Lawrence Ave. East, Scarborough, Ontario M1E 2S2

OFFICES IN THE UNITED KINGDOM:

Kenya: Tel: (44 171) 355 3144 Fax: (44 171) 495 8656
25 Brook's Mews, off Davis St., Mayfair, London W1Y 1LGF, England

Lesotho: Tel: (44 171) 242 3131
433 High Holborn House, 52 High Holborn, London WC1V 6RB, England

Malawi: Tel: (44 171) 4914172/7 Fax: (44 171) 491 9916
336 Grosvenor St. London W1X 0DE, England

Seychelles: Tel: (44 171) 224 1670 Fax: (44 171) 487 5756
2nd Floor, Eros House, 111 Baker St., London W1M 1FE, England

South Africa: Tel: (44 181) 944 8080 Fax (44 181) 944 6705
5-6 Alt Grove, London SW19 4DZ, England

Swaziland:
58 Pont St., Knightsbridge, London SW1, England

Tanzania: Tel: (44 171) 499 7727
77 South Audley St., London W1Y 5TA, England

Zambia: Tel: (44 171) 589 6343/4 Fax: (44 171) 225 3221
2 Palace Gate, Kensington, London W8 5NG, England

Zimbabwe: Tel: (44 171) 836 7755 Fax: (44 171) 379 1167
Zimbabwe Tourist Office c/o Zimbabwe High Commission,
429 Strand, London WC2R 0SA, England

OFFICES IN THE UNITED STATES:

Kenya: Tel: (212) 486-1300/3 Fax: (212) 688-0911
Office of Tourism
424 Madison Ave., New York, NY 10017

Tel: (310) 274-6635 Fax: (310) 859-7010
Doheny Plaza, Suite 111, 9150 Wilshire Blvd., Suite 160,
Beverly Hills, CA 90212
http://www.africanvacation.com/kenya
E-mail: kenya2day@aol.com

Seychelles: Tel: (212) 687-9766 Fax: (212) 922-9177
820 Second Ave., Suite 900-F, New York, NY 10017

South Africa: Tel: (310) 641-8444 or (800) 782-9772
Office of Tourism (SATOUR)

9841 Airport Blvd., Suite 1524, Los Angeles, CA 90045

Tel: (212) 730-2929 or (800) 822-5368 Fax: (212) 764-1980
Suite 2040, 500 Fifth Ave., New York, NY 10010

Zambia: Tel: (212) 972-7200 Fax: (212) 972-7360
National Tourist Board, 800 Second Ave., New York, NY 10017

Zimbabwe: Tel: (800) 621-2381 or (212) 332-1090
Fax: (212) 332-1093
Tourist Office, 1270 Avenue of the Americas, Suite 2315,
New York, NY 10020

TRAVELERS CHECKS

American Express, Thomas Cook's, MasterCard and Visa travelers checks are widely accepted. Stay away from lesser known companies; you may have difficulty cashing them.

VACCINATIONS

Check with the tourist offices or embassies of the countries you wish to visit for current requirements. If you plan to visit one or more countries in endemic zones (i.e., in Africa, South America, Central America or Asia), be sure to mention this when requesting vaccination requirements. Many countries do not require any vaccinations if you are only visiting the country directly from the United States, Canada or Western Europe, but if you are also visiting countries in endemic zones, there may very well be additional requirements.

Then check with your doctor and preferably an immunologist, or call your local health department or the Centers for Disease Control in Atlanta, Georgia at (404) 639-3311 for information. They will probably recommend some vaccinations in addition to those required by the country you will be visiting.

Make sure you are given an International Certificate of Vaccinations showing the vaccinations you have received.

Malarial prophylaxis (pills) is highly recommended for all the countries included in this guide except for Lesotho. However, international travelers must at least pass through South Africa en route to Lesotho.

VISA REQUIREMENTS

Travelers from most countries must obtain visas to enter many of the countries included in this guide. Apply for visas with the closest diplomatic representative or through a visa service well in advance and check for all current requirements (see **DIPLOMATIC REPRESENTATIVES** on next page).

VISA REQUIREMENTS CHART

	Citizenship					Requirements/Restrictions
	AUS	CAN	NZ	UK	USA	
Botswana	No	No	No	No	No*	*Maximum visit of 90 days.
Burundi	Yes	Yes	Yes	Yes	Yes	Onward ticket; sponsorship for business visa.
Kenya	Yes	Yes	No	No*	Yes	*UK citizens of Asian origin need visa. Visitor's pass issued upon arrival.
Lesotho	No	Yes	No	No	Yes	
Malawi	No	No	No	No	No	Maximum visit of 90 days
Mauritius	No	No	No	No	No	Maximum 1 - month stay.
Namibia	No	No	No	No	No	
Rwanda	Yes	Yes	Yes	Yes	Yes	
Seychelles	No	No	No	No	No	*Maximum visit of 90 days.
South Africa	No	No	No	No	No	Letter from employer for business visa.
Swaziland	No	No	No	No	No	
Tanzania	Yes*	Yes	Yes	Yes*	Yes	*Visitor's pass required. For business visa, letter of invitation.
Uganda	No	No	No	No	No*	*Must have vaccination certificate for yellow fever, cholera & typhoid.
Congo	Yes	Yes	Yes	Yes	Yes	Certified sponsorship letter from government for business visa.
Zambia	No	No	No	No	Yes	
Zimbabwe	No	No	No	No	No	Require a return ticket.

Visa regulations change frequently-check with embassy or a visa service prior to traveling.

WILDLIFE ASSOCIATIONS

African Wildlife Foundation, 1400 16th St. NW, Suite 120, Washington, D.C. 20036; tel: (202) 939-3333.

David Shepherd Conservation Foundation, Winkworth Farm, Hascombe, Godamling, Surrey GU8 4JW, England; tel: Hascombe 220.

Dian Fossey Gorilla Fund, 45 Inverness Dr. East, Englewood, CO 80112-5480; tel: (303) 790-2345.

Endangered Wildlife Trust, c/o Mike Delvin, 346 Smith Ridge Road, New Canaan, CT 06840; tel: (203) 966-1981.

Fauna and Flora Preservation Society, c/o Zoological Society of London, Regents Park, London NW1 4RY, England.

World Wildlife Fund, 1250 24th Street N.W., Washington, D.C. 20037; tel: (202) 293-4800.

SAFARI GLOSSARY

ablution block — a building containing showers, toilets and sinks, most often with separate facilities for men and women.

adaptation — the ability, through structural or functional characteristics, to improve the survival rate of an animal or plant in a particular habitat.

age (approx.) — mammals

1) adult — eight years and older
2) juvenile — three to eight years
3) infant — birth to three years

arboreal — living in trees.

banda — a basic shelter or hut, often constructed of reeds, bamboo, grass, etc.

boma — a place of shelter, a fortified place, enclosure, community (East Africa).

browse — to feed on leaves.

calving season — period when young of a particular species are born. Not all species have calving seasons. Most calving seasons occur shortly after the rainy season commences. Calving seasons can also differ for the same species from one park or reserve to another.

camp — camping sites; also refers to lodging in chalets, bungalows or tents in a remote location.

caravan — a trailer.

carnivore — an animal that lives by consuming the flesh of other animals.

carrion — remains of dead animals.

diurnal — active during the day.

endangered — refers to an animal that is threatened with extinction.

gestation — duration of pregnancy.

grazer — an animal that eats grass.

habitat—an animal or plant's surroundings that has everything it needs in order to live.
habituated — an animal that has been introduced to and accepted the presence of human beings.
herbivore — an animal that consumes plant matter for food.
hide — a camouflaged structure from which one can view wildlife without being seen.
kopje (pronounced *kopee*) — rock formations which protrude from the savannah, usually caused by wind erosion (southern Africa).
koppie — same as kopje (East Africa).
kraal — same as boma (southern Africa).
mammals — warm-blooded animals that produce milk for their young.
midden — usually an accumulation of dung in the same spot as a scent-marking behavior.
nocturnal — active by night.
omnivore — an animal that eats both plants and animals.
pan — hard-surface flatlands that collect water in the rainy season.
plunge pool— a very small swimming pool.
predator — an animal that hunts and kills other animals for food.
prey — animals hunted by predators for food.
pride — a group or family of lions.
rondavel — an African-style structure for accommodation.
ruminant — mammals that have complex stomachs and therefore chew the cud.
rutting — behavioral pattern exhibited by males of a species over a time period during which mating is most prevalent (e.g., impala, wildebeest).
savannah — open grassy landscape with widely scattered trees.
scavenger — an animal that feeds on carrion or remains of animals killed by predators or that have died from other causes.
species — a group of plants or animals with specific characteristics in common, including the ability to reproduce among themselves.
spoor — a track (i.e., footprint) or trail made by animals.
symbiosis — an association of two different organisms in a relationship that may benefit one or both partners.
tarmac — asphalt-paved roads.
territory — the home range or domain which an animal may defend against intruders of the same or other species.
toilet, long-drop — a permanent bush toilet or "outhouse" in which a

toilet seat has been placed over a hole dug about 6 feet (2 m) deep.
toilet, short-drop — a temporary bush toilet, usually a toilet tent used on mobile tented safaris in which a toilet seat has been placed over a hole dug about 3 feet (1 m) deep.
tracking — following and observing animal spoor by foot.
tribe — a group of people united by traditional ties.
troop — a group of apes or monkeys.
ungulate — hoofed animal.
veld — a southern African term for open land.
wallow — the art of keeping cool and wet, usually in a muddy pool (i.e., rhinoceros, buffalo and hippopotamus).

LATIN/SCIENTIFIC NAMES OF MAMMALS, REPTILES, BIRDS AND TREES

MAMMALS

Aardvark (antbear)	*Orycteropus afer*
Antelope, roan	*Hippotragus equinus*
Antelope, sable	*Hippotragus niger*
Baboon	*Papio anubis*
Baboon, chacma	*Papio ursinus*
Bongo	*Boocercus eurycerus*
Buffalo	*Syncerus caffer*
Bushbaby, greater	*Galago crassicaudatus*
Bushbuck	*Tragelaphus scriptus*
Bushpig	*Potamochoerus porcus*
Caracal	*Caracal caracal*
Cheetah	*Acinonyx jubatus*
Chimpanzee	*Pan troglodytes*
Civet	*Viverra civetta*
Colobus, black and white or guereza	*Colobus guereza*
Dikdik, Kirk's	*Rhynchotragus kirki*
Dog, African wild	*Lycaon pictus*
Duiker, grey bush	*Sylvicapra grimmia*
Eland, Patterson's	*Taurotragus oryx*
Elephant, African	*Loxodonta africana*
Fox, bat-eared	*Otocyon megalotis*

Gazelle, Grant's	*Gazella granti*
Gazelle, Thomson's	*Gazella thomsoni*
Gemsbok or oryx	*Oryx gazella*
Genet	*Genetta tigrina*
Giraffe, Masai	*Giraffa camelopardalis tippelskirchi*
Giraffe, reticulated	*Giraffa camelopardalis reticulata*
Giraffe, Rothschild's	*Giraffa camelopardalis rothschildi*
Gorilla, lowland	*Gorilla gorilla graveri*
Gorilla, mountain	*Gorilla gorilla beringei*
Hare, African	*Lepus capensis*
Hare, spring	*Pedetes capensis*
Hartebeest	*Alcelaphus buselaphus*
Hippopotamus	*Hippopotamus amphibius*
Hog, giant forest	*Hylochoerus meinertzhageni*
Hyena, brown	*Hyaena brunnea*
Hyena, spotted	*Crocuta crocuta*
Hyena, striped	*Hyaena hyaena*
Hyrax, bush	*Dendrohyrax brucei*
Hyrax, rock	*Procavia johnstoni*
Hyrax, tree	*Dendrohyrax arboreus*
Impala	*Aepyceros melampus*
Jackal, black-backed	*Canis mesomelas*
Jackal, golden	*Canis aureus*
Jackal, side-striped	*Canis adustus*
Klipspringer	*Oreotragus oreotragus*
Kongoni	*Alcelaphus buselaphus*
Kudu, greater	*Tragelaphus strepsiceros*
Lechwe	*Kobus lechwe*
Leopard	*Panthera pardus*
Lion	*Panthera leo*
Mongoose, banded	*Mungos mungo*
Mongoose, dwarf	*Helogale parvula*
Mongoose, slender	*Herpestes sanguineus*
Mongoose, white-tailed	*Ichneumia albicauda*
Monkey, Patas	*Erythrocebus patas*
Monkey, vervet	*Cercopithecus aethiops*
Nyala	*Tragelaphus angasi*
Oribi	*Ourebia ourebi*
Oryx, fringe-eared	*Oryx beisa*

Pangolin, Temminck's ground	*Manis temmincki*
Porcupine, crested	*Hystrix africae-australis*
Ratel	*Mellivora capensis*
Reedbuck, mountain	*Redunca fulvorufula*
Rhinoceros, black	*Diceros bicornis*
Rhinoceros, white	*Ceratotherium simum*
Serval	*Leptailurus serval*
Sitatunga	*Tragelaphus spekei*
Steenbok	*Raphicerus campestris*
Topi	*Damaliscus korrigum*
Tsessebe	*Damaliscus lunatus*
Waterbuck, common	*Kobus ellipsiprymnus*
Waterbuck, Defassa	*Kobus defassa*
Wildebeest	*Connochaetes taurinus*
Zebra, Burchell's	*Equus burchelli*
Zebra, Grevy's	*Equus grevyi*
Zorilla	*Ictonyx striatus*

REPTILES

Chameleon	*Chamaelo dilepis*
Crocodile, Nile	*Crocodylus niloticus*
Monitor, Nile	*Varanus niloticus*
Python	*Python sebae*

BIRDS

Avocet	*Recurvirostra avosetta*
Barbet, d'Arnaud's	*Trachyphonus darnaudi*
Barbet, black-collared	*Lybius torquatus*
Barbet, yellow-fronted tinker	*Pogoniulus chrysoconus*
Bee-eater, carmine	*Merops nubicoides*
Bee-eater, swallow-tailed	*Merops hirundineus*
Bustard, kori	*Ardeotis kori*
Cormorant, reed	*Phalacrocorax africanus*
Cormorant, white-breasted	*Phalacrocorax carbo*
Coucal, coppery-tailed	*Centropus cupreicaudus*
Crane, blue	*Anthropoides paradisea*
Crane, crowned	*Balaearica regulorum*

Crane, wattle	*Grus carunculata*
Cuckoo shrike, black	*Campephaga sulphurata*
Darter, African	*Anhinga rufa*
Dikkop, water	*Burhinus vermiculatus*
Dove, Cape Turtle	*Streptopelia capicola*
Duck, white-faced	*Dendrocygna viduata*
Eagle, bateleur	*Terathopius ecaudatus*
Eagle, black	*Aquila verreauxii*
Eagle, brown snake	*Circaetus cinereus*
Eagle, fish	*Haliaeetus vocifer*
Eagle, lesser spotted	*Aquila pomarina*
Eagle, martial	*Polemaetus bellicosus*
Eagle, tawny	*Aquila rapax*
Eagle, Verreaux	*Aquila verreauxii*
Eagle, Wahlberg's	*Aquila wahlbergi*
Eagle, western banded snake	*Ciraetus cinerascens*
Egret, cattle	*Bulbulcus ibis*
Egret, little	*Egretta garzetta*
Egret, slaty	*Egretta vinaceigula*
Flamingo, greater	*Phoenicopterus ruber*
Flamingo, lesser	*Phoenicopterus minor*
Flycatcher	*Muscicapidae*
Fody, Mauritius	*Foudia rubra*
Francolin, crested	*Francolinus sephaena*
Francolin, Swainson's	*Francolinus swainsonii*
Goose, Egyptian	*Alopochen aegyptiacus*
Goose, Spur-winged	*Plectropterus gambensis*
Guinea fowl, crested	*Guttera pucherani*
Guinea fowl, helmeted	*Numida meleagris*
Gull, grey-headed	*Larus cirrocephalus*
Hamerkop	*Scopus umbretta*
Heron, goliath	*Ardea goliath*
Heron, green-backed	*Butorides striatus*
Heron, purple	*Ardea purpurea*
Hornbill, ground	*Bucorvus leadbeateri*
Hornbill, yellow-billed	*Tocus flavirostris*
Ibis, bald	*Geronticus calvus*
Ibis, sacred	*Threskiornis aethiopicus*
Jacana, African	*Actophilornis africanus*

Kestrel, Dickenson's	*Falco dickinsoni*
Kestrel, Mauritius	*Falco punctatus*
Kingfisher, pied	*Ceryle rudis*
Kingfisher, striped	*Haycyon chelucuti*
Kite, yellow-billed	*Milvus migrans parasitus*
Lammergeyer	*Gypaetus barbatus*
Lourie, grey	*Corythaixoides concolor*
Merle	*Hypsipetes olivacea*
Nightjar, dusky	*Caprimulgus fraenatus*
Olive white-eye	*Zosterops chloronotos*
Ostrich	*Struthio camelus*
Owl, Pel's fishing	*Scotopelia peli*
Oxpecker, red-billed	*Buphagus erythrorhynchus*
Oxpecker, yellow-billed	*Buphagus africanus*
Parakeet, rose-ringed	*Psittacula krameri*
Parrot, Meyer's	*Poicephalus meyeri*
Pelican, pink-backed	*Pelecanus rufescens*
Pelican, white	*Pelecanus onocrotalus*
Pic-pic	*Zosterops borbonica*
Plover, blacksmith	*Vanellus armatus*
Plover, long-toed	*Vanellus crassirostris*
Plover, white-crowned	*Vanellus albiceps*
Quelea, red-billed	*Quelea quelea*
Roller, lilac-breasted	*Coracias caudata*
Sand grouse, Namaqua	*Pterocles namaqua*
Sand grouse, yellow-throated	*Sagittarius serpentarius*
Sandpiper, common	*Tringa hypoleucos*
Sandpiper, wood	*Tringa glareola*
Secretary bird	*Sagittarius serpentarius*
Shrike, crimson-breasted	*Laniarius atrococcineus*
Shrike, long-tailed	*Corvinella melanoleuca*
Skimmer, African	*Rynchops flavirostris*
Snipe, painted	*Rostratula benghalensis*
Spoonbill, African	*Platalea alba*
Spurfowl, grey-breasted	*Francolinus rufopictus*
Starling, glossy	*Amprotornis nitens*
Starling, long-tailed	*Lamprotornis mevesii*
Starling, superb	*Spreo superbus*
Stilt, black-winged	*Himantopus himantopus*

Stork, marabaou	*Leptoptilos crumeniferus*
Stork, saddle-billed	*Ephippiorhynchus senegalensis*
Stork, whale-headed	*Balaeniceps rex*
Stork, yellow-billed	*Mycteria ibis*
Sunbirds	*Nectariniidae*
Vulture, Egyptian	*Neophron percnopterus*
Vulture, hooded	*Neophron monachus*
Vulture, lappet-faced or Nubian	*Torgos tracheliotus*
Vulture, Ruppell's	*Gyps rueppelli*
Vulture, white-backed	*Gyps africanus*
Vulture, white-headed	*Trigonoceps occipitals*
Woodhoopoe, red-billed	*Phoeniculus cyanomelas*

TREES

Acacia, apple ring	*Acacia albida*
Acacia, stinkbark	*Acacia clavigera*
Acacia, umbrella	*Acacia tortillis*
Acacia, yellow bark	*Acacia xanthaphloea*
Aloe	*Aloe chabaudii*
Baobab	*Adansonia digitata*
Candelabra tree	*Euphorbia ingens*
Chestnut, African star	*Sterculia africana*
Croton, lavender	*Croton macrostachys*
Date, desert	*Balanites aegyptiaca*
Ebony, diospyros	*Diospyros abyssinica*
Fig, sycamore	*Ficus sycamorus*
Leadwood	*Combretum imberbe*
Mahogany	*Trichilia emetica*
Mopane	*Colophospermum mopane*
Msasa	*Brachystegia boehmii*
Palm, fan	*Hyphaene ventricosa*
Palm, wild date	*Phoenix relinata*
Rain tree	*Lonchocarpus capassa*
Sausage tree	*Kigelia africana*
Tamarind	*Tamarindus indica*
Terminalia, silver	*Terminalia sericea*
Thorn, wait-a-bit	*Acacia mellifera*
Thorn, whistling	*Acacia drepanolobium*

SUGGESTED READING LIST

WILDLIFE – GENERAL

Through a Window, J. Goodall, 1990 (Boston: Houghton Mifflin) (O/P).

Field Guide to the Larger Mammals of Africa, J. Dorst and P. Dandelot, 1996 (Capetown, South Arica: New Holland).

Field Guide to the Birds of East Africa, J. G. Williams and N. Arlot, 1963 (London: Collins).

The Behavior Guide to African Mammals, R. D. Estes, 1991 (Berkeley: University of California Press).

Survivors Song, D. Owens and M. Owens, 1992 (Boston: Houghton Mifflin).

Africa's Vanishing Wildlife, Chris and Tilde Stuart, 1996 (Johannesburg, South Arica: Southern).

Africa Natural History, Chris and Tilde Stuart, 1995 (Johannesburg, South Arica: Southern).

African Elephants, Daryl and Sharna Balfour, 1997 (Capetown, South Africa: Struik).

Cats of Africa, Paul Bosman and Anthony Hall-Martin, 1997 (Capetown, South Africa: Fernwood Press).

African Insect Life, A. Skaiffe, John Ledger and Anthony Barnister, revised 1997 (Capetown, South Africa: Struik).

Wildlife of Southern Africa, V. Carruthers, 1997 (Johannesburg, South Arica: Southern).

Field Guide to the Mammals of Southern Africa, Chris and Tilde Stuart, 1996 (Capetown, South Africa: Struik).

Field Guide to the Larger Mammals of Southern Africa, Chris and Tilde Stuart, 1996 (Capetown, South Africa: Struik).

Smithers Mammals of Southern Africa, Peter Apps, 1996 (Johannesburg, South Arica: Southern).

Roberts Birds, Gordon Maclean, 1993 (Johannesburg, South Arica: Southern).

Field Companion to Roberts Birds, G. Maclean, 1996 (Johannesburg, South Arica: Southern).

Sasol Birds of Malawi, by Newman/Madland and Johnstone-Stewart.

Sasol Birds of Southern Africa, Ian Sinclair, 1995 (Capetown, South Africa: Struik).

Birds of Kenya & Tanzania, Zimmerman, Turner and Pearson, 1996 (A & C Black) (Johannesburg, South Africa: Russel Friedman Books).

Field Guide to the Mammals of Africa, H. Diller, 1977 (London: Collins).

A Safari Companion, A Guide to Watching African Mammals, Richard D. Estes, 1993 (VT., USA: Chelsea Green Publishing).

The Behavior Guide to African Mammals, Richard Despard Estes, 1991 (London: University of California Press).

On Safari in East Africa, Ernest Neal, 1991 (London: Collins) (O/P).

The African Safari, P. Jay Fetner, 1987 (New York: St. Martins Press) (O/P). Lots of photos and information on wildlife.

Conservation and Wildlife Management in Africa, edited by R. H. V. Bell and E. McShane Caluzi, 1984 (Washington, D.C.: World Wildlife Fund) (O/P). Research.

Safari: The East African Diaries of a Wildlife Photographer, Gunter Ziesler and Angelika Hofer, 1984 (New York: Facts on File) (O/P).

The Chimpanzees of Gombe, Patterns of Behavior, Jane Goodall, 1986 (Cambridge, MA: Harvard University Press). Chimpanzee research.

Gorilla: Struggle for Survival in the Virungas, Michael Nichols, 1989 (New York: Aperture Press). Color photo book.

Ngorongoro, Reinhard Kunkel, 1992 (London, U.K.: Harper Collins). (O/P).

Among the Predators and Prey, Hugo Van Lawick, 1986 (London: Elm Tree Books).

Savage Paradise: The Predators of Serengeti, Hugo Van Lawick, 1983 (London: William Collins) (O/P).

The Leopards Tale, Jonathan Scott, 1988 (London: Elm Tree Books) (O/P).

Cheetah, Katherine and Karl Ammann, 1985 (New York: Arco Pub.) (O/P).

Great Cats, J. Seidensticker, 1991 (Emmaus, PA: Rodale Press) (O/P).

The Great Migration, Jonathan Scott, 1989 (Emmaus, PA: Rodale Press) (O/P).

Elephants: Majestic Creatures of the Wild, Jeheskez Shoshani, 1992 (Emmaus, PA: Rodale Press) (O/P).

African Game Trails, T. Roosevelt, 1983 (New York, U.S.A.: St. Martins Press).

Fate of the Elephant, Douglas H. Chadwick, 1993 (London, U.K.: Viking Penguin).

A Field Guide to the Birds of West Africa, W. Serle and G. Morel, 1977 (London, U.K.: Harper Collins).

Field Guide to the Mammals of Africa Including Madagascar, T. Haltenorth and H. Diller, 1980 (London, U.K.: Harper Collins).

Southern, Central, and East African Mammals, Chris and Tilde Stuart, 1992 (Johannesburg, South Africa: Struik). Photo guide.

Elephant Memories, Cynthia Moss, 1989 (New York: Fawcett) (O/P).

The Kingdon Field Guide to African Mammals, Jonathan Kingdon, 1997 (London, U.K.: Harcourt Brace).

Running Wild, John McNutt and Lesley Boggs, 1996 (Capetown, South Africa: Southern Book Publishers).

AFRICA – GENERAL

Travel Survival Guides to Africa (by country), various authors, 1992 (Victoria, Australia: Lonely Planet).

Last Chance to See, D. Adams and M. Carwardine, 1991 (New York: Harmony Books) (O/P).

I Dreamed of Africa, K. Gallman, 1991 (New York: Penguin Books).

The Africans, D. Lamb, 1987 (New York: Vintage Books).

Origins Reconsidered, R. E. Leakey and R. Lewin, 1992 (New York: Doubleday) (O/P).

Maasai, Tepilit Ole Saitoti, 1997 (U.S.A.: Franklin Watts).

Africa Timeless Soul, Wilby, 1996 (U.K.: Pan MacMillian).

African Folklore, Best of, A. Savoury, 1972 (Johannesburg, South Africa: Struik).

African Silences, P. Matthiessen, 1992 (U.K.: Collins).

Africa's Vanishing Wildlife, Chris and Tilde Stuart, 1996 (Capetown, South Africa: Southern).

North of South, Shiva Naipaul, 1994 (U.K.: Penguin).

The Blue Nile, Alan Moorehead, 1983 (U.K.: Penguin).

The Making of Mankind, Richard Leakey, 1981 (Michael Joseph) (O/P).

The White Nile, Alan Moorehead, 1973 (U.K.: Penguin).

The Besieged Desert, Mitch Reardon (U.K.: Collins) (O/P).

Shadows of Sand, Colin Mead (Johannesburg, South Africa).

The Tree Where Man Was Born, Peter Matthiessen, 1997 (New York: E.P. Dutton).

No Man's Land: The Last of White Africa, John Heminway, 1983 (U.K.: Harcourt Brace Jovanovich) (O/P). Remarkable account of one man's journey through Africa.

Africa: Natural History, Leslie Brown, 1965 (Random House).

The Long African Day, Norman Myers, 1972 (MacMillan).

The End of the Game, Peter Beard, 1996 (San Francisco, U.S.A.: Chronicle Bodius).

Safari — A Chronicle of Adventure, Bartle Bull, 1992 (London, U.K.: Penguin Books).

Africa — A Continent Revealed, Rene Gordon, 1997 (New Holland, London, U.K.: Camerapix).

The African Adventurer, Peter Capstick, 1992 (New York, U.S.: St. Martins Press).

Survivors Song — Life and Death in the African Wilderness, Mark and Delia Owens, 1993 (London, U.K.: Harper Collins).

African Laughter, Doris Lessing, 1992 (London, U.K.: Flanimero).

SOUTHERN AFRICA

Complete Book of South African Birds, Peter Ginn, revised 1996 (Capetown, South Africa: Struik).

Complete Book of South African Mammals, Gus Mills and Lex Hes, 1997 (Capetown, South Africa: Struik).

Long Walk to Freedom, Nelson Mandela, 1995 (Abacus, Little Brown, London, U.K.: McDonald).

Newman's Birds of Southern Africa, Kenneth Newman, 1983 (Johannesburg, South Africa: Southern Book Publishers).

Trees of Southern Africa, Keith Coates Palgrave, 1977 (Capetown, South Africa: Struik).

Southern African Trees — A Photographic Guide, Piet van Wyk, 1993 (Capetown, South Africa: Struik).

Guide to Southern African Game and Nature Reserves, Chris and Tilde Stuart, 1992 (Capetown, South Africa: Struik).

Living Deserts of Southern Africa, Barry Lovegrove, 1993 (Capetown, South Africa: Fernwood Press).

Top Birding Spots in Southern Africa, Hugh Chittenden, 1992 (Johannesburg, South Africa: Southern Books).

Field Guide to Snakes and Reptiles of Southern Africa, Bill Branch, 1992 (Capetown, South Africa: Struik).

National Parks of Southern Africa, Anthony Bannister and Brendon Ryan, 1993 (Capetown, South Africa: Struik).

South Africa — The Beautiful, Brian Johnson Barker, 1992 (Capetown, South Africa: Struik).

Traveller's Guide to South Africa, Peter Joyce, 1997 (Capetown, South Africa: Struik).

Driving South, David Robbins, 1993 (Johannesburg, South Africa: Southern Books).

Field Guide to Mammals of Southern Africa, C. Stuart and T. Stuart, 1991 (Cape Town, South Africa: Struik Publishers).

Land Mammals of Southern Africa: A Field Guide, R. H. N Smithers, 1992 (Johannesburg, South Africa: Southern Book Publishers).

BOTSWANA

Botswana, Brush with the Wild, Paul Augustinus 1987 (Johannesburg, South Africa: Acorn Books).

Beyond the Endless Mopane, Harvey, 1997 (Swan Hill).

Field Guide to Mammals of Botswana, P. Comley and S. Meyer, 1994 (Kasane, Botswana: Africa Window).

Okavango — Sea of Land, A. Bannister, 1996 (Cape Town, South Africa: Struik).

Wild About the Okavango, Duncan Butchant, 1995 (Johannesburg, South Africa: Southern).

Running Wild, John McNutt and Lesley Boggs, 1996 (Johannesburg, South Africa: Southern Book Publishers).

Plants of the Okavango Delta, Karen and William Ellcry, 1997 (Dalbridge, Kwa-Zulu Natal, South Africa: Tsaro).

Shell Field Guide to the Common Trees of the Okavango Delta, Veronica Roodf 1993 (Botswana: Shell).

Visitors Guide of Botswana, J. Fowles and M. Main, 1993 (Johannesburg, South Africa: Southern).

Cry of the Kalahari, Mark and Delia Owens, 1984 (Boston: Houghton Mifflin).

Okavango: Jewel of the Kalahari, Karen Ross (New York: Macmillan) (O/P).

Okavango: Sea of Land, Land of Water, P. Johnson and A. Bannister, 1977 (Cape Town, South Africa: Struik Publishers). Large photo book.

Okavango: African's Last Eden, Frans Lanting, 1993 (Johanessburg, South Africa: Chronicle U.S.–Russel Friedman Books) (O/P).

The Bushmen, P. Johnson, A. Bannister and A. Wallenburgh, 1979 (Cape Town, South Africa: Struik Publishers) (O/P). Large photo book.

The Heart of the Hunter (series), Laurens Van der Post, 1980 (Kent, U.K.: Harcourt Brace Jovanovich).

The Lions and Elephants of the Chobe, Bruce Aitken, 1986 (Capetown, South Africa: Stramill).

Kalahari — Life's Variety in Dune and Delta, Michael Main, 1990 (Johannesburg, South Africa: Southern Books) (O/P)

The Crowded Desert — The Kalahari National Park, Wilf Nussey, 1993 (South Africa: William Waterman Pub.) (O/P).

Nature of Botswana — A Guide to Conservation and Development, Alec Cambell, 1992 (Garborone, Botswana U.K.: IUCN) (O/P).

This Is Botswana, Peter Joyce, 1993 (Capetown, South Africa: Struik).

ZAMBIA AND ZIMBABWE

Kakuli, Norman Carr, 1995 (Corporate Brochure Co., Oxford, U.K.: Gondwana).

Mukiwa, Peter Godwin, 1996 (London, U.K.: Picador).

Songs to an African Sunset, Seki Nednza Shand, 1996 (London, U.K.: Lonely Planet).

Visitor's Guide to Zimbabwe, M. Maurel, 1995 (Johannesburg, South Africa: Southern).

Visitor's Guide to Zambia, N. Plewman and B. Dooley, 1995 (Johannesburg, South Africa: Southern).

Zambezi, L. Watermeyer, J. Dabbs and Y. Christian, 1988 (Harare, Zimbabwe: Albida Samara Pvt. Ltd.). Large photo book.

Zambezi — The River of the Gods, Jan and Fiona Teede, 1991 (England, London, U.K.: Andic Deutsch).

Zambezi — A Journey of a River, Michael Main, 1990 (Johannesburg, South Africa: Southern Book Publishers).

The Spirit of the Zambezi, Jeff and Veronica Stutchbury, 1991 (Oxford, U.K.: The Corporate Brochure Company).

The Leopard Hunts in Darkness (and other series), Wilbur Smith, 1992 (London, U.K.: Mandarin).

Livingstone's African Journal, I. Schapers.

Eye of the Elephant, Mark and Delia Owens, 1992 (Boston, U.S.A.: Houghton Mifflan). Biography of their time in North Luangwa.

Guide to the Wildlife of the Luangwa Valley, Norman Carr (BP Zambia Ltd.).

Zambia, Ian Murphy and Richard Vaughan, 1992 (Oxford, U.K.: Corporate Brochure Company) (O/P).

Zimbabwe, Ian Murphy and Richard Vaughan, 1993 (Oxford, U.K.: Corporate Brochure Company) (O/P).

This Is Zimbabwe, Gerald Cubitt and Peter Joyce, 1992 (Capetown, South Africa: Struik).

African Laughter, Doris Lessing, 1992 (London, U.K.: Harper Collins). Biography of her return visits to Zimbabwe.

MALAWI

Guide to the Mulanje Massif, Frank Eastwood and Malawi Wildlife Society (Lilonene, Malawi).

Birds of Malawi, Newman/Madland and Johnstone-Stewart 1992 (Capetown, South Africa: Southern Books).

NAMIBIA

Desert Adventure, Paul Augustinus, 1997 (Johannesburg, South Africa: Acorn Books).

Skeleton Coast, Benedict Allen, 1997 (London, U.K.: BBC).

Namibia Beautiful Land, David Bristow 1992 (Capetown, South Africa: Struik).

This Is Namibia, Peter Joyce and Gerald Cubitt (Capetown, South Africa: Struik).

Running Wild, John McNutt and Lesley Boggs, 1996 (Johannesburg, South Africa: Southern Book Publishers).

Namibia — Africa's Harsh Paradise, A. Bannister and P. Johnson, 1978 (Cape Town, South Africa: Struik Publishers). Large photo book.

The Besieged Desert, Mitch Reardon (U.K.: Collins) (O/P).

Shadows of Sand, Colin Mead (Johannesburg, South Africa).

Skeleton Coast, Amy Schoeman, 1996 (Johannesburg, South Africa: Southern Book Publishers). Pictorial and informative.

Sands of Silence — On Safari in Namibia, P. Capstick, 1991 (Berkshire, U.K.: St. Martins Press).

Etosha, Daryl and Shanna Balfour, 1992 (Cape Town, South Africa: Struik).

Himba — Nomads of Namibia, Margaret Jacobsen, 1991 (South Africa: Struik).

Journey Through Namibia, M. Amin, D. Willetts and T. Shah, 1993 (Capetown, South Africa: Struik) (O/P).

This Is Namibia, Gerald Cubitt and Peter Joyce, 1992 (Capetown, South Africa: Struik).

SOUTH AFRICA

Long Walk to Freedom, Nelson Mandela, 1995 (Little Brown, London, U.K.: Abacus).

Traveller's Guide to South Africa, Elaine Hurford and Peter Joyce, 1996 (Capetown, South Africa: Struik).

This Is South Africa, Peter Borchert, 1995 (Capetown, South Africa: Struik).

Magnificent South Africa, Hurford and Joyce, 1996 (Capetown, South Africa: Struik).

South African Landmarks & Popular Places, P. Joyce, 1995 (Capetown, South Africa: Struik).

Lightning Bird: One Man's Journey into Africa, Lyall Watson, 1983 (Hants, U.K.: Touchstone, S&S) (O/P).

The Washing of the Spears: The Rise and Fall of the Zulu Nation, Donald R. Morris, 1995 (Hants, U.K.: Touchstone, S&S).

The Covenant, James A. Michener, 1980 (New York, U.S.A.: Random House).

The Last Wilderness, Nicholas Luard (O/P).

The Heart of the Hunter (series), Laurens Van der Post 1987 (London, U.K.: Chattos Windis).

When the Lion Feeds, 1986 (series) Wilbur Smith
(London, U.K.: Heimemann).

My Chocolate Redeemer, Christopher Hope 1989
(London, U.K.: Heimemann) (O/P).

My Traitor's Heart, Rian Malan 1990
(New York, U.S.A.: Vintage Books).

EAST AFRICA

Illustrated Checklist Birds of East Africa, B. von Perlo 1995
(London, U.K.: Collins).

Safari Guide to Common Birds of East Africa, D. Hosking, 1996
(London, U.K.: Collins).

Safari Guide to Larger Mammals of East Africa, D. Hoskin, 1996
(London, U.K.: Collins).

Field Guide to the Birds of East Africa, J. G. Williams and N. Arlot, 1963 (London, U.K.: Collins).

Guide to Mt. Kenya and Kilimanjaro, edited by Iain Allen, 1981
(Nairobi, Kenya: Mountain Club of Kenya) (O/P).
Rock and ice routes.

Field Guide to the National Parks of East Africa, John G. Williams, 1967 (London: Collins).

A Field Guide to the Birds of East and Central Africa, J. G. Williams, 1995 (London: Collins).

The Tree Where Man Was Born, Peter Matthiessen, 1995
(London, U.K.: Panther) (O/P).

Field Guide to the Birds of East Africa, J. G. Williams and N. Arlott, 1995 (London, U.K.: Harper Collins).

Field Guide to the Wild Flowers of East Africa, Michael Blundell, 1992 (U.K.: Harper Collins).

Portraits in the Wild: Animal Behavior in East Africa, Second Edition, Cynthia Moss, 1982
(Chicago: University of Chicago Press) (O/P).

KENYA

Nine Faces of Kenya, E. Huxley, 1990 (New York: Penguin Books) (O/P).

Facing Mount Kenya, J. Kenyatta, 1962 (New York: Random House).

Kingdom of Lions, Jonathan Scott, 1992 (Kyle Cathie) (London, U.K. and Johannesburg, South Africa: Russel Friedman Books).

Kenya Pioneers, Errol Trzebinski, 1991 (London, U.K.: Mandarin).

Kenya the Beautiful, Brett Michael (Capetown, South Africa: Struik).

Kenya — Magic Land, M. Amin and D. Willetts (Johannesburg, South Africa: Southern).

Birds of Kenya & Tanzania, Zimmerman, Turner and Pearson, 1996 (A & C Black) (Africa: Russel Friedman Books).

Illustrated Checklist Birds of East Africa, B. von Perlo 1995 (London, U.K. Collins).

Safari Guide to Common Birds of East Africa, D. Hosking, 1996 (London, U.K. Collins).

Safari Guide to Larger Mammals of East Africa, D. Hosking, 1996 (London, U.K. Collins).

Journey through Kenya, M. Amin and B. Tetley, 1994 (Capetown, South Africa: Struik).

A & C Black (London, U.K. & Johannesburg, South Africa: Russel Friedman Books).

Born Free, Joy Adamson, 1960 (New York: Harcourt, Brace and World) (O/P).

Out of Africa, Isak Dinesen, 1989 (London, U.K.: Penguin Books).

The Flame Trees of Thika, Elspeth Huxley, 1998 (London, U.K.: Pimlico) (O/P).

West with the Night, Beryl Markham, 1987 (London, U.K.: Virago).

The Lunatic Express, Charles Miller, 1971 (Macmillan) (O/P).

The Marsh Lions, Brian Jackman, 1982 (London: Elm Tree Books) (O/P).

Shepherds of the Desert, David Keith Jones, 1984 (London: Elm Tree Books) (O/P).

Elephant Memories Portraits in the Wild, Cynthia Moss, 1988 (New York: Fawcett Columbine) (O/P).

I Dreamed of Africa, Kuki Gallman, 1991 (London, U.K.: Penguin).

The Great Safari — The Lives of George and Joy Adamson, William Morrow 1993 (New Jersey, U.S.A.: Adrian House).

Journey Through Kenya, M. Amin, D. Willetts and B. Tetley, 1982 (U.K.: Camerapix).

Kingdom of Lions, Johnathan Scott, 1992 (London, U.K.: Kyle Cathie).

TANZANIA

Kilimanjaro: The White Roof of Africa, Harald Lange, 1985 (Seattle, WA: The Mountaineers Books). Large photo book.

Among the Elephants, Iain and Ona Douglas-Hamilton, 1975 (London, U.K.: Viking). Elephant research at Lake Manyara National Park, Tanzania.

Serengeti Shall Not Die, Bernard and Michael Grzimek, 1960 (London: Hamish Hamilton).

Barefoot Over the Serengeti, David Read, 1979. Autobiography about growing up in the northern Serengeti/southern Masai Mara.

Golden Shadows, Flying Hooves, George B. Schaller, 1989 (Chicago, IL, U.S.A.: University of Chicago Press) Personal account of the author's famous study of the lions of the Serengeti.

Sand Rivers, Peter Matthiessen, 1981. A walking safari in the Selous Game Reserve.

My Kalulu, H. M. Stanley, 1873 (New York: Scribner, Armstrong & Co.).

The Chimpanzees of Gombe, Patterns of Behavior, Jane Goodall 1986 (Cambridge, MA: Harvard University Press). Chimpanzee research.

Journey Through Tanzania, M. Amin, D. Willetts and B. Marehall, 1993 (Capetown, South Africa: Struik).

Ngorongoro, Reinhard Kunkel, 1992 (London, U.K.: Harper Collins).

RWANDA

Gorillas, Karl Ammann, 1996
(Johannesburg, South Africa: Southern).

Lake Regions of Central Africa, Richard Burton
(New York, U.S.A. Dover Publishers).

Gorillas in the Mist, Dian Fossey, 1989
(London, U.K.: Penguin Books) (O/P).

UGANDA

Uganda/Rwenzori, David Pluth, 1997
(Stafa, Switzerland: Little Wolf).

Bonogo,The Forgotten Ape, Frans De Waal, 1997
(West Sussex, U.K.: University of California Press).

Mountains of the Moon, Patrick Synge, 1986
(New York: Hippocrene Books). Travel in Uganda, 1934.

CONGO

Congo Journey, Redmond O'Henlon, 1996
(London, U.K.: Hamish Hamilton).

Guide to the Ruwenzori, H. A. Osmaston and D. Pasteur, 1972
(Reading, Berks, U.K.: West Col Productions) (O/P). Rock and ice routes.

The Forest People, Colin Turnbull, 1994 (Herts, U.K.: Pocket Books).
On pygmies of the Ituri Forest.

The River Congo, Peter Fobath, 1977(Massachusettes, U.S.A.:
Houghton Mifflin) (O/P). History.

MAIN INDEX

MAIN INDEX

C

D

E

F

T

U

V

ACCOMODATIONS INDEX

ACCOMMODATIONS INDEX

A

B

C

D

J

K

L

M

Q

R

S

ABOUT MARK NOLTING, AUTHOR & AFRICA EXPERT

Mark Nolting wanted adventure. He found it as an Olympic sportscaster, international businessman, oil engineer and Hollywood actor. But it wasn't until he traveled through Africa that he found the excitement he was looking for.

Mark Nolting heads up The Africa Adventure Company, Ft. Lauderdale, Florida. He is the author of two award-winning books, *Africa's Top Wildlife Countries* and *Travel Journal Africa*.

Known as *the* "Travel Expert of Africa Travel" in the industry, Nolting and his experienced staff arrange tours for travelers who want to go on an African safari.

It all began in 1975. Nolting had graduated from Florida State University the previous year with a degree in business administration and minors in chemistry, physics, math and biology. For a year and a half, he had worked for a South Florida marketing firm, but the call of the wild beckoned.

"One morning," said Nolting, "I just woke up and realized I wanted to travel around the world. And I decided, if I don't go, I'll always regret it, and if I don't go now, I never will."

Two weeks later, he departed for Luxembourg. During the 1976 Winter Olympics in Innsbruck, Austria, he worked for ABC Sports. Next he found a job in middle management with the world's third-largest mail order catalog house, located in Germany.

But Nolting wasn't trying to become a European businessman. He was out to see the world. Although his itinerary called for him to head for India, Nepal and the Far East, he took a six-month detour through Africa and traveled across the Sahara Desert and on through Central and East

Africa. He toured several parks and reserves and fell in love with the "safari experience."

Then he found his way to the Mideast and was fast-tracked through a program for oil-drilling engineers. He eventually came back to the United States — Los Angeles. It occurred to Nolting that he'd never tried acting, so he decided to give it a shot and wound up working for four years.

Yet the yearning for more in-depth travel through Africa was still with him. He couldn't shake the memory of the wildlife and the spectacular terrain he had seen there. And so, once again, he was off, heading for Africa, a purpose in mind.

He returned to Africa and traveled for two years through 16 countries, from Cairo to Cape Town, gathering material for his books and establishing contacts with safari companies and tour guides. On his return to the United States in 1985, he wrote his books and established The Africa Adventure Company.

In July 1992 he married Alison Wright, whom he had met a few years previously at a safari camp she was running in Zimbabwe. In July 1993 they had their first child, Miles William Nolting, and in 1996, their second child, Nicholas Hamilton Nolting.

His many visits have included touring the antiquities of Egypt and scuba diving off the Sinai Peninsula; crossing Lake Nasser and the deserts of Sudan; experiencing the multitude of lodge safaris and authentic African mobile tented safaris to the wildlife reserves of Kenya and Tanzania; climbing Mt. Kenya, Mt. Kilimanjaro in Tanzania and the Ruwenzoris in the Congo; visiting the beautiful Kenyan coast; gorilla trekking and mountain climbing in Rwanda; hunting with pygmies, gorilla trekking and game viewing in the Congo; and taking the ferry from Bujumbura (Burundi) to Kigoma (Tanzania).

In southern Africa his adventures have included walking safaris from bush camp to bush camp and day and night game drives in Zambia; one- and seven-day white-water rafting safaris (fifth class) on the Zambezi River; viewing Victoria Falls at different times of the year; kayak safari upstream of Victoria Falls; several canoeing safaris on the lower Zambezi River; walking with top professional guides and game viewing by boat and open vehicle on day and night game drives in Zimbabwe; flying safaris to the major reserves of Botswana; mokoro safaris in the Okavango Delta; a fly-in safari to the Skeleton Coast and visiting Etosha Pan and other parks in Namibia; driving the Garden Route, sightseeing in Cape Town and visiting the private reserves and parks in South Africa; pony trekking in Lesotho; traveling through Swaziland; and holidaying in the beautiful island countries of Mauritius and the Seychelles.

Mark continues to travel to Africa yearly to update information and explore new areas. Hard-to-find information on Africa is always at his fingertips, and he loves to take the time to talk to people about the adventures that can be found in Africa.

The Publishers

WHAT OTHERS SAY ABOUT *AFRICA'S TOP WILDLIFE COUNTRIES* AND THEIR SAFARIS WITH THE AFRICA ADVENTURE COMPANY

"For six consecutive years we have travelled to Africa on safaris planned by Mark Nolting and the staff of the Africa Adventure Company (AAC). For flying safaris, mobile tented safaris, game drives (in open or closed vehicles, by boat, canoe, mokoro, etc.) or a safari on foot, we can attest that no one plans a safari better than Mark! In addition to planning excellent larger group and "package safaris" to all the well-known African national parks and game reserves, the AAC is especially experienced and adept at designing private safari experiences for small parties in very remote areas, game ranches, small camps (whether permanent, temporary or mobile) and native villages. From personal experience we have learned that Mark *knows* Africa, and is both well-known and trusted by those in Africa. Through the AAC we have been able to stay in the best game viewing areas with the best guides and accommodations. We have enjoyed our times in the famous and highly visited (usual) game parks and areas in East and Southern Africa. But only through the AAC's expert knowledge and careful planning could we have gone mountain gorilla trekking in Uganda; chimpanzee trekking in Tanzania; exploring deserts and parks in Namibia; gone camel trekking in Northern Kenya; done backpacking, canoeing and white-water rafting in Zimbabwe; gone on walking safaris in Zambia, Namibia, Zimbabwe, Tanzania, Botswana, Kenya and Uganda; explored the Okavango Delta, Savute and Chobe areas in Botswana; explored volcanic craters (Empakaii, Olmoti) as well as the remote Ruaha National Park, Tarangire National Park and the Selous Game Reserve in Tanzania; investigated the local cultures in non-commercialized visits to remote villages throughout Southern and East Africa. Thank you Mark for these unforgettable experiences!

We can also attest to the fact that the books written by Mark Nolting are accurate, well documented and up-to-date on all the areas we have visited. They form a valuable planning tool and a good source of information while on Safari. Bravo!"

Steve and Phyllis Brady
Wichita, Kansas

The Africa Adventure Company has been tops in our book and we are happy to recommend the company to anyone interested in a trip to Africa. We are anxious for our grandchildren to get old enough for us to introduce them to the wonders of a safari. We look forward to traveling with you again in the near future. Your knowledge of the country and attention to details can't be beat!

Roger and Jane Tillman
Chicago, Illinois

Thanks for a truly great experience. This was my second trip with your company and my fourth safari in Africa. I have recommended you to several of my friends and will be a return customer in the future. Keep up the good work. I'm looking forward to future Africa Adventures!

Jerry Chase, MD
Colorado

We have just returned from Botswana — the third trip that you have arranged for us into Southern Africa. I can't tell you how pleased we are. As good as one was, the next has been better. Your choice of local operators, guides, sites and timing has been exceptional. With your personal advice, recommendations, and guidance you have made our experiences unforgettable. It is for these reasons and more we have been so comfortable in recommending you to so many of our friends. Keep up the splendid work and looking forward to our next trip.

Flo and Burt Fink
Encino, California

My wife and I have recently returned from our safari to Zimbabwe and Botswana. Simply put, this has been the best trip we have ever taken. Every step of the way we were met by courteous, competent and friendly personnel arranged by your company. It was a huge relief to see someone holding a sign with our name on it when in a strange airport. The camps that you recommended were first rate and the food was excellent. All the guides were very knowledgeable and personable.

Gene and Denise Brown
Washington

Just wanted to let you know that the trip you planned for Susan and me exceeded our wildest dreams — it was fabulous! — Thank you so much for your invaluable help and time spent listening to us in the planning stages.

We'll be back!

Gretchen Daily
Stanford, California

Someone told me before I went on my first safari that once I went to Africa I would not be able to stay away. Of course I did not believe that. However, since that first trip I have been obsessed with Africa; it is something I cannot explain. I now understand what they meant! Mark and his staff have done a superb job in arranging my safaris. Since I prefer the smaller remote camps, Mark always seems to find these wonderful places. Each safari has just gotten better and better. I am always amazed while out in the bush how things come together — vehicles, people and vouchers just appear!

Gwyn Baumgarten
Houston, Texas

I know I'm "gushing" but we had such a wonderful time and there is so much to tell. Let me emphasize how much we appreciate the smoothness of such complex arrangements. And your recommendations for parks, lodging, etc. were impeccable. There is no question that we have been bitten by the bug and will return. Our only quandary is how soon and we will definitely contact you to help us so keep us on your mailing list.

Ronnie Cantor and David Deutsch
Honolulu, Hawaii

We had a terrific safari to Kenya and Tanzania. The itinerary you arranged for us was indeed fabulous, as we got to see a great deal of both countries during one trip. Talking to other travelers at the lodges, we had the impression that we were seeing more game and wildlife than most of them, and we attributed this to our excellent itinerary. We will certainly recommend AAC to all of our friends here in Kuwait.

Warren and Sue King
Kuwait

I have visited Africa twice with the Africa Adventure Company. In 1994, my honeymoon was to Zimbabwe and Botswana. In 1997, my daughter and I visited Uganda (gorilla trekking) and Kenya. Both trips I found myself in the best camps with the best guides. I love adventure travel and African wildlife safaris are the best. Mark Nolting is well respected in the USA and in Africa as the expert and he deserves it! All of our safaris have been super! Once Africa is in your blood it calls you back often. I look forward to my next safari with Mark Nolting and his superb staff.

Kevin Hessee
North Palm Beach, Florida

The trip could not have been planned any better, and I feel that we got enormous value for our money. I also can't say enough for your entire staff; everyone at the Africa Adventure Company was friendly, professional and extremely helpful. And the little "extras" you provide — the frequent communications, the safari bag, and the follow-up after our return - set the Africa Adventure Company as a truly class operation.

John and Deb Nowell
Park Ridge, Illinois

African
SAFARI JOURNAL

Mark Nolting has explored and researched the African Continent for over 25 years and is also the author of **Africa's Top Wildlife Countries**, an award winning 600+ page travel guide currently in its fifth edition.

Having spent hours in preparation for each of his earlier safaris, and in the end having to carry with him several heavy resource books on mammals, reptiles, birds and trees,as well as maps, phrase books and a diary, the idea of consolidating all this vital information into one book, the **African Safari Journal** was formed.

Many safaris have very strict baggage limitations (i.e. 25-33 lbs.) making this an all-the-more-valuable resource.

The **AFRICAN SAFARI JOURNAL** is the perfect Africa companion. Don't go on safari without it!

ORDER FORM

Please rush me . . .

__________ Copies of *AFRICAN SAFARI JOURNAL* @ $16.95 each.

__________ Copies of *AFRICA'S TOP WILDLIFE COUNTRIES* @ $18.95 each.

Make checks and money orders payable to Global Travel Publishers, Inc. Mail to Global Travel Publishers, Inc., 5353 N. Federal Highway, Suite 300, Ft. Lauderdale, FL 33308, U.S.A. Call (954) 491-8877 or toll-free 1-800-882-9453 (1-800-882-WILD) or fax your order to (954) 491-9060 and charge to Visa/MasterCard/Amex

______Check/M.O. Enclosed ____Visa ____MasterCard____Amex

Card No. ______________________________ Exp. ____/_____

Telephone Day: (____) ____________ Home: (____)____________

Signature____

Name____

Company____

Street Address____

City_________________________ State______ Zip_________

AFRICAN SAFARI *JOURNAL* (@ $16.95)	$ ____________
AFRICA'S TOP WILDLIFE COUNTRIES (@ $18.95)	$ ____________
Purchase Total	$ ____________
Sales Tax (see next page)	$ ____________
Shipping & Handling (see next page)	$ ____________
TOTAL	$ ____________

FREE SHIPPING WITHIN THE U.S.A.!

*Florida residents add 6% sales tax.
** For items shipped to Canada, add $2.00 for the first item, $1.00 for each additional item for shipping and handling.
For overseas orders, call, fax or e-mail for a quote.

_____ We would like one of your Africa travel experts to contact us to discuss safari options for our vacation, expedition, business, group or incentive trip (please include a daytime telephone number where you can be reached). If you have an idea of what you would like your safari to include please enclose details. We can also be reached Monday—Friday 9.00am—5.30pm Eastern Time toll free at 800-882-9453 or 954-491-8877, by fax at 954-491-9060, by e-mail at **noltingaac@aol.com**, or visit our website at **www.africa-adventure.com** and e-mail us a completed questionaire.

_____ We would like Mark Nolting to speak to our club, organization, business, etc. We have enclosed a brief description of our request.

Name ____

Company ____

Address ____

Daytime Telephone No. _____________________________

Fax ____

E-mail ____